# MOVIE WESTER

## Hollywood Films the Wild, Wild West

# MOVIE WESTERNS
## Hollywood Films the Wild, Wild West

by John Howard Reid

HOLLYWOOD CLASSICS 4

Lulu Press, Inc.
2006

# HOLLYWOOD CLASSICS NUMBER FOUR

Previously published in this series:

1. New Light on Movie Bests
2. "B" Movies, Bad Movies, Good Movies
3. Award-Winning Films of the 1930s
5. Memorable Films of the Forties
6. Popular Pictures of the Hollywood 1940s
7. Your Colossal Main Feature Plus Full Support Program
8. Hollywood's Miracles of Entertainment
9. Hollywood Gold: Films of the Forties and Fifties
10. Hollywood "B" Movies: A Treasury of Spills, Chills & Thrills
11. Movies Magnificent: 150 Must-See Cinema Classics
12: These Movies Won No Hollywood Awards

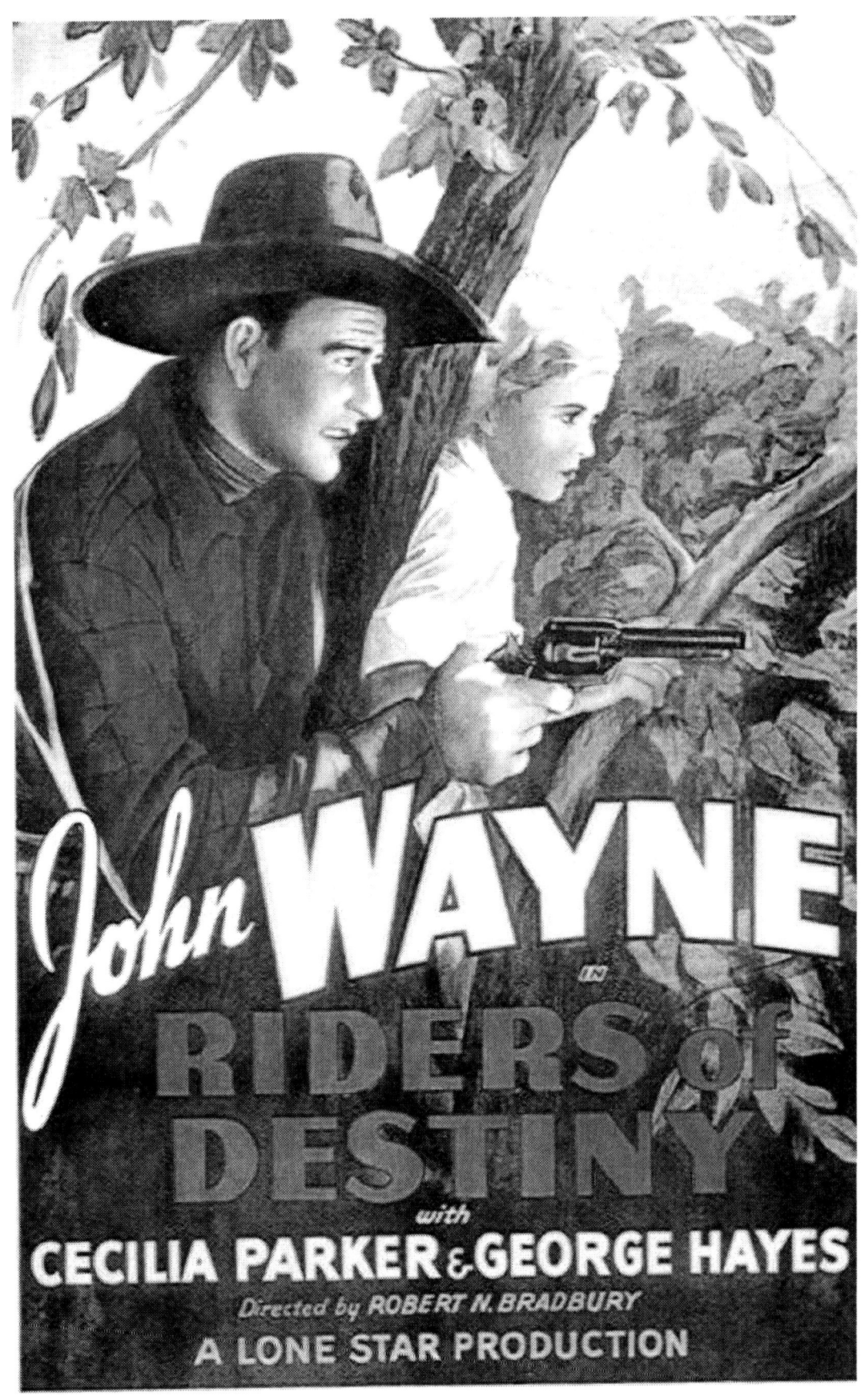

# Across the Badlands

**Charles Starrett** (Steve Ransom/Durango Kid) **Smiley Burnette** (Smiley Burnette), **Helen Mowery** (Eileen Carson), **Stanley Andrews** (Sheriff Crocker), **Bob Wilke** (Duke Jackson/Keeno Jackson), **Dick Elliott** (Rufus Downey), **Hugh Prosser** (Jeff Carson), **Robert W. Cavendish** (Bart), **Charles Evans** (Gregory Banion), **Paul Campbell** (Pete), **Harmonica Bill** (himself), **Dick Alexander** (tough), **Bob Woodward** (henchman and stunt double), **Jock Mahoney** (stunt double).

Director: **FRED F. SEARS**. Original screenplay: **Barry Shipman**. Photography: **Fayte Browne**. Film editor: **Paul Borofsky**. Art director: **Charles Clague**. Set decorator: **Fay Babcock**. Make-up: **Leonard Engleman**. Hair styles: **Helen Hunt**. Camera operator: **Emil Buddy Harris**. Music director: **Mischa Bakaleinikoff**. Music supervisor: **Paul Mertz**. Stills: **Bill Crosby**. Grip: **Ray Rich**. Gaffer: **Bud Williams**. Production manager: **Jack Fier**. Assistant director: **Lee Lukather**. Set continuity: **Dorothy Wilson**. Sound recording: **Jack Haynes**. Producer: **Colbert Clark**.

Copyright 31 August 1950 by Columbia Pictures Corp. No New York opening. U.S. release: 14 September 1950. U.K. release: 21 March 1955 (sic). Not released theatrically in Australia. 55 minutes. U.K. release title: *The CHALLENGE*.

SYNOPSIS: Steve Ransom, alias the Durango Kid, exposes a gang making attacks on surveyors laying a new railway line. Plenty of action and thrills plus some tuneful songs.

COMMENT: Starrett's 116th western turns out as one of the better Durango Kid entries, skilfully directed by Fred F. Sears. Although the chases are filmed from fixed camera positions instead of the more exciting (and more expensive) running inserts, the angles have been carefully chosen with horses' hooves panning right into the camera and a stuntman falling from his mount and rolling down an incline perfectly centred. Sears uses an occasional crane shot effectively in the studio back lot sequences (the pan along the enormous banner welcoming Duke Jackson and down to Dick Elliott and drawing back to take in the dozen extras that constituted the crowd) and we like the nice little dolly back from a close-up of Burnette's mouth after cutting from a poster advertising the dance. Barry Shipman's script has good dialogue and characterizations and keeps interest at a high level by astutely hiding the identity of the mastermind. The acting is good, though casting is (praiseworthily) a little off-beat with Bob Wilke a more subdued villain than usual, Hugh Prosser in an unmenacing role; Dick Elliott as an unscrupulous buffoon; and Stanley Andrews making the most of one of the meatiest parts that ever came to his way. Charles Starrett seems a little puzzled to find himself in such sterling company, but Mr. Burnette is in especially good form (and voice), his foolery forming an integral part of the plot instead of being tacked on in crudely-written additional scenes. Despite her standing in the cast list, Helen Mowery plays only a minor part in the story. There is plenty of action, though two sequences give evidence of hasty shooting. If you look hard you can see the rope tied at the back of the Durango Kid's double as he jumps into the saddle and even a ten-year-old could spot the double used for the villain in the climactic fist-fight atop the cliff! These quibbles aside, production values are extremely able.

# Adventures of Chico

**Chico** (himself).

Directors, photographers, writers, film editors, producers: **STACY WOODARD, HORACE WOODARD**. Music score: **Dr Edward Kilenyi**. RCA Sound System.

Copyright 2 December 1937 by Woodard Productions. New York opening at the 55th Street Playhouse: 25 February 1938. U.S. release through Monogram: 10 April 1938. Never theatrically released or broadcast in Australia. 6 reels. 60 minutes.

SYNOPSIS: A young Mexican boy and his father on a dusty farm encounter various animals including quail, armadillos, wild board, deer, coatis, a rattlesnake, a coyote, a mountain lion, a raccoon, and most especially a roadrunner.

NOTES: When they had finished their work on *The River*, late in 1936, Stacy and Horace Woodard packed up their cameras and headed for Mexico. The entire expedition consisted of the two brothers and a couple of cameras with lenses, reflectors and reels of negative. They were in Mexico more than a year, during which time they shot more than 100,000 feet of film. To edit this footage down to 60 minutes, took yet another four months.

The Woodards created the "Struggle to Live" nature series and won awards from The Academy of Motion Picture Arts and Sciences in 1933 and 1935. Stacy was chief cameraman on *The River*.

COMMENT: If you want to know what a roadrunner really looks like, this is the made-to-order movie for you. Lots of close-ups too. In fact too many close-ups by far. A roadrunner has only two expressions — feathers up and feathers down — and he is not a particularly attractive bird either.

Of course there are other birds and animals in the movie as well. But once again the Woodards delight in serving up too much of a good thing. The inquisitive coatis, for instance, are entertaining enough when we first sight them. But enough is enough, we cry, when the brothers bring them back for an extremely lengthy encore.

Even Chico himself tends to out-stay his welcome. There are too many intercut shots of Chico looking puzzled, Chico smiling, Chico downcast, Chico pensive, Chico eager, Chico asleep.

Nonetheless, the fascinating footage does outweigh the tedious. What a pity the Woodards didn't take the scissors to another ten or even twenty minutes of Chico's adventures!

OTHER VIEWS: With loving artistry and the budgetary supervision of no man, the brothers have fashioned a gently humorous, pleasantly sentimental pastorale. Though it has an excellent music score by Dr Edward Kilenyi, the picture's best music and all of its poetry are merely the wonder of a child at the endlessly enchanting world of animals and the pure, almost abstract love of life.

If this is not the best animal picture ever made, we hope someone will tell us where to go to look for its equal.

— The New York Times.

# Ambush

**Robert Taylor** (Ward Kinsman), **John Hodiak** (Captain Ben Lorrison), **Arlene Dahl** (Ann Duverall), **Don Taylor** (Lieutenant Linus Delaney), **Jean Hagen** (Martha Conovan), **Bruce Cowling** (Tom Conovan), **Leon Ames** (Major Breverly), **John McIntyre** (Frank Holly), **Pat Moriarity** (Sergeant Mack), **Charles Stevens** (Diablito), **Chief Thundercloud** (Tana), **Ray Teal** (Captain J. R. Wolverson), **Robin Short** (Lieutenant Storrow), **Richard Bailey** (Lieutenant Tremaine).

Directed by **SAM WOOD** from a screenplay by **Marguerite Roberts** based on the short story of the same title by **Luke Short**, originally published in "The Saturday Evening Post". Photographed by **Harold Lipstein**. 2nd unit director: **John D. Waters**. Camera operator: **David Ragin**. Art directors: **Cedric Gibbons** and **Malcolm Brown**. Set decorations: **Edwin B. Willis** and **Ralph S. Hurst**. Music score: **Rudolph G. Kopp**. Film editor: **Ben Lewis**. Production manager: **Dave Friedman**. Assistant director: **John Waters**. Script supervisor: **Leslie Martinson**. Hair stylist: **Sydney Guilaroff**. Make-up: **Jack Dawn**. Grip: **Hap Constable**. Costumes designed by **Walter Plunkett**. Still photographer: **Bert Lynch**. Technical advisor: **Colonel Charles E. Morrison**. Sound recording supervisor: **Doulgas Shearer**. Sound engineer: **James K. Brock**. Producer: **Armand Deutsch**.

Copyright by Loew's Inc., 12 December 1949. U.S. release date: 13 January 1950. New York opening at the Capitol: 18 January 1950. U.K. release: 26 June 1950. Australian release: 6 July 1950. 7,988 feet. 89 minutes. An M-G-M picture.

SYNOPSIS: A civilian scout, assigned to a mission to rescue a white girl captured by a renegade Apache, has a falling out with the cavalry captain in charge of the mission.

NOTES: Sam Wood's last film. Armand Deutsch's first film.
   Luke Short is the pseudonym of Fred Dilley Glidden.

VIEWERS' GUIDE: Adults.

COMMENT: An interesting film, if not one of Wood's best, though it does round out his career quite honorably. *Ambush* represents a transition stage between the big budget studio westerns of the *California, Union Pacific* school and the smaller scale location westerns of the Anthony Mann-Daves-Sturges tradition. In fact, the scene of Taylor and McIntyre's escape down the gap between the boulders that are only wide enough for one horse, could well have been cut from one of Mann's films and the climax, the actual *Ambush* itself, is brilliantly staged in the scrubby desert foliage with the Indian chief singling out Taylor for his revenge as his lips form the word "Kinsman" while he lies pretending death and the cavalry sweeps in.

   Against this, one notices that Arlene Dahl (then at her most gorgeous and also at the peak of her modest career) never leaves the studio and the film could well have used color. The story is intelligent, with the sub-plot of the officer in love with the drunken soldier's wife well integrated. The dialogue scenes are handled in the flexible multi-face groupings characteristic of Wood's major films. Notice also the way the scout's death is not noticed until after the action, and the realistically grimy fort.

— B.P.

OTHER VIEWS: From its opening pre-credits tracking shot to its suspensefully edited, breathtakingly staged finale, this is a stylish western, a fitting tribute to the career of director Sam Wood who died over three months before the film's release. The story itself is a collection of standard western plots, but interest is kept at a high level by the large number of plots used and by the fact that most of them are resolved in an unexpected way. They all build in fact to a stunning series of climaxes culminating in the Indian attack so sweepingly and vigorously staged by 2nd unit director John D. Waters.

The characters too have something more of real flesh and blood than the usual western stereotypes. The relationships between the people involved are more interesting and more complex than the usual stylised (or clichéd) characters and their dialogue has a refreshing ring of authenticity. The majority of the players, unfortunately, are not quite equal to the script's demands, though Don Taylor and Jean Hagen seize their opportunities, giving portrayals of more scope and vigor than those generally allotted to them.

The direction has visual flair and style and the pace is very astutely judged. Production values are absolutely first-class, with superlative location photography and skilled film editing. This last is of special significance as Wood died before editing was completed.

— J.H.R.

A robust western in the best tradition, with Robert Taylor in fine form as the hero.

— M.F.B.

Plenty of action in this film with Robert Taylor and John Hodiak giving their characters more depth than one usually encounters in second echelon westerns. The direction is fine, likewise the photography.

— E.V.D.

# Ambush Trail

**Bob Steele** (Curley Thompson), **Syd Saylor** (Sam Hawkins), **I. Stanford Jolley** (Hatch Bolton), **Lorraine Miller** (Alice Rhodes), **Charles King** (Al Craig), **Bob Carson** (Ed Blane), **Budd Buster** (Jim Haley), **Kermit Maynard** (Walter Gordon), **Frank Ellis** (Frank Owen), **Edward Cassidy** (Marshal Dawes).

Directed by **HARRY FRASER** from an original screenplay by **Elmer Clifton**. Photographed by **Jack Greenhalgh**. Settings (= art director): **E. H. Reif**. Film editor: **Ray Livingston**. Music scored and directed by **Lee Zahler**. Assistant director: **Seymour Roth**. Sound recording: **Glen Glenn**. Producer: **Arthur Alexander**.

Copyright by Pathé Industries, Inc., 21 June 1946. Distributed by P.R.C. U.S. release date: 17 February 1946. No New York opening. 6 reels. 60 minutes.

COMMENT: One of Bob Steele's last starring roles, this is a very routine, minor western with far too much dialogue and too little action. The story is a familiar old chestnut that is unimaginatively developed and despite the presence of some attractive players (Steele himself, Charles King, Kermit Maynard), the film is at best only a fair offering for the lower half of an action double bill.

— E.S.

OTHER VIEWS: Sub-standard, undistinguished and wearisome western about the villain who tires to ruin local cattlemen and who is foiled by our hero.

— E.V.D.

# Ambush Valley

**Bob Custer** (Bob Manning), **Victoria Vinton** (Mary), **Eddie Phillips** (Clay), **Wally Wales** (Joel), **Oscar Gahan** (Diggs), **Edward Cassidy** (nester), **Denver Dixon** (2nd nester), **Wally West** (3rd nester), and **Jack Anderson, Jack Gilman, Roger Williams, John Elliott, Vane Calvert.**

Directed by **RAYMOND SAMUELS** (= Bernard B. Ray) from a screenplay by **Forrest Sheldon**, based on an original story by **Bennett Cohen**. Photographed by **Paul Ivano**. Assistant director: **William Nolte**. Film editor: **Fred Bain**. Associate producer: **Harry S. Webb**. Executive producer: **William Steiner**. Producer: **Bernard B. Ray.**

Produced and distributed by Reliable Pictures Corporation. Not copyrighted. No New York opening. U.S. release date: 1 November 1936. 56 minutes.

COMMENT: Mildly entertaining low-budget western. The picture has some curiosity value in that Bob Custer was quite a popular cowboy star in the late days of silents and the early days of sound. But his career had gone well down from its zenith at this stage (in fact Reliable Pictures closed its door soon after this film was made). Custer retired in 1938 and now seems to be completely forgotten even by the most devoted western fans.

— E.S.

# Americana

20th Century-Fox, 1939.

A western to have been directed by Fritz Lang and produced by Darryl F. Zanuck on which the director did a considerable amount of research. The idea was to tell one hundred years of the country's history through the story of a lost mine — an idea that was partly realized by producer/director S. Sylvan Simon in *Lust For Gold* (1949) at Columbia. Unfortunately, Lang's version never reached the shooting stage.

# American Empire

**Richard Dix** (Dan Taylor), **Leo Carillo** (Domique Beauchard), **Preston Foster** (Paxton Bryce), **Frances Gifford** (Abby Taylor), **Robert H. Barrat** (Crowder), **Jack LaRue** (Pierre), **Guinn "Big Boy" Williams** ("Sailaway"), **Cliff Edwards** (Runty), **Meril Guy Rodin** (Paxton Bryce, Junior), **Chris-Pin Martin** (Augustin), **Richard Webb** (Crane), **William Farnum** (Louisiana judge), **Etta McDaniel** (Willa May), **Hal Taliaferro** (=Wally Wales) (Malone), **Tom London** (onlooker).

Directed by **WILLIAM McGANN** from a screenplay by **J. Robert Bren, Gladys Atwater** and **Ben Grauman Kohn**, based on an original story by **J. Robert Bren** and **Gladys Atwater**. Photographed by **Russell Harlan**. Film editors: **Carrol Lewis** and **Sherman A. Rose**. Music composed by **Gerard Carbonara** and directed by **Irvin Talbot**. Art director: **Ralph Berger**. Assistant director: **Glenn Cook**. Sound engineer: **William Wilmarth**. Western Electric Sound System. Associate producer: **Dick Dickson** (= Richard Dix). Producer: **Harry Sherman**. A Harry Sherman Production, released through United Artists.

Copyright by United Artists Productions, Inc., 30 December 1942. U.S. release date: 13 December 1942. U.K. release date: 15 February 1943. U.S. length: 7,359 feet (= 82 minutes). U.K. length: 7,200 feet (= 80 minutes). New York opening at the Rialto: 13 January 1943. Australian release: 29 April 1943. Australian length: 7,302 feet.

U.K. release title: *MY SON ALONE*. Re-issue title: *MEN OF DESTINY*.

COMMENT: A period western about a Texas cattle breeder, set in the aftermath of the Civil War. The storyline is routine, but the action sequences are vigorously staged and a fine cast led by Richard Dix (then near the close of his career but still presenting a ruggedly masculine image), help considerably to give the film an above average interest.

— E.V.D.

OTHER VIEWS: Following the Civil War, three men, Dix, Foster and Carrillo, the latter incongruously playing a French Creole, establish a vast cattle ranch in Texas. Carillo is caught selling off part of the herd and is sent on his way but he keeps raiding the cattle, making a fortune from his rustling, then enticing Foster into his schemes until hero Dix stands alone against them, his only ally being Gifford, his sister and Foster's wife. Superior action film with high production values, excellent photography and a good script where the dialogue rings true without cliché.

— *Motion Picture Guide*.

For the bulk of his lengthy screen career, Richard Dix was overshadowed by his work in *Cimarron* (1931). As a further example of this fact, this World War II vintage release, produced by Harry "Pop" Sherman, was a later attempt to cash in on Dix's self-sustaining image. It was an elaborate production, by United Artists standards, and the New York Times noted that Sherman "has climaxed an otherwise well-behaved drama with a reel that explodes in all directions."

In the accepted parlance of Western screenlore, *American Empire* offered a vivid panorama of frontier country, grazing cattle, and stern men battling it out with dastardly rustlers. Within this format, Dix is Dan Taylor who, after the Civil War, goes to Texas where he settles down and raises cattle, developing an empire there during the Reconstruction period. Vermin such as Preston Foster's Paxton Bryce make it difficult for the likes of staunch Dix. Frances Gifford, who would later move to M-G-M but never receive her due there, makes a fetching diversion from the horses and gunplay.

Certainly producer Sherman was more intent on capturing a flavor of the Old West (as movie fans expected it to be) than on depicting the frontier times as they actually were. There are plenty of flaws in the presentation, but with square-jawed Dix at the helm it hardly seems to matter.

After appearing as the Indian hero of *The Vanishing American* (1925), Dix had quite a career in the film genre. He was Joaquin Murietta in *The Gay Defender* (1928) and an Indian again in *Redskin* (1929). After the epic *Cimarron*, resolute Richard performed similar chores in *The Conquerors* (1932), RKO's attempt to follow-up the success of its Edna Ferber story. RKO would employ Dix as Pecos Smith in Zane Grey's *West of the Pecos* (1934), as a marshal in *The Arizonian*, and as a miner in *Yellow Dust* (1936). Dix turned to a comedy as a faded cowboy star in Columbia's *It Happened in Hollywood* (1936), but returned to his established form in Republic's expansive *Man of Conquest* (1939), playing the great Texan, Sam Houston. Moving on into the forties, Dix was an Oklahoma Territory marshal in *Cherokee Strip* (Paramount, 1940), a rancher in *The Roundup* (Paramount, 1941), and received special billing as Wild Bill Hickok in *Badlands of Dakota* (Universal, 1941). Next he was Wyatt Earp in *Tombstone, the Town Too Tough to Die* (Paramount, 1942), a gunfighter in *Buckskin Frontier* (United Artists), and a marshal in *The Kansan* (United Artists, 1943) his final oater.

— Parish and Pitts: *The Great Western Pictures*.

# Angel and the Badman

**John Wayne** (Quirt Evans), **Gail Russell** (Prudence Worth), **Harry Carey** (Wistful McClintock), **Bruce Cabot** (Laredo Stevens), **Irene Rich** (Mrs. Worth), **Lee Dixon** (Randy McCall), **Stephen Grant** (Johnny Worth), **Tom Powers** (Dr Mangrum), **Paul Hurst** (Carson), **Olin Howlin** (Bradley), **John Halloran** (Thomas Worth), **Joan Barton** (Lila), **Craig Woods** (Ward Withers), **Marshall Reed** (Nelson), **Hank Worden** (townsman), **Pat Flaherty** (Baker), **Fred Graham** (Wayne's stuntman), **Geraldine Farnum, Rosemary Bertrand** (saloon girls), **Wade Crosby** (another Baker), **Ken Terrell, Symona Boniface** (brawl spectators), **Jack O'Shea** (barfly), **Rex Lease** (roulette croupier), **Bob Burns** (man at meeting), **Jack Kirk** (Carson ranch hand), **Louis Faust** (tree-tumbled outlaw).

An original screenplay written and directed by **JAMES EDWARD GRANT**. 2nd unit director: **Yakima Canutt**. Photography: **Archie Stout**. Production design: **Ernst Fegte**. Music composed by **Richard Hageman**, directed by **Cy Feuer**. Songs, including "A Little Bit Different" by **Kim Gannon** and **Walter Kent**. Film editor: **Harry Keller**. Set decorations: **Charles Thompson** and **John McCarthy, Jr**. Special effects: **Howard Lydecker, Theodore Lydecker**. Stunts: **Chuck Roberson, Henry Wills, John Hudkins**. Make-up: **Bob Mark**. Hair styles: **Peggy Gray**. Costumes: **Adele Palmer**. Set continuity: **Catalina Lawrence**. Production assistant: **Al Silverman**. Assistant director: **Harvey Dwight**. Sound recording: **Vic Appel**. Producer: **John Wayne**. Executive producer: **Herbert J. Yates**. RCA Sound System. A John Wayne Production.

Copyright 10th December, 1946 by Republic Pictures (Corp. U.S. release date: 15th February, 1947. New York opening at the Gotham: 2 March 1947. U.K. release through British Lion: March 1947. Australian release through British Empire Films: 12 February 1948. 9,269 feet. 103 minutes.

SYNOPSIS: An agnostic cowboy is befriended by a Quaker family.

NOTES: Wayne's debut as a producer, Grant's as a director.

VIEWER'S GUIDE: Suitable for all but the most tender-hearted.

COMMENT: An off-beat western, written and directed by James Edward Grant with some splendid assistance on 2nd unit by Yakima Canutt and some rugged backgrounds beautifully captured in the gray, dust-swirled photography of Archie Stout. Although the bizarre and religious touches may puzzle the fans, they will be more than delighted by the many thrillingly-staged action spots, including a terrific fight in a saloon and a breathtaking chase sequence that not even inserted studio close-ups can eclipse. A judiciously-chosen support cast does full justice to Grant's nicely-observed characters, while Miss Russell herself appears in the full bloom of youth and beauty. The music is a contributing factor to the film's success, with its lyrical romantic leitmotif and its excellent underscoring of the action scenes (I particularly like Cabot's tinkling the piano before the climactic gun-duel). The film was produced by Wayne himself and as might be expected, production values are first-class.

OTHER VIEW: A prolific screenwriter, James Edward Grant directed only three or four films, of which this is the first and the best. The Quakers are observed most sympathetically and the characters for the most part hold the interest and are neatly etched, despite a certain superficiality of approach, Miss Russell is charming, Mr. Wayne more than adequate, and the predictable romance is not allowed to obtrude too much on the action, splendidly staged by 2nd unit director Canutt against some impressive natural backgrounds.

Although not nominated for recognition by The Academy of Motion Picture Arts and Sciences, I thought Stout's black-and-white cinematography was certainly the best Hollywood effort of the year and definitely had the edge over the two American films that were nominated in this section: Lang's *The Ghost and Mrs Muir* and Folsey's *Green Dolphin Street*. And it's good to see that Republic have taken good care of the master negative. 2004 prints are just as beautiful as those struck in the year of release.

For a debut director, Grant has handled the movie with gratifying assurance and flair. Admittedly he was helped out by action specialist and long-time Wayne ally, Yakima Canutt. But he has certainly drawn sympathetic and/or enthralling performances from all his players. Of course his writing and dialogue have considerable appeal too. But it's hard to imagine any other players but Wayne and Russell in the lead roles, Carey as the philosophical marshal, and Cabot as the irredeemably mean bad guy. And no-one but Olin Howlin could handle a cowardly blatherskite with as much conviction and personal charisma as Olin Howlin.

And for his behind-the-camera debut, producer Wayne has actually invaded John Ford territory and has brilliantly succeeded in equaling the master on his own turf.

# the Appaloosa

**Marlon Brando** (Matt Fletcher), **Anjanette Comer** (Trini), **John Saxon** (Chuy Medina), **Emilio Fernandez** (Lazaro), **Alex Montoya** (Squint-Eye), **Frank Silvera** (Ramos), **Rafael Campos** (Paco), **Miriam Colon** (Ana), **Larry D. Mann** (priest), **Argentina Brunetti** (Yaqui woman).

Director: **SIDNEY J. FURIE**. Screenplay: **James Bridges, Roland Kibbee**. Based on the 1963 novel by **Robert MacLeod**. Photographed in Technicolor and Techniscope by **Russell Metty**. Film editor: **Ted J. Kent**. Art directors: **Alexander Golitzen, Alfred Sweeney**. Set decorations: **John McCarthy, Oliver Emert**. Make-up: **Bud Westmore**. Costumes: **Rosemary Odell, Helen Colvig**. Hair styles: **Larry Germain**. Music: **Frank Skinner**. Music supervision: **Joseph Gershenson**. Assistant director: **Douglas Green**. Production managers: **Wallace Worsley, William S. Gilmore**. Sound: **Waldon O. Watson, Lyle Cain**. Producer: **Alan Miller**.

Additional credits: Camera operator: **Edwin Pyle**. Assistant cameraman: **Ledger Haddow**. Set co-ordinator: **Virgil Clark**. Assistant film editor: **Peter Colbert**. Choreography: **Poppy Del Vando**. Additional sound men: **William Griffith, James Alexander, Bruce Smith**. 2nd assistant director: **Carl Beringer**. 3rd assistant director: **James Welch**. Script supervisor: **Robert Forrest**. Wardrobe: **Olive Koenitz, Norman Mayreis, David Watson**. Make-up artists: **Mark Reedall, Hank Edds, Phil Rhodes, Sherrie Rose**. Hairdresser: **Clara Holgate**. Special effects: **Ben McMahon**. Technical advisor: **Salvador Baquez**. Dialogue coach: **Celia Webb**. Still photographs: **Chic Donchin**. Gaffer: **Max Nippell**. Grips: **Charles Cowie, Ken Smith**. Props: **Bill Nunley, John Faltis**. Main titles by Pacific Title. Westrex Sound System. Executive producer: **Edward Muhl**.

Copyright 15 October 1966 by Universal Pictures. New York opening at the Baronet and the DeMille: 14 September 1966. U.K. release: 2 December 1966. Sydney opening at the Victory. 8,820 feet. 98 minutes.

U.K. and Australian release title: *SOUTHWEST TO SONORA*.

SYNOPSIS: After avenging the murder of his Indian wife, buffalo hunter Matt Fletcher enters a church in the border town of Ojo Prieto. He plans to unburden his sins and begin life anew by using his magnificent Appaloosa stallion to start a horse breeding farm. But his hopes are dashed when a beautiful young woman named Trini uses his appearance to further her own ends. Trini has been sold by her parents to a Mexican bandit, Chuy Medina, and, as a ruse to escape, she tells him that Matt molested her in the church. Then, when Chuy also enters the church, she rides off on Matt's Appaloosa. But she is quickly captured and returned by Chuy's pistoleros. And Matt's hopes are completely shattered when Chuy steals the Appaloosa.

NOTES: Location scenes filmed in St George, Utah; Lancaster, California; and in the San Bernardino Mountains near Wrightwood, California.

VIEWERS' GUIDE: Strictly adults.

COMMENT: Stylishly and inventively directed, this off-beat western, beautifully photographed and played with surprising effectiveness by a stand-out support cast (Brando is much his usual self), emerges as one of the best films of the year. Some critics have objected to Furie's mannered camera angles and compositions, complaining that they obtruded into and slowed down the action, but we feel they are a major factor in creating the film's atmosphere — that together with the music score and the impressive natural locations they give the film a visual and a dramatic impact that lifts it right out of the class of the ordinary western.

OTHER VIEWS: A stylized western with some absorbing character studies — particularly impressive are Marlon Brando as the hero, Anjanette Comer as the double-dealing heroine and John Saxon as an oily Mexican bandit. Furie's direction emphasises character rather than action with the result that the pace is at times too slow. Still it makes a change to see stock-types in real depth.

—E.V.D.

Here's good old Mumbles Marlon up to his usual vocal tricks on the other side of the border. However, his is by no means the worst performance. That honor belongs to John Saxon, incredibly hammy and doubly as unconvincing as a Mexican villain. Anjanette Comer seems similarly out of place. Some of the native Mexican actors like Emilio Fernandez and Alex Montoya are more at home, though their forcefulness is undermined both by the unimportance of their roles and by the slow-moving, lingering close-ups style employed by the director.

The film's lack of sustained and sustainable suspense must be laid to the director's account. True, he does always try to fill up his widescreen with something or other, be it sombrero (his favorite device) or bottle or pillar or post, but he fails to keep the film moving. Not only is there too much meaningless dialogue, but it is too slowly delivered. Whole scenes could be ruthlessly cut (especially those involving Comer and Colon with our hero) to tremendous advantage. Even the introductory scene between Brando and Montoya should go. It has atmosphere and tension, but it does nothing to advance the plot and takes far too long to make its one rather insignificant point.

# Arizona

**Jean Arthur** (Phoebe Titus), **William Holden** (Peter Muncie), **Warren William** (Jefferson Carteret), **Porter Hall** (Lazarus Ward), **Paul Harvey** (Solomon Waters), **George Chandler** (Haley), **Byron Foulger** (Pete Kitchin), **Regis Toomey** (Grant Oury), **Edgar Buchanan** (Judge Bogardus), **Wade Crosby** (Longstreet), **Frank Hill** (Mano), **Nina Campana** (Teresa), **Addison Richards** (Captain Hunter), **Paul Lopez** (Estevan Ochoa), **Colin Tapley** (Bert Massey), **Uvaldo Varela** (Hilario Gallego), **Earl Crawford** (Joe Briggs), **Griff Barnett** (Sam Hughes), **Ludwig Hardt** (Meyer), **Patrick Moriarty** (Terry), **Frank Darien** (Joe), **Syd Saylor** (Timmins), **Silver Tip Baker** (barfly), **Kermit Maynard** (Bill Oury), **Ralph Peters** (bartender), **Al Rhein** (dealer), **Carleton Young** (Lieutenant Chapin), **Emmett Lynn** (Leatherface), **Jack Ingram** (courier), **Clarence Morrow** (Indian interpreter), **Iron Eyes Cody** (Indian), **Michael Cruz** (barber), **Earle S. Dewey** (Bill Coombs), **Jerry Fletcher** (Harry Coombs), **William Harrigan** (Union commanding officer), **Gayle DeCamp** (Mowry), **Bob Bell** (U.S. cavalryman), **Forrest Burns** (Mike), **Frank Brownlee** (Weaver), **Walter Baldwin** (declares for the South), and **Victor Adamson, I. Stanford Jolley.**

Producer/director: **WESLEY RUGGLES**. Screenplay: **Claude Binyon**. Based upon the novel by **Clarence Budington Kelland**. Photography: **Joseph Walker**. 2nd unit photography : **Harry Hallenberger, Fayte Browne**. Film editors: **Otto Meyer, William Lyon**. Art director: **Lionel Banks**. Music composed by **Victor Young**, directed by **M. W. Stoloff**. Additional music: **Paul Mertz**. Orchestrations: **Herman Hand, Sidney Cutner**. 2nd unit director: **Sam Nelson**. Assistant director (main unit): **Norman Deming**.

Assistant directors: **Cliff Broughton, Earl Bellamy, Richard McWhorter, William McGarry, Bud Brill, Joe Dill.** Associate art director: **Robert Peterson**. Set decorator: **Frank Tuttle**. Costumes: **Kalloch**. Stunts: **Danny Sands**. Stills: **Irving Lippman**. Sound recording: **George Cooper**.

Copyright 29 November 1940 by Columbia Pictures Corp. New York opening at the Radio City Music Hall, 6 February 1941. U.S. release 25 December 1940. Australian release: 6 March 1941. 14 reels. 127 minutes. (Cut to 120 minutes in Australia).

SYNOPSIS: Girl freight-line operator wants to own the biggest cattle ranch in Arizona.

NOTES: No fewer than ten films tied for first place at the U.S. boxoffice in 1940, all with an initial domestic rentals gross of $1½ million. The others: *Buck Benny Rides Again, The Fighting 69th, Kitty Foyle, Northwest Mounted Police, North West Passage, Rebecca, Santa Fe Trail, Strange Cargo, Strike Up the Band.* Coming in a close second: *The Road to Singapore.*

Nominated for awards from The Academy of Motion Picture Arts and Sciences for Black-and-White Art Direction (won by *Pride and Prejudice*) and Best Original Music Scoring (won by *Pinocchio*).

William Holden's first western. (The role was originally intended for Gary Cooper).

Negative cost: $2 million.

The character played by Paul Harvey, Solomon Waters, was originally called Solomon Warner in the script. The name was changed for obvious reasons. Jean often calls him Sol or Wat in the actual movie. Also changed was a bit of dialogue in which Jean refers to him when overcharging her 25 cents for a needle as "an old Jew". This became "an old Scotsman". (Mind you, in my opinion the film would be improved a whole lot if most of the Harvey-Arthur material, which is dull both in the writing and in the acting, were cut out completely).

Norman Deming, who is billed here as assistant director, co-directed with this movie's 2nd unit director Sam Nelson, two Columbia 1939 serials, *Mandrake the Magician* and *Overland With Kit Carson*. (I'm glad to say that the action material in Arizona is a vast improvement over *Mandrake*. I particularly like Nelson's pleasing habit of riding horses and wagons over the camera).

COMMENT: An attractively rolling title introduces this long, lavishly-budgeted epic western in which the players do wonders to overcome their somewhat cliched dialogue and formularised roles (though in 1940 they were probably less familiar as stock types of western characters). It's good to see George Chandler in a fair-sized part as Hall's henchman. William plays the villain with his usual smooth assurance and Porter gives us his delightful characterization as a small-time crook. Holden is effective too and even gets to sing "I Dream of Jeanie" (which is then used as a romantic theme throughout) right through and a few bars of "Kiss Me Quick and Go" in a pleasing light tenor all his own. Miss Arthur repeats herself from *The Plainsman*. There's plenty of action superbly directed by Sam Nelson with lots of running inserts as Indians bite the dust. Ruggles makes a commendable attempt to spice up the over-talky Jean Arthur scenes with tracking shots and often lots of extras milling around in the background. In fact, the opening series of tracking shots as Holden and his wagon train come into Tucson is a classic sequence which belongs on anyone's list of memorable scenes. No expense has been spared to recapture the epic sweep of *Cimarron*, though non-Arizonians might well be bored by the constant plugs for the ideals and aspirations of the Arizona Territorians. It all comes to an effectively directed shoot-out climax though many western fans may feel cheated that it is shown through Miss Arthur's eyes and not through that of the protagonists. I thought it effective anyway. Paul Harvey has a major role which he plays somewhat indifferently. Addison Richards does not seem to be in the 127-minute release print. Most attractively photographed, with realistic sets that convey the primitive squalor of the early west.

OTHER VIEWS: Long, sprawling western with plenty of action and splendid photography. Ruggles gets the best out of his cast, particularly Arthur, Holden, William and Buchanan.

— E.V.D.

# Arizona Bad Man

**Reb Russell** (the Association man), **Lois January** (the girl), **Charles "Slim" Whitaker** (the stepfather), **Edmund Cobb** (the border rustler), **Dick Botiller** (Pedro), **Tommy Bupp** (the crippled boy), **Anne Howard** (Min, a saloon floozy), **Walter James** (bartender), **Loyal Underwood** (dance caller), **Lionel Backus, Silver Tip Baker, Barney Beasley, Eva McKenzie, Fay McKenzie, Ray Henderson** (people at dance), **Jack Jones, Johnny Luther** (musicians), **Ben Corbett, Tracy Layne** (wranglers), and the voice of **Smiley Burnette**.

Director and film editor: **S. ROY LUBY**. Original story, "Black Bart's Fall" by **Eric Howard**. Photography: **James S. Brown**. Title song, "Reb and His Old Pal, Rebel", composed and sung by **Smiley Burnette**. Stunts: **Jack Jones**. Assistant director: **William O'Connor**. Sound recording: **Dave Stoner**. Recording facilities: **California Studios**. Producer: **Willis Kent**.

Not copyrighted by Willis Kent Productions. U.S. release through various independent state's rights exchanges: 1935. 58 minutes.

SYNOPSIS: Girl unwillingly aids her stepfather in his cattle rustling activities in order to prevent him ill-treating her crippled young brother.

COMMENT: Lois January hardly comes across as an ideal Hollywood heroine, but that is one of the charms of this grittily realistic little western, starkly photographed against unattractive scenery and set in particularly drab interiors. Hero and villain do all their own fighting and though a few punches are obviously pulled, enough hit home to hurt. Considering the film's sparse budget, Luby's direction is uncommonly effective. True, he wastes a lot of time on the introductory square dance, but once Edmund Cobb enters the picture, interest perks up considerably. In fact, Cobb's ingratiating portrait of the good badman undoubtedly ranks as one of his best performances in talkies. Whitaker too makes the most of his opportunities. As for our hero, he definitely rates as personable, though we see very little (thank goodness) of "his pal, Rebel."

# Arizona Legion

**George O'Brien** (Boone Yeager), **Lorraine Johnson** (Letty Meade), **Carlyle Moore Jr** (Lieutenant Ives), **Chill Wills** (Whopper Hatch), **Edward Le Saint** (Judge Jeade), **Harry Cording** (Whiskey Joe), **Tom Chatterton** (Commissioner Teagle), **William Royle** (Dutton), **Glenn Strange** (Kirby), **Monte Montague** (Dawson), **Joe Rickson** (Dakota), **Robert Burns** (Tucson Jones), **John Dilson, Lafe McKee, Guy Usher, Bob Kortman, Wilfred Lucas, Jim Mason, Art Mix**.

Director: **DAVID HOWARD**. Screenplay: **Oliver Drake**. Story: **Bernard McConville**. Photography: **Harry J. Wild**. Film editor: **Frederic Knudtson**. Music director: **Roy Webb**. RCA Sound System. Producer: **Bert Gilroy**.

Copyright 20 January 1939 by RKO Radio Pictures, Inc. U.S. release: 20 January 1939. No recorded New York opening. Australian release: 15 June 1939. 6 reels, 58 minutes.

SYNOPSIS: Bandits take over a town.

NOTES: McConville's original story was called "The Stagecoach Stops at Pinyon Gulch".

Lorraine Johnson is better known as Laraine Day.

VIEWERS' GUIDE: Okay for all.

COMMENT: Director David Howard gets plenty of pace and action into this one, even though the story is pretty routine. O'Brien himself daringly stunts on the speeding stagecoach during the routing-the-heavies finale. The young Miss Day makes a most agreeable heroine. All told, a very entertaining minor league western, on a par with *The Renegade Ranger*.

# Bad Men of Arizona

**Richard Dix** (Wyatt Earp), **Kent Taylor** (Doc Holliday), **Edgar Buchanan** (Curly Bill Brocius), **Frances Gifford** (Ruth Grant), **Don Castle** (Johnny Duane), **Clem Bevans** (Tadpole), **Victor Jory** (Ike Clanton), **Rex Bell** (Virgil Earp), **Charles Halton** (Dan Crane), **Harvey Stephens** (Morgan Earp), **Chris-Pin Martin** (Chris), **Dick Curtis** (Frank McLowery), **Paul Sutton** (Tom McLowery), **Donald Curtis** (Phineas Clanton), **Wallis Clark** (Ed Schieffelin), **James Ferrara** (Billy Clanton), **Charles Stevens** (Indian Charley), **Jack Rockwell** (Bob Paul), **Hal Taliaferro** (Mason), **Emmett Vogan** (John), **Spencer Charters** (judge), **Mickey Eissa, Beryl Wallace, Charles Middleton**.

Director: **WILLIAM McGANN**. Screenplay: **Albert Shelby LeVino, Edward Paramore**. Based on the 1939 book *Tombstone, the Toughest Town in Arizona* by **Walter Noble Burns**. Photography: **Russell Harlan**. Film editors: **Carroll Lewis, Sherman A. Rose**. Supervising art director and associate producer: **Lewis Rachmil**. Producer: **Harry Sherman**. A Harry Sherman Production.

Copyright 12 June 1942 by Paramount Pictures Inc. New York opening at the Rialto: 26 July 1942. U.S. release: 13 June 1942. Australian release: 1 October 1942. 8 reels. 7,150 feet. 79 minutes.

U.S. and U.K. release title: *TOMBSTONE, THE TOWN TOO TOUGH TO DIE.*

SYNOPSIS: Two prospectors, Tadpole (Clem Bevans) and Ed Schieffelin (Wallis Clark), discover silver in the Arizona hills and they name the spot "Tombstone".

Years later, they establish the Schieffelin and Foster Mining Properties and with this as a centre, the two rich partners create a town which soon grows big enough to sport "The Epitaph", a newspaper. The editor of the paper writes editorials to chide "the Mayor and his phoney peace officers", because Curly Bill (Edgar Buchanan) and his circle of outlaws really run the town. The gang consists principally of Ike Clanton (Victor Jory), Billy Clanton (James Ferrara), Tom McLowery (Paul Sutton) and Frank McLowery (Dick Curtis).

Things become so tough in the town that Wyatt Earp (Richard Dix), one of three brothers from the Southwest, is pressed into service as Sheriff. Curly and his gang are worried and manufacture a plot with Mayor Crane (Charles Halton), who has been forced by the newspaper to make Wyatt Sheriff, to eliminate Wyatt and his two brothers, Virgil (Rex Bell) and Morgan (Harvey Stephens).

Crane orders Wyatt to go out collecting taxes from the toughest cowboys of the territory. He introduces Johnny (Don Castle), a stranger looking for a job, as a tax appraiser who will accompany Wyatt on his journey. The plan is for some angry outlaw to kill Earp while he is forcing him to pay up. Johnny will make sure that, if Wyatt does collect money, Curly will get the sum. Meanwhile, Doc Holliday (Kent Taylor), a cold killer-friend of Wyatt, comes to town and joins up with Morgan, Virgil and Wyatt as a deputy.

NOTES: See *Frontier Marshal* in this book for other Earp movies.

Locations at Long Valley in the High Sierras, and Lone Pine in the Alabama Hills.

VIEWERS' GUIDE: Okay for all.

COMMENT: Here's Wyatt Earp, Doc Holliday and all our other friends of the O.K. Corral, this time directed by Bill McGann. Although it doesn't quite achieve the epic stature it's obviously aiming for, and suffers by comparison with the other versions, particularly *My Darling Clementine* and *Frontier Marshal*, it's still a fascinating, suspenseful, action-packed piece of entertainment.

OTHER VIEWS: Exciting, historically inaccurate, fast-paced western. Dix comes across superbly as Earp, but Taylor's Doc leaves much to be desired.

— *Motion Picture Guide.*

# Belle Starr's Daughter

**George Montgomery** (Marshal Tom Jackson), **Rod Cameron** (Bob "Bitter Creek" Yauntis), **Ruth Roman** (Rose of Cimarron, Belle Starr's daughter), **Wallace Ford** (Lafe Bailey), **Charles Kemper** (Gaffer), **William Phipps** (Yuma), **Edith King** (Mrs Allen), **Jack Lambert** (Bronc), **Fred Libby** (Slim), **Isabel Jewell** (Belle Starr), **J. Farrell**

MacDonald (Doc Benson), **Chris-Pin Martin** (Spanish George), **Kenneth MacDonald** (Jim Davis), **William Perrott** (Loftus), **William Ruhl** (Chris), **Frank Darien** (old man), **Larry Johns** (Jed Purdy), **Harry Harvey** (drunk citizen), **Charles Stevens** (Cherokee Joe), **Paul E. Burns** (Clearwater doctor), **Lane Chandler** (Marshal Evans), **Mary Foran** (Bonnie), **Henry Hull** (old marshal), **Bill Kennedy** (Kiowa marshal), **John Cason** (Kiowa posseman), **Christine Larsen** (saloon girl), **Hank Patterson** (townsman), and **Alvin Hammer**.

Director: **LESLEY SELANDER**. Original screenplay: **W.R. Burnett**. Photography: **William A. Sickner**. Camera operator: **John Martin**. Art director: **Lucius Croxton**. Set decorator: **Dave Milton**. Music composed and directed by **Dr Edward Kilenyi**. Film editor: **Jason Bernie**. Production manager: **Wesley Barry**. Assistant director: **Harry Mancke**. Script supervisor: **Bill Shank**. Hair stylist: **Fay Smith**. Make-up: **Webb Overlander**. Grip: **Bill Johnson**. Still photographer: **Ed Jones**. Special effects: **Ray Mercer**. Sound recording: **Tom Lambert**. Associate producer: **Jack Jungmeyer Jr**. Producer: **Edward L. Alperson**. Alson Productions, Inc. Released through 20th Century-Fox Film Corp.

Copyright 3 November 1948 by 20th Century-Fox Film Corp. New York opening at the Globe: 8 January 1949. U.S. release: November 1948. U.K. release: 28 March 1949. Australian release: 2 June 1949. 7,760 feet. 86 minutes.

SYNOPSIS: Colorful Western in which Belle Starr, a notorious Wild West bandit, is killed by Bob Yauntis, one of her own men, who lays the blame on a marshal. Belle's daughter, Rose, turns bandit in order to take vengeance on the marshal, until he proves his innocence. Rod Cameron gives an excellent performance as the bad man, with good work coming from George Montgomery and Ruth Roman.

— *Picture Show*.

NOTES: A Fox release and follow-up to the highly successful *BELLE STARR*.

COMMENT: A-grade western with an exciting script by W.R. Burnett (author of *Little Caesar* and *The Asphalt Jungle*) and direction by Lesley Selander that is far more slick and stylish than his usual standard. There's plenty of action and the pace is fast.

Rod Cameron and Fred Libby contribute interesting character portrayals. Ruth Roman fills the title role quite agreeably, while George Montgomery lends some skilful horsemanship to the climactic chase. (A pity that his fist fight with Jack Lambert is so obviously staged with doubles).

The supporting cast is strong and production values, including the atmospheric photography by William Sickner, excellent.

# Bells of San Angelo

**Roy Rogers**, **Bob Nolan** (themselves), **Dale Evans** (Lee Madison), **Andy Devine** (Cookie), **John McGuire** (Rex Gridley), **Olaf Hytten** (Lionel Bates), **David Sharpe** (Gus Ulrich), **Fritz Leiber** (padre), **Hank Patterson** (old timer), **Fred S. Toones** (cook), **Eddie Acuff** (bus driver), **Bob Nolan, Pat Brady, Tim Spencer, Karl Farr, Hugh Farr**

**[The Sons of the Pioneers]** (themselves), **Keefe Brasselle** (Ignacio), **Dale Van Sickel** (Mike, a henchman, and stunt double for John McGuire), **Charles Sullivan** (Roberts, a henchman), **Fred Graham, Roy Bucko, Whitey Christy, Post Park, Eddie Parker, James Linn, Kansas Moehring, Doc Adams, Art Dillard** (mine henchmen), **Victor Cox** (bus passenger), **Jay Kirby** (rider), **Rex Rossi** (Ramon), **Ray Turner** (Buck), **Luana Walters** (lodge clerk), **Joe Yrigoyen** (stunt double for Roy Rogers), and "Trigger".

Director: **WILLIAM WITNEY**. Screenplay: **Sloan Nibley**. Original screen story: **Paul Gangelin**. Photographed in Trucolor by **Jack Marta**. Film editor: **Les Orlebeck**. Art director: **Gano Chittenden**. Set decorators: **John McCarthy Jr, Helen Hansard**. Make-up: **Bob Mark**. Special effects: **Howard Lydecker, Theodore Lydecker**. Music director: **Morton Scott**. Orchestrations: **Mort Glickman**. Songs: "Bells of San Angelo" (chorus), "Hot Lead" (Pioneers), "A Cowboy's Dream of Heaven" (Rogers), "I Love the West" (Evans), "Gee, But I Love To Get Up Early in the Mornin' " (Toones, Evans, Rogers, Hytten, Devine), "Lazy Days" (Pioneers). All songs by **Tim Spencer** and **Jack Elliott**. Stunts: **Fred Graham, Eddie Parker**. Assistant director: **Jack Lacey**. Sound recording: **Fred Stahl**. RCA Sound System. Associate producer: **Edward J. White**. Executive producer: **Herbert J. Yates**.

Copyright 7 May 1947 by Republic Pictures Corp. No recorded New York opening. U.S. release: 15 April 1947. U.K. release through British Lion: 20 August 1949. Never released in Australia, either theatrically or to television. 78 minutes.

SYNOPSIS: "Border investigator" (are there such things?) exposes a silver smuggling operation. (Why the villains go to such an enormous amount of trouble and take such elaborate precautions is not explained. Rogers and his chums and the padre move quite freely across the border without once being challenged or passing through any kind of customs check).

COMMENT: It's odd that this one was never released in some countries as it's just about as good as the Republic "B" western ever got and that's a mighty high standard indeed. Attractively color-photographed locales, plenty of action, the fights vigorously staged, the chases thrillingly augmented by stuntwork and running inserts, some catchy songs, ingratiating players, and above all a script that doesn't take itself too seriously, often cleverly lampooning the mystery novel and providing opportunities for some nice touches of comedy and romance between the two well-delineated principals.

Whether fist-fighting or singing or hard-riding or light romancing, Rogers is in especially fine form. His opposite number Dale Evans looks marvelously attractive in color and plays with an absolutely entrancing sparkle and animation. The rest of the comedy is in the capable hands of Andy Devine and Olaf Hytten, whilst the villains are enacted by John McGuire and our favorite stuntman David Sharpe. The only sour note in this ensemble is struck by Fritz Leiber. Evidently nobody told old Fritz that this was a light romantic adventure. His performance is so hammily heavy-handed, he throws all his scenes off-balance. Fortunately there are not many of them as his part is mercifully small.

Also brief, in fact virtually fleeting, is the part played by Bob Nolan. He doesn't even figure much with his Sons of the Pioneers, where most of the singing is handled by Pat Brady, the Farr brothers (Hugh and Carl), Lloyd Perryman and Tim Spencer.

William Witney has directed with an admirably sure hand, balancing the light comedy-romance episodes with vigorously staged action to perfection. The songs are nicely presented too. Other credits and production values are far above the studio's usual "B" average.

# the Big Country

**Gregory Peck** (James McKay), **Jean Simmons** (Julie Maragon), **Carroll Baker** (Patricia Terrill), **Charlton Heston** (Steve Leech), **Burl Ives** (Rufus Hannassey), **Charles Bickford** (Major Henry Terrill), **Alfonso Bedoya** (Ramon), **Chuck Connors** (Buck Hannassey), **Chuck Hayward** (Rafe Hannassey), **Buff Brady** (Dude Hannassey), **Jim Burk** (Cracker Hannassey), **Dorothy Adams** (Hannassey woman), **Chuck Roberson, Bob Morgan, John McKee** and **Jay Slim Talbot** (Terrill cowboys), **Ralph Sanford, Harry V. Chesire, Dick Alexander** (guests), **Jonathan Peck, Stephen Peck, Carey Paul Peck** (boys), **Donald Kerr** (liveryman).

Director: **WILLIAM WYLER**. Screenplay: **James R. Webb, Sy Bartlett** and **Robert Wilder**. Adaptation: **Jessamyn West** and **Robert Wyler**. Based on the 1957 novel and *Saturday Evening Post* serial "Ambush at Blanco Canyon" by **Donald Hamilton**. Photography: **Franz F. Planer**. Sound: **John Kean** and **Roger Heman**. Music: **Jerome Moross**. Art direction: **Frank Hotaling**. Set decoration: **Edward G. Boyle**. Costumes: **Emile Santiago** and **Yvonne Wood**. Hairstyles: **Joan St Oegger**. Make-up: **Dan Greenway** and **Harry Maret Jr.** Assistant director: **Ivan Volkman**. Second unit director: **John Waters** and **Robert Swink**. Second unit photography: **Wallace Chewning**. Technirama. Technicolor. Supervising film editor: **Robert Swink**. Film editors: **Robert Belcher, John Faure**. 2nd assistant director: **Ray Gosnell**. 3rd assistant director: **Henry Hartman**. Sound editor: **Del Harris**. Filmed on the Drais Ranch, near Stockton, California. A William Wyler Production for Anthony-Worldwide Productions. Released by United Artists. Producers: **William Wyler** and **Gregory Peck**.

Copyright 1958 by Anthony-Worldwide Productions. New York opening at the Astor: 1 October 1958. U.S. release: 15 August 1958. U.K. release: 1 March 1959. Australian release: 2 July 1959. 165 minutes.

SYNOPSIS: Back in the carefree movie days of the 1920s, fledgling Director William Wyler made one western a week for a whole year. "Every Friday I would be given a new script", he recalls. "The actors were real cowboys, and the films followed a set formula: action at the beginning, a plot, and big action at the end." The formula has changed little, but everything else has changed considerably. For *The Big Country*, Director Wyler had a $3,000,000 budget, a year of preparation before he began shooting, five more months to film it, and a gaudy troupe of players led by Gregory Peck (also co-producer). He has not squandered his resources. *Big Country* is a starkly beautiful, carefully written, classic western that demands comparison with *Shane*.

In both *Shane* and *High Noon*, the plot tautened in one spare, straight line — the hero awaiting an unwanted showdown with an implacable enemy — and the characters tightroped their way toward their inevitable destination. The setting may have been Dry Gulch, but the town sage was Aristotle. In contrast, Wyler's panorama is as broad as his movie's title indicates, and his drama hinges not on a fate-decreed clash of incompatible forces, but on a succession of real choices to be made by each of the characters, each choice affecting the lives of all the others and creating in turn new sets of choices. The construction is taken from life, and Director Wyler, working with a bone-hard, uncluttered script by James Webb, Sy Bartlett and Robert Wilder, proves himself a master builder.

True to the old formula, the film begins with action. A gentleman from Baltimore (Gregory Peck), togged out in a sooty city suit, arrives in the Southwestern village of San Rafael to claim the hand of Pat (Carroll Baker), daughter of Rancher Henry Terrill (Charles Bickford), richest man west of the Rothschilds. Peck is barely out of the stagecoach before he is set upon by a liquored-up gang of Hannassey boys, whose father has long feuded with Terrill over water rights. But Peck's is a different code: he refuses to fight back or to show off his manhood by trying to ride a bumpy stallion.

But if hatred is poison, suggests Wyler, pacifism is not necessarily an antidote. Enraged by the Hannasseys' rough stuff, and spurred on by a foreman (Charlton Heston) who himself cottons to Carroll, Bickford's men pillage the Hannassey ranch. Reprisal bounces back on reprisal as in some brutal pingpong game, until the scattered feud pulls together into one pitched battle for control of the Big Muddy ranch, access to whose river had been warily shared by the two ranchers; now it must be held by one or the other.

The movie's story is acted out against a landscape in which the splash of blood provides the only bright color. Photographer Franz Planer, working extensively in wide-angle long shots, has caught the muted tans, browns and faded yellows of West Texas with unsurpassed exactness — an accomplishment partly due to the fact that the film was shot near the Mojave Desert in Southern California, which pictorially appears more Texan than Texas. Co-Producer Peck plays the hero as if he were not so much peace-loving as merely sleepy, but Burl Ives wakes him up with a portrayal of Old Man Hannassey that has dignity, simplicity, and roars to the canyon tops. Director Wyler has earned a Friday off.

— *Time*.

NOTES: Burl Ives won the Academy Award for Best Supporting Actor, defeating Theodore Bikel in *The Defiant Ones*, Leo Jacoby in The *Brothers Karamazov*, Arthur Kennedy in *Some Came Running*, and Gig Young in *Teacher's Pet*.

Jerome Moross was nominated for an Oscar for his Music Score, losing to Dimitri Tiomkin's *The Old Man and the Sea*.

The New York Film Critics nominated the film for Best Picture and Wyler for Best Director, both losing to *The Defiant Ones*.

Burl Ives, Best Supporting Actor — Hollywood Foreign Press.
Best Western of the year — Film Daily annual poll of American film critics.
Best Western of 1958 — *New York Daily News*.
Best Western of 1958 — *Time*.
Best Western of 1958 — *New York Journal American*.
Best Western of 1958 — *New York World-Telegram*.
Best Western of 1958 — *New York Post*.
"Simply the best film ever made. My number one favorite film." — President Dwight D. Eisenhower.

VIEWERS' GUIDE: Adults.

COMMENT: An epic western directed by William Wyler in an obvious attempt to recapture the success of *The Westerner*. That the attempt is not wholly successful is due more to the stock characters in the script than to Wyler's somewhat old-hat technique. What makes *The Big Country* really outstanding is Jerome Moross's invigorating music score — one of the most exciting ever composed for a motion picture.

OTHER VIEWS: For a simple story, *The Big Country* had the lengthiest writing credits of a Wyler movie — screenplay by James R. Webb, Sy Bartlett, and Robert Wilder; adapted by Jessamyn West and Robert Wyler from the Donald Hamilton story *Ambush at Blanco Canyon*. Webb was a prolific western writer, the scripter of such Robert Aldrich yarns as *Vera Cruz* and *Apache*, who had just written *Pork Chop Hill* for Lewis Milestone (he was also to write the Ford-Hathaway-George Marshall Cinerama western *How the West Was Won* and Ford's *Cheyenne Autumn*). Bartlett was the former newsman who had helped Wyler get into the Air Force, now a screenwriter-producer forming a partnership with Peck (in 1967, he was to hire Wilson to write *Che*). Wilder was a novelist friend of Robert's, the author of *Flamingo Road*, which Curtiz had adapted in 1949, and of *And Ride Tiger*. Increasingly, credits were "arbitrated" by the Writers' Guild of America (WGA), the successor of the old Screen Writers' Guild. Wyler was to remember little of who wrote what on *The Big Country* and even to express astonishment at finding Jessamyn West among the names. His fights with the WGA over who should have his or her name on the screen were far from over.

"It was a good story and I got a big cast together," Wyler recalled. "Secondary people were all top actors and actresses. We built a whole western town near Stockton, California. We needed wide open stretches but also fertile country. The canyon battle was shot in the Mojave Desert and Red Rock Canyon, some of the same locations as *Hell's Heroes*."

*The Big Country* started in August 1957. Wyler loved his big screen and Technicolor and lovingly shot a lone tree in a yellow-brown prairie, horsemen tracing their arabesques against dusty plains, bone-white canyons and cruel mesas. He had Planer put the wide-angle lenses on the camera and film muted hues — browns, faded yellows, early dawns, and perspectives stretching to the horizon. At the screening of the dailies — Bob Swink had been upped to "supervising editor" and the cutters were Robert Belcher and John Faure — he realized there was a danger, that the open country was *too* big, that it actually dwarfed the actors and, in a sense, made the story puny and irrelevant.

He worked painstakingly, demanding perfection from actors and technicians alike. The premise was as tough as the theme of *Friendly Persuasion* — just how much violence must a peaceable man use to preserve peace — and his *mise en scéne* would have to say that also. To make the point, violence had to be expert. It also had to carry the exact weight. When McKay rouses the foreman out of bed to fight him with no one to watch them in the moonlight, the script had it ending in a draw and McKay, gasping for air, say, "Well, what has it proved?" Very simple on paper, but once fleshed out by Peck and Heston, the scene didn't necessarily have the same weight. And now this huge screen. Shot in closeup, the fisticuffs looked ugly. Wyler chose to shoot it in long shots that made the fight pointless, tiny figures in the expanse of the landscape.

It was a big picture. By the time it opened at the Astor on Broadway, 1 October 1958, it was a $3.1 million production and a two-and-three-quarter-hours-long movie that United Artists was nervous about. Would it click? The reviews ranged from disastrous to sublime. Bosley Crowther said that despite its mighty pretentions, *The Big Country* did not get "beneath the skin of its conventional western situation and its stock western characters. It skims across standard complications and ends on a platitude. Peace is a pious precept but fightin' is more excitin'. That's what it proves."

— Axel Madsen: *William Wyler*.

The story is a mass of inconsistencies. So is Wyler's direction... We never understood *anybody*. Why do the Terrills hate the Hannasseys and vice versa? Why does Patricia Terrill love her father more than her fiancee? Why does Peck love her? Why does he later love her school teacher friend?... Why, why, why? The motivations do not spring from the characterizations, and the characterizations did not spring from the thoughtful minds of skilful authors. Peck's performance is his standard one. So is Burl Ives', but Ives' standard performance has not yet become so familiar as Peck's (it's well on the way). Bickford seemed aware his part was inconsistently written and seemed unhappy in it. I thought it valiant of Charlton Heston to try as hard as he did to make his part make sense. Miss Baker's inability to act was painful to watch... She looks awful in Technicolor... Jean Simmons, to my surprise, was better than usual. Her chronic frigidity seemed to be thawing. Just a bit, of course. The real star of this expensive film is Wallace Chewning... Some of [the exteriors] are the most beautiful color photography I've ever seen in a Western.

— Courtland Phipps in *Films In Review*.

A large-scale, meticulously produced, obviously expensive Western... For all its familiar Western trappings, it is a fairly complex and sophisticated affair... Seeks to underline, as did *Friendly Persuasion*, the virtues of non-violence. It might be called a Jessamyn Western... Wyler has done his utmost to give it epic stature... Has set forth [the plot] against backgrounds of unparalleled beauty and with a technical precision that is literally breathtaking... Editing has a flow and rhythm to it that is almost infectious. Clearly, Wyler has mastered the problems of composing and directing for the new screen shapes beyond any of his contemporaries. What he has failed to do is obtain performances of matching force and effectiveness from his large, expensive cast. Peck underplays to the point of listlessness, Ives intones his lines flatly and heavily, while Carroll Baker, Jean Simmons, and Charlton Heston are little more than adequate... For this, however, the writers must share responsibility. In their eagerness to point a moral, they overlooked the necessity of exploring, explaining, and making credible their characters.

— Arthur Knight in *Saturday Review*.

*The Big Country* was the first film on which Gregory Peck's name would appear as "producer" and, Peck told an interviewer during the picture's production, it was in Rome that he had caught the producing bug — from William Wyler.

Out of their mutually pleasant experience making *Roman Holiday* grew the Peck-Wyler co-production partnership responsible for *The Big Country*. After this, their second picture together, was completed, however, Wyler told a newspaper reporter in New York, "I'll never make another picture with Greg Peck... and you can quote me." Dissolve partnership.

As Peck has observed, *The Big Country* is "a sort of *Grand Hotel* Western," with "a whole gallery of characters. They all have big scenes and fit into the main theme."

Producers Peck and Wyler spared no expense to make the picture live up to its name. A part of Wyler's attraction to this project was his keen desire to use the setting, the vast landscape of "the big country," as a counterpoint to the small-minded creatures who inhabit it and fight against its stunning beauty.

For Peck, producing the picture brought him, he says, a new awareness of production details to which someone who was only acting would usually remain oblivious. A producer, he found, is "always aware of money going down the drain."

The disagreement between Peck and Wyler arose, in fact, over costs, specifically, what Peck considered Wyler's extravagance: "He overshot by an hour's length, which had to be cut." They wound up with a picture just under three hours long and "went way over our budget." The original budget, projected for $3 million, was revised to $3.5 million. "We spent," says Peck, "4.1 million."

Neither Peck nor Wyler is the sort of man to carry a grudge very far, if at all, and the attrition of time has eroded whatever strain the picture made on their mutual regard.

— John Griggs: *The Films of Gregory Peck.*

# Big Jack

**Wallace Beery** (Big Jack Horner), **Richard Conte** (Dr Alexander Meade), **Marjorie Main** (Flapjack Kate), **Edward Arnold** (Mayor Mahoney), **Vanessa Brown** (Patricia Mahoney), **Clinton Sundberg** (C. Petronius Smith), **Charles Dingle** (Mathias Taylor), **Clem Bevans** (Saltick Joe), **Jack Lambert** (Bud Valentine), **Will Wright** (Will Farnsworth), **William "Bill" Phillips** (Toddy), **Syd Saylor** (Pokey), **Vince Barnett** (Tom Speed), **Trevor Bardette** (John Oakea), **Andy Clyde** (Putt Cleghorn), **Edith Evanson** (Widow Simpson), **Tom Fadden** (Sheriff Summers), **Robert B. Williams** (Jed), **Eddie Dunn** (coachman), **Francis McDonald** (prisoner), **Minerva Urecal** (Mrs Summers), **Ann Doran** (Sarah), **Hank Bell** (driver), **Dick Alexander, Lynn Farr, Jimmy Martin, Lane Bradford, Casey McGregor, Cactus Mack, Carl Sepulveda, Bill Dix, Bob Filmer, Fred Gilman** (bandits), **Jim Pierce** (man in buggy), **Helen Dickson** (woman in buggy), **Carol Henry, Frank McCarroll, Hollis Bane, Frank McGrath** (posse members).

Director: **RICHARD THORPE**. Screenplay: **Gene Fowler, Marvin Borowsky, Otto Van Eyss**. Story: **Robert Thoeren**. Suggested by the 1937 book *Doctors on Horseback: Pioneers of American Medicine* by **James Thomas Flexner**. Photography: **Robert Surtees**. Film editor: **George Boemler**. Music: **Herbert Stothart**. Supervising art director: **Cedric Gibbons**. Camera operator: **A. Lindsley Lane**. Associate art director: **Randall Duell**. Set decorations: **Edwin B. Willis, Hugh Hunt**. Music directed by **Andre Previn**. Production manager: **Al Shenberg**. Assistant director: **Al Jennings**. Script supervisor: **John Banse**. Hair styles: **Sydney Guilaroff**. Make-up: **Jack Dawn**. Grip: **Albert Hunter**. Costumes: **Valles**. Still photographs: **S.C. Manatt**. Sound: **Douglas Shearer, John A. Williams**. Western Electric Sound System. Producer: **Gottfried Reinhardt**.

Copyright 24 February 1949 by Loew's Inc. An M-G-M picture. U.S. release: April 1949. U.K. release: 6 March 1950. New York opening at the Gotham: 21 May 1949. Australian release: 25 August 1949. 7,750 feet. 86 minutes.

SYNOPSIS: Big Jack and his outlaw gang save a young doctor from a hanging party.

NOTES: Wallace Beery's final fling. He died of a heart attack in his Hollywood home on the night of 15 April 1949.

Seventh pairing of Beery with Marjorie Main. Their ill feeling was mutual. She always complained he never spoke his lines as written, whilst he retorted that she could never remember hers. "She's blown her lines already thirteen times on this one take," Beery complained to a reporter. "If I have to make another picture with her, so help me I'll have a heart attack!"

COMMENT: A promising script ruined by Richard Thorpe's typically lacklustre direction. In his last film performance, Beery is allowed to act in a somewhat more hammy fashion than usual. The support cast, with the exception of Marjorie Main and Syd Saylor, is not particularly strong. The best feature of the film is Robert Surtees' fine photography.

# the Big Stampede

**John Wayne** (John Steele), **Noah Beery** (Sam Crew), **Mae Madison** (Ginger Malloy), **Luis Alberni** (Sonora Joe), **Berton Churchill** (Governor Lew Wallace), **Paul Hurst** (Arizona), **Sherwood Bailey** (Pat Malloy), **Hank Bell** (member of Sonora Joe's band), **Lafe McKee** (Cal Brett), **Joseph Girard** (Major Parker), **Frank Ellis**, "Duke".

Director: **TENNY WRIGHT**. Screenplay: **Kurt Kempler**. Based on the 1927 original screenplay *The Land Beyond the Law* by **Marion Jackson**. Photography: **Ted McCord**. Film editor: **Frank Ware**. Western Electric Sound System. Associate producer: **Sid Rogell**. Producer: **Leon Schlesinger**. A **Leon Schlesinger** "Four Star Western".

Copyright 28 September 1932 by Vitagraph Pictures, Inc. Released through Warner Bros. No New York showcase. U.S. release: 8 October 1932. U.K. release: March 1933. 54 minutes.

SYNOPSIS: A bandit (Alberni) aids a new deputy sheriff (Wayne) in cleaning up a gang of rustlers organised by a big land owner (Beery) in New Mexico.

NOTES: A re-make of *The Land Beyond the Law* (1927) starring Ken Maynard as Steele, Dorothy Dwan as Ginger, Tom Santschi as Crew, Noah Young as the bandit chief, Gibson Gowland as Crew's vicious henchman, Billy Butts as the youngster, and "Tarzan" the horse as himself. Directed by Harry J. Brown, photographed by Sol Polito for Charles R. Rogers Productions.

Re-made again in 1936 under the original title, this time with Dick Foran.

VIEWERS' GUIDE: Okay for all.

COMMENT: The original Ken Maynard effort must have been one spectacular movie. True, some of the stock footage was undoubtedly lifted from earlier films, but it's still mighty impressive. This Wayne re-make would certainly have knocked the socks off most spectators who must have a wondered how a little "B" western could afford such exceptionally lavish effects.

And it's not that *The Big Stampede* relies to all that great an extent on stock footage either! Impressively adding to the tautness and suspense of the script are a fine roster of players, led by the personable Wayne, the delightfully villainous Beery and the psycho-comic Hurst. (Love the way the cast is introduced in the credit titles: Wayne chatting to "Duke", Hurst glowering at a laughing Beery, Miss Madison looking uncomfortable whilst Master Bailey stares self-consciously at the camera).

Wright has directed with considerable flair and panache, making the most of the many action sequences (especially the saloon appointment) staged especially for this movie.

For the most part, the stock material is cleverly integrated. It's only the speed of the silent footage that gives the game away — though all the same it's still hard to tell where some *Land Beyond* shots stop and *Big Stampede* begins (the gunning down of Lafe McKee, for instance).

Realistic sets and locations allow ace cinematographer Ted McCord to present a series of pictures that are always fascinating or appealing.

# Billy the Kid Returns

**Roy Rogers** (Roy Rogers), **Roy Rogers** (Billy the Kid), **Mary Hart** (Ellen Moore), **Fred Kohler Sr** (Matson), **Morgan Wallace** (Morganson), **Edwin Stanley** (Moore), **Wade Boteler** (Sheriff Pat Garrett), **Smiley Burnette** (Frog Millhouse), **Joseph Crehan** (Marshal Conway), **Robert Emmett Keane** (Page), **Jack Kirk** (Morganson henchman), **Chris-Pin Martin** (desk clerk), **George Montgomery, Fred Burns, Jack Kirk, Art Dillard** (henchmen), **Ray Nichols** (Tommy Miller), **Al Taylor** (Burton), **Betty Jane Hainey, Patsy Lee Parsons** (Miller's daughters), **Rudy Sooter, Oscar Gahan** (musicians), **Tex Phelps, Betty Roadman, Fern Emmett, Fred Parker, Silver Tip Baker** (townspeople), **Jim Corey** (Bart), **Frank O'Connor** (store customer), **Bob McKenzie** (storekeeper), **Lloyd Ingraham** (Conway's deputy), **Ralph Dunn, Bruce MacFarlane** (army officers), **Bob Card** (soldier), **Bob Burns, Al Haskell, George Morrell** (homesteaders), **Tom Smith** (Garrett's deputy), **Dorothy Vaughan** (Mrs Allen), and "Trigger".

Director: **JOSEPH KANE**. Screenplay: **Jack Natteford**. Photography: **Ernest Miller**. Film editor: **Lester Orlebeck**. Music director: **Cy Feuer**. Music composed by **Foy Willing, Tim Spencer, Alberto Colombo, William Lava, Sid Robbin**. Songs: "Born to the Saddle" (Rogers), "When the Sun Is Settin' on the Prairie" (Rogers, reprised Rogers and chorus), "When I Camped under the Stars" (Rogers), "Dixie Instrument Song" (Burnette and chorus), "Dixie Brand" (Burnette and chorus), "Sing a Little Song about Anything" (Rogers and Burnette). Songs composed by **Smiley Burnette** and **Eddie Cherkose**. Production manager: **Al Wilson**. Unit manager: **Arthur Siteman**. RCA Sound System. Associate producer: **Charles E. Ford**. Executive producer: **Herbert J. Yates**.

Copyright 4 September 1938 by Republic Pictures Corp. No recorded New York release date. U.S. release date: 4 September 1938. U.K. release through British Lion. Never theatrically released in Australia. 6 reels. 54 minutes.

SYNOPSIS: A lawman impersonates Billy the Kid in order to stop a rancher hassling nesters.

NOTES: Rogers' 14th film and second starring vehicle.
  Mary Hart is sometimes billed under her real name, Lynne Roberts.

COMMENT: A singing Billy the Kid? Well no, it's actually Leonard Slye's Roy Rogers impersonating Billy the Kid — though he does play in a straight fashion Billy himself as well. The two characters never appear on screen together as the real Billy is shot before the Rogers character appears on the scene. Aside from this unusual intro, it's a likable enough if thoroughly routine offering. Fred Kohler does the honors as the villain's chief henchman, the heroine is pretty, Mr Rogers does a bit of fast riding culminating in a spectacular horse-and-rider leap from cliff-top into a lake, whilst Mr Burnette's foolery and novelty numbers are fairly tolerable. A couple of Mr Rogers' songs are melodic enough to deserve more than the somewhat perfunctory treatment they're given here. Not that this will worry the fans. What will disappoint the juvenile audience is that there's no action climax. The villains are captured by a ruse and quietly, hang-doggedly submit. Direction and other credits are competent but thoroughly routine. Production values are firmly "B".

# Bitter Creek

**Wild Bill Elliott** (Clay Tyndall), **Carleton Young** (Quentin Allen), **Beverly Garland** (Gail Bonner), **Claude Akins** (Vance Morgan), **Jim Hayward** (Dr Prentiss), **John Harmon** (A. Z. Platte), **Veda Ann Borg** (Whitey), **Dan Mummert** (Jerry Bonner), **John Pickard** (Oak Mason), **Forrest Taylor** (Harley Pruitt), **Dabbs Greer** (sheriff), **Mike Ragan** (Joe Venango), **Zon Murray** (2nd rider), **John Larch** (gunman), **Joe Devlin** (Pat Cleary), **Earl Hodgins** (Charles Hammond), **Florence Lake** (Mrs Hammond), **Jane Easton** (Oak's girl), **Frank Tyler, Pat Cleary, James Dent**.

Director: **THOMAS CARR**. Screenplay: **George Waggner**. Film editor: **Sam Fields**. Photography: **Ernest Miller**. Dialogue supervisor: **Stanley Price**. Art director: **James West**. Music: **Raoul Kraushaar**. Assistant director: **Melville Shyer**. Set continuity: **Donna Norridge**. Special photographic effects: **Ray Mercer**. Sound recording: **Charles Cooper**. Producer: **Vincent M. Fennelly**. Executive producer: **Bill Elliott**. A Westwood Production for Allied Artists.

Copyright 21 February 1954 by Allied Artists Pictures Corp. Released in the U.S.A. on the same date by Monogram Pictures Corp. U.K. release through Associated British-Pathé: floating from April 1957 (sic). Australian release through Paramount: 12 September 1957 (sic). 6,689 feet. 74 minutes.

SYNOPSIS: Clay Tyndall, arriving in the Bitter Creek country to avenge the death of his rancher brother, suspects the criminals are the Lazy Q men, working for Quentin Allen.

Clay questions Gail Bonner (who is engaged to Quentin Allen), Doc Prentiss, and an old-time stage-driver named Platte.

COMMENT: Tame Poverty Row western. Except for a held-too-long burst of gun-fire in a darkened corridor, Thomas Carr's direction is noticeably lacking in distinction.

George Waggner's screenplay is fair. It has some good dialogue (particularly in the confrontation scene between Elliott and Young) and situations that could have amounted to something in the hands of a better director — and a better cast! Beverly Garland is one of the least attractive heroines we have met in many a day, and Mr Elliott is rather glum — understandably, perhaps, as he seems to have put up some of the money for this effort.

There's not much action and production values are generally as dreary as Ernest Miller's flat photography. Only Raoul Kraushaar's music score is a cut above the average.

RECOMMENDED VIEWING PROCEDURE: Turn up the sound for the credits and following rolling title, then turn down for the opening gun-fire in the darkened corridor sequence, then turn the whole thing off!

— G.A.

# Black Aces

**Buck Jones** (Ted Ames), **Kay Linaker** (Sandy McKenzie), **Fred Mackaye** (Len Stoddard), **W. E. Laurence** (Boyd Loomis), **Robert Frazer** (Homer Truesdale), **Raymond Brown** (Henry Kline), **Bob Kortman** (Wolf Whalen), **Bernard Phillips** (Jake Stoddard), **Frank Campeau** (Ike Bowlaigs), **Charles LeMoyne** (Sheriff Potter), **Charles King** (Jess), **Arthur Van Slyke** (Silver Tip Joe), **Bob McKenzie** (Hank Farnum), **Ben Corbett** (the outlaw look-out), and "Silver".

Produced and directed by **BUCK JONES**. Co-director: **Lesley Selander**. Screenplay: **Frances Guihan**. Based on the novel by **Stephen Payne**. Photographed by **Allen Thompson** and **William Sickner**. Film editor: **Bernard Loftus**.

Copyright 29 June 1937 by Universal Pictures Co., Inc. Released in the U.S.A. 5 September 1937. No New York opening. 6 reels. 59 minutes.

COMMENT: Another unusual film from the Buck Jones western stable, this one has some really extraordinary photography which defies all Hollywood conventions:— Fully half the film is shot in almost total darkness (including the opening and the climax) and another quarter of it in the eerie twilight just before sunset or just after sunrise. Jones' direction is more than competent and incorporates at least one striking image (Jones rides down a slight incline and is surrounded by a complete circle of badmen). Jones' production eschews flamboyance and has a realistic drabness about it which is very effective.

The script reveals the identity of the "boss" a little too early in the narrative, but the slack is taken up by some fine character studies, particularly from Kay Linaker as the unusually spirited heroine, Fred Mackaye as the card-cheating saloon proprietor, and Bernard Phillips as his personable brother. Comedian Corbett has a straight role for once.

# Black Bart

**Yvonne DeCarlo** (Lola Montez), **Dan Duryea** (Charles E. Boles), **Jeffrey Lynn** (Lance Hardeen), **Percy Kilbride** (Jersey Brady), **Lloyd Gough** (Sheriff Gordon), **Frank Lovejoy** (Lorimer), **John McIntire** (Clark), **Don Beddoe** (J. T. Hall), **Ray Walker** (MacFarland), **Soledad Jimenez** (Teresa), **Eddy C. Waller** (Mason), **Anne O'Neal** (Mrs Harmon), **Chief Many Treaties** (Indian), **Douglas Fowley** (Sheriff Mix), **Paul Maxey, Milton Kibbee, Ray Harper, Wayne Treadway, Earl Audet, William Norton Bailey, Kenneth Ross-MacKenzie** (men), **Eddie Acuff** (Elkins), **Ray Teal** (Pete), **Marshall Ruth** (band leader), **Bert Davidson** (Blake), **Russ Conway** (Agent Clayton), **Ray Bennett** (Henry), **Nina Caompana** (Mamasita), **Bill O'Leary** (Wells Fargo man), **George Douglas** (Alcott), **Everett Shields** (killer), **Reed Howes** (bartender).

Director: **GEORGE SHERMAN**. Screenplay: **Luci Ward, Jack Natteford, William Bowers**. Original story: **Luci Ward, Jack Natteford**. Photographed in Technicolor by **Irving Glassberg**. Technicolor color consultants: **Natalie Kalmus, Clemens Finley**. Art direction: **Bernard Herzbrun, Emrich Nicholson**. Film editor: **Russell Schoengarth**. Sound: **Leslie I. Carey, Corson Jowett**. Set decorations: **Russell A. Gausman, William L. Stevens**. Costumes: **Yvonne Wood**. Hair stylist: **Carmen Dirigo**. Make-up: **Bud Westmore**. Choreography: **Val Raset**. Assistant director: **William Holland**. Dance music: **Frank Skinner**. Camera operator: **Edward Sharp**. Music score: **Frank Skinner**. Script supervisor: **Pat Betz**. Production manager: **Howard Christie**. Grip: **Dean Paul**. Still photographs: **Ed O'Toole**. Produced by **Leonard Goldstein**.

Copyright 24 March 1948 by Universal Pictures Co., Inc. New York opening at the Winter Garden: 3 May 1948. U.S. release: April 1948. U.K. release through Eros (the film was turned down by Rank): floating from November 1949. Australian release: 12 August 1948. 7,247 feet. 80 minutes.

U.K. release title: *BLACK BART, HIGHWAYMAN*.

SYNOPSIS: This film is based on the adventures of Charles E. Bolton, poet-highwayman who committed 28 hold-ups before he was apprehended, and Lola Montez, the internationally famous dancer. That they ever did meet is not impossible but highly improbable, for Lola was touring the U.S. under the direction of P. T. Barnum at the time Black Bart was on the rampage. This is a dashingly-played (particularly by Dan Duryea and lovely Yvonne De Carlo), fast-moving and very exciting melodrama, very competently directed with appealing Technicolor photography.

— E.V.D.

VIEWERS' GUIDE: Okay for all.

COMMENT: Quite an entertaining "B", photographed in most attractive Technicolor by Irving Glassberg, this classy Universal entry features an interesting and highly rewarding group of players, led by Yvonne De Carlo, Dan Duryea, Jeffrey Lynn and Percy Kilbride. Very capably directed by George Sherman from a taut, well-constructed and peopled-with-interesting-characters screenplay (to which William Bowers doubtless made a major contribution), *Black Bart* (despite its off-putting title) rates as a must-see western.

# Blazing Across the Pecos

**Charles Starrett** (Steve Blake, the Durango Kid), **Smiley Burnette** (himself), **Patricia White** (Lola Carter), **Paul Campbell** (Jim Traynor), **Charles Wilson** (Ace Brockway), **Thomas Jackson** (Matt Carter), **Jack Ingram** (Buckshot Thomas), **Chief Thunder Cloud** (Chief Bear Claw), **Pat O'Malley** (Mike Doyle), **Jacques O'Mahoney** [Jock Mahoney] (Bill Wheeler), **Frank McCarroll** (Gunsmoke Ballard), **Pierce Lyden** (Jason), **Paul Conrad** (Sleepy Larsen), **Red Arnall and the Western Aces** (themselves), **Ralph Bucko** (messenger), **Jack Evans, Jack Tornek, Blackie Whiteford** (townsmen), **Post Park** (stage driver). Narrated by **Fred F. Sears**.

Director: **RAY NAZARRO**. Screenplay: **Norman S. Hall**. Original story: **Normal S. Hall**. Photography: **Ira H. Morgan**. Film editor: **Richard Fantl**. Art director: **Charles Clague**. Set decorator: **Sidney Clifford**. Music: **Paul Sawtell**. Songs: "Home Cookin" and "Popcorn" by **Smiley Burnette**; "Going Back to Texas" by **Red Arnall**. Script supervisor: **Wyonna O'Brien**. Grip: **Al Becker**. Still photos: **Irving Lippman**. Camera operator: **Gert Anderson**. Assistant director: **Gilbert Kay**. Sound technician: **Jack Goodrich**. Western Electric Sound System. Producer: **Colbert Clark**.

Copyright 17 June 1948 by Columbia Pictures Corp. No recorded New York opening. U.S. release: 1 July 1948. U.K. release: September 1952. Not theatrically released in Australia. 6 reels. 55 minutes. U.K. release title: *UNDER ARREST*.

SYNOPSIS: Gambling czar's efforts to seize control of the town are foiled by the Durango Kid.

COMMENT: Above average Durango Kid western. There's plenty of action including a stagecoach chase with exciting running inserts and some good stunt-work (Jock Mahoney who has a brief two-or-three-line role doubles for the Kid) and some spectacular Indians-on-the-warpath stock footage. The patter-type musical numbers rendered by Mr Burnette and Red Arnall are very pleasant too, and Mr Burnette's foolery is fairly amusing. Charles Starrett does his usual competent job and we liked Charles Wilson's rubber-faced villain. Nazarro's direction is a cut above his usual standard and production values are generally adequate. Despite his prominence in the cast list, Thomas Jackson has only a minor role, the bulk of the support work being carried by Jack Ingram as Buckshot and Paul Campbell as Jim Traynor, neither of whom figure in the credits at all!

OTHER VIEWS: A gambler wants to build a private empire out of Pecos Flats, so he bribes a band of Indians to terrorize the townsfolk and raid the wagon trains. Of course the Durango Kid sorts him out in time. Much the usual Starrett standard western, with plenty of pace and little subtlety.

— E. Victor Dyer.

# Blue Montana Skies

**Gene Autry** (himself), **Smiley Burnette** (Frog Millhouse), **June Storey** (Dorothy Hamilton), **Harry Woods** (Eddie Hendricks), **Tully Marshall** (Steve), **Al Bridge**

(marshal), **Glenn Strange** (Bob Causer), **Dorothy Granger** (Molly Carter), **Edmund Cobb** (Joe Brennan), **Robert Winkler** (Wilbur), **Jack Ingram** (Frazer), **John Beach** (corporal, North West Mounted), **Walt Schrum and His Colorado Hillbillies** (themselves), **Augie Gomez** (Blackfeather), **Elmo Lincoln** (Curly, the warehouse manager), **Allan Cavan** (2nd customs officer), **Ted Mapes** (a Mountie), **Curley Dresden** (henchman in armor), **Jack Kenny** (curio shop proprietor), **Frankie Marvin** (Cookie), **Buffalo Bill Jr**, and "Champion".

Director: **B. REEVES EASON**. Screenplay: **Gerald Geraghty**. Story: **Norman S. Hall, Paul Franklin**. Photography: **Jack Marta**. Film editor: **Lester Orlebeck**. Music director: **Raoul Kraushaar**. Songs: "Blue Montana Skies" by **Gene Autry, Fred Rose** and **Johnny Marvin**; "I Just Want You" by **Gene Autry, Fred Rose** and **Johnny Marvin**; "Away Out Yonder" by **Fred Rose**; "Old Geezer"; "Rocking in the Saddle". Assistant director: **Philip Ford**. Production manager: **Al Wilson**. Associate producer: **Harry Grey**. Executive producer: **Herbert J. Yates**.

Copyright 4 May 1939 by Republic Pictures Corp. No recorded New York opening. U.S. release: 4 May 1939. U.K. release through British Lion. No Australian theatrical release. 6 reels. 59 minutes.

SYNOPSIS: Autry and Frog track down fur smugglers in the Canadian snow country.

NOTES: Autry's 32nd of his 94 films.

COMMENT: June Storey is an attractive little heroine and it's nice to see some of our favorite villains like Harry Woods, Glenn Strange, Eddie Cobb and Jack Ingram on deck. Al Bridge is in the cast too but this time firmly on the side of the law! There are some pleasant songs and now and again there is a brief spurt of action, but though the film is directed by the well-known 2nd unit action director B. Reeves Eason, surprisingly the action spots are rather tamely staged and never amount to much. Even the climax is disappointingly short. Mr Burnette's comedy routines are similarly lacking in sparkle, but at least *their* brevity is a blessing.

# Borderland

**William Boyd** (Hopalong Cassidy), **James Ellison** (Johnny Nelson), **George Hayes** (Windy), **Morris Ankrum** (Loco), **Charlene Wyatt** (Molly Rand), **Nora Lane** (Grace Rand), **Trevor Bardette** (Colonel Gonzales), **Al Bridge** (Dandy Morgan), **George Chesebro** (Tom Parker), **John Beach, Earle Hodgins, John St Polis, Edward Cassidy, Slim Whitaker, Cliff Parkinson, Karl Hackett, Robert Walker, Frank Ellis**.

Director: **NATE WATT**. Screenplay: **Harrison Jacobs**. Based on the 1931 novel *Bring Me His Ears* by **Clarence E. Mulford**. Photography: **Archie Stout**. Film editor: **Robert Warwick**. Art director: **Lewis J. Rachmil**. Assistant directors: **Derwin Abrahams, Harry Knight**. Associate producer: **Eugene Strom**. Producer: **Harry Sherman**. A Harry Sherman Production, presented by **Adolph Zukor**.

Copyright 26 February 1937 by Paramount Pictures, Inc. No recorded New York showcase. U.S. release: 26 February 1937. 9 reels. Yes, 9 reels — the novel runs over 300 pages. 82 minutes.

SYNOPSIS: Hoppy goes undercover as an outlaw. His quarry: a murderous border gang, led by Morris Ankrum (also playing a pretend role as a harmless half-wit).

NOTES: Don Miller says this one holds the record as the longest "B" series western ever made.
   Number 9 of the 66-picture series.

VIEWERS' GUIDE: Okay for all.

COMMENT: Solely of curiosity value, this early Hopalong Cassidy has little to recommend it save some nice exterior photography by Archie Stout. The film is poorly directed by Nate Watt and the action sequences are some of the wettest we've seen (though the climax with Hoppy holding a bleeding gun-wound in his leg has a certain novelty value). Screenplay by Harrison Jacobs does a disservice to Clarence E. Mulford's novel.

OTHER VIEWS: *Borderland* had a strong plot, a strong villain (Morris Ankrum again) and was strung out to 82 minutes, longest of all series Westerns. It was also the last appearance by Ellison as Johnny Nelson. He had been getting a buildup of sorts, including the role of Buffalo Bill in DeMille's *The Plainsman*, and his desire to step forward to greener pastures was granted by Sherman.

— Don Miller.

# Border Patrol

**William Boyd** (Hopalong Cassidy), **Andy Clyde** (California Carlson), **Jay Kirby** (Johnny Travers), **Russell Simpson** (Orestes Krebs), **Claudia Drake** (Inez), **Duncan Renaldo** (commandante), **Cliff Parkinson** (Don Enrique), **George Reeves** (Mexican officer), **Robert Mitchum, Herman Hack, Pierce Lyden** (henchmen), **Merrill McCormack**.

Director: **LESLEY SELANDER**. Screenplay: **Michael Wilson**. Based on characters created by **Clarence E. Mulford**. Photography: **Russell Harlan**. Film editor: **Sherman A. Rose**. Art director: **Ralph Berger**. Music director: **Irvin Talbot**. Associate producer: **Lewis J. Rachmil**. Producer: **Harry Sherman**. A Harry Sherman Production for Paramount Pictures. Released through United Artists, who purchased the film outright from Paramount in order to take up the slack in a product shortage caused by the war.

Copyright 11 December 1942 by United Artists Productions, Inc. No *New York Times* review, though the movie did open in New York. U.S. release: 2 April 1943. Australian release: 24 June 1943. 6,054 feet. 67 minutes.

SYNOPSIS: *Border Patrol*, originally titled "Missing Men", spotted unbilled Mitchum as a henchman for a ruthless silver-mine operator (Russell Simpson), who has been using Mexicans for slave labor. Hoppy and sidekicks California Carlson (Andy Clyde) and

Johnny Travers (Jay Kirby) are Texas Rangers out to bring the villains to justice, but are instead framed for murder and only saved from hanging when a Mexican girl helps them make a getaway in time for the standard blood and thunder finale. George Reeves (later television's "Superman") and Duncan Renaldo (better known as the movies' "Cisco Kid") play Mexican army officers in this outing.

— Alvin H. Marill: *Robert Mitchum on the Screen.*

NOTES: Number 45 of the 66-picture series, and film debut of Robert Mitchum. Negative cost: $87,285. Initial worldwide rentals gross: $132,406.

COMMENT: A more appealing than average Hoppy entry, thanks not only to the easy-to-spot presence of Robert Mitchum as a bad guy, but to better acting all around. The script by none other than Michael Wilson — *Five Fingers, A Place in the Sun, Friendly Persuasion, The Bridge on the River Kwai, Planet of the Apes*, etc — is realistically suspenseful, providing some fascinating characters with plenty of opportunities to generate drama and conflict. Tensely directed by Lesley Selander, with the aid of fine photography by Russell Harlan and suitable mood music scored by Irvin Talbot.

OTHER VIEWS: In the mid-thirties, independent producer Harry "Pop" Sherman obtained the rights to the Hoppy stories from Cassidy's creator, Clarence Edward Mulford. In the 1930s, the series made money, but eventually costs rose and revenue declined. At this stage, Boyd bought out Sherman and acquired all the production and television rights to Hoppy, putting himself in complete control of the radio and later television series as well as the last dozen theatrical adventures.

The Hoppy series followed a standard formula, except that its good-guy hero was dressed completely in black, making a striking, if somewhat fatherly figure, astride his all-white horse, "Topper". True to the trio form, staple of the "B" western of the 1930s and 1940s, Hoppy rode with a young, good-looking sidekick (at various times, James Ellison, Russell Hayden, Brad King, Jay Kirby, Jimmy Rogers, and Rand Brooks) and, for comedy relief, a crusty, jack-of-all-trades partner (George "Gabby" Hayes, Britt Wood, and finally Andy Clyde). Usually Hoppy would be found in various locales, to avoid boring his ever-faithful followers, and occasionally he would not be seen as foreman of the Bar 20 Ranch but as the local sheriff or riding with the Texas Rangers.

Of all the young actors who gained film experience in the Hoppy stock company, none moved to greater stardom than the laconic, droopy-eyed, two-fisted bad guy (and once-in-awhile hero), Bob Mitchum.

"It's not a slipshod Western," Dorothy Masters wrote in the New York *Daily News*, "but one that has [Boyd's] first-rate acting and a believable story... With good production and good acting, *Border Patrol* is a darned good Western."

— Alvin H. Marill.

# Border Romance

**Armida** (Conchita), **Don Terry** (Bob Hamlin), **J. Frank Glendon** (Buck Adams), **Marjorie "Babe" Kane** (Nina), **Victor Potel** (Slim), **Wesley Barry** (Victor Hamlin), **Nita Martan** (Gloria), **Harry von Meter** (captain), **William Costello** (lieutenant).

Director: **RICHARD THORPE**. Original story and screenplay: **John Francis Natteford**. Photography: **Harry Zech**. Additional photography: **Ted McCord**. Film editor: **Richard Cahoon**. Art director: **Ralph De Lacy**. Music director: **Al Short**. Songs by **Will Jason** and **Val Burton**: "Song of the Rurales" (chorus), "The Girl from Topolombo" (Kane), "Yo Te Adoro" (Armida and Terry), "My Desert Rose" (Terry). Sound engineer: **J. Stransky Jr**. RCA Sound System. Producer: **Lester F. Scott**.

Copyright 13 May 1930 by Tiffany Productions, Inc. New York opening at the Colony: 25 May 1930. U.S. release: 18 May 1930. 7 reels. 5,974 feet. 66 minutes. Print under review is the re-issue presented by Amity Pictures.

SYNOPSIS: Bob Hamlin, his younger brother Victor and their helper Slim are horse-traders in Mexico. Their horses are stolen. Whilst pursuing bandits, they themselves are seemingly hunted by the rurales who want to question them about a tavern shooting in which a Mexican was killed. Bob still finds time to romance both Conchita, a diminutive yet spirited senorita, and Gloria, a bar-girl friend of the horse bandit; whilst Slim, who has saved some money, is vigorously pursued by his ex-wife Nina, a singer in the local cantina.

NOTES: Also released in a silent version.

COMMENT: This remarkably curious film certainly whets our appetite for more of the same. By the standards of the independent early sound western, it is not only lavishly produced but technically quite accomplished. There are no odd cuts, washed out photography or other evidences of primitive sound recording. Zech's rich photography exhibits a nice range of contrasts, the film editing is reasonably deft, and the recording of the songs, whilst obviously dubbed, is still agreeably proficient.

Even more curious is that the film belongs not to the William S. Hart and *The Covered Wagon* traditions of the silent western, but is firmly in the camp of *Rio Rita* and *Girl of the Golden West*. Not only do the characters break into incongruous if pleasing song at every likely and unlikely opportunity, but they play to each other as if they were acting on a stage. They project their voices with stage emphases, they exaggerate their facial expressions, and their movements are blocked out within invisible but still potent stage confines.

This said, Armida makes a most attractive little heroine. Fans of "Babe" Kane will not be disappointed either, though she has only the one quick song, followed by a typically snappy dance. Don Terry is a bit wet as the hero, whilst Potel and Barry overact as his sidekicks — particularly Potel, though he does have one or two genuinely funny lines.

If it's action and not song or comedy you're after, you will probably be a bit disappointed, despite the long shoot-out, riding-to-the-rescue climax. Which brings us to our final curiosity. It's an odd western indeed in which the comedy, romance and music are obviously regarded by all concerned as far more important than chases, fights and gunplay. In fact the songs are very tuneful indeed. Notice also that the music tends to play under the dialogue scenes whilst the action spots are left to the mercy of primitive sound effects.

**The director:** Richard Thorpe had already directed over sixty western features before *Border Romance*. A devotee of the don't-make-it-good-make-it-Monday school of film-making, Thorpe was noted for his celerity in printing takes that other directors would have described as less than perfect. Thorpe always believed that striving for perfection was a waste of money and time. Mr and Mrs Average Picturegoer didn't know and couldn't tell the difference between Thorpe's okay first or second take and William Wyler's masterly 37th or 49th. Usually his films are staged with reasonable vigor but little imagination. *Border Romance*, however, is less vigorous but more imaginative.

# the Boy from Oklahoma

**Will Rogers, Jr** (Tom Brewster), **Nancy Olson** (Katie Brannigan), **Lon Chaney** (Crazy Charlie), **Anthony Caruso** (Barney Turlock), **Wallace Ford** (Wally Higgins), **Clem Bevans** (Pop Pruty), **Merv Griffin** (Steve), **Louis Jean Heydt** (Paul Evans), **Sheb Wooley** (Pete Martin), **Slim Pickens** (Shorty), **Tyler MacDuff** (Billy the Kid), **Skippy Torgerson** (Johnny Neil), **James Griffith** (Joe Downey), **Charles Watts** (Harry), **Britt Wood** (prisoner), **Joan Weldon** (saloon girl on porch), **George Chesebro, George Lloyd** (barflies), **Harry Lauter** (Jim), **Guy Wilkerson** (Huey Mitchell), **Denver Pyle** (blacksmith), **Forrest Taylor** (doctor), **Montie Montana** (Roper), **John L. Cason** (henchman).

Director: **MICHAEL CURTIZ**. Screenplay: **Frank Davis** and **Winston Miller**. Based on a Saturday Evening Post story by **Michael Fessier**. Photographed in WarnerColor by **Robert Burks**. Film editor: **James Moore**. Art director: **Leo K. Kuter**. Set decorations: **Emile Kuri**. Wardrobe: **Howard Shoup**. Music composed by **Max Steiner**, orchestrated by **Murray Cutter**, directed by **Ray Heindorf**. Make-up artist: **Gordon Bau**. Dialogue director: **Norman Stuart**. Assistant director: **Oren Haglund**. Sound: **Stanley Jones**. RCA Sound System. Producer: **David Weisbart**. Presented by Warner Bros.

No New York opening. Not copyrighted. U.S. release: 27 February 1954. U.K. release: 31 May 1954. Australian release: 10 March 1955. 7,922 feet. 88 minutes.

SYNOPSIS: Quiet-mannered sheriff restores law and order in Black Rock.

NOTES: Curtiz's last film under his Warner contract.
  Although Warners, Curtiz and Will Rogers, Jr. all claimed that this was only his second film, the actor had in fact played his father in David Butler's *Look For the Silver Lining* (1949).

COMMENT: A minor but very accomplished Western. True, the central, idea of a mild-mannered sheriff is not new (see *Destry*). Likewise when this film was originally released, many of its other elements were labelled familiar and or quite ordinary. But time has given *The Boy from Oklahoma* a new freshness and lease of life. Broadcast no less than three times on Australian television in 1994, it has found a responsive audience.
  Superbly photographed both indoors — Burks can be justly proud of such suspenseful low-key lighting as the sequences in the barn — and out (Curtiz gets the most in dramatic value out of some only moderately attractive locations by using tightly composed shots with lots of pans and running inserts, all sharply cut together), and lensed on a sizable budget with lots of extras milling about its large sets, *The Boy from Oklahoma* is a western with pace, charm, style and artistry.

Of course a lot of that charm is contributed by a very attractive cast. Not least in this department is Will Rogers himself. Though he is obviously no youngster, Rogers displays a pleasant, thoroughly likeable personality. He is very agreeably supported by Nancy Olson. And it's nice to see Clem Bevans in a major part -- and figuring prominently in a really suspenseful moment at the climax too. Lon Chaney Jr provides a wealth of those Old Testament quotes (without which no vintage Hollywood movie is complete), whilst Wallace Ford has a wonderfully roguish part as a cowardly Caruso henchman. Caruso of course makes a breathtakingly villainous heavy. And we love James Griffith's cameo as the drunk and willing stooge. Merv Griffin however has but a few tiny spots early on before dropping out altogether. There are other players like Slim Pickens who volunteer more than their quota of entertainment, but these we will leave for you to discover yourself.

Curtiz was a marvelous all-rounder who could successfully direct all genres of film from historical epics and swashbucklers through musicals and soap operas to farces and westerns. *The Boy from Oklahoma* is Curtiz's attempt at a "B", with all the familiar ingredients given a new impetus and meaning by his classy style. What with in-depth compositions, tight frame arrangements, effective camera set-ups (there's even an unobtrusive long take, disguised by its deep focus, low-key lighting and the seemingly natural movements of players and camera) and sharply smooth film editing, *The Boy from Oklahoma* is a very accomplished "B" indeed. Moreover, Curtiz and his scriptwriters have had a bit of fun with the usual "B" conventions by exaggerating them. Thus the villain is both more brutally and more schemingly villainous, whilst the clean-cut hero is even more mild-mannered (even bookish) and philosophical. In a Charles Starrett western, for example, there's no way you could get away with such scenes as Caruso belting into Ford (an excellent no-dialogue touch) and then attempting to murder old nice guy Clem Bevans. Nor would the hero's run-ins and romance with boyish heroine Nancy Olson be welcomed.

All the same, the film certainly has enough action to satisfy any western fan. The introductory horse race is excitingly staged, despite obvious studio inserts, whilst the climax is all location action filmed with thrilling running inserts and some great stunts, all especially staged for this film. There is not a single foot of stock footage.

While the aim was undoubtedly to make a lighthearted "B" with an "A" budget, it still achieves some powerful moments of tension and suspense. It is precisely because characters like Rogers and Bevans are so naturally likeable that the audience really feels with them in their fight. No doubt it was a challenge to Curtiz to bring off a western that strikes just the right balance between light romantic comedy and heavy drama, but he succeeds brilliantly. Curtiz was keen to make a star of Rogers (whom he had directed in his official debut *The Story of Will Rogers*), so here he does marvellously by a script ingeniously re-tailored by Frank Davis to fit Rogers' personality giving every frame the full Curtiz treatment. Unlike Curtiz's next film *The Egyptian* where his style is often swamped under CinemaScope and a stifling over-budget, *The Boy from Oklahoma* is recognisably and obviously a Curtiz film.

Other technical credits, capped by a rousing Steiner score, are equally adept.

Why did Warners lose interest in the film? No New York opening, no copyright, little publicity. One, it was Curtiz's last film under his 30-year Warner Bros contract. No studio likes to trumpet the wares of its rivals. And two, it was undoubtedly felt that the movie lacked star power and had nothing to offer the 1954 teenage market. On the other hand, it was far too unsophisticated for the art house circuit. As for Rogers, pleasant and likeable though he may be, there was no place for a peace lover in the 1954 of the Cold War, Senator McCarthy and Korea. The last frame of the film in which Rogers and young Joey ride into the sunset, surely that's a symbol of Curtiz's Warners career at its end. (Of course he did make one return to his old studio — in 1957 for *The Helen Morgan Story*).

# Brimstone

**Rod Cameron** (Johnny Tremaine), **Adrian Booth** (Molly Bannister), **Walter Brennan** (Pop Courteen), **Forrest Tucker** (Sheriff Henry McIntyre), **Jack Holt** (Marshal Walter Greenside), **Jim Davis** (Mick Courteen), **James Brown** (Bud Courteen), **Guinn "Big Boy" Williams** (Art Benson), **Jack Lambert** (Luke Courteen), **Will Wright** (Martin Treadwell), **David Williams** (Todd Bannister), **Harry V. Cheshire** (Calvin Willis), **Hal Taliaferro** (Dave Watts), **Herbert Rawlinson** (storekeeper), **Stanley Andrews** (Winslow), **Charlita** (Chiquita), **Jody Gilbert** (fat lady on stage), **George Chesebro** (saloon keeper), **Charles Cane** (bartender), **Hank Bell** (shotgun guard), **Sam Flint** (Dr Cane), **Helen Brown** (Mrs Inslow), **Teddy Infuhr** (young boy), **Emmett Lynn** (stage driver), **Ted Mapes** (cowhand).

Director: **JOSEPH KANE**. Screenplay: **Thames Williams**. Story: **Norman S. Hall**. Photographed in Trucolor by **Jack Marta**. Film editor: **Arthur Roberts**. Art director: **Frank Arrigo**. Set decorators: **John McCarthy Jr, Charles Thompson**. Costumes: **Adele Palmer**. Make-up: **Bob Mark**. Hair styles: **Peggy Gray**. Special effects: **Howard Lydecker, Theodore Lydecker**. Optical effects: Consolidated Film Industries. Music composed by **Nathan Scott**, orchestrated by **Stanley Wilson**. Sound recording: **T.C. Carman, Howard Wilson**. RCA Sound System. Associate producer: **Joseph Kane**. Executive producer: **Herbert J. Yates**.

Copyright 17 August 1949 by Republic Pictures Corp. New York opening at the Palace: 6 October 1949. U.S. release: 15 August 1949. U.K. release through Associated British-Pathé. Australian release through 20th Century-Fox: 27 October 1950. 8,376 feet. 93 minutes.

SYNOPSIS: The makers of this film landed themselves in something of a quandary. When the film was all ready for release, someone in Republic's publicity department pointed out that the title meant nothing. There was not a single reference to brimstone, in any shape or allegorical form throughout the entire movie. A Foreword was hastily added in which the early settlers were commended for fighting Indians, drought — and outlaws like "Brimstone" Courteen. In the movie, however, the character is not called "Brimstone" but "Pop" Courteen, a title that masks a viciously vengeful rancher who, together with his three sons, is waging a secret war against the community in general, homesteaders in particular.

COMMENT: I don't know why Adrian Booth gets such prominent billing here. Her role is so small, you would expect to find her name well down the cast list. But then Jack Holt's part is so fleeting, he's hardly in the movie at all.

Two players have the lion's share of the action:

Number one, Rod Cameron, an indifferent performer, but rugged enough to acquit himself honorably in the action scenes (with the help of a stunt double, of course).

Number two, Walter Brennan, who emerges as the real star of the film.

Admittedly, you can't always rely on Brennan. True, he's given some engrossingly charismatic portraits in the past, but some directors seem to have been afraid of him and unable to keep him under control.

We could cite quite a few films in which Brennan has hammed it up to a really obnoxious degree (though in the actor's defense it must be said that in many of these cases the script was so weak that many players would feel the only way to strengthen the part was by over-indulging in scene-chewing and other hammy mannerisms).

But here in *Brimstone*, Brennan is not only perfectly cast, but perfectly controlled. It's a good meaty part, and though Walter plays it to the hilt, he doesn't overplay it, or project it on just the one monotonously menacing note. He shades the role well. He can temper open hostility and incredibly mean-spirited viciousness with sly cunning, subterfuge and even a seemingly transparent if rough yet rascally charm. Yes, Brennan has a great role. He plays it superbly.

Oddly, the next most impressive performance is handed out by Hal Taliaferro. A long-time western star, under the name Wally Wales, Taliaferro must have played hundreds of miniscule roles in the 1940s. His name often appears towards the bottom of cast lists, but it is usually very difficult to pick him out in the crowd. Here for once, he has a comparatively sizable role. Although he makes an extremely late entrance, he provides an extra ingredient in the climax, agreeably complicating the shoot-out and adding a few nice touches to the suspense.

Jack Lambert contributes his usual strong characterization as a surly but none-too-bright offspring, Guinn "Big Boy" Williams turns in a bit of slightly forced comic relief, while Forrest Tucker adequately holds down a none-too-large but unusual role as an opportunistic sheriff.

Production values are unusually good by Republic standards (even if they are helped out by some blue tinted stock and matching main footage in the introductory episode), with locations near Sacramento, a fair bit of action, and above all, as said, Walter Brennan's riveting performance.

OTHER VIEWS: Despite indifferent direction by Joseph Kane and somewhat flat color photography, *Brimstone* is helped out by a fairly entertaining, plot-twisting script and a stand-out portrait by Walter Brennan as an irredeemably mean badman. Rod Cameron makes a fair-fisted hero.

— G.A.

# Cabin in the Cotton

**Richard Barthelmess** (Marvin Blake), **Dorothy Jordan** (Betty Wright), **Bette Davis** (Madge Norwood), **Henry B. Walthall** (Old Elph), **Berton Churchill** (Lane Norwood), **Walter Percival** (Cleve Clinton), **William Le Maire** (Jake Fisher), **Hardie Albright** (Roland Neale), **Tully Marshall** (Old Slick Harkness), **Clarence Muse** (old blind negro), **Edmund Breese** (Holmes Scott), **John Marston** (Russ Carter), **Erville Alderson** (Sock

Fisher), **Dorothy Peterson** (Lilly Blake), **Snowflake** (Ezzy Daniels), **Russell Simpson** (Uncle Joe), **Harry Cording** (Ross Clinton), **Virginia Hammond** (Mrs Norwood), **Florine McKinney** (Liza), **Dennis O'Keefe** (dance extra), **Libby Taylor** (Norwood's maid), and **Trevor Bardette, Charles King, David Landau, J. Carroll Naish**.

Director: **MICHAEL CURTIZ**. Associate director: **William Keighley**. Screenplay: **Paul Green**. Based on the novel "Cabin in the Sky" by **Harry Harrison Kroll**. Photography: **Barney McGill**. Film editor: **George Amy**. Art director: **Esdras Hartley**. Costumes: **Orry-Kelly**. Love theme composed by **Harry Warren**. Song, "Old Folks at Home" by **Stephen Foster**. Music orchestrated by **Ray Heindorf**, played by The Vitaphone Orchestra conducted by **Leo F. Forbstein**. Assistant cameramen: **William P. Whitley, Kenneth Green**. Stills: **William Walling**. Assistant director: **Al Alleborn**. Sound recording: **Earl Sitar**. Associate producer: **Hal B. Wallis**. Executive producer: **Jack L. Warner**. In charge of production: **Darryl F. Zanuck**.

Copyright 15 October 1932 by First National Pictures, Inc. U.S. release: 1 October 1932. New York opening at the Strand: 29 September 1932. 8 reels. 79 minutes.

SYNOPSIS: A wealthy planter takes an interest in an impoverished sharecropper's son who wants to educate himself, takes him into his home and gives him a job as bookkeeper. The young man discovers that the planter has been cheating his tenants. Another complication is that he is madly in love with the planter's daughter!

NOTES: Keighley says he was "dialogue director" on this film. See "Films in Review" October 1974.

COMMENT: Although the Foreword is careful to point out that this film isn't going to take sides between the planters and the peckerwoods, it is pretty clear which side the scriptwriters favor. Certainly the planters do get a few arguments in but Berton Churchill who plays his characteristic role of blustering double-dealing is hardly an ideal spokesman.

Still, leaving aside the question of the rights and wrongs on either side — which is now only of historical interest anyway — the film has an engrossing story which is just as exciting to-day as when it was first presented back in 1932. If anything the film is much less dated than the usual plantation drama thanks to the skilled direction of Michael Curtiz which concentrates on a crisp and realistic handling and the script's development of character and its avoidance of some of the more usual melodramatic clichés.

Two aspects I like are the genuine affection that obviously exists between father and daughter, never overtly stated but plain from their bearing and attitude towards each other, and the fact that Bette Davis receives no more than a climactic snub for her "sin" — actually none of the participants are punished for their crimes. Yes, this realistic script is a far cry from the tinselly, if idealistically "moral" reversions of normal human behavior that Hollywood was to turn out under the repressive hand of the Motion Picture Production Code.

Curtiz's realistic handling is hampered in the early stages by the use of obvious stock shots and process backgrounds. Fortunately, this practice ceases quite early on. Curtiz directs the whole film in short, brisk takes (superlatively edited by George Amy).

Barney McGill's exquisite photography also ranks as a major asset not only for his broodingly atmospheric night scenes and the sparkle and whiteness of the plantation house episodes, but for the wonders he has done with Bette Davis.

Davis certainly looks most attractive in this made-to-order part of the rich and spoilt daughter. She acts with appealing vivacity too, making the most of such lines as "I'd like to kiss you, but I've just washed my hair!" Co-star Richard Barthelmess is inclined to over-do the facial expressions indicating indecision and is not too believable as a poor sharecropper (he is too well-groomed and speaks too well), but I like him. He has a personality that is exactly right for this kind of role. The rest of the cast is most capable.

# Canyon Passage

**Dana Andrews** (Logan Stuart), **Brian Donlevy** (George Camrose), **Susan Hayward** (Lucy Overmire), **Patricia Roc** (Caroline Marsh), **Ward Bond** ( Honey Bragg), **Andy Devine** (Ben Dance), **Rose Hobart** (Marita Lestrade), **Halliwell Hobbes** (Clenchfield), **Lloyd Bridges** (Johnny Steele), **Stanley Ridges** (Jonas Overmire), **Dorothy Petersen** (Mrs Dance), **Vic Cutler** (Van Blazier), **Fay Holden** (Mrs Overmire), **Tad Devine** (Asa Dance), **Dennis Devine** (Bushrod Dance), **Hoagy Carmichael** (Linnet), **Onslow Stevens** (Lestrade), **James Cardwell** (Gray Bartlett), **Ray Teal** (Neil Howison), **Virginia Patton** (Liza Stone), **Francis McDonald** (Cobb), **Erville Alderson** (judge), **Ralph Peters** (Stutchell), **Jack Rockwell** (teamster), **Joseph P. Mack, Gene Stutenroth, Karl Hackett, Jack Clifford, Daral Hudson, Dick Alexander** (miners), **Wallace Scott** (MacIvar), **Chief Yowlachi** (Indian spokesman), **Jack Ingram, Peter Whitney, Eddie Dunn** (men), **Chester Clute** (Portland storekeeper), **Frank Ferguson** (preacher), **Rex Lease, Willy Kaufman** (card players), **Jay Silverheels** (Indian who breaks mandolin), **Harry Shannon** (McLane), **Sherry Hall** (clerk), **Calvin Spencer** (stunt double for Lloyd Bridges), and **Janet Ann Gallow, Mary Newton.**

Directed by **JACQUES TOURNEUR**. Associate producer: **Alexander Golitzen**. Screenplay by **Ernest Pascal**. Based on the *Saturday Evening Post* story by **Ernest Haycox**. Technicolor consultant: **Natalie Kalmus**. Director of photography: **Edward Cronjager**. Special photography: **David S. Horsley**. Technicolor associate: **William Fritzsche**. Art directors: **John B. Goodman** and **Richard H. Riedel**. Film editor: **Milton Carruth**. Sound director: **Bernard B. Brown**. Sound technician: **William Hedgcock**. Set decoration: **Russell A. Gausman** and **Leigh Smith**. Costumes: **Travis Banton**. Director of make-up: **Jack P. Pierce**. Hair stylist: **Carmen Dirigo**. Assistant director: **Fred Frank**. Music director: **Frank Skinner**. Dialogue director: **Anthony Jowitt**.

Songs: "Ole Buttermilk Sky" by **Hoagy Carmichael** and **Jack Brooks**; "Rogue River Valley", "I'm Gettin' Married in the Morning", "Silver Saddle", — all by **Hoagy Carmichael**. Producer: **Walter Wanger**.

Copyright 18 July 1946 by Universal Pictures Co., Inc. New York opening at Loew's Criterion: 7 August 1946. U.S. release: 26 July 1946. U.K. release: 18 November 1946. Australian release: 19 December 1946. 8,288 feet. 92 minutes.

SYNOPSIS: It is the year 1856, and Logan Stewart (Dana Andrews), at the request of his close friend Camrose (Brian Donlevy), prepares to make a trip and take his friend's fiancée, Lucy Overmire (Susan Hayward), from Portland to Jacksonville, Oregon, to join Camrose.

Logan, a transient mule-train owner who has a store in Jacksonville, is in love with Lucy, but avoids her out of loyalty to his friend, and courts Caroline (Patricia Roc), daughter of nearby settlers, Mr and Mrs Dance (Andy Devine and Dorothy Peterson).

Their first stop is the Dances' cabin, and Caroline is not exactly thrilled to see Logan in Lucy's company. After a rest, Logan and Lucy resume their journey to Jacksonville.

Meanwhile, Camrose, losing a lot of money at poker, steals from miners' pokes entrusted to him in order to pay his debt, and ends up killing one of the miners.

NOTES: Hayward's first movie for Walter Wanger was this beautiful and different western, which is unjustly ignored when discussing western films and "how the west was won." Filmed on location, mostly at the Umpqua National Forest, the Oregon scenery was shown in all its splendid beauty.

Susan, a good rider, had to learn how to ride sidesaddle for this movie, which was her second with Brian Donlevy, and the last where she got third billing. From now on it was strictly first or second billing for her.

— Eduardo Moreno: *Susan Hayward*.

COMMENT: At the time this film was made, Alexander Golitzen was Universal's supervising art director. He had worked closely with Wanger on *Arabian Nights*. Here we find him billed as associate producer and although he is not credited for art direction, it is obvious that this sphere was closely supervised by him. The sets are not only lavish, they also contrive to look frontier realistic, yet are artistic and dazzle the eye at the same time. Outdoors Oregon is beautifully captured in the Technicolor photography of Eddie Cronjager.

The story is a little weak and is predictably conventional, but it incorporates enough action to satisfy the fans and it is earnestly enough acted. Ward Bond is particularly good as the villain of the piece, while Hoagy Carmichael gets to sing snatches of three or four songs including "Ole Buttermilk Sky" which was nominated for an Academy Award (unaccountably — it's a catchy song but we only get to hear four bars of it — and those right at the conclusion while people are stampeding towards the popcorn concession).

The credit titles read "Introducing Patricia Roc", though surely she needed no introduction at this stage of her career with starring roles in maybe a dozen or more British films behind her. However, this turned out to be her only Hollywood film, which is not surprising — she doesn't really fit in here and it is hard to credit such an obvious glamor-puss as a frontier woman — Susan Hayward maybe, but Patricia Roc definitely no. Miss Hayward is effective and makes the most of her role, even though her fans will be upset that she is often not very flatteringly photographed. Tourneur's direction has style and pace.

OTHER VIEWS: RKO, with whom I had a contract, lent me to Universal for *Canyon Passage*, which had the biggest budget I had worked with to that date. The music and songs by Hoagy Carmichael were especially remarkable. One of them, "Ole Buttermilk Sky", was nominated for Best Song, but lost out to Harry Warren and Johnny Mercer's "On the Atchison, Topeka and Santa Fe".

— Jacques Tourneur.

# the Capture

**Lew Ayres** (Vanner), **Teresa Wright** (Ellen), **Victor Jory** (Father Gomez), **Jacqueline White** (Luana), **Jimmy Hunt** (Mike), **Barry Kelley** (Mahoney), **Duncan Renaldo** (Carlos), **Edwin Rand** (Tevlin), **William Bakewell** (Tobin), **Milton Parsons** (thin man), **Frank Matts** (Juan), **Felipe Turich** (Valdez).

Director: **JOHN STURGES**. Original story and screenplay: **Niven Busch**. Photography: **Edward Cronjager**. Supervising film editor: **George Amy**. Production designer: **William E. Flannery**. Set decorators: **John McCarthy Jr, Charles Thompson**. Miss Wright's costumes: **Mary Wills**. Make-up: **Bob Mark**. Hair styles: **Peggy Gray**. Assistant make-up artist and hairdresser: **Louise Landmier**. Assistant make-up man: **Howard Smit**. Music composed by **Daniele Amfitheatrof**, orchestrated by **David Tamkin**. Special effects: **Howard Lydecker, Theodore Lydecker**. Optical effects: Consolidated Film Industries. Technical advisor: **Tena Menard**. Assistant director: **John Grubbs**. Stills: **Frank Bjeering**. Camera operator: **Henry Cronjager, junior**. Grip: **Glen Kaiser**. Gaffer: **Don Carstenson**. Set continuity: **Dorothy Yutzi**. Sound recording: **Richard E. Tyler, Howard Wilson**. RCA Sound System. Associate producer: **Edward Donahoe**. Producer: **Niven Busch**. A Niven Busch Production.

Copyright 21 April 1950 by Showtime Properties, Inc. Filmed on locations in Mexico and at Republic Studios, Hollywood. Released through RKO Radio Pictures. New York opening at the Rivoli: 21 May 1950. U.S. release: 8 April 1950. U.K. release: 26 June 1950. Australian release: 21 July 1950. 8,173 feet. 91 minutes.

SYNOPSIS: Oil company employee mistakes innocent man for a bandit.

COMMENT: Niven Busch (*Duel in the Sun, Pursued*) made this movie with his own money. Generally it's an interesting and creditable effort, though it does have a few odd shortcomings. That normally reliable player Victor Jory gives a mechanical and unconvincing performance, and there are moments in the script when the circumlocutions of the dialogue become too repetitious and predictable to sustain interest. Fortunately these moments are few and Mr Jory's part is small.

Perhaps it could also be argued that Mr Busch has attempted to crowd too many elements into his script. On the credit side, however, he has plotted some intriguing and original twists into this Mexican western. And he and director John Sturges, assisted by cinematographer Edward Cronjager, have filmed the story against appropriately atmospheric, striking backgrounds.

Lew Ayres does plausibly by the part of the tortured hero, whilst Miss Wright is likewise convincing in an equally difficult role.

Jacqueline White, the unforgettable heroine of the later *The Narrow Margin*, has a rather different role here. After an elaborate introduction, she drops out to make room for the Teresa Wright character.

Barry Kelley is perfectly cast as the heavy, whilst Milton Parsons makes the most of his two limited opportunities.

All in all, *The Capture* emerges as a compelling thriller with strikingly film noirish location production assets.

# Carolina

**Janet Gaynor** (Joanna Tate), **Lionel Barrymore** (Bob Connelly), **Henrietta Crosman** (Mrs Connelly), **Robert Young** (Will Connelly), **Mona Barrie** (Virginia), **Almeda Fowler** (Geraldine), **Richard Cromwell** (Allan), **Russell Simpson** (Richards), **Alden Chase** (Jack Hampton), **Ronald Cosbey** (Harry Tate), **John Cosbey** (John Tate), **Stepin Fetchit** (Scipio), **Anita Brown** (Essie), **James Ellison** (dancer), **Beulah Hall, Clinton Rosemond** (singers), **Mary Forbes** (Aunt Catherine), **Joe Young** (officer), **Shirley Temple** (girl), **Roy Watson** (Jefferson Davis), **John Elliott** (General Robert E. Lee), **John Webb Dillon** (General Stonewall Jackson), **J.C. Fowler** (General Leonidas Polk), **Andre Cheron** (General Beauregard), **Jerry Stewart** (checkers player), **Edna Herd** (woman), **Frances Curry, Beas Eblow, Mary King, Bernice Pilot** (singers).

Director: **HENRY KING**; based on the play *The House of Connelly* by **Paul Green**. Screenplay: **Reginald Berkeley**. Camera: **Hal Mohr**. Film editor: **Robert Bassler**. Music director: **Louis E. de Francesco**. Songs: **Lew Brown, Jay Gorney, L.E. de Francesco, Frederick Hollander, William Kernell**. Sound recording: **Joseph Aiken**. Producer: **William Fox**.

Copyright 2 February 1934 by Fox Film Corp. New York opening at the Radio City Music Hall: 15 February 1934 (ran one week). 7,600 feet. 83 minutes.

SYNOPSIS: Conflict in an old Southern family after the Civil War when the heir to an impoverished plantation marries an equally poor tenant farmer.

NOTES: The play opened on Broadway at the Martin Beck on 28 September 1931 and ran a satisfactory 83 performances. Franchot Tone, Morris Carnovsky, Art Smith, Mary Morris, Stella Adler, J. Edward Bromberg, Robert Lewis and Clifford Odets and others were directed by Lee Strasberg and Cheryl Crawford. The play was the first production of The Group Theatre.

COMMENT: Well acted but somewhat dated melodrama with an over-talkative script that betrays its stage origins. Mostly of curiosity interest, particularly for fans of Janet Gaynor and Lionel Barrymore. The eagle-eyed will spot young Shirley Temple in a bit role.

# Challenge of the Range

**Charles Starrett** (Steve Roper), **Smiley Burnette** (himself), **Paula Raymond** (Judy Barton), **William Halop** (Reb Watson), **Steve Darrell** (Cal Matson), **Henry Hall** (Jim Barton), **Robert Filmer** (Grat Largo), **George Chesebro** (Lon Collins), **John McKee** (cowpuncher), **Frank McCarroll** (Dugan), **John Cason** (Spud Henley), **Freddie Daniel, M.H. Richman, Eddie Wallace, J.D. Sumner [The Sunshine Boys]** (themselves), and **Edmund Cobb**.

Director: **RAY NAZARRO**. Original screenplay: **Ed. Earl Repp**. Photography: **Rex Wimpy**. Film editor: **Paul Borofsky**. Art director: **Charles Clague**. Set decorator: **David**

Montrose. Songs by **Smiley Burnette**; **Doris Fisher** and **Allan Roberts**. Make-up: **Gordon Hubbard**. Hair styles: **Dotha Hippe**. Camera operator: **Fayte Brown**. Stills: **Bill Crosby**. Grip: **Al Becker**. Gaffer: **Bill Johnson**. Set continuity: **Frances McDowell**. Production manager: **Jack Fier**. Assistant director: **Paul Donnelly**. Sound recording: **Russell Malmgren**. RCA Sound System. Producer: **Colbert Clark**.

Copyright 3 February 1949 by Columbia Pictures Corp. No New York opening. U.S. release: 3 February 1949. U.K. release: August 1951. No theatrical release in Australia. 5,069 feet. 56 minutes.

U.K. release title: *MOONLIGHT RAID*.

SYNOPSIS: A mystery band of armed men are intimidating ranchers. The local Farmers' Association hires Steve Roper to investigate.

NOTES: Starrett's 103rd western.

COMMENT: Just a bit above average Durango Kid western. Production values are a bit thin, though there is plenty of action. The interior sets are drab, however, and the songs are not much. Script, acting and direction (save for one inventive shot when the camera tracks in on a crack in the door) are strictly routine.

# Code of the West

**James Warren** (Bob Wade), **Debra Alden** (Ruth), **John Laurenz** (Chito Rafferty), **Steve Brodie** (Saunders), **Rita Lynn** (Pepita), **Robert Clarke** (Harry), **Carol Forman** (Milly), **Harry Woods** (Marshal Hatfield), **Raymond Burr** (Boyd Carter), **Harry Harvey** (Stockton), **Phil Warren** (Wescott), **Emmett Lynn** (Doc Quinn), **Forrest Taylor** (Ira Meeker), **Archie Butler, Allen Lee, Clem Fuller, Eddie Juaregui, John Hudkins** (cowboys), **Jason Robards** (Morley), **William Desmond** (settler), **Harry Cheshire** (Judge Culver), **Budd Buster** (hotel clerk), **Philip Morris** (Webster), **Perc Launders** (stagecoach driver), **Tom Steele** (stunt double for James Warren), **Bud Wolfe** (stunt double for Raymond Burr), and the singing voice of **Doreen Tryden**.

Director: **WILLIAM BERKE**. Screenplay: **Norman Houston**. Based on the 1924 novel by **Zane Grey**. Photography: **Jack Mackenzie**. Film editor: **Ernie Leadlay**. Music: **Paul Sawtell**. Song, "Rainbow Valley" (Laurenz) by **Lew Pollack** and **Harry Harris**. Song, "Oo! La! La!" (Forman, dubbed by Tryden) by **Walter Jurmann**. Music director: **Constantin Bakaleinikoff**. Art directors: **Albert S. D'Agostino** and **Lucius O. Croxton**. Set decorators: **Darrell Silvera** and **Tom Oliphant**. Special effects photography: **Russell A. Cully**. Assistant director: **Grayson Rogers**. Sound recording: **Jean L. Speak, Roy Granville**. RCA Sound System. Producer: **Herman Schlom**.

Copyright 12 February 1947 by RKO Radio Pictures, Inc. U.S. release: 2 February 1947. No New York opening. U.K. release: 14 February 1949. Australian release: 20 May 1948. 5,194 feet. 57 minutes.

SYNOPSIS: Raymond Burr plays a ruthless saloon-owner (why are publicans always the heavies in these movies?) who wants to control all the land in the Strip, but his plans are thwarted by the return of a young settler (James Warren, naturally)!

COMMENT: If the synopsis of the 1925 silent version of Zane Grey's novel (starring Owen Moore and Constance Bennett, directed by the great William K. Howard for Paramount) is anything to go on, this sound picture bears little resemblance to the original book. Never mind, it's a most entertaining movie anyway. Director William Berke tries really hard to follow in the shadow of William K. Howard, and excels himself both in the dialogue (long tracking shots) and action spots (running inserts, good stuntwork). Norman Houston's able screenplay maintains solid interest throughout. Photography and other technical credits rate as really first class, whilst production values appear welcomely expansive. And it's good to see Raymond Burr contributing his usual impressive performance as the heavy.

# Colorado Sunset

**Gene Autry** (Gene Autry), **Smiley Burnette** (Frog Millhouse), **June Storey** (Carol Haines), **Barbara Pepper** (Ginger Bixby), **Larry "Buster" Crabbe** (Dave Haines), **Robert Barrat** (Dr Blair), **William Farnum** (Sheriff Glenn), **Purnell Pratt** (Hall), **Kermit Maynard** (Drake), **Elmo Lincoln** (Burns), **Patsy Montana** (Patsy), **Frankie Marvin** (Frankie), **Jack Ingram** (Clanton), **CBS-KMBC Texas Rangers,** including **Captain Bob Crawford, Irish Mahaney, Dave May** and **Tookie Cronenbold** (themselves), **Fred Burns, George Morrell** (radio fans), **Jack Kirk, Ralph Peters, Rose Plummer** (townsfolk), **Budd Buster** (outlaw spotter), **Francis Ford** (drunk), **Ed Cassidy, Reginald Barlow, Murdock MacQuarrie** (dairymen), **Chuck Baldra** (cowboy), **Slim Whitaker** (cigar fancier), **Ethan Laidlaw** (poster man), **Al Taylor** (henchman), **Cactus Mack** (extra man), **Bill Yrigoyen** (stunt double for Gene Autry), and "Champion".

Director: **GEORGE SHERMAN**. Associate producer: **William Berke**. Story: **Luci Ward, Jack Natteford**. Screenplay: **Betty Burbridge, Stanley Roberts**. Camera: **William Nobles**. Editor: **Les Orlebeck**. Music supervisor: **Raoul Kraushaar**. "Colorado Sunset" composition: **Con Conrad, Wolfe Gilbert**. Gene Autry also sings "Seven Years with the Wrong Woman". Other songs: "Vote for Autry" (chorus), "On Our Merry Old Way Back Home" and "Poor Little Dogies". Production manager: **Al Wilson**. RCA Sound System. Executive producer: **Herbert J. Yates**.

Copyright 31 July 1939 by Republic Pictures Corp. No recorded New York opening. U.S. release: 31 July 1939. U.K. release through British Lion: No Australian theatrical release. 7 reels. 64 minutes.

SYNOPSIS: Gene and his Texas Troubadors quit barnstorming as they purchase what they think is a Colorado cattle ranch, only to discover that the stock consists of milk cows. This puts them in the midst of a dairy war, with some well-concealed power hijacking the dairy trucks and destroying them in an effort to force them into a combine.

NOTES: Number 34 of Autry's 94 motion pictures.

COMMENT: *Colorado Sunset* is by no means the incongruous mixture that Fenin and Everson's illustration in *The Western* makes out. In fact it is one of Autry's best westerns, full of action which is directed in a lively, zestful manner by George Sherman with lots and lots of fast running inserts and lots and lots of thrilling stunt falls. It is also one of the most spectacularly produced of all Autry's films with not a single clip of stock footage and the deployment of hundreds of extras against some striking natural locations. The spectacular climax itself with its employment of scores of hard-riding, pistol-shooting horsemen and the crashing of dozens of milk-wagons would be enough in itself to lift the film into the "A" category, but there are some other action sequences that are almost equally exciting — the destruction of Autry's ranch in which cross-cutting is used effectively, and the rescue of Kermit Maynard right at the beginning of the film with Autry's obligatory chase after a runaway wagon (a sequence that is incorporated into almost all his films).

The cast too puts the film firmly in the "A" class and is one of the most interesting ever assembled for an Autry western. Autry himself is a more colorful personality here than in most of his films. The TV print has doubtless dropped some of his songs (as well as Patsy Montana and her Cowgirls) though he has three or four pleasant numbers and there is a rousing election march complete with baton-twirling cuties.

The whole film has a no-expense-spared look about it. The photography is of much better quality than usual, the film being most attractively lit throughout. The film editing is sharp.

Mr Burnette is his usual amiable self and a sequence in which he rewires the amplifiers at an election rally is quite amusing. Miss Storey is not a particularly attractive heroine but Barbara Pepper is a delightful sub, exchanging dialogue (chiefly with Burnette) with an infectious enthusiasm.

The rest of the cast also enter into their parts with zest — Robert H. Barrat makes a colorful villain and Larry Buster Crabbe is always at his best in villainous roles such as here. William Farnum has a good scene as the sheriff which he plays with true professionalism while Kermit Maynard plays the wagon driver whom Autry rescues at the beginning of the film. Couldn't spot Elmo Lincoln of Tarzan fame but nice to see Jack Ingram up to his usual dirty work as leader of the band of marauders.

OTHER VIEWS: Another "modern" western with six-shooting sheriff Autry tangling with bandits hijacking milk trucks, features a grandly crowded chase climax with running inserts and the very personable Larry Buster Crabbe as the villain's chief henchman. June Storey has a more sizable part than in *Mountain Rhythm* and screams delightfully at the appropriate moments in Gene's novelty song, "Seven Years With the Wrong Woman", while Smiley clowns with the equally delightful Barbara Pepper (who alas disappears from the action for just about all the second half). Robert Barrat leads an interesting contingent of support players. Credits and production values (including Sherman's and/or his stunt director's vigorous use of real locations) are well above standard.

# Colorado Trail

**Charles Starrett** (Grant Bradley), **Iris Meredith** (Joan Randall), **Edward LeSaint** (Jeff Randall), **Al Bridge** (Mark Sheldon), **Robert Fiske** (Deacon Webster), **Dick Curtis**

(Slash Driscoll), **Bob Nolan** (Bob), **Lloyd Perryman** (Lloyd), **Hank Bell** (Tombstone Terry), **Edward Peil, Sr** (Hobbs), **Edmund Cobb** (Cameron), **Jack Clifford** (Judge Bennett), **Sons of the Pioneers, George Chesebro, Dick Botiller, Stanley Brown**.

Director: **SAM NELSON**. Original screenplay: **Charles Francis Royal**. Photography: **Benjamin Kline**. Film editor: **William Lyon**. Music director: **Morris W. Stoloff**. Songs composed by **Bob Nolan**. Western Electric Sound System. Producer: **Harry Decker**.

Copyright 27 August 1938 by Columbia Pictures Corp of California. No recorded New York opening. U.S. release: 8 September 1938. No Australian theatrical release. 6 reels. 55 minutes.

SYNOPSIS: See review below.

NOTES: Starrett's 21st of his 142 westerns.

COMMENT: Although it is not a member of the series of course (they didn't start until some years later and here Charles Starrett sports the unusual Christian name of "Grant" instead of the customary "Jeff"), here is gathered together as fine a gallery of the players who were later to figure in the Durango Kid series as one could wish. Even George Chesebro is present — in a one line bit as a rancher in the crowd, but our main interest is in that delightful trio of villains, Al Bridge, Richard Fiske and Dick Curtis.

Eddie Cobb has a small part as a rancher — on the right side of the law unfortunately. Hank Bell has a fairly large part as the provider of the comic relief. Bob Nolan and the Sons of the Pioneers sing some pleasant songs. Edward LeSaint plays the heroine's father and the heroine is the lovely Iris Meredith.

The film itself is a bit short on action and long on talk (even excepting a lively court sequence with a cranky judge), but there is a climactic shoot-out and Charles Starrett wears an enormous white sombrero and rides a striking palomino.

The direction and other credits are routine. The script is the usual chestnut — in fact it combines two chestnuts — the one about the do-gooder stranger being the son of the local bad man and the one about the town villain fencing off the pass so that the ranchers are forced to sell their beef to him. There's a bit of location photography and a nice bit of stunt-work at the start when our hero's double leaps on board a runaway coach.

The dialogue comes across as stilted as the plot.

# Dead Man's Trail

**Johnny Mack Brown** (Johnny), **Jimmy Ellison** (Dan), **Barbara Allen** (Mrs Winslow), **I. Stanford Jolley** (sheriff), **Terry Frost** (Kelvin), **Lane Bradford** (Brad), **Gregg Barton** (Yeager), **Richard Avonde** (Stewart), **Stanley Price** (Blake), **Dale Van Sickel** (Walt).

Director: **LEWIS COLLINS**. Original story and screenplay: **Joseph F. Poland**. Photography: **Ernest Miller**. Film editor: **Sam Fields**. Music: **Raoul Kraushaar**. Set continuity: **Melville Shyer**. Producer: **Vincent M. Fennelly**. A Frontier Pictures Production.

Copyright 22 June 1952 by Monogram Pictures Corp. No New York opening. U.S. release: 20 July 1952. U.K. release through associated British-Pathé: March 1955 (sic). Never theatrically released in Australia. 5,286 feet. 58½ minutes.

SYNOPSIS: When an escaped convict is killed by former gangster associates, his brother helps a Texas Ranger.

NOTES: A "B" western that will interest not only the usual run of oater fans but will especially capture the attention of serial devotees as well, since writer Joseph F. Poland worked on **every** Republic serial from *King of the Royal Mounted* all the way through to *The Purple Monster Strikes*. I imagine there's a fortune to be made from this little western at serial conventions alone, so I'm amazed no enterprising distributor has bought up the rights.

COMMENT: Johnny Mack Brown turns sleuth for this whodunit western. Gunplay takes second place to some neat detection when he trails an escaped convict to find the secret hiding place of his loot.

It's a modest, juvenile-styled adventure, with Brown making an excellent heavyweight hero.

The picture also boasts something new in heroines in Barbara Allen, a fragile old lady, who would charm a herd of buffalo.

# Deputy Marshal

**Jon Hall** (Ed Garry), **Frances Langford** (Janet Masters), **Russell Hayden** (Bill Masters), **Dick Foran** (Joel Benton), **Julie Bishop** (Claire Benton), **Clem Bevans** (Doc Vinson), **Joe Sawyer** (Eli Cresset), **Forrest Taylor** (Sheriff Lance), **Mary Gordon** (Mrs Lance), **Kenne Duncan** (Kyle Freeling), **Vince Barnett** (hotel reception clerk), **Stanley Blystone** (Leo Hanald), **Roy Butler** (Weed Toler), **Wheaton Chambers** (Harley Masters), **Tom Greenway** (bartender), **Ted Adams** (telegrapher), **Ray Jones** (townsman).

Narrated by **Clem Bevans**.

Director: **WILLIAM BERKE**. Screenplay: **William Berke**. Based on the 1947 novel *Deputy Marshall* (sic) by **Charles Heckelmann**. Photography: **Carl Berger**. Film editor: **Edward Mann**. Art director: **Martin Obzina**. Set decorator: **Ted Offenbecker**. Music director: **Mahlon Merrick**. Songs: "Levis, Plaid Shirt and Spurs" (Langord), "Hideout in Hidden Valley" (Langford) by **John Stephens** (lyrics), **Irving Bibo** (music). Music supervisor: **David Chudnow**. Make-up: **Paul Stanhope**. Special effects: **Charles Duncan, J.R. Glass**. Grip: **Noble Craig**. Camera operator: **Al Myers**. Stills: **Buddy Longworth**. Assistant director: **Melville Shyer**. Sound recording: **Frank McWhorter**. Sound engineer: **Walter Dalgleish**. Photographed with the Garutso Balanced Lens. RCA Sound System. Associate producer: **Murray Lerner**. Producer: **William Stephens**. Executive producer: **Robert L. Lippert.**

Copyright 15 October 1949 by Lippert Productions, Inc. New York opening at the Palace (accompanying the usual vaudeville bill): 10 November 1949. U.S. release through Screen Guild Productions: 28 October 1949. U.K. release through Pathé: 16 January

1949. Australian release through 20th Century-Fox: 12 October 1951 (sic). Running times: 72 minutes (US & UK), 75 minutes (Aust).

SYNOPSIS: A railroad survey map is stolen by a mystery killer.

COMMENT: Aside from the facts that it offers an unusually large role to Clem Bevans (which that lovable oldtimer mercilessly takes full advantage of by shamelessly hogging the camera at both start and fade-out) and that one of our favorite singers, Frances Langord, is on hand, there's not much to get excited about in this rather routine, low-budget western. Miss Langford is poorly photographed and costumed to boot, whilst her songs though pleasant enough are totally undistinguished.

Doubtless a fine man in real life, Berke the Jerk as I call him was never any great shakes as a director. He doesn't even rate a mention in Todd McCarthy's 325 filmographies in *Kings of the Bs*. I've not struck him as a writer before, but needless to say, the screenplay is just as dull. However, it does provide some splendid opportunities for Joe Sawyer, one of the best heavies in the business. And it's good to see Russell Hayden too, though Dick Foran (strikingly but too appropriately dressed all in black) is largely wasted. As for stoic Jon Hall, he's pretty much a take-him-or-leave-him hero.

The last statement just about sums up our attitude to the movie as well.

OTHER VIEWS: Mild western fare. One or two good fights, plus a few poorly staged chases through uninteresting countryside. The plot has possibilities (though all its ingredients have been far more tautly exercised in other films), but lacklustre staging robs the script of most of its potential suspense. Both leads and support players are hampered by the generally slow pacing and lack of vigor in Berke's direction as well as by their cliched dialogue. Joe Sawyer, the always reliable Julie Bishop, and surprisingly Russell Hayden come off best.

— G.A.

**The Director:** Considering his meager budgets and hasty shooting schedules, William Berke was usually efficient enough, but only very occasionally surpassed the routine. His best known films are *Dick Tracy* (1945) and *Jungle Jim* (1948).

# Desert Pursuit

**Wayne Morris** (Ford Smith), **Virginia Grey** (Mary Smith), **George Tobias** (Ghazili), **Anthony Caruso** (Hassan), **John Doucette** (Kafan), **Emmett Lynn** (Leatherface), **Frank Lackteen** (Indian chief), **Gloria Talbot, Billy Wilkerson, Robert Bice** (Indians).

Director: **GEORGE BLAIR**. Screenplay: **W. Scott Darling**. Based on the 1937 novel *Desert Voices* by **Kenneth Perkins**. Photography: **William Sickner**. Film editor: **Leonard W. "Ace" Herman**. Music director: **Edward J. Kay**. Special effects: **Ray Mercer**. Set continuity: **Ilona Vas**. Assistant director: **Rex Bailey**. Sound recording: **Frank Webster**. Associate producers: **Wayne Morris, Leonard W. "Ace" Herman**. Producer: **Lindsley Parsons**.

Copyright 21 April 1952 by Monogram Pictures Corp. No recorded New York opening. U.S. release: 11 May 1952. U.K. release through Pathe: 10 August 1953. No Australian theatrical release. 70 minutes.

SYNOPSIS: A gold prospector tries to escape three pursuing bandits by riding across Death Valley.

COMMENT: This is certainly a cut above the usual Monogram "B" western, doubtless because it is based on a novel rather than an original screen story geared to the usual western clichés. The plot has a number of extremely novel (pun intended) twists, yet manages to pack in plenty of action for its 70 minutes. The ruggedly rocky and sandy desert locations in which seemingly all the movie was lensed are not only particularly impressive in themselves, but serve the story well.

Both principals revel in the greater depth provided for their characters, whilst Tobias, Caruso and Doucette make a wonderfully hissable trio of villains. Emmett Lynn over-acts to an irritating degree but fortunately isn't in the movie long enough to make too bad a lasting memory.

Blair handles the action vigorously. Sickner's cinematography is — by Monogram standards — superb.

OTHER VIEWS: There is no credit for art direction or set decoration as this film was shot entirely on location and has no interiors. It is extremely well served by photographer William Sickner. The direction, however, is considerably less distinguished and the script, especially the opening scene with Emmett Lynn, is inclined to over-talkativeness. However, there is enough action to satisfy the fans and generally the acting is good enough to get by. Camels in Death Valley is a novel touch as well as the idea of making the villains Arabs and the indigenous people Mission Indians whom the Spanish padres left to fend for themselves when recalled to Spain.

Summing up, this is an agreeable and generally creditable little offering in Wayne Morris' Monogram series.

# the Desperado

**Wayne Morris** (Sam Garrett), **James Lydon** (Tal Cameron), **Beverly Garland** (Lauren Bannerman), **Rayford Barnes** (Roy Novack), **Daabs Greer** (Sheriff Jim Langley), **Lee Van Cleef** (Buck Creyton/Paul Creyton), **Nestor Paiva** (Captain Thornton), **Roy Barcroft** (Martin Novack), **John Dierkes** (Sergeant Rafferty), **Richard Shackleton** (Pat Garner), **I. Stanford Jolley** (Garner), **Charles Garland** (trooper), **Florence Lake** (Mrs Cameron), **Harry Hayden** (schoolmaster), **Robert Shayne** (Wilson), **Lyle Talbot** (judge), **Tristram Coffin** (attorney), **William "Bill" Phillips** (bartender), **Stanley Price** (witness), **George Eldredge** (Bannerman), **John Eldredge** (Cameron).

Director: **THOMAS CARR**. Screenplay: **Geoffrey Homes** (pseudonym of **Daniel Mainwaring**). Based on the novel by **Clifton Adams**. Photography: **Joseph M. Novak**. Film editor: **Sam Fields**. Art director: **James West**. Set decorator: **Vincent A. Taylor**. Music: **Raoul Kraushaar**. Set continuity: **Mary Chaffee**. Dialogue supervisor: **Stanley Price**. Special photographic effects: **Ray Mercer**. Assistant director: **Melville Shyer**. Sound recording: **John K. Keen**. Western Electric Sound System. Producer: **Vincent M. Fennelly**.

A Silvermine Production, released through Allied Artists Pictures Corp. Copyright 20 June 1954 by Allied Artists Pictures Corp. No New York opening. U.S. release: 20 June 1954. U.K. release through Associated British-Pathe: 23 April 1954. No Australian theatrical release. 7,210 feet. 80 minutes.

SYNOPSIS: Fleeing from the State Police under the corrupt administration of the 1870s, a young Texan is befriended by gunman Sam Garrett.

COMMENT: Wayne Morris was the last of the "B" western heroes and *The Desperado* is the second last of the "B" western series. It's a shame it's not the official last as it's a much superior a film to *Two Guns and a Badge*. With *The Desperado* the series "B" western would have gone out in really grand style.

Blessed with an intriguing script by none other than Daniel Mainwaring, *The Desperado* is probably the best-written "B" western ever made. Gone are all the usual "B" stereotypes of plot, setting and characterization. Instead we are presented with a fascinating and unusually complex story, involving real, believable people.

Director Thomas Carr has risen to the occasion nobly, drawing ingratiating performances and character studies from unlikely players like Wayne Morris, Jimmy Lydon, Rayford Barnes and even Dabbs Greer. One of our favorite heavies Lee Van Cleef has a major dual role, while Nestor Paiva is unusually effective in a deep-dyed villainous role with absolutely no comic undertones whatever. John Dierkes also makes a wonderfully sadistic bully-boy, but Roy Barcroft fans will be disappointed to find him in a minor sympathetic role as a too law-abiding ex-sheriff.

Production values are better than the usual Silvermine level. There are plenty of scene changes, extras, a fair amount of action, and some reasonably effective locations. Technical credits including staging, lighting and music scoring are also impressive by Monogram's usual standards.

Oddly, *The Desperado* is not listed in Mainwaring's credits as published in *Backstory 2: Interviews with Screenwriters of the 1940s and 1950s* edited by Pat McGilligan (University of California Press, 1991). Whilst certainly a lesser effort than classics like *Out of the Past, The Lawless* and *Invasion of the Body Snatchers*, it's most definitely worthy of inclusion.

OTHER VIEWS: This better-than-average Allied Artists western moves at a good clip, boasts an interesting cast and will please most action fans. Although it starts off with the usual time-wasting rolling Foreword title (underlined by Kraushaar's customarily plodding score), production values are pretty fair, while Carr's direction is slightly more imaginative than his usual norm.

# Destry Rides Again

**Marlene Dietrich** (Frenchy), **James Stewart** (Thomas Jefferson Destry Jr), **Mischa Auer** (Boris Callahan), **Charles Winninger** (Washington Dimsdale), **Brian Donlevy** (Kent), **Allen Jenkins** (Bugs Watson), **Warren Hymer** (Gyp Watson), **Irene Hervey** (Janice Tyndall), **Una Merkel** (Lily Belle Callahan), **Billy Gilbert** (Loupgerou, the bartender), **Samuel S. Hinds** (Hiram J. Slade), **Jack Carson** (Jack Tyndall), **Tom**

Fadden (Lem Claggett), **Virginia Brissac** (Sophie Claggett), **Edmund MacDonald** (Rockwell), **Lillian Yarbo** (Clara), **Joe King** (Sheriff Joseph Keogh), **Dickie Jones** (Eli Whitney Claggett), **Ann Todd** (Claggett girl), **Harry Cording** (Rowdy cowboy), **Dick Alexander, Bill Steele Gettinger** (cowboys), **Minerva Urecal** (Mrs DeWitt), **Bob McKenzie** (doctor), **Billy Bletcher** (pianist), **Lloyd Ingraham** (Turner, the express agent), **Harry Tenbrook** (stage rider), **Bud McClure** (stage driver), **Chief John Big Tree** (Indian in saloon), **Philo McCullough** (bartender), **Alex Voloshin** (assistant bartender), **Carmen D´Antonio** (dancer), **Bill Cody Jr** (small boy), **Loren Brown** and **Harold De Carro** (jugglers), **Dora Clemant, Mary Shannon** (women), **George Chesebro** (bar patron), **Robert Keith, Duke York**.

Director: **GEORGE MARSHALL**. Screenplay: **Felix Jackson, Gertrude Purcell, Henry Myers** (from a screen story by **Felix Jackson** derived from the novel by **Max Brand**). Photographer: **Hal Mohr**. Art directors: **Jack Otterson, Martin Obzina**. Editor: **Milton Carruth**. Music: **Frank Skinner**. Songs: "Little Joe the Wrangler" (Dietrich), "You've Got That Look That Leaves Me Weak" (Dietrich), "The Boys in the Back Room" (Dietrich), all by **Frederick Hollander** and **Frank Loesser**. Music director: **Charles Previn**. Set decorator: **Russell A. Gausman**. Costumes: **Vera West**. Hair styles: **Nellie Manley**. Assistant director: **Vernon Keays**. Sound recording: **Bernard B. Brown**. Sound technician: **Robert Pritchard**. Associate producer: **Islin Auten**. Producer: **Joe Pasternak**.

Copyright 8 December 1939 by Universal Pictures Co., Inc. New York opening at the Rivoli: 29 November 1939. U.S. release: 29 December 1939. Australian release: 25 April 1940. 10 reels. 8,453 feet. 94 minutes.

SYNOPSIS: Kent, a suave gambler (Brian Donlevy) runs the lawless frontier town of Bottle Neck, utilizing the services of his barroom entertainer, Frenchy (Marlene Dietrich), to cheat suckers like Lem Claggett (Tom Fadden) out of their ranches so that he can collect a tariff on all cattle driven through.

When Sheriff Keogh (Joe King) learns that Claggett has been cheated at cards, he tries to enforce the law but is shot, and in the commotion the Mayor of Bottle Neck, Hiram J. Slade (Samuel S. Hinds), informs the patrons of the Last Chance Saloon that the sheriff has gone out of town. He and Kent appoint Wash Dimsdale (Charles Winninger), the town drunk, as the new sheriff. Wash, once deputy to the famous lawman Thomas Jefferson Destry, suddenly reforms and sends for his old pal's son Tom (James Stewart) to come to Bottle Neck as his deputy.

The mild-mannered Mr Destry arrives by stagecoach with Janice Tyndall (Irene Hervey) and her headstrong brother Jack (Jack Carson), a cattleman. Wash introduces Tom to the townsfolk in the Last Chance Saloon, and when Kent tries to take Tom's guns away from him, they learn that he doesn't carry any. Frenchy hands the new deputy a mop and pail to help clean up Bottle Neck.

The town thinks Destry is too mild a deputy to be a threat to Kent's gang, but he nevertheless attempts to clean up Bottle Neck by looking for Sheriff Keogh's body.

NOTES: "Max Brand" is the pseudonym of Frederick Faust. His novel was previously filmed in 1932 with Tom Mix as Destry opposite Claudia Dell's Frenchy. In 1954 Universal remade the film simply as *Destry* with Audie Murphy in the title role opposite

Mari Blanchard. Many of the novel's plot devices turn up in other westerns, for example *The Boy from Oklahoma* (1954), *Frenchie* (1950).

Universal's top boxoffice attraction of 1939-40.

COMMENT: In any other year but 1939, *Destry Rides Again* would have figured mightily on the nation's "Ten Best" lists. A smash with both critics and public, it marked a turning point in Dietrich's career, re-establishing her as a major star. As this hard-as-nails bar belle, she is ideally cast. Her song, "See What the Boys in the Back Room Will Have", became a classic which is now synonymous with her name. In the title role, James Stewart is also absolutely perfect.

The definitive version of the novel, this one is not only lavishly produced, but forcefully directed. Brisk film editing carries the viewer with admirable celerity through necessary but dull continuity scenes in order to concentrate our attention on the much more interesting material when Dietrich and Stewart strike sparks, and such fine character actors as Charles Winninger, Samuel S. Hinds, Allen Jenkins and Warren Hymer have their charismatic innings.

OTHER VIEWS: *Destry Rides Again* presents Marlene Dietrich as a *Blue Angel* of the Far West. Not only does she play Frenchy with panache and style, but she emerges here as a fine comedian, registering just as strongly in the comic sequences as in the dramatic. In short, she is marvellous.

— Francois Timmory in L'Ecran Francais.

Stewart brings humor and sound characterization to a boots-and-saddle variation of a typical Stewart role — the apparently easy-going softy who turns hard when it will do the most good.

— *Newsweek*.

James Stewart, who had just turned in the top performance of his cinematurity as Jefferson Smith in *Mr Smith Goes to Washington*, turns in as good a performance or better as Thomas Jefferson Destry.

— *Time*.

# the Duel at Silver Creek

**Audie Murphy** (Silver Kid), **Faith Domergue** (Opal Lacey), **Stephen McNally** (Lightning Tyrone), **Susan Cabot** (Dusty Fargo), **Gerald Mohr** (Rod Lacey), **Eugene Iglesias** (Johnny Sombrero), **Kyle James [James Anderson]** (Rat Face Blake), **Walter Sande** (Peter Fargo), **Lee Marvin** (Tinhorn Burgess), **George Eldredge** (Jim Ryan), **Steve Darrell** (sheriff), **Wheaton Chambers** (Dr Hargrove), **Griff Barnett** (Pop), **Harry Harvey** (Father Cromwell), **Frank Wilcox** (doctor at fort), **Monte Montague** (man at bar), **Cactus Mack** (member of posse), **Stanley Blystone** (voice of civilian).

Narrated by **Stephen McNally**.

Director: **DON SIEGEL**. Screenplay: **Gerald Drayson Adams, Joseph Hoffman**. Story: **Gerald Drayson Adams**. Photographed in Technicolor by **Irving Glassberg**.

Film editor: **Russell Schoengarth**. Art directors: **Bernard Herzbrun, Alexander Golitzen**. Set decorators: **Russell A. Gausman, Joseph Kish**. Costumes: **Bill Thomas**. Make-up: **Bud Westmore**. Hair styles: **Joan St Oegger**. Music: **Hans J. Salter**. Music director: **Joseph Gershenson**. Technicolor color consultant: **Richard Mueller**. Stunts: **Johnny Carpenter**. Sound recording: **Leslie I. Carey, Corson Jowett**. Western Electric Sound System. Producer: **Leonard Goldstein**.

Copyright 12 June 1952 by Universal Pictures Co., Inc. New York opening at the Palace: 1 August 1952. U.S. release: August 1952. U.K. release on the lower half of a double bill: September 1952. Australian release: 6 February 1953. 77 minutes.

SYNOPSIS: The marshal of Silver City joins up with Luke Crowell, alias the Silver Kid, to apprehend claim jumpers.

COMMENT: Curious in that this is one of Audie Murphy's best films — even though he isn't the real star! That honor belongs to Stephen McNally as the town marshal, though Murphy is equally ingratiating — perhaps even more so — as his sidekick. In fact this unlikely partners routine gets a very appealing workout here — and like the best of these it's not without its fair share of humor.

Also curious is the fact that Miss Domergue effectively plays a thoroughly evil femme fatale, — one who doesn't have a single redeeming quality! Miss Cabot does okay by the obligatory tomboyish "other gal".

Despite his position way down in the cast list, Lee Marvin can be easily spotted. In fact he has a few nice bits as a saloon loafer. We also like the guy who plays the oldtime deputy, Dan Music. Acting honors on the other side of the law belong firmly to Eugene Iglesias who makes his Johnny Sombrero a wonderfully greasy ne'er-do-well. Gerald Mohr is more conventional, though still effective, as a smiling villain. Siegel himself can be spotted as one of the bushwackers who waylay Murph.

Drayson and Hoffman have concocted an unusually rich script with lots of interlocking incidents and characters. This appealing script has been given an unusually lavish production by producer Goldstein, with lots of extras milling around, excellent locations, and polished technical credits.

Director Siegel takes ample advantage of all this budget largesse. The running inserts are marvellously effective in the action scenes.

All told, highly engrossing.

OTHER VIEWS: Vigorous direction, lusty playing and an unusually interesting scenario make this one of the top westerns of the year. Despite its "B" rating, technical credits and production values are more than creditable enough for an "A".

# Dumb Bell of the Yukon

Director: **JACK KING**. Story: **Harry Reeves, Homer Brightman**. Animation: **Don Towsley, Fred Kopietz, Ed Aardal, Sandy Strother**. Lay-outs and backgrounds: **Ernie Nordli**. Music: **Oliver Wallace**. Color by Technicolor. RCA Sound System. Producer: **Walt Disney**.

Copyright 5 April 1946 by Walt Disney Productions. A Walt Disney "Donald Duck" cartoon, released through RKO Radio Pictures. 1 reel.

COMMENT: One of the best of Jack King's Donald Ducks, this one has a bright story idea which introduces a couple of most engaging characters in the delightfully hesitant Baby Bear and his truly fearsome Mother (one clever upside-down shot of her ferociously slavering jaw had the whole theatre screaming). For a second there it looks as if the story is going to take a not unexpected but unwelcomely grisly turn but it is ingeniously tracked into an amusing series of running gags in which the fast-thinking Donald is almost continually outwitted by the slow and/or appealingly naive bears.

# Five Came Back

**Chester Morris** (Bill, the pilot), **Lucille Ball** (Peggy, the good-time girl), **Wendy Barrie** (Alice Melhorne, the secretary), **John Carradine** (Crimp, the bounty collector), **Kent Taylor** (Joe, the co-pilot), **Joseph Calleia** (Vasquez, the anarchist), **Sir C. Aubrey Smith** (Professor Henry Spenger, the anthropologist), **Elisabeth Risdon** (Mrs Martha Spengler), **Patric Knowles** (Judson Ellis, the millionaire), **Casey Johnson** (Tommy, the young boy), **Allen Jenkins** (Pete, the boy's minder), **Dick Hogan** (Larry, the steward), **Robert Homans** (police captain), **Selmer Jackson** (airline manager), **Pedro De Cordoba** (Latin official), **Tiny Jones** (flower lady), **Frank Mills** (taxi-driver), **Ronald R. Rondell** (page with package), **Charlie Hall** (airport worker), **Pat O'Malley** (young Tommy's father), **Frank Faylen** (photographer),

Director: **JOHN FARROW**. Screenplay: **Jerry Cady, Dalton Trumbo, Nathanael West**. Original screen story: **Richard Carroll**. Photography: **Nicholas Musuraca**. Film editor: **Harry Marker**. Music: **Roy Webb**. Special photographic effects: **Vernon L. Walker**. Art directors: **Van Nest Polglase, Albert S. D'Agostino**. Costumes: **Edward Stevenson**. Production executive: **Lee Marcus**. Montage: **Douglas Travers**. Assistant directors: **Argyle Nelson, Sam Ruman**. Sound recording: **John E. Tribby**. RCA Sound System. Producer: **Robert Sisk**.

Copyright 23 June 1939 by RKO Radio Pictures, Inc. New York opening at the Rialto: 4 July 1939. U.S. release: 23 June 1939. Australian release: 28 September 1939. 75 minutes.

SYNOPSIS: An airplane carrying twelve passengers and crew is forced to crashland in the Amazon jungle.

NOTES: Although produced on a "B" picture budget of only $225,000, this movie turned out to be a "sleeper" — a movie that to the studio's surprise took off with both critics and public. Boxoffice receipts in the U.S.A. and Canada alone were well over a million dollars, returning RKO a handsome profit of $262,000 after paying all advertising, print, studio overhead and distribution costs.

COMMENT: Despite the naivety of its script and the lapse into needless and unconvincing moralising at the conclusion, this is a superior version of the tale than the remake *Back To Eternity* despite the fact that both were directed by Farrow. Here his direction has an invigorating freshness due to the long takes using fluid camera movement and the pace with which the characters are introduced and dialogue delivered that contrasts with the stale professionalism of the re-make. Lucie Ball is delightfully seductive and all told we much prefer this cast to that of the remake with the possible exception of Rod Steiger who has the Joseph Calleia part, a role for which he is not really suited. Interesting that the plot of both films is exactly the same, as are the characters and that all Latimer did was to rewrite the dialogue. He may have made it a bit more convincing, but he also made it less interesting. An obvious model is used for the crash, but the sets are fairly convincing. Notice that Farrow uses Lewton's later much used device of not showing the headhunters until the final shot and then only their feet as the camera tracks through the foliage and then sweeps up to show the plane flying into the clouds, a corny but effective fade-out.

OTHER VIEWS: The five that came back were the survivors of a party of twelve who crashed in an airliner somewhere in the wilds near the source of the Amazon. How some of them died, how the others lived for the day when the aeroplane could be mended for the flight, and how at the last moment some of them had their hopes dashed, is told very quietly in this simple yet compelling film. The director has an able cast with which to build up the tense atmosphere in which that oddly assorted little community spend long days in waiting, and the actors must be praised for the restraint with which thy sink their sometimes strong idiosyncrasies for the good of the film as a whole. The film moves so smoothly to its moving conclusion that the director's considerable art is imperceptible except in retrospect: then it is possible to see the degree of skill with which it has been staged and acted.

# Frontier Marshal

**Randolph Scott** (Wyatt Earp), **Nancy Kelly** (Sarah Allen), **Cesar Romero** (Doc Halliday), **Binnie Barnes** (Jerry), **John Carradine** (Ben Carter), **Edward Norris** (Dan Blackmore), **Eddie Foy Jr** (Eddie Foy), **Ward Bond** (town marshal), **Lon Chaney Jr** (Pringle), **Chris-Pin Martin** (Pete), **Joe Sawyer** (Curly Bill), **Harry Hayden** (Mayor Henderson), **Ventura Ybarra** (Pablo), **Charles Stevens** (Indian Charlie), **Tom Tyler** (Buck Newton), **Del Henderson** (proprietor of Bella Union Cafe), **Si Jenks** (prospector), **Gloria Roy** (dance hall girl), **Margaret Brayton** (mother), **Pat O'Malley** (customer), **Harry Woods, Dick Alexander** (Curly Bill's men), **John Bleifer, Hank Mann, Edward Le Saint, Heinie Conklin, George Melford** (men), **Fern Emmett** (hotel maid), **Kathryn Sheldon** (Mrs Garvey), **Ferris Taylor** (doctor), **John Butler** (harassed man), **Arthur Aylesworth, Eddie Dunn** (card players), **Philo McCullough, Ethan Laidlaw** (toughs), **Dick Elliott** (Jerry's propositioner), **Hank Bell** (man at bar), **Harlan Briggs** (editor).

Director: **ALLAN DWAN**. Screenplay: **Sam Hellman**. Based on the 1931 biography *Wyatt Earp, Frontier Marshal* by **Stuart N. Lake**. Photography: **Charles G. Clarke**. Film editor: **Fred Allen**. Art directors: **Richard Day, Lewis H. Creber**. Set decorator: **Thomas Little**. Costumes: **Herschel**. Music director: **Samuel Kaylin**. Sound recording: **George Leverett, William H. Anderson**. RCA (sic) Sound System. Producer: **Solomon M. Wurtzel**.

Copyright 28 July 1939 by 20th Century-Fox Film Corp. New York opening at the Roxy: 28 July 1939. U.S. release: 28 July 1939. Australian release: 28 September 1939. 6,429 feet. 71 minutes.

SYNOPSIS: Wyatt Earp cleans up Tombstone, Arizona.

NOTES: Wyatt Earp (1848-1929) was actually not a marshal at this stage of his career, but a deputy sheriff of Pima County, centered in Tombstone, Arizona. Other screen impersonations of him include Walter Huston in *Law and Order* 31, Richard Dix in *Tombstone* 42, Henry Fonda in *My Darling Clementine* 46, Joel McCrea in *Wichita* 55, Burt Lancaster in *Gunfight at the OK Corral* 57, James Stewart in *Cheyenne Autumn* 64, James Garner in *Hour of the Gun* 67, Harris Yulin in *Doc* 70. There was also a long-running TV series starring Hugh O'Brian.

This movie is actually a re-make of the Lake novel originally filmed in 1934 with George O'Brien as Earp and Alan Edwards as Doc. It was re-made again in 1946 with Henry Fonda and Victor Mature under the title *My Darling Clementine*. And re-made yet again in 1953 under the title *Powder River*.

Although permission had been obtained from Earp's estate (and a fee of $5,000 duly paid) to use his name, lawyers for the estate sued Fox anyway, claiming that Earp's screen romance with "Sarah Allen" was entirely fictitious.

Until *Gunfight at the OK Corral* (1957), this *Frontier Marshal* was the definitive exposition of the Earp legend, so far as Australian audiences were concerned. Randolph Scott was always the "A"-grade king of the cowboys, whereas Henry Fonda never rated at Australian ticket windows.

VIEWERS' GUIDE: Adults.

COMMENT: A lavishly-produced western, though most of the money seems to have been spent on the first half of the film. The climax at the O.K. Corral is somewhat skimped — especially in comparison with other versions — and the film as a whole is considerably inferior to Ford's greatly expanded re-make, *My Darling Clementine*. Still *Frontier Marshal*, despite the fact that it is largely studio-bound and that its action sequences are not handled as vigorously as in the other Earp films, has some good things going for it in the cast department. Eddie Foy is a stand-out here. His presence alone is worth the price of admission and his absence from the other versions is to be deplored. And this must be the last occasion that Binnie Barnes, who was to continue as a western heroine throughout the early forties, was photographed sufficiently attractively (skilful make-up and costumes also helped) to justify her casting. Randolph Scott does well by Wyatt Earp while Cesar Romero is in many respects a more convincing Doc Halliday than Victor Mature. Nancy Kelly makes an appealing heroine, while John Carradine, Lon Chaney Jr and Joe Sawyer make an admirable trio of villains (in fact we should have liked to see more of them, especially Chaney and Carradine). Dwan's direction has some imaginative touches (Scott's suddenly being accosted by the vigilante group; his odd entrance from above) and the musical numbers (including Miss Barnes' delightful rendition of "Heaven Will Protect the Working Girl") are handled with gusto. Charles Stevens plays the same role in this film as he does in Ford's re-make, but otherwise the cast is completely dissimilar. Charles Clarke's photography is consistently a thing of beauty, the art direction is pleasing and other production credits are top-drawer.

# the Frontiersman

**William Boyd** (Hopalong Cassidy), **George "Gabby" Hayes** (Windy), **Russell Hayden** (Lucky), **Evelyn Venable** (June Lake), **Clara Kimball Young** (Amanda Peters), **William Duncan** (Buck Peters), **Charles A. "Tony" Hughes** (Judson Thorpe), **Dickie Jones** (Artie Peters), **Roy Barcroft** (Sutton), **Emily Fitzroy** (Miss Snook), **John Beach** (Quirt), St Brendan Boys' Choir (school kids), **Blackjack Ward** (rustler), **George Morrell** (townsman), **Jim Corey** (Bar 20 cowboy), **Jesse Cavan** (townsman), **Robert B. Mitchell** (himself).

Director: **LESLEY SELANDER**. Screenplay: **Norman Houston**. Additional dialogue: **Harrison Jacobs**. Based on an original story by **Clarence E. Mulford**. Photography: **Russell Harlan**. Film editor: **Sherman A. Rose**. Art director: **Lewis J. Rachmil**. Assistant directors: **Derwin Abrahams, Theodore Joos**. Producer: **Harry Sherman**. Presented by **Adolph Zukor**. The St Brendan Boys' Choir directed by **Robert B. Mitchell**.

Copyright 16 December 1938 by Paramount Pictures, Inc. No New York showcase. U.S. release: 16 December 1938. Australian release: 22 June 1939. 6,656 feet. 74 minutes.

Copyright title and Australian release title: *The Frontiersmen*.

SYNOPSIS: Hopalong Cassidy sets out to trace down a cattle rustler, known as Dan Rowley, and to tame spoiled Artie Peters, the ten-year-old nephew of Buck Peters, the owner of Bar 20.

When the local school teacher, a battle-axe of a woman, quits her post in protest against the behavior of the kids, Hoppy imports a beautiful new teacher, June Lake, without consulting Mayor Thorpe, whom Hopalong suspects is really Rowley.

Miss Lake's beauty precipitates a violent competition for her attentions, into which everyone but Hoppy enters. Disappointed, the girl turns to the suave mayor.

NOTES: Number 20 of the 66-picture series.
 Locations in the San Jacinto Mountains.
 From 1937 through to 1941, William Boyd was 2nd only to Gene Autry on the North American exhibitors' list of money-making "Western" stars.

VIEWERS' GUIDE: Okay for all.

COMMENT: It wasn't until television was launched in Australia in October 1956 and his old films suddenly hit the airwaves, that Bill Boyd/Hopalong Cassidy became a household name in that country. True, these movies had originally played in cinemas, but "B" westerns were never highly regarded in the land of Oz and were used almost exclusively in Saturday matinees designed wholly for kids. Even here, Hoppy was not well thought of, the moppets preferring Gene Autry or Wild Bill Elliott or even Roy Rogers as second league cowboy heroes. (The first league was dominated by Randy Scott and John Wayne).

*The Frontiersman* is not exactly a typical Hoppy anyway, produced on a far more lavish budget than usual, using a really novel and off-beat script. Unfortunately, despite the interest generated by the originality of the story, combined with Russell Harlan's most attractively photographed exteriors, the movie fails the vital action test. The action eps are not only pretty tame but the villains are uncommonly dull. And there's too much tiresome, tedious (and sometimes downright nauseating) talk all around.

OTHER VIEWS: Bill Boyd was the strangest person I ever worked with. It's hard to say who he hated most — kids or horses. He despised actors and acting too, and hated producers, directors and newsmen as well. He believed his success was entirely due to his ingratiating personality. He was convinced he only had to smile into the camera, or give out with his charming laugh, and audiences would be enchanted. It's hard to say who disliked who the most: Boyd, Sherman, or Sherman, Boyd. It was all Boyd's idea to radically change the Cassidy character. Instead of the hard, scrappy gunslinger of Mulford's novels, Boyd played Hoppy as a dandy, dressed all in black — "a monkey suit," Pop Sherman called it. But Boyd was established in the role, the series was making money, so Pop let Boyd have his way... As for *The Frontiersman* which to my shame I directed, that was just plain bad. Pop had this bright idea of marking the hundredth anniversary of choral singing in American schools by casting the St Brendan Boys' Choir in the picture!

— Lesley Selander.

# Fury at Furnace Creek

**Victor Mature** (Cash), **Coleen Gray** (Molly Baxter), **Glenn Langan** (Rufe), **Reginald Gardiner** (Captain Walsh), **Albert Dekker** (Leverett), **Fred Clark** (Bird), **Charles Kemper** (Peaceful Jones), **Robert Warwick** (General Blackwell), **George Cleveland** (judge), **Roy Roberts** (Al Shanks), **Willard Robertson** (General Leads), **Griff Barnett** (Appleby), **Frank Orth** (Evans), **J. Farrell MacDonald** (Pops), **Charles Stevens** (Artego), **Jay Silverheels** (Little Dog), **Robert Adler** (Leverett henchman), **Harry Carter** (clerk), **Mauritz Hugo, Howard Negley** (defense counsels), **Harlan Briggs** (prosecutor), **Si Jenks** (jury foreman), **Guy Wilkerson, Edmund Cobb** (court clerks), **Kermit Maynard** (scout), **Paul Newlan** (bartender), **Ted Mapes** (man), **George Chesebro, Al Hill, Jerry Miley** (card players), **Minerva Urecal** (Mrs Crum), **Ray Teal** (sergeant), **Alan Bridge** (lawyer), **Oscar O'Shea** (jailer), **Robert Williams** (stranger), **James Flavin** (judge advocate).

Narrated by **Reed Hadley**.

Director: **H. BRUCE HUMBERSTONE**. Screenplay: **Charles G. Booth**. Additional dialogue: **Winston Miller**. Based on the 1938 novel *Four Men and a Prayer* by **David Garth**. Photography: **Harry Jackson**. Film editor: **Robert Simpson**. Art directors: **Lyle Wheeler, Albert Hogsett**. Set decorator: **Thomas Little**. Costumes: **René Hubert**. Special photographic effects: **Fred Sersen**. Make-up: **Ben Nye, George Lane**. Music director: **Alfred Newman**. Music composed by **David Raksin**, orchestrated by **Herbert Spencer** and **Maurice de Packh**. Wardrobe director: **Charles Le Maire**. Sound recording: **Eugene Grossman, Harry M. Leonard**. Western Electric Sound System. Producer: **Fred Kohlmar**.

Copyright 21 April 1948 by 20th Century-Fox Film Corp. New York opening at the Globe: 11 July 1948. U.S. release: May 1948. U.K. release: 17 January 1949. Australian release: 21 October 1948. 7,906 feet. 88 minutes.

SYNOPSIS: A U.S. cavalry officer, accused of provoking an Indian massacre in order to facilitate the operations of a mining syndicate on Indian land, dies at his court martial. His two sons, one a goody-goody cavalry man, the other a quick-on-the-drawer gambler, set out to clear his name.

COMMENT: It's always amazed me that this lavishly produced, excitingly scripted and thrillingly staged western has no following. Perhaps it's the cast that has failed to attract the fans. Victor Mature is always acknowledged to have delivered a fine portrayal in Ford's *My Darling Clementine*, but he's just as effective here, even if the role is less showy. Heroine Coleen Gray is never numbered among the greats, yet she too has given a number of telling portraits. We enjoyed her characterization here. With the support players of course there are fewer cavils. No critic in his right mind would fail to praise the likes of Reginald Gardiner, Albert Dekker, Fred Clark, Charles Kemper, Charles Stevens and company. Gardiner has the most showy role, but all contribute engrossing performances.

Lucky Humberstone has directed in an appropriately bravura style, assisted by Harry Jackson's striking studio and Arizona location cinematography. The large sets are equally impressive. So is Newman's score. This is a handsomely mounted and produced western which still comes across with tremendous force and power.

OTHER VIEWS: Despite its catchpenny title, *Fury at Furnace Creek* rates as director Bruce Humberstone's masterpiece, breathtakingly photographed with a strong plot line and spectacular action sequences. The large cast acquits itself well and production credits are honorable in all departments. Humberstone's forte is action, but he handles the dialogue confrontations with equal ease. The script is peopled with interesting characters and only a somewhat conventional romantic interest dulls an otherwise really outstanding production. The climax is a tour-de-force of edge-of-the-seat excitement, the absence of music and the high contrast photography contributing to the dramatic effect. Both stationary camera angles and running inserts are used in the chase sequences — in Humberstone's expert hands, both are equally effective.

# Grand Canyon

**Richard Arlen** (Mike Adams), **Mary Beth Hughes** (Terry Lee), **Reed Hadley** (Mitch Bennett), **James Millican** (Tex Hartford), **Olin Howlin** (Windy), **Grady Sutton** (Halfnote), **Joyce Compton** (Mabel), **Charlie Williams** (Bert), **Margia Dean** (script girl), **Anna May Slaughter** (little girl), **Stanley Price** (make-up man), **Holly Bane** (Rocky), **Frank Hagney** (first thug), **Kid Chissel** (second thug), **Zon Murray** (Morgan), **Murray Lerner, Robert L. Lippert** (producers looking at rushes).

Director: **PAUL LANDRES**. Screenplay: **Jack Harvey, Milton Luban**. Original screen story: **Carl K. Hittleman**. Photography: **Ernest W. Miller**. Supervising film editor: **Paul Landres**. Film editor: **Edward Mann**. Art director: **Frank Sylos**. Wardrobe: **Al Berke**.

Make-up: **Paul Stanhope**. Hair styles: **Loretta Franzel**. Special effects: **Ray Mercer**. Sound effects: **Harry Coswick**. Dialogue director: **Milton Luban**. Casting director: **Yolanda Molinari**. Executive assistant: **Murray Lerner**. Script supervisor: **Moree Herring**. Inserts: **Earl Hays**. Music score: **Albert Glasser**. Songs: "Love Time in Grand Canyon", "Serenade to a Mule" by **Katherine Glasser** (lyrics) and **Albert Glasser** (music). Camera operator: **Archie R. Dalzell**. Grip: **Noble Craig**. Stills: **Milton Gold**. Assistant director: **Frank Fox**. Sound engineers: **Garry Harris, Walter Dalgleish**. RCA Sound System. Producer: **Carl K. Hittleman**. Executive producer: **Robert L. Lippert**.

Copyright 1 October 1949 by Lippert Productions, Inc. Released in the U.S. through Screen Guild Productions: 12 August 1949. No recorded New York opening. U.K. release through Falcon-Exclusive: 26 February 1951. Australian release through 20th Century-Fox: 18 January 1952 (sic). 65 minutes.

SYNOPSIS: A muleteer is promoted to leading man in a Poverty Row movie allegedly shooting in Arizona's Grand Canyon.

NOTES: Original theatrical prints were released in sepia.

COMMENT: Although it will not be apparent to the viewers who sit through this adventure/romance/comedy with a moving picture background, this film is something of an oddity.

The company around which the fictitious story is framed happens to be Lippert itself. Much is made of the notion that the picture's limited shooting schedule, constrained budget and poor production values, require the enhancement of actual location shooting. But in point of fact, of course, the real main unit never strays far from the home studio and the adjacent Hollywood hills.

True, we do see a bit of the Grand Canyon, but mainly through stock and 2nd unit shots, as well as the ever-ready back projection.

In order to forestall this sort of criticism, Lippert's publicity department actually put out a story that the film was made mostly in the studio because bad weather forced the location company's premature return from the real Grand Canyon. Marvelous what alibis these guys can think up!

Okay, so we see very little of the real Grand Canyon after all. This would be okay, if we saw and heard a reasonably sharp and punchy satire. But we don't. The script comes over like unflavored ice cream, depending a great deal on the charisma of the players to give it taste and appeal. Which, fortunately, they do manage to accomplish.

Our main entertainment problems arise when the script detours into forced comedy. Arlen's two verbose sidekicks, Olin Howland (or Howlin, if you like) and Grady Sutton are especially wearisome. Joyce Compton is also forced to act the comic stooge. And a long scene with a potential Shirley Temple in the person of Anna May Slaughter is also allowed to drag.

Flat-footed direction must also be blamed for the film's very middling success, despite the promise of its central idea. It's indeed fortunate that the photography is so attractive, that Arlen is such a personable hero, that Mary Beth Hughes is one of our favorite "B" heroines, that Reed Hadley has such an entrancing voice, that James Millican makes such a delightfully surly villain, and that one of our top character actors, Charles Williams, has such a fairly sizable role as the assistant director.

# the Great Barrier

Richard Arlen (Hickey), Antoinette Cellier (Mary Moody), Barry Mackay (Steve), Lilli Palmer (Lou), Roy Emerton (Moody), J. Farrell MacDonald (Major Rogers), Ben Weldon (Joe), Jock MacKay (Bates), Ernest Sefton (magistrate), Henry Victor (Bulldog Kelly), Frank McGlynn Sr (Sir John MacDonald, prime minister of Canada), and as members of the C.P.R. board: Reginald Barlow (James Hill), Arthur Loft (William Van Horne), Gilbert Emery (George Stephen), Howard C. Hickman (Donald Smith), William Kuhl (Thomas Shaughnessy), Lestrange Millman (R.B. Angus).

Director: **MILTON ROSMER**. Screenplay: **Michael Barringer, Milton Rosmer**. Dialogue: **Ralph Spence, Milton Rosmer**. Based on the novel *The Great Divide* by **Alan Sullivan**. Photography: **Glen MacWilliams, Bob Martin, Sepp Allgeier**. Additional studio interiors directed by **Geoffrey Barkas**, photographed by **Arthur Crabtree**. Film editors: **Charles Frend, B.H. Hipkins**. Music: **Hubert Bath**. Music director: **Louis Levy**. Art director: **Walter W. Murton**. Wardrobe: **Marianne**. Sound recording: **Phillip Dorte**. British Acoustic Film Sound System. Producer: **Gunther Stapenhorst**.

Copyright 4 February 1937 by Gaumont British Picture Corp. of America. New York opening at the Criterion: 25 March 1937 (ran two days). U.S. release through Gaumont-British: 29 April 1937. U.K. release through Renown: February 1937. London opening at Haymarket: 4 February 1937. Australian release through 20th Century-Fox. 9 reels. 83 minutes.

U.S. release title: *SILENT BARRIERS*.

SYNOPSIS: Construction of the Canadian Pacific Railway is halted at the Rockies.

COMMENT: A rip-roaring, action-paced, vigorously staged Canadian western whose continuous thrills are halted only by an occasional sub-title, a bit of mild romance with the attractive Miss Cellier and the equally attractive but villainous Lilli Palmer, and three pleasant-enough songs (two from Mr Mackay). The action is staged on the grandest of scales with lots of rioting extras, rugged locations, real rolling stock and lots of destruction (both natural and man-made). Production values rate as extremely lavish.

The players in this action feast acquit themselves most capably (Roy Emerton is especially forceful). The direction from Milton Rosmer is surprisingly swift and sure. The lighting photography not only catches the eye, but the work of four cameramen blends so perfectly it's impossible to tell who did what. The film editing is ultra-pacey yet smooth. The plot moves so fast, the script has little time for character development and other such subtleties. But the players give their roles plenty of color nonetheless.

All told, a must for action fans, railroad buffs, and Canada-lovers.

# Guns of the Timberland

Alan Ladd (Jim Hadley), Jeanne Crain (Laura Riley), Gilbert Roland (Monty Welker), Frankie Avalon (Bert Harvey), Lyle Bettger (Clay Bell), Noah Beery, Jr (Blackie), Verna Felton (Aunt Sarah), Alana Ladd (Jane Peterson), Regis Toomey

(Sheriff Taylor), **Johnny Seven** (Vince), **George Selk** (Amos Stearnes), **Paul E. Burns** (Bill Burroughs), **Henry Kulky** (logger), **George J. Lewis** (Jud), **Steve Pendleton** (Sam Peterson).

Director: **ROBERT D. WEBB**. Screenplay: **Aaron Spelling, Joseph Petracca**. Based on the 1955 novel by **Louis L'Amour**. Photographed in Technicolor by **John Seitz**. Film editor: **Tom McAdoo**. Art director: **John Beckman**. Set decorator: **Frank M. Miller**. Costumes: **Marjorie Best**. Make-up: **Gordon Bau**. Music composed by **David Buttolph**, orchestrated by **Maurice de Packh**. Songs: "Gee Whizz Willikens Golly Gee" (Avalon) and "The Faithful Kind" (Avalon), both by **Mack David** (music), **Jerry Livingston** (lyrics); "Cry Timber" (chorus) by **Sy Miller**. Production manager: **John Veitch**. Stunts: **Russell Saunders, Paul Baxley**. Assistant director: **Dick Moder**. Sound recording: **Francis M. Stahl**. Associate producer: **George C. Bertholon**. Producer: **Aaron Spelling**. Executive producer: **Alan Ladd**. A Jaguar Production.

Copyright 1960 by Jaguar Films. Released through Warner Bros. No New York opening. U.S. release: March 1960. U.K. release: May 1960. Australian release: 25 August 1960. Running times: 93 minutes (Aust), 91 minutes (USA), 88 minutes (UK).

SYNOPSIS: Logging partners Jim Hadley and Monty Welker arrive in the Northwest country of 1895 with a government contract permitting them to cut down the trees in a dense mountain range. Opposing them are some ranchers of a nearby valley who fear their grazing land will be destroyed by the lumbermen. Led by Laura Riley, one of the largest landowners, the ranchers organize and dynamite the loggers' timber road. Hadley wants to retaliate by legal means but the headstrong Welker resorts to violence which results in the serious injury of a young rancher, Bert Harvey, who had been friendly toward the lumbermen. Eventually, Hadley, influenced by both the ranchers' arguments and his growing love for Laura, splits with Welker.

NOTES: Location scenes filmed in Northern California.
Film debuts of rock star Frankie Avalon, and Alan Ladd's daughter Alana.

COMMENT: Arriving a little late for our screening, I missed the credits. To my dismay I thought I was watching a 16mm ex-CinemaScope print. The color was fuzzy and Alan Ladd's face looked bloated in close-up – a distortion often produced when unsqueezing CinemaScope prints for TV. When the film was over and our panel started writing up their comments, I found to my amazement I was mistaken. The film was not made in any anamorphic system. What we saw on our screen was a full aperture reduction straight from 35mm. Ladd's face would have looked even worse on a theatre screen when the frame was cropped top and bottom and the image blown up for widescreen. No wonder the distributor didn't dare open the movie in New York, the home of critical antipathy to Mr Ladd. What a roasting he would have received from *The New York Times* and the other newspapers!

Disregarding Mr Ladd's jaded appearance, *Guns of the Timberland* is pretty much a Ladd vehicle. This time our hero sees the error of his logging ways and comes down firmly on the side of the environmentalists. This action is not only the catalyst for Romance (in the person of Jeanne Crain, looking very beautiful here) but Conflict with his longtime partner and friend, forcefully yet sympathetically played here by Gilbert Roland. A fair amount of action ensues, culminating in a rip-roaring forest fire.

Another surprise was my belated discovery that the film was supposed to be set in 1895. I thought it was more or less contemporary. There's no period flavor about the movie at all. The costumes, the props, the furnishings could pass for backwoods modern. Mr Avalon even has a couple of songs that certainly don't jive with 1895!

In addition to Mr Roland and Miss Crain, it's always good to see Lyle Bettger. Producer Ladd doubtless cast him in the movie because of his small size, but he's big enough to run rings around Alan in the acting department. His role is comparatively small and not exactly characteristic (he's one of the goodies this time), but with his distinctive voice and forceful manner he's a guy you remember long after Ladd's more routine dramatics have faded from memory.

The director is at his best in the action spots. These are suspensefully staged. Production values also benefit from extensive location lensing. I love the conclusion on the logging train when Ladd's companions snatch up Miss Crain and the ensemble steams off into the distance to a rousing chorus of "Cry Timber". This is the sort of stuff director Webb does best -- including of course that frighteningly realistic forest fire in which both Ladd and Roland seem to be doing their own death-defying stunts. They're braver men than I am, that's for sure!

# Haunted Gold

**John Wayne** (John Mason), **Sheila Terry** (Janet Carter), **Erville Alderson** (Benedict), **Harry Woods** (Joe Ryan), **Otto Hoffman** (Simon), **Martha Mattox** (Mrs Herman), **Edgar "Blue" Washington** (Clarence), **Slim Whitaker** (Slim), **Bob Burns** (Bob), **Ben Corbett** (Ben), **Jim Corey** (Ed), **Tom Bay** (Tom), **Bud Osborne** (Bud), **Mack V. Wright** (Mack), **Blackjack Ward** (henchman), **Charles Le Moyne** (cowhand), and "Duke".

Director: **MACK V. WRIGHT**. Screenplay: **Adele Buffington**. Based on her 1928 screenplay *The Phantom City*. Photography: **Nick Musuraca**. Film editor: **William Clemens**. Music score: **Leo F. Forbstein**. Associate producer: **Sid Rogell**. Western Electric Sound System. Presented by **Leon Schlesinger**. A Four Star Western.

Copyright 7 February 1933 by Vitagraph, Inc. A Warner Bros. picture. No New York opening. U.S. release: 17 December 1932. U.K. release: May 1933. 57 minutes.

SYNOPSIS: Hampered by bandits, two heirs try to find a missing fortune in an abandoned gold mine.

NOTES: A re-make of the 1928 silent *The Phantom City* which starred Ken Maynard and Eugenia Gilbert. The director was Albert Rogell, the photographer Ted McCord. "Blue" Washington repeats his original role.

COMMENT: It would be wrong to exaggerate the virtues of this little western, but the fact is that on a first viewing — despite some clumsy effects that don't quite come off — it's a mighty entertaining little piece. It's only on a second look that you realize the reason for the mismatched cuts, under-cranking and too dark location photography is that the producer has liberally spliced in footage from the 1928 silent version *The Phantom City*. Not only have whole action sequences — including an elaborate chase in which our hero foils his pursuers by pulling a whole house down in their tracks, plus a wonderfully exciting ascent up a mine shaft with displaced beams falling right into the camera, plus a truly astonishing series of stunts from a bucket suspended over a canyon, plus an amazing bit of business when "Duke" (the horse, not Wayne) forces one of the heavies over a cliff — been incorporated, but even background and establishing shots.

Nonetheless, that first viewing is certainly a marvellous entertainment experience. You think to yourself, how can they afford all this excitement, all this elaborate staging on a "B" budget? True, the players are strictly second-rate, though Wayne himself gives a likeable and ingratiating performance. By contrast, the other players are somewhat traditionally stiff.

Although heavy-handed and even at times inept, the direction tries mightily to get plenty of spooky atmosphere out of the sets and situations. In some scenes Wright successfully employs an unusually large variety of odd camera angles. Musuraca's shadow-laden photography is also an asset.

# Heaven Only Knows

**Robert Cummings** (Mike), **Brian Donlevy** (Duke), **Marjorie Reynolds** (Ginger), **Jorja Cartwright** (Drusilla), **Bill Goodwin** (Plumber), **Stuart Erwin** (sheriff), **John Litel** (reverend), **Peter Miles** (Speck O'Donnell), **Edgar Kennedy** (Jud), **Gerald Mohr** (Treason), **Lurene Tuttle** (Mrs O'Donnell), Ray Bennett (Freel), **Will Orlean** (Kansas City Kid), **Arlene Gray, Gary Gray, Jimmy Hawkins, Timmy Hawkins** (kids in schoolroom), and **Glenn Strange.**

Director: **ALBERT S. ROGELL**. Screenplay: **Art Arthur, Rowland Leigh**. Adaptation: **Ernest Haycox**. Story: **Aubrey Wisberg**. Photography: **Karl Struss**. Film editor: **Edward Mann**. Art director: **Martin Obzina**. Set decorator: **A. Roland Field**. Wardrobe: **Bill Edwards**. Make-up: **Ern Westmore, Don Cash**. Hair styles: **Marjorie Lund**. Music composed and directed by **Heinz Roemheld**, supervised by **David Chudnow**. Camera operator: **Robert Gough**. Dialogue coach: **Lee Frederic**. Special photographic effects: **Ray Binger**. Special effects: **Rocky Cline**. Production manager: **Joe Popkin**. Assistant director: **Jack Voglin**. Sound recording: **Corson Jowett**. Western Electric Sound System. Producer: **Seymour Nebenzal**. Executive producer: **Seymour Nebenzal**.

Copyright 12 September 1947 by Nero Films, Inc. Released through United Artists. New York opening at the Broadway: 13 November 1947. U.S. release: 12 September 1947. U.K. release: 16 February 1948. Australian release: 1 April 1948. 8,982 feet. 100 minutes.

Early in 1948 the U.S. release title was changed to *MONTANA MIKE*.

SYNOPSIS: Angel reforms local western crime boss.

COMMENT: Another entry in the Hollywood-finds-angels cycle, though this one is surprisingly amusing and entertainingly intriguing. It's also most ingratiatingly acted.

Donlevy, an uneven performer, is especially believable here. Direction and other credits are thoroughly skilled, whilst production values (particularly by the standard of independent movies) are breathtakingly elaborate.

In the difficult central role, Robert Cummings acquits himself particularly well. The part requires him to be a figure of fantasy yet thoroughly believable, keep a judicious balance between drama and comedy, and change pace near the conclusion from what is essentially a light part to one that is dramatically yet triumphantly sorrowful.

The director manages to keep the changing moods of the script on an even keel so that the "heavy" finale caps the whole picture in a satisfyingly forceful way. Although obviously derived from *La Charrette Fantome* (1939), this final sequence is one of the most memorable in the American cinema.

Cummings has excellent support in Stu Erwin as a philosophical sheriff, Marjorie Reynolds and Jorja Cartwright. Even the smallest roles are faultlessly filled.

An inspiring and moving motion picture which runs the gamut from satire to slapstick, from action to tears. Rogell's masterpiece. And a lasting memorial too of the finely atmospheric work of that cinematographer's cinematographer, Karl Struss.

# Indian Paint

**Johnny Crawford** (Nishko), **Jay Silverheels** (Chief Hevatanu), **Pat Hogan** (Sutamakis), **Robert Crawford, Jr** (Wacopi), **George J. Lewis** (Nopawallo), **Joan Hollmark** (Amatula), **Bill Blackwell** (Sutako), **Robert Crawford, Sr** (Motopi), **Al Doney** (Lataso), **Cinda Siler** (Petala), **Suzanne Goodman** (Lataso's widow), **Marshall Jones** (comanche leader), **Warren L. Dodge** (2nd comanche).

Director: **NORMAN FOSTER**. Screenplay: **Norman Foster**. Based on the 1942 book by **Glenn Bach**. Photographed in Eastman Color by **Floyd Crosby**. Film editors: **Robert Crawford, Sr, George White**. Music: **Marlin Skiles**. Song "Song of Nishko" (Crawford) by **Ted Saizis** and **Vincent Saizis**. Song, "Painted Pony" by **Marlin Skiles** (music) and **Norman Foster** (lyrics). Set decorator: **Jack Glover**. Make-up: **Dan Greenway**. Production manager: **James Howard Joslin**. Assistant director: **Foster H. Phinney**. Property master: **Jack Glover**. Wardrobe: **Majuanta Jo Miller**. Script supervisor: **May Wale**. Editorial assistant: **Ned Shaheen**. Sound effects: **Del Harris**. Music editor: **Edna Bullock**. 2nd unit photography: **Ted Saizis, Vincent Saizis**. Assistant cameraman: **Sam Noto**. Key grip: **Lou Kusley**. Chief electrician: **Robert S. Comer**. Sound supervisors: **Ted Saizis, Vincent Saizis**. Sound mixer: **Walter James Jr**. Sound re-recording: **Glen Glenn Sound Company, Inc**. Producer: **Eugene W. Goree**. Executive producer: **Robert T. Callahan**. Associate producers: **Jay Richards, Robert Crawford Sr, James A. Sullivan**.

Copyright 7 April 1965 by Tejas Productions, Inc. No New York opening. U.S. release through Eagle American Films and Crown International Pictures: 8 April 1965. U.K. release through BLC/ British Lion: 5 August 1966. No Australian theatrical or TV release. 91 minutes. Cut to 77 minutes in the UK.

SYNOPSIS: Nishko, the son of the chief of the Arikara tribe, trains the foal of a domesticated mare and a wild stallion. When mature, the colt is torn between loyalty to his young trainer and his instinct to return to his father's herd.

NOTES: Filmed in and around Cleburne, Texas, in 1963.

COMMENT: A story with plenty of exciting incidents, including some amazing animal footage, all beautifully photographed. Norman Foster's direction with its over-use of close-ups is inclined to be dull, whilst the acting, not to be too unkind, is second-rate. *Indian Paint* holds the interest but all the same its appeal is likely to be limited. It falls between two stools, — not arty enough for the art-house circuit, yet too un-Hollywood for general release. Of the speaking players, only Hogan and Silverheels are genuine Indians.

# In Old California

**John Wayne** (Tom Craig), **Binnie Barnes** (Lacey Miller), **Albert Dekker** (Britt Dawson), **Helen Parrish** (Ellen Sanford), **Patsy Kelly** (Helga), **Edgar Kennedy** (Kegs McKeever), **Dick Purcell** (Joe Dawson), **Harry Shannon** (Carlin), **Charles Halton** (Hayes), **Emmett Lynn** (Whitey), **Bob McKenzie** (Bates), **Milt Kibbee** (Tompkins), **Paul Sutton** (Chick), **Anne O'Neal** (Mrs Tompkins), **Minerva Urecal** (Mrs Carson), **Robert E. Homans** (marshal), **Hooper Atchley** (Higgins), **Pearl Early** (Mrs Bates), **Ruth Robinson** (Mrs Higgins), **Frank Jacquet** (Dr Glaggett), **Jack O'Shea** (saloon patron), **Jack Kirk, Frank Ellis** (wagon drivers), **James C. Morton** (Red, bartender at Sacramento), **Forrest Taylor** (man with Carlin in saloon), **Dick Alexander** (Clem), **Donald Curtis** (Pike), **George Lloyd** (San Francisco sheriff), **Stanley Blystone** (San Francisco deputy), **Slim Whitaker** (pedestrian), **Frank Hagney, Ed Brady** (angry citizens in lynch mob), **Wade Crosby** (San Francisco bartender), **Guy Usher** (first boat captain), **Martin Garralaga** (Alvarez), **Esther Estrella** (Maria Alvarez), **Matt Willis** (joker at bar), **Fern Emmett** (Mrs Coggins), **Blackie Whiteford** (man in crowd), **Emily LaRue** (Rosita Alvarez), **Dorothy Granger** (saloon girl), **Rex Lease** (gold strike rider), **Karl Hackett** (Charlie), **Cecil Weston** (Mrs Marvin), **Fred Walburn** (Archie Higgins), and **Merrill McCormack, Frank McGlynn, Art Mix, Lynne Carver, Chester Conklin, Horace B. Carpenter, Olin Howland, Ralph Peters, Bud Osborne.**

Director: **WILLIAM McGANN**. Writers: **Gertrude Purcell, Frances Hyland** from a screen story by **J. Robert Bren, Gladys Atwater**. Cinematographer: **Jack Marta**. Art director: **Russell Kimball**. Supervising editor: **Murray Seldeen**. Editor: **Howard O'Neill**. Music: **David Buttolph**. Music director: **Cy Feuer**. Costumes: **Adele Palmer**. RCA Sound System. Associate producer: **Robert North**. Executive producer: **Herbert J. Yates**.

Copyright 31 May 1942 by Republic Pictures Corp. New York opening at Loew's Criterion: 17 June 1942. U.S. release: 31 May 1942. U.K. release through British Lion: 11 January 1943. Australian release through British Empire Films: 18 November 1943. 8,116 feet. 90 minutes.

SYNOPSIS: Wayne reported back to Republic for *In Old California* to play Tom Craig, a young Bostonian who meets an attractive dance hall singer Lacey Miller (Binnie Barnes) en route to Sacramento where he plans to set up as a pharmacist. She is engaged to Britt Dawson (Albert Dekker), the boss of Sacramento politics who lives off tribute exacted from ranchers in the area. Dawson tries to make it impossible for Wayne to find a site for his pharmacy but is foiled when Lacey goes into partnership with him. Wayne becomes a popular fellow as he cures the local aches and pains but he remains aloof from Lacey because of her engagement to Dawson and instead takes an interest in Ellen (Helen Parrish), a girl of highly respectable background. When Wayne leads the ranchers in revolt against Dawson, the latter places poison in a tonic that Wayne prescribes.

COMMENT: A disappointing Wayne movie all around. Firstly the script makes him a druggist of all things. Nothing macho about a druggist — particularly in Hollywood movies where either surly Charles Halton or bright but dim Irving Bacon have this profession sewn up. Then our hero is constantly bested by the villain but never gets the chance to even the score. A strange characterization indeed! Thirdly, he is forced to play opposite Binnie Barnes, a lively girl in her day, but so poorly photographed here she looks old enough to play Wayne's mother! Fourthly, he is constantly upstaged by a lot of knockabout comic relief perpetrated by Edgar Kennedy and Patsy Kelly.

OTHER VIEWS: A lavishly produced western, competently directed and photographed, with a large roster of favorite support players including George Lloyd as a sheriff, Charles Halton a blacksmith, and Robert Homans the marshal.

— C.F.

Not one of Wayne's brightest vehicles. True, there are some large crowd scenes, and exciting action spots including a saloon slug-fest between Wayne and Dekker (and their doubles, though these are so well integrated they are difficult to detect) and a climax in which a troop of baddies pour down over the hills to attack the wagon train (there are some nice stunts here too, though the whole sweeping effect is a bit spoilt by some very obvious studio cut-ins). But Binnie Barnes is too old to be playing heroines (she is none too flatteringly photographed, either) and the script with Wayne cast in the unlikely role of a druggist leading to a climax in which he leads a train of medical supplies to the victims of typhoid at a gold mining camp is, despite a few bright lines of dialogue, sheer hoke whose plot is as unconvincing as its dialogue is cliché-written. The comic relief provided by Edgar Kennedy and Patsy Kelly is wearisomely predictable and is not helped by director William McGann's unimaginative handling. Only the direction of the action scenes excels — and these were doubtless megaphoned by Yakima Canutt. However, other production values are not even up to Mr McGann's standard of competence. The photography especially, is careless and slip-shod (when the light is turned right down at the Higgins shack, it makes not the slightest difference to the lighting on the set) and the sets are for the most part neither eye-pleasing nor lavishly appointed. Process work is poor, the film looks as if it has been edited with a meat-axe, and the sound has been recorded on such a low level it is necessary to turn the volume control right up increasing the level of surface noise.

# In Old Monterey

**Gene Autry** (Gene), **Smiley Burnette** (Frog), **June Storey** (Jill), **George Hayes** (Gabby Whittaker), **Stuart Hamblen** (Bugler), **Billy Lee** (Jimmy), **Jonathan Hale** (Stevenson), **Robert Warwick** (Major Forbes), **William Hall** (Gilman), **Eddie Conrad** (proprietor), **Frank Kettering, Ken Trietsch, Paul Trietsch, Charles Ward** (Hoosier Hotshots), **Edna Earle Wolson** (Sarie), **Margaret Waters** (Sally), **The Ranch Boys** (themselves), **Forrest Taylor** (colonel), **Curley Dresden, Jack Kirk** (cowhands), **Ralph Bucko, Roy Bucko, Victor Cox, Jim Corey, Frank Ellis, Dan White** (townsmen), **Curley Bradley, Ken Carson, Shorty Carlson, Jack Ross** (Ranch Boys), **Bob Wilke** (man on wagon), **Hal Price** (wagon driver), **Reverend Neal Dodd** (clergyman), **Jack O'Shea** (miner), **James Mason, Tom Steele** (henchman), **Rex Lease, George Montgomery** (soldiers), **Edward Earle** (captain), **Fred Burns** (Fred), **Bill Yrigoyen** (stunt double for Gene Autry), and "Champion" the horse.

Director: **JOSEPH KANE**. Story: **Gerald Geraghty, George Sherman**. Screenplay: **Gerald Geraghty, Dorrell McGowan** and **Stuart McGowan**. Camera: **Ernest Miller**. Editor: **Edward Mann**. Music supervisor: **Raoul Kraushaar**. Music: **Paul Sawtell**. Songs: "It Happened In Monterey" and "Little Pardner" by **Gene Autry**, "Tumbling Tumbleweed", "Born in the Saddle", "Columbia the Gem of the Ocean", "The Vacant Chair". Composers and lyricists: **Frank Marvin, Billy Rose, Mabel Wayne, Gus Kahn, Walter Donaldson, Bob Nolan, Fred Rose**. Stunts: **Tom Steele**. Production manager: **Al Wilson**. RCA Sound System. Associate producer: **Armand Schaefer**. Executive producer: **Herbert J. Yates**.

Copyright 14 August 1939 by Republic Pictures Corp. No recorded New York opening. U.S. release: 14 August 1939. U.K. release through British Lion. Australian release through British Empire Films: 11 April 1940. 8 reels. 6,553 feet. 73 minutes.

SYNOPSIS: Gene, as an army man, is assigned to try and straighten out the difficulties with the ranchers who occupy a section the government wants to use a proving grounds for bombing planes. With a bunch of army buddies Gene joins the ranchers using his experience as a former cowhand to win them over to the government's point of view. But the owner of a large and profitable borax works does not want the army to come in. With his henchman he tries to make it appear that the army fliers are using ruthless tactics to frighten the ranchers. The latter determine to offer armed resistance to the take over. They throw up a barricade in the town but Gene comes up with proof that the borax owner and his gang are responsible for the dirty work.

NOTES: Autry's 35th of his 94 movies.

COMMENT: An unusual Autry vehicle in a number of ways. The plot is used as a peg on which to hang a great deal of patriotic talk and a defence of the superior fighting force concept that still figures strongly even in present-day (2004) politics. The villains kill the heroine's kid brother. There are no less than seven songs (we enjoyed them) plus a zingy musical interlude by the Hoosier Hot Shots. Comic relief is cut to a minimum once the plot gets into stride and Burnette's part virtually disappears (he has no songs either). There is nonetheless a fair amount of action topped by one of the most large-scale climactic action sequences ever filmed for a B-western — a shoot-out involving hundreds of extras and considerable location filming. The locations are quite strikingly used in a few shots too. Some of the earlier action pieces use stock footage but the climax is all-new material. Autry is in good voice and even does one of his own stunts though a stand-in is rather obviously used in an early bronco-busting sequence. Burnette and Hayes turn in their usual characterizations. Miss Storey makes a pretty heroine, though her part is small. Hale does a much more convincing job here as the villain than he does as Mr Dithers in the Blondie films. The direction is fast-paced and other credits are equally smooth.

# Jack McCall, Desperado

**George Montgomery** (Jack McCall), **Angela Stevens** (Rose Griffith), **Douglas Kennedy** ("Wild" Bill Hickok), **James Seay** (Bat McCall), **Eugene Iglesias** (Grey Eagle), **William Tannen** (Spargo), **Jay Silverheels** (Red Cloud), **John Hamilton** (Colonel Cornish), **Selmer Jackson** (Colonel Braud), **Stanley Blystone** (judge), **Gene Roth** (attorney), **Alva Lacy** (Hisega), **Joe McGuinn** (U.S. marshal), **Emory Parnell** (2$^{nd}$ judge), **Kenne Duncan** (renegade), **Victor Adamson** (barfly).

Director: **SIDNEY SALKOW**. Screenplay: **John O'Dea**. Story: **David Chandler**. Photographed in Technicolor by **Henry Freulich**. Film editor: **Aaron Stell**. Music director: **Mischa Bakaleinikoff**. Art director: **Paul Palmentola**. Set decorator: **Sidney Clifford**. Technicolor color consultant: **Francis Cugat**. Unit manager: **Herbert Leonard**. Assistant director: **Paul Donnelly**. Sound engineer: **George Cooper**. RCA Sound System. Producer: **Sam Katzman**.

Copyright 13 March 1953 by Columbia Pictures Corp. (In notice: 1952). No New York opening. U.S. release: April 1953. U.K. release: 20 April 1953. Australian release: 3 February 1955 (sic). 6,822 feet. 75 minutes.

SYNOPSIS: A Southerner, fighting in the Union army, is framed as a spy.

COMMENT: With plenty of action and sufficiently fast-moving to satisfy undemanding fans, this one also managed to capture good reviews. True, it's shot in pleasing, if not particularly artistic color, and boasts more production values than your average Katzman "B". Though the introductory sequence is reprised (no doubt for the benefit of latecomers), there is little if any stock footage, even though a large number of costumed extras battle and chase each other (occasionally with running inserts) across real location countrysides. Frequent changes of set and locale add to the fast pace which helps to offset the pulp novel story with its limited characterizations and elemental plot.

The film would also have risen to higher entertainment heights with a couple of more personable villains. Yes, it's surprising to see Wild Bill Hickok as the treacherous heavy, but Douglas Kennedy is not all that convincing. Not that he is the worst actor in the piece, though the support players here are definitely a fourth-rate bunch (including Gene Roth in a one-shot bit as the prosecutor). The embarrassingly wooden Jay Silverheels takes that honor. The girl is okay, though bland. Her role is rather small anyway.

Montgomery has a bit of presence, though obviously doubled for his fights and stuntwork.

Despite all the action, sets and crowds, and Mr Salkow's admirably fast pacing, *Jack McCall* offers little more than the least demanding audience might expect. Unless you're a rabid Western or Montgomery fan, the impression you take away will be bland and unmemorable.

# Jedda

**Ngarla Kunoth** (Jedda), **Robert Tudawali** (Marbuck), **Betty Suttor** (Sarah McMann), **Paul Reynell** (Joe), **George Simpson-Lyttle** (Douglas McMann), **Constable Tas Fitzer** [of the Northern Territory Police] (Peter Wallis), **Wason Byers, Willie Farrar** and aborigines of the Pitjantara, Aranda, Pintudi, Yungman, Djauan, Waugite and Tiwi tribes of North and Central Australia.

Director: **CHARLES CHAUVEL**. Original screenplay: **Charles Chauvel, Elsa Chauvel**. Photographed in Gevacolor by **Carl Kayser**. Cameraman: **Phil Pike**. Film editors: **Alec Ezard, Jack Gardiner, Pam Bosworth**. Art director: **Ronald McDonald**. Music composed and conducted by **Isador Goodman**. Producer: **Charles Chauvel**.

Copyright 1956 by Charles Chauvel Productions. U.S. release through Distributors Corporation of America: 12 June 1956. New York opening at the 46th Street Embassy: 27 February 1957. U.K. release through Independent/British Lion: 13 August 1956. Australian release through Columbia: 5 May 1955. Sydney opening at the Lyceum: 5 May 1955. 9,046 feet. 100 minutes. Cut to 88 minutes in the U.S.A, 73 minutes in the U.K.

U.S. release title: *Jedda the Uncivilized*.

SYNOPSIS: Reared as a white girl, orphaned Jedda still feels some longings for the life of her own people. Her inherited emotions are stirred by corroboree music... and when hand-some black Marbuck "sings" her to his blanket, she cannot resist. Marbuck takes her from homestead, is chased by Jedda's loved one, a station worker who is partly black. Returning with Jedda to his tribe, Marbuck is chastised for breaking blood laws, is "sung" by the elders. Driven insane by the "singing", he drags Jedda with him as he falls from a cliff.

NOTES: Charles Chauvel's final feature. After completing *Jedda*, he shot 13 eps for the television series *Australian Walkabout*. He died in 1959.

Number 24 at Australian ticket windows for 1955.

VIEWERS' GUIDE: Unsuitable for children.

COMMENT: Surprising to notice *Jedda* had a "General Exhibition" certificate on original release. It certainly wouldn't get such an all clear in 2006. Obviously filmed without the cooperation of the Royal Society for the Prevention of Cruelty to Animals, the film graphically shows animals being shot and killed. Not as emotionally disturbing, but still irritating are crude technical elements such as obvious post-synching (including a ridiculously phoney voice for the narrator) and a disappointingly Mickey Mouse music score from the famed Isador Goodman. Director Chauvel manages to get some breathtaking scenery in front of the camera, but his skills with the players are much less impressive. Tudawali comes across best. Betty Suttor and George Simpson-Lyttle are especially bad, leaving the viewer to wonder how such abominably hammy performances could have survived a screening of the initial rushes in the cutting-room.

The story is so drawn out that the chase is uninvolving. It's the location photography that really impresses, the great red canyons of the Northern Territory that Kayser has so finely captured in a color system that obviously favors reds by day and purples by night. [Eric Porter is credited for "additional photography", though actually his contribution is limited to the animation of the jedda birds before "The End" title — and very obvious animation it is too!]

OTHER VIEWS: Audience appeal: Charles Chauvel has made a film which enobles and dignifies the Australian north, and its native inhabitants. The color photography is at most times magnificent, often in its panoramas reaching beyond Hollywood standards. There's some fine action, and the human story, very uneven in quality, is at best compelling.

Boxoffice rating: Shouldn't be hard to bring topline business with this exploitable Australian production — the first local fiction pic in color.

The acting is not the most commendable aspect of *Jedda*, cast as it was largely from full-blooded aborigines and other folk who actually live in the Territory.

But through sheer animal magnificence, Robert Tudawali emerges as a strong screen personality. He's the aborigine who plays Marbuck, a nomadic badman. The character is based closely on fact.

In his handling of the aborigines as a whole, Chauvel has done wonders in an almost impossible task — trying to transpose their feelings and characteristics onto celluloid in a form and style that will be acceptable to the average movie-goer; for *Jedda*, though often naturalistic and certainly close to the truths of nature, is primarily a story film, not a documentary or an exposition of any anthropological theory.

And in story line and detail of incident and characterization, it is a good outdoor adventure.

But we must mention one of its more obvious limitations: the sound-track often depends on music and an informative narration, rather than lip-sync.
— *Film Weekly*.

# Jivaro

**Fernando Lamas** (Rio), **Rhonda Fleming** (Alice Parker), **Brian Keith** (Tony), **Lon Chaney, Jr** (Pedro), **Richard Denning** (Jerry Russell), **Rita Moreno** (Maroa), **Marvin Miller** (Kovanti), **Morgan Farley** (Vinny), **Pascual Pena** (Sylvester), **Nestor Paiva** (Shipley), **Charles Lung** (padre), **Gregg Barton** (Edwards), **Kay Johnson** (Umari), **Rosa Turich** (native woman), **Marian Mosick** (Sylvester's wife), **Richard Bartell** (locket native), **Eugenia Paul** (Indian girl).

Director: **EDWARD LUDWIG**. Screenplay: **Winston Miller**. Story: **David Duncan**. Suggested by the 1886 novel *King Solomon's Mines* by **Sir Henry Rider Haggard**.

Photographed in Natural Vision Three-Dimension and Technicolor by **Lionel Lindon**. Film editor: **Howard Smith**. Art directors: **Hal Pereira, Earl Hedrick**. Set decorators: **Sam Comer, Grace Gregory**. Costumes: **Edith Head**. Make-up: **Wally Westmore**. Technicolor color consultant: **Richard Mueller**. 2nd unit photography: **W. Wallace Kelley**. Special photographic effects: **John P. Fulton**. Process photography: **Farciot Edouart**. Music score: **Gregory Stone**. Assistant director: **William McGarry**. Sound recording: **Harold Lewis, Gene Garvin**. Western Electric Sound System. Producers: **William Howard Pine, William C. Thomas**. A Pine-Thomas film, produced and released by Paramount Pictures.

Copyright 1 February 1954 (in notice: 1953) by Paramount Pictures Corp. New York opening (flat) at the Palace: 12 February 1954. U.S. release: February 1954. U.K. release on the lower half of a double bill: April 1954. Australian release (flat): 11 March 1955. Sydney opening on a double bill at the Victory. 8,228 feet. 91 minutes.

U.K. and Australian release title: LOST TREASURE OF THE AMAZON.

SYNOPSIS: A cool but not overbright beauty comes looking for her fiancé who is lost in the Amazon jungle.

NOTES: Paramount's last 3-D feature played flat in most situations, though it did have some 3-D showings in Britain and the U.S.A.


COMMENT: Not exactly one of the Most Boring films ever made, but it certainly runs the Top of the Tedious pretty close. The swaggering Fernando Lamas, one of the most egotistical yet least personable of Hollywood's minor stars, is here joined by that regular Pine-Thomas lesser light, Rhonda Fleming in a cutdown variation of *King Solomon's Mines*. Even in its 3-D version, the film comes across as a lackluster, snail-paced affair. It doesn't help that there are few 3-D effects — a shrunken head is thrust at the camera and a chair or two is thrown into the lens — and that the 2nd unit work is so grainy it was obviously blown up from 16mm. Many scenes like those with longwinded Lamas and frippery Fleming on the boat are completely superfluous and unnecessary. One wonders why the editor left them in, especially as at 91 or 93 minutes the film is too long for a "B" feature anyway.

The support players come across as a trifle more interesting than the pedestrian principals, though only villainous Brian Keith gets much in the way of a dramatic opportunity. Cult hero, Lon Chaney, is confined to just one scene — true, it's one of the most exciting in the movie — near the beginning, while Rita Moreno has virtually no part at all.

Ludwig's direction manages the difficult feat of bringing a dull script to an even less animated life.

Production values are strictly "B".

In short, a waste of time. Even the Amazonian locations look synthetic. Although mildly stimulated by the opening scenes, desperate action fans will have deserted the movie long before the long-promised jivaro-attack climax. Maybe rabid followers of the loquacious Lamas and/or that equally dreary, equally unconvincing heroine, Miss Rhonda Fleming, a so meticulously groomed fashion clotheshorse of the studio backlot jungle — maybe fans of these two spoilers will get something out of *Jivaro*. Maybe.

# Juarez

**Paul Muni** (Benito Pablo Juarez), **Bette Davis** (Empress Carlotta von Habsburg), **Brian Aherne** (Maximilian von Habsburg), **Claude Rains** (Louis Napoleon), **John Garfield** (Porfirio Diaz), **Donald Crisp** (Marechal Bazaine), **Gale Sondergaard** (Empress Eugenie), **Joseph Calleia** (Alejandro Uradi), **Gilbert Roland** (Colonel Miguel Lopez), **Henry O'Neill** (Miguel Miramon), **Pedro de Cordoba** (Riva Palacio) **Montagu Love** (Jose de Montares), **Harry Davenport** (Dr Samuel Basch), **Walter Fenner** (Achille Fould), **Alex Leftwich** (Drouyn de Lhuys), **Robert Warwick** (Major DuPont), **John Miljan** (Mariano Escobedo), **Irving Pichel** (Carbajal), **Walter Kingsford** (Prince Metternich), **Monte Blue** (Lerdo de Tejada), **Louis Calhern** (LeMarc), **Vladimir Sokoloff** (Camilo), **Georgia Caine** (Countess Battenberg), **Gennaro Curci** (Senor de Leon), **Bill Wilkerson** (Tomas Mejia), **Hugh Sothern** (John Bigelow), **Fred Malatesta** (Senor Salas), **Carlos de Valdez** (tailor), **Frank Lackteen** (coachman), **Walter O. Stahl** (Senator del Valle), **Frank Reicher** (Duc de Momy), **Holmes Herbert** (Marshall Randon), **Egon Brecher** (Baron von Magnus), **Manuel Diaz** (Pepe), **Mickey Kuhn** (Augustin Iturbide), **Lillian Nicholson** (Josefa Iturbide), **Noble Johnson** (Regules), **Grant Mitchell** (Harris), **Charles Halton** (Roberts), **Martin Garralaga** (Negroni), **Dewey Robinson** (soldier collecting signatures). [Cutting-room floor players: William Edmunds (Italian minister), Gilbert Emery (ambassador)].

Directed by **WILLIAM DIETERLE**. Screenplay by **John Huston, Aeneas MacKenzie, Abem Finkel** and **Wolfgang Reinhardt**. Based in part on a 1926 play *Juarez and Maximilian* by **Franz Werfel** and a 1934 book *Phantom Crown* by **Bertita Harding**. Photographed by **Tony Gaudio**. Musical score by **Erich Wolfgang Korngold**. Musical direction by **Leo F. Forbstein**. Dialogue director: **Irving Rapper**. Film editor: **Warren Low**. Art director: **Anton Grot**. Set decorator: **George James Hopkins**. Costumes by **Orry-Kelly**. Technical adviser: **Ernest Romero**. Make-up: **Perc Westmore**. Hair styles: **Margaret Donovan**. Orchestral arrangements by: **Hugo Friedhofer** and **Milan Roder**. Historical research: **Professor Jesse John Dossick**. Assistant art director: **Leo Kuter**. Properties: **James Gibbens**. Head of research: **Herman Lissauer**. Head of publicity: **Charles Einfeld**. Assistant directors: **Jack Sullivan** (first), **John Prettyman**. Sound by **C.A. Riggs** and **G.W. Alexander**. Executive producer: **Hal B. Wallis**. Associate producer: **Henry Blanke**.

Copyright 10 June 1939 by Warner Brothers Pictures, Inc. New York opening at the Hollywood: 25 April 1939. U.S. release: 10 June 1939. U.K. release: November 1939. Australian release: 12 October 1939. 132 minutes.

SYNOPSIS: It is 1863. The French army, in Mexico as an armed bill collector, is failing its purpose. The liberal constitutional government under the Zapotecan Indian, Benito Pablo Juarez, a brilliant, honest statesman and president, will not pay because it cannot. The treasury has been emptied, the country all but ruined by the dictators and militarists who, through the centuries have preceded him in office.

Napoleon III of France, his Empress Eugenie, and his ministers hit upon a new plan. They will force the people of Mexico, at gun and sword point, to overthrow the Juarez government, vote for monarchial rule. Mexico shall have an Emperor. That Emperor will be named and controlled by Napoleon. They decide that Maximilian von Hapsburg, brother of Franz Josef of Austria, shall be that man.

After a year of preparation and intrigue, the plebiscite, by force, is held and on May 28th, 1864, Maximilian and his lovely young empress, Carlotta, land in Vera Cruz and are taken to the palace of Chapultepec. Juarez and his loyal cabinet members and generals are forced to flee to the northern part of the country, but not before Juarez has sent a prophetic message to Maximilian; a message that is a challenge.

Not many months pass before Maximilian, at heart an honest man, sincerely eager to give Mexico a just rule, realizes that he has been duped by Napoleon and the other European rulers. He refuses to sign edicts that would take the land from the people, return it to those wealthy few from whom Juarez has wrested it. He tries, in fact, to see Juarez, to propose that Juarez become Secretary of State.

NOTES: Negative cost: around $1.4 million. Brian Aherne was nominated for Best Supporting Actor, losing to Thomas Mitchell in *Stagecoach*.

Number 8 on the Film Daily's annual survey of American film critics.

COMMENT: Controversial in its day because of its many historical distortions (and indeed fabrications), *Juarez* is best viewed as a superlative piece of dramatic entertainment. Superbly set and photographed, with brilliant performances, masterly direction, and a Korngold score, what more could you ask? Yes, two more things — and *Juarez* has them: a riveting script, breathtakingly paced.

OTHER VIEWS: A quite impressive film, the two parts of Juarez and Maximilian are well written and admirably acted by Paul Muni and Brian Aherne (Mr Muni's make-up is extraordinarily impressive: he is an Indian to the very shape of the skull and the stony Aztec profile).

I have not usually been an admirer of Mr Aherne's acting: his personality has always seemed to go with a pipe and Harris tweeds and a boundless complacency, but here he nearly acts Mr Muni off the set. With his forked and silky beard, the blond whiskers and curls, the gentle worried inflexibility, he is every inch a Hapsburg, and the film is his from that first puzzled inquiry at Vera Cruz — 'Why are the streets so empty?' — to his long, careful frock-coated stride up the rocky hill of the death-place. (Bette Davis's Carlota simply does not exist beside him).

Mr Muni as the whitewashed Juarez has a smaller and easier part: he has only to be simple, kindly, ruthless from the best ideological motives: he is preaching to the converted. He hasn't got to put over such an unfashionable doctrine as the divine right of kings to be the servant of their people, and when he defines democracy to General Porfirio Diaz every Left Book Club heart will beat a little faster (who cares or knows about the ruined schools and churches?). Many of my colleagues have objected to the dialogue, which they call stilted: it seemed to me to go admirably with the stiff dated Hapsburg court set down, like a millionaire's purchase from Europe, with its gold-leaf and scarlet hangings, its ushers and rules of precedence, in the dry savage countryside, where we watch a vulture peck at a child's body in a ruined village. The cameramen have for once resisted the temptation to make Mexico picturesque — there are hardly any cactuses and no sky-lined peons.

— Graham Greene.

# the Kettles in the Ozarks

**Marjorie Main** (Ma Kettle), **Arthur Hunnicutt** (Sedge Kettle), **Ted de Corsia** (Professor), **Una Merkel** (Miss Bedelia Baines), **Richard Eyer** (Billy Kettle), **David O'Brien** (conductor), **Joe Sawyer** (Bancroft Baines), **Richard Deacon** (Cod Head), **Sid Tomack** (Benny), **Pat Goldin** (Small Fry), **Harry Hines** (Joe), **Jim Hayward** (Jack Dexter), **Olive Sturgess** (Nancy Kettle), **George Arglen** (Freddie), **Eddie Pagett** (Sammy), **Cheryl Calloway** (Susie), **Pat Morrow** (Sally), **Bonnie Franklin** (Betty), **Louis DaPron** (mountaineer), **Sarah Padden** (Miz Tinware), **Roscoe Ates** (man), **Kathryn Sheldon** (old woman), **Stuart Holmes** (bald-headed man), **Elvia Allman** (meek man's wife), **Paul Wexler** (Reverend Martin), **Robert Easton** (Lafe).

Director: **CHARLES LAMONT**. Original story and screenplay: **Kay Lenard**. Based on characters created by **Betty MacDonald** in her 1945 autobiography *The Egg and I*. Photography: **George Robinson**. Film editor: **Edward Curtiss**. Music supervision: **Joseph Gershenson**. Art directors: **Alexander Golitzen, Alfred Sweeney**. Set decorators: **Russell A. Gausman, Ruby R. Levitt**. Costumes: **Marjorie Main, Jay Morley Jr**. Make-up: **Bud Westmore**. Hair styles: **Joan St Oegger**. Assistant director: **Joseph E. Kenny**. 2nd assistant director: **Gordon McLean**. Sound recording: **Leslie I. Carey, Robert Pritchard**. Western Electric Sound System. Producer: Richard Wilson.

Copyright 1955 by Universal Pictures Co., Inc. A Universal-International picture. No New York opening. U.S. release: April 1956. U.K. release through J. Arthur Rank Film Distributors: November 1955. Australian release: 9 March 1956. 7,253 feet. 81 minutes. Cut to 71 minutes in Australia so that it could easily fit on the lower half of a double bill.

SYNOPSIS: Ma Kettle and thirteen of her sixteen children visit her lazy brother-in-law's rundown farm in the Ozarks.

NOTES: Ninth of Universal's ten-picture "Ma and Pa Kettle" series.

Percy Kilbride by this time was heartily sick of playing Pa. Minor injuries received in an auto accident gave him a good excuse to bow out of the series. He retired permanently from the screen and even refused $1 million to appear in a TV version of the Kettles. Ironically he was killed in December 1964 when struck by a car whilst crossing the street.

COMMENT: This attempt to get by without Pa is not overly successful. Not only is Kilbride sadly missed, but the scriptwriter injudiciously calls our attention to his absence on no less than three occasions including two long letters which Ma Main reads. As might be expected, Miss Main carries the whole burden of this entry. Hunnicutt has no personality and is even outclassed by a goose wearing galoshes. Exaggerated slapstick abounds. But the movie signally lacks wit and charm. Heavy-handed direction and meat-axe film editing don't help.

Miss Main was determined to continue the series without Kilbride. "I'd stand on my head to make people laugh," she said at the time. "That's all I have to live for. I don't want to retire." Unfortunately, the popularity of the series was now on the wane. Never highly regarded by the critics who found the cornball slapstick tedious and the lack of production values irritating, the Kettle movies were now being upstaged by a number of

TV imitators such as *The Real McCoys, The Beverly Hillbillies, Green Acres* and *Petticoat Junction*.

OTHER VIEWS: About the only claim to fame this entry can muster is the presence of that personable stuntman Dave O'Brien (the perennial fall-guy of *Pete Smith Specialties*) as a Kettle-kids-harassed train conductor. These sequences occur quite early in the film. If you think this railroad slapstick embarrassingly inept, be warned it's all downhill from there. And to think that producer Richard Wilson, a long-time associate of Orson Welles, was assistant director on *Citizen Kane* and an associate producer of *The Lady from Shanghai*.

# King of Dodge City

**Bill Elliott** (Wild Bill Hickok), **Tex Ritter** (Tex Rawlings), **Judith Linden** (Janice Blair) **Dub Taylor** (Cannonball), **Guy Usher** (Morgan King), **Rick Anderson** (Judge Lynch), **Kenneth Harlan** (Jeff Carruthers), **Pierce Lyden** (Reynolds), **Francis Walker** (Carney), **Harrison Greene** (Stephen Kimball), **Jack Rockwell** (Martin), **Edmund Cobb, George Chesebro** (gamblers), **Steve Clark** (Samuels), **Tris Coffin** (crooked gambler), **Jack Ingram** (Bill Lang), **Ed Coxen** (Sheriff Daniels), **Lee Prather** (man at meeting), **Ned Glass** (bank teller), and **Tex Cooper, Russ Powell, Jay Lawrence, Frosty Royce.**

Director: **LAMBERT HILLYER**. Original screenplay: **Gerald Geraghty**. Photography: **Benjamin Kline**. Film editor: **Jerome Thoms**. Music: **Mischa Bakaleinikoff, Sidney Cutner, Ben Oakland.** No further credits either on the movie itself or issued by Columbia publicity. Producer: **Leon Barsha**.

Copyright 14 August 1941 by Columbia Pictures Corp. No New York opening. U.S. release: 14 August 1941. Australian release: 3 December 1942. 6 reels. 5,720 feet. 63 minutes.

SYNOPSIS: Morgan King is out to control the whole territory, but Wild Bill Hickok is out to stop him.

NOTES: First of a series of eight westerns starring Wild Bill Elliott and Tex Ritter.

COMMENT: An enjoyable western, with good action and songs. The basic plot is familiar, but the writer gives it a few new twists and adds some interesting characters, agreeably played by Elliott, Ritter, Linden and Taylor. The support players though are not much and we would have appreciated a much more personable heavy than the almost zero-rating Guy Usher. Hillyer directs at a reasonably brisk pace and has a good eye for the picturesque.

# the Last of the Mohicans

**James Gordon** (Colonel Munro, commander of Fort William Henry on Lake George), **Barbara Bedford** (Cora Munro, his eldest daughter), **Lillian Hall** (Alice Munro, his youngest daughter), **Henry Woodward** (Major Heyward, Alice's fiancé), **Wallace Beery**

(Magua, a "friendly" messenger from Fort William Henry), **Albert Roscoe** (Uncas), **Theodore Lorch** (Chingachgook, Uncas' father), **George Hackathorne** (Captain Randolph), **Nelson McDowell** (David Gamut, a lay preacher), **Harry Lorraine** (Hawkeye), **Sidney Deane** (General Webb), **Jack MacDonald** (Tamenund), **Boris Karloff** (Indian), and **Joseph Singleton.**

Director: **MAURICE TOURNEUR**. Associate director: **Clarence Brown**. Screenplay: **Robert A. Dillon**. Based on the 1826 novel by **James Fenimore Cooper**. Photographed in black-and-white by **Philip R. Dubois** and **Charles Van Enger**. Art director: **Floyd Mueller.** Producer: **Maurice Tourneur**. A Maurice Tourneur Production.

Copyright by 16 November 1920 by Maurice Tourneur. Released through Associated Producers in the U.S.A. New York opening at the Strand: 2 January 1921. 77 minutes at sound speed (which is slightly too fast. At correct speed, film should run 85-90 minutes).

SYNOPSIS: Betrayed by a cowardly officer, Fort William Henry falls to the French and their barbaric Indian allies. One traitorous Indian captures the colonel's two daughters, but is pursued by the eldest daughter's lover, Uncas, the last of the Mohicans.

NOTES: First film version of the Cooper novel, a top money-maker worldwide.

COMMENT: Handsomely realised on the grandest of scales, this superb picturisation of the second *Leatherstocking Tale* is a grippingly suspenseful narrative from start to finish. Tourneur has directed in his usual, meticulously picturesque style, each frame both beautifully and dramatically composed. Making marvellous use both of outdoor locations and man-made sets, the picture constantly engages the eye as much as it grips the heart and the emotions.

The use of white actors in Indian roles (which Hollywood is still doing even in 1999) was much criticised at the time of the film's release. Fortunately, we are now so used to this convention, that we can enjoy the film far more than contemporary critics. Wallace Beery, in fact, gives a typically villainous performance as the evil Magua. Opposite him, Barbara Bedford makes a feisty heroine, whilst solid support is offered by George Hackathorne as the cowardly Randolph. The only player I was a little unhappy with was Albert Roscoe, whom I thought a little stiff as Uncas.

The photography (aided in the print under review by wonderful tinting) is a joy to behold.

As stated, the budget is unstinting, the action scenes especially being staged on the most elaborate scale. The camera rarely moves, but when it does as in the rapid tracking shots during the massacre sequence, it is more than routinely effective.

The novel has been translated to the screen with such admirable fidelity that its realism is too potent for children and adolescents.

# Lawless Nineties

**John Wayne** (John Tipton), **Ann Rutherford** (Janet Carter), **Harry Woods** (Charles K. Plummer), **George "Gabby" Hayes** (Major Carter), **Al Bridge** (Steele), **Lane Chandler** (Bridger), **"Snowflake" [Fred Toones]** (Mose), **Etta McDaniel** (Mandy Lou), **Tom Brower** (Marshall), **Cliff Lyons** (Davis), **Jack Rockwell** (Smith), **Al Taylor** (Red),

**Charles King** (Hartley), **George Chesebro** (Green), **Tom London** (Ward), **Sam Flint** (Pierce), **Earl Seaman** (Teddy Roosevelt), **Tracy Layne** (Belden), **Philo McCullough** (outlaw leader), **Chuck Baldra** (Tex), **Lloyd Ingraham** (Palmer), **Monte Blue** (outlaw), **Jimmie Harrison** (telegraph operator), **Lew Meehan, Sherry Tansey, Steve Clark, Jim Corey, Art Dillard, Bud Osborne, Tex Palmer, Pascale Perry, Jack Kirk** (henchmen), **Henry Hall** (mayor), **Rose Plummer, Emma Tansey** (homesteaders' wives), **Bud Pope, James Sheridan** (deputies), **Curley Dresden, Edward Hearn, George Morrell** (townsmen), **Bob Burns** (settler), **Horace B. Carpenter** (dynamite thrower), **Yakima Canutt** (stunt double for John Wayne).

Director: **JOSEPH KANE**. Screenplay: **Joseph Poland**. Original screen story: **Joseph Poland, Scott Pembroke**. Photography: **William Nobles**. Supervising film editors: **Joseph H. Lewis, Murray Seldeen**. Film editor: **Lester Orlebeck**. Stock music by **Heinz Roemheld** and **Arthur Kay**, directed by **Lee Zahler**. Stunts: **Cliff Lyons**. Assistant director: **Robert Emmett Tansey**. Sound engineer: **Terry Kellum**. Associate producer: **Paul Malvern**. Producer: **Trem Carr**. Executive producer: **Herbert J. Yates**.

Copyright 27 April 1936 by Republic Pictures Corp. New York opening at the Rialto: 26 June 1936. U.S. release: 15 February 1936. U.K. release through British Lion: August 1936. 6 reels. 58 minutes.

SYNOPSIS: Lawless elements try to prevent Wyoming joining the Union.

COMMENT: This one and *Santa Fe Stampede* were the only Wayne "B" westerns to be reviewed by *The New York Times*. Certainly this one has some claim to such attention. On the surface at least it's rather lavishly mounted, though some of the spectacular action footage doesn't bear too close attention. Most of it is obviously stock material which has been spliced in somewhat randomly whether the moment was appropriate or not, or even whether the footage quite matched its description or not. This is why we have Lewis as supervising editor. Still for unsophisticated audiences the effect must have been quite exciting. It certainly makes for a more lively outing than the usual Wayne "B". Moreover director Kane has risen to the occasion with some slightly more imaginative directorial touches than was his norm, assisted by some fine stuntwork and even what looks like genuine night-for-night photography by William Nobles. (It's not that easy to tell. The video print under review is dupey and washed out. It's from the Republic Pictures Collection too, with a claim on the box: "Mastered from original film negatives." My guess is that it's a dupe from a primitive television print complete with tinny 16mm sound. If this has been mastered from original 35mm negatives, someone sure did a lousy job).

The support cast is lavishly appointed too, with no fewer than four of our all-time favorite villains — and all with some good opportunities for nastiness too. Wayne shoots a pistol out of King's hand, Chesebro picks a fight with our hero, Bridge leads the marauders while Woods directs operations. Tom London is on hand to back up Chesebro too, and it's good to see Jack Rockwell back on the right side of the law. We will pass over the somewhat labored comic relief provided by Etta McDaniel and Snowflake, and even the relaxed, almost agreeably perky heroine enacted by Ann Rutherford to concentrate our remaining attention on George Hayes. He's good. We love him. This time he gives a startlingly accurate Walter Huston impersonation, not just in make-up, but right down to the very timbre of his voice. It suits and matches the role so perfectly that casual picturegoers may well have marveled what Huston was doing in a "B" western. It's interesting that although Hayes had introduced his "Gabby" oldtimer in *The Lucky Texan* back in 1933, he is still playing other character roles at this stage of his career. (Another interesting career note is that Lane Chandler who played Wayne's buddy in *Sagebrush Trail* (1933) has a similar but very considerably smaller part here).

OTHER VIEWS: Produced on a far more lavish scale than the usual western "B", this is lively, exciting fare with plenty of action and even some good acting — particularly from George Hayes as a crusading newspaper publisher. This is a stock role, but Hayes plays it not only with conviction but with unexpected dignity and restraint.

# Lawless Range

**John Wayne** (John Allen/John Middleton), **Sheila Mannors** (Anne Mason), **Earl Dwire** (Emmett, the storekeeper), **Frank McGlynn Jr** (Carter, the banker), **Wally Howe** (Hank Mason), **Jack Curtis** (marshal), **Yakima Canutt** (Burns), **Glenn Strange** (Burns' offsider), **Julia Griffin** (Mrs Mason), **Fred Burns** (Allen), **Charley Sargent** (Shorty), **Bob Kortman** (Shorty's pal), **Jack Kirk, Charles [Chuck] Baldra, Charles [Slim] Whitaker** (outlaws), **Bob Burns** (Bert), **Charles Brinley** (townsman), **Frank Ellis** (member of necktie party), **Sam Flint** (Sam Middleton), **Herman Hack** (robber), **Ray Henderson** (gambler), **John Ince** (Clem), **George Ovey** (Shorty, a ranch hand), **Francis Walker** (cowhand), **Pascale Perry** (henchman), **Tex Palmer** (deputy), **Frank Parker, James Sheridan** (townsmen), and **The Wranglers** (singing cowhands).

Director: **ROBERT NORTH BRADBURY**. Original story and screenplay: **Lindsley Parsons**. Photography: **Archie Stout**. Film editor: **Carl Pierson**. Art director: **E.R. Hickson**. Music composed by **Sam Perry** and **Clifford Vaughan**. Songs: "Blood A-Runnin'" (Wayne dubbed by Smith Ballew); "On the Banks of the Sunny San Juan" (Wayne dubbed by Smith Ballew); "Down That Old Dusty Road" (male chorus). Stunts: **Francis Walker**. Sound recording: **Dave Stoner**. Balsley and Phillips Sound System. Producer: **Paul Malvern**. Executive producer: **Trem Carr**.

Copyright 18 November 1935 by Republic Pictures Corp. A Trem Carr Production for Monogram/Lone Star, released by Republic in the U.S.: 4 November 1935. U.K. release through British Lion: March 1937. 6 reels. 59 minutes.

SYNOPSIS: A ruthless gang of outlaws seems determined to drive every rancher from the valley. Why?

NOTES: Wayne's final Lone Star western — though the movie was not released as such. Monogram had become part of the new Republic Pictures organization.

COMMENT: Here is Wayne signing off his Lone Star career with a snatch from the very same song with which he started off in *Riders of Destiny*. But in addition to the opening lines from "Blood a' Runnin' ", Wayne (obviously dubbed by extra-deep-voiced Smith Ballew) sings "On the Banks of the Sunny San Juan" right through. It's the longest musical interlude in any Wayne film. And as if that were not enough in the melody line, we are also treated to a chorus of cowpunchers standing around "That Old Dusty Road".

Not that *Lawless Range* is short on action. That we have in plenty too. Lots of hard riding (in running inserts yet) and guns blazing ("Popping" would actually be a better word) plus a couple of impressive stunts including a high dive from a cliff (reprised from 1934's *The Trail Beyond*) and a jump from saddle to saddle. Unfortunately, a fair amount of the action footage is obviously stock — which makes for some confusing continuity. Still, unsophisticated fans will probably find the action sufficient and the pacing brisk enough to satisfy their needs — though few will fail to tumble to the identity of the big boss quite early on in the piece.

Wayne as usual makes an engaging hero, Miss Manners/Mannors/Bromley is a plucky heroine (even when offering such lines as "I think his disappearance is part of some scheme") and it's good to see Wally Howe doing a Gabby Hayes impersonation as the kidnapped rancher. (Because they have all obviously copied from each other, just about every reference book tells us this role was played by Earl Dwire. Which is dead wrong. Mr Dwire plays the town storekeeper).

A few picturesque location shots augment a very middling budget. Despite one or two of his irritating whip pans, director Bradbury generally if humbly hits home. His tracking shots with the lynch mob are particularly effective.

# a Lawless Street

**Randolph Scott** (Calem Ware), **Angela Lansbury** (Tally Dickinson), **Warner Anderson** (Hamer Thorne), **Jean Parker** (Cora Dean), **Wallace Ford** (Dr Amos Wynn), **John Emery** (Cody Clark), **James Bell** (Asaph Dean), **Ruth Donnelly** (Molly Higgins), **Michael Pate** (Harley Baskam) **Don Megowan** (Dooley Brion), **Jeanette Nolan** (Mrs Dingo Brion), **Peter Ortiz** (Hiram Hayes) **Don Carlos** (Juan Tobrez), **Frank Hagney** (Dingo Brion), **Charles Williams** (Willis), **Frank Ferguson** (Abe Deland), **Harry Tyler** (Tony Cabillo). **Harry Antrim** (Mayor Kent), **Jay Lawrence, Reed Howes, Guy Teague** (townsmen), **Pat Collins** (gambler), **Hal K. Dawson** (hotel clerk), **Frank Scannell** (bartender), **Edwin Chandler** (man), **Stanley Blystone** (rancher), and **Barry Brooks.**

Director: **JOSEPH H. LEWIS**. Screenplay: **Kenneth Gamet**. Based on the 1953 novel *The Marshal of Medicine Bend* by **Brad Ward** (pseudonym of **S. Peeples**). Photographed in Technicolor by **Ray Rennahan**. Film editor: **Gene Havlick**. Art director: **George Brooks**. Set decorator: **Frank Tuttle**. Music composed and conducted by **Paul Sawtell**. Song, "Mother Says I Mustn't" (Lansbury). Technicolor color consultant: **Henri Jaffa**. Choreography: **Jerry Antes**. Assistant to the producer: **David Breen**. Assistant director: **Abner E. Singer**. Sound supervisor: **John Livadary**. Sound recording: **Frank Goodwin**. Western Electric Sound System. Associate producer: **Randolph Scott**. Producer: **Harry Joe Brown**. A Scott-Brown Production.

Copyright 1955 by Producers-Actors Corporation. Released through Columbia Pictures Corp. No New York opening. U.S. release: 15 December 1955. U.K. release: 13 February 1956. Australian release: 27 July 1956. Sydney opening at the Victory. 78 minutes.

SYNOPSIS: Veteran marshal is threatened by both gunmen and businessmen.

COMMENT: After a slow start, the plot settles down okay, working in sufficient action for the fans. The dialogue on the other hand remains stubbornly clichéd and pretentious, as well as more than a little verbose. Director Joseph H. Lewis does what he can with it, filming in long takes to get it over with as fast as possible, and even having the actors often turn their backs on it literally to the camera. Typically, Lewis stages the action spots most vigorously, though a stand-in is obviously doing duty for Randy in his big saloon brawl with Megowan (who slugs it out most effectively without benefit of any cover). Scott is believable, as usual, and receives pleasant to middling support. Pate makes a charmingly chilling villain, whilst Miss Lansbury, who is inclined to ham it up a trifle (well, she is playing an actress after all), at least has a song, which turns out to be one of the film's highlights. Superbly staged, choreographed and directed with the camera starting in on the tacky orchestra and then tracking back slowly through the whole auditorium, this visual delight is an excellent recreation in music and sound which offers pointers to *Heller in Pink Tights*.

Rennahan's color photography looks a bit garish with its reddish dissolves. Some over-upholstered sets don't help. The hotel lobby is far too chintzily grand. And there are other signs of hasty shooting using such budget conscious measures as standing sets. Nonetheless, despite its faults, *A Lawless Street* offers more than its fair share of entertainment.

OTHER VIEWS: An interesting support cast including Jean Parker, Jeanette Nolan, James Bell, John Emery, Ruth Donnelly, Michael Pate and Frank Hagney help to prop up a somewhat uncomfortable performance by Angela Lansbury and a none too charismatic chief villain in lacklustre Warner Anderson. Some judicious cutting to eliminate the worst of Randy's scenes with cliched Ruth Donnelly and almost risibly over-intense Angela Lansbury would help. The climactic action ends a little abruptly, but otherwise the gun duels and fist fights deliver strongly. In fact, Don Megowan who does his own brawling, registers so strongly he threatens to tip our interest away from Scott himself.

# Law of the Badlands

**Tim Holt** (Dave), **Joan Dixon** (Velvet), **Robert Livingston** (Dirkin), **Leonard Penn** (Cash), **Harry Woods** (Conroy), **Larry Johns** (Simms), **Robert Bray** (Benson), **Kenneth MacDonald** (Captain McVey), **John Cliff** (Madigan), **Richard Martin** (Chito Rafferty), **Sam Lufkin** (bank teller), **Danny Sands** (boy), **Art Felix** (henchman), **Booger McCarthy** (another henchman), **Roy Gordon** (secretary of the treasury).

Director: **LESLEY SELANDER**. Original screenplay: **Ed Earl Repp**. Photography: **George E. Diskant**. Film editor: **Desmond Marquette**. Music composed by **Paul Sawtell** and **Roy Webb**, conducted by **Constantin Bakaleinikoff**. Art directors: **Albert S. D'Agostino, Feild Gray**. Set decorators: **Darrell Silvera, William Stevens**. Sound recording: **John Cass, Clem Portman**. RCA Sound System. Producer: **Herman Schlom**.

Copyright 27 December 1950 by RKO Radio Pictures, Inc. No recorded New York opening. U.S. release: 24 February 1951. Australian release: 29 January 1953 (sic). 60 minutes.

SYNOPSIS: Two Texas Rangers masquerade as outlaws in order to capture a counterfeiting ring.

NOTES: Negative cost: $98,000. After print, advertising and distribution costs, RKO still lost $20,000 of this modest outlay.

COMMENT: Passably entertaining Tim Holt western of no special distinction, competently directed, with the standard fights and chases and some attractive location photography. RKO's "B" westerns had a professional gloss that was often noticeably absent from the output of Poverty Row studios. Despite its comparatively modest budget, *Law of the Badlands* is no exception.

## the Law of the 45's

**Guinn "Big Boy" Williams** (Tucson Smith), **Molly O'Day** (Joan Hayden), **Al St John** (Stoney Martin), **Ted Adams** (Gordon Rontell), **Lafe McKee** (Charlie Hayden), **Fred Burns** (sheriff), **Curley Baldwin** (deputy), **Martin Garralaga** (Joe Sanchez), **Sherry Tansey** (Toral), **Broderick O'Farrell** (Sir Henry Sheffield), **Glenn Strange** (Monte, a ranch hand), **Ace Cain** (Saunders), **Jack Evans, Herman Hack, Ralph Bucko, Buck Morgan, Merrill McCormick, Tex Palmer, Art Felix** (Rontell's henchmen), **Francis Walker** (ranch hand), **Bill Patton** (argumentative rancher), **George Morrell** (townsman), **William McCall** (the doctor), **Budd Buster** (ticket clerk), **Jack Kirk** (singing wrangler), **Chuck Baldra** (the guitar player), and **The Singing Wranglers** [**Jack Jones, Jack Kirk, Chuck Baldra, Glenn Strange**].

Director: **JOHN P. McCARTHY**. Screenplay: **Robert Emmett Tansey**. Based on the novel by **William Colt MacDonald**. Photography: **Robert Cline**. Film editor: **Holbrook N. Todd**. Songs: "On a Lonely Trail", "Las Golondrinas", "Sunset Trail". Stunts: **Jack Jones**. Assistant director: **Myron Marsh**. Production manager and associate producer: **Max Alexander**. Producer: **Arthur Alexander**.

Not copyrighted by Normandy Pictures Corp. U.S. release through First Division: 1 December 1935. 57 minutes. U.K. release title: *the Mysterious Mr Sheffield*.

COMMENT: One of the better "Big Boy" efforts, this one has been produced on a much higher budget than usual and features plenty of newly staged action (along with the usual parade of wonky stock footage). A young Al St John capably backs up "Big Boy" more for riding and shooting than comedy relief, the heroine is reasonably attractive, our old friend Lafe McKee does himself credit in a decent role, and the villain positively shimmers with deep-dyed intensity. Effective use of locations also helps maintain the rage.

## L'il Abner

**Granville Owen** (Li'l Abner), **Martha O'Driscoll** (Daisy Mae), **Mona Ray** (Mammy Yokum), **Johnnie Morris** (Pappy Yokum), **Buster Keaton** (Lonesome Polecat), **Bill Seward** (Cousin Delightful), **Kay Sutton** (Wendy Wilecat), **Maude Eburne** (Granny

Scraggs), **Edgar Kennedy** (Cornelius Cornpone), **Charles A. Post** (Earthquake McGoon), **Bud Jamison** (Hairless Joe), **Dick Elliott** (Marryin' Sam), **Johnny Arthur** (Montague), **Walter Catlett** (barber), **Lucien Littlefield** (the sheriff/Mr Oldtimer), **Frank Wilder** (Abijah Gooch), **Chester Conklin** (Mayor Gurgle), **Mickey Daniels** (Cicero Grunts), **Doodles Weaver** (Hannibal Hoops), **Marie Blake** (Miss Lulubell), **Billy Bevan** (m.c.), **Renie Riano** (Sarah Jones), **Al St John** (Joe Smithpan), **Eddie Gribbon** (Barney Bargrease), **Heinie Conklin, Hank Mann, Eddie Borden** (bachelors), **Vic Potel** (Fantastic Brown), **Joan Standing** (Kitty Hoops), **Ed Brady, Tiny Jones, Jim Mason** (townspeople), **George Morris** (bandsman), and "Salomey".

Director: **ALBERT S. ROGELL**. Screenplay: **Charles Kerr, Tyler Johnson**. Original story: **Al Capp**. Based on the United Features comic strip written and drawn by **Al Capp**. Photography: **Harry Jackson**. 2nd unit director: **Herman Raymaker**. 2nd unit photography: **Paul Eagler**. Film editors: **Otto Ludwig, Donn Hayes**. Art director: **Ralph Berger**. Music director: **Lud Gluskin**. Title song (chorus) by **Ben Oakland, Milton Drake, Milton Berle**. RCA Sound System. Associate producer: **Herman Schlom**.

Copyright 1 November 1940 by Vogue Pictures, Ltd. No New York opening. U.S. release through RKO Radio Pictures: 1 November 1940. Never released in Australia, either theatrically or on television. 78 minutes.

U.K. release title: *TROUBLE CHASER*.

SYNOPSIS: Suffering a bout of indigestion after eating a Dagwood Bumstead sandwich, Li'l Abner is told by a mischievous barber that he has only 24 hours to live.

NOTES: The plot of this one bears little relationship to the 1959 Paramount musical which was based on the very successful 1956 Broadway play.

COMMENT: Here's a movie that fully deserved its poor reputation. In fact it's plain awful in just about every way. That's a pity because the producer had at least one worthwhile idea. By handing out parts to old-time comedians like Buster Keaton and Chester Conklin in theory he should have gladdened the hearts of picturegoers worldwide. Unfortunately, the witless script lets them down. In fact, aside from the decorative Martha O'Driscoll, the only featured player to give an attractive performance is Walter Catlett. I suspect he wrote his lines himself. Certainly he delivers them with a panache and style that serves to point up the amateurishness and signal lack of talent of most of the other players. I could go through the cast list awarding dishonorable mentions right and left, but it's most simpler to list those few such as Kay Sutton and Dick Elliott who are halfway competent. Indeed the introduction to Kay Sutton with the camera zeroing in on her eyes is just about the only touch of genuine flair the direction displays throughout. Fortunately the producer extended his love for the veteran slapstick comedians to the silent period generally, for he has given a job to Herman Raymaker, a successful director of the mid-twenties (e.g. the Rin-Tin-Tin feature, *The Night Cry*), who was forced into an early retirement a few years after the coming of sound (one of his last films, *Trailing the Killer*, made in 1932, starred Heinie Conklin who has a small part here). Raymaker directed the Walter Catlett scene as well as the climactic Sadie Hawkins Day race — and maybe even the Skunk Hollow chase as well. These scenes are certainly livelier than the rest of this tediously disappointing, elephantine movie. Hard to believe the waffley, non-satiric, schoolboyish story came from the pen of Al Capp himself. How could he disappoint his fans with such limpid tosh?

# the Lonely Trail

**John Wayne** (Captain John Ashley), **Cy Kendall** (General Benedict Holden), **Bob Kortman** (Captain Hayes), **Ann Rutherford** (Virginia Terry), **Snowflake [Fred Toones]** (Snowflake), **Etta McDaniel** (Mammy), **Sam Flint** (Governor), **Denny [Dennis Moore] Meadows** (Dick Terry), **Jim Toney** (Jed), **Yakima Canutt** (Horell), **Lloyd Ingraham** (Tucker), **Bob Burns, Jack Card** (ranchers), **James Marcus** (mayor), **Rodney Hildebrand** (captain of cavalry), **Eugene Jackson** (dancer), **Floyd Shackleford** (Armstrong), **Jack Kirk, Jack Ingram, Bud Pope, Tex Phelps, Tracy Layne, Clyde Kenney** (troopers), **Leon Lord** (Blaine), **Horace B. Carpenter** (wagon loader), **Oscar Gahan** (townsman), **Francis Walker, Murdock MacQuarrie** (ranchers), **Nina Mae McKinney** (dancer), **Clifton Young** (son of murdered rancher), **Charles King** (sentry), **Henry Hall** (officer), **Lafe McKee** (prisoner who is shot).

Director: **JOSEPH KANE**. Screenplay: **Bernard McConville, Jack Natteford**. Original screen story: **Bernard McConville**. Photography: **William Nobles**. Film editor: **Robert Jahns**. Supervising film editor: **Murray Seldeen**. Music supervisor: **Harry Grey**. Stock music composed by **Heinz Roemheld**. Song, "Old Folks at Home" by **Stephen Foster**, sung by **Etta McDaniel**. Sound recording: **Terry Kellum**. Sound re-recording: **Roy Granville**. Associate producer: **Paul Malvern**. Producer: **Nat Levine**. A Nat Levine Production.

Copyright 25 May 1936 by Republic Pictures Corp. No New York opening. U.S. release: 25 May 1936. U.K. release through British Lion: April 1937. 6 reels. 58 minutes.

SYNOPSIS: A carpetbagger and his ruthless henchmen are exposed by a former Union officer in post-Civil War Texas.

COMMENT: Much of interest in this western including a night-time climax with our heroes fighting the villains in silhouette and insurgents carrying torches dynamiting the gates of the fort. Wayne and his sidekick Toney (called "Tony" in the credits, but then Etta McDaniel is given an "s" in her surname so the official spelling is none too reliable) make a late entrance, after a montage of spectacular Civil War stock footage and a lot of material in which the heavies led by Cy Kendall (love his broad-brimmed hats) establish their oppression. The bad guys as usual have it all over the goodies in charisma. Wayne is pleasant enough, but squawky-voiced Rutherford is a pain and Mr Meadows/Moore is bland to the point of somnambulism. As for Mr Toones, we will pass over his stereotype in silence. Yes, give us dyed-in-brutality Bob Kortman and his naive but willing henchman Yakima Canutt any day. The one thing the nice folks have going for them is an ingenious series of musical look-outs, featuring Stephen Foster's "Camptown Races". Another pleasant musical device has a fine choir singing "Swing Low, Sweet Chariot" as the faithful retainers stage a mock funeral.

A rather extensive support cast list has been provided for this one by Republic's publicity boys, but why no credit for Charles King as the sentry? And isn't that Lafe McKee in a cameo part as the father prisoner?

For all the threats and on-camera opportunism, there is not a great deal of gutsy action in this one. Even the climax is resolved with disappointing rapidity. The presence of Yakima Canutt in the cast often guarantees thrilling stuntwork, but even that is limited to a couple of falls and a good leap from horseback on to a fleeing buckboard. Joseph Kane has directed this chase with some welcome running inserts, and has generally handled the film competently, making fair use of his Lone Pine locations. (That is Mount Whitney you can see in a couple of backgrounds, even though this is supposed to be Texas).

Incidentally, former stuntman turned producer Paul Malvern was a crack shot. He and Wayne insisted on actually shooting the dipper out of Duke's hand. Kane refused to direct such an "idiotic" stunt, so Malvern himself took over for this one shot. (Actually it required two. The first shot hit the dipper all right, but failed to knock it out of Wayne's hand).

# the Lost Trail

**Johnny Mack Brown** (Nevada), **Raymond Hatton** (Sandy), **Jennifer Holt** (Jane Burns), **Riley Hill** (Ned Turner), **Kenneth MacDonald** (John Corbett), **Lynton Brent** (Hall), **John Ince** (Bailey), **John Bridges** (Dr Brown), **Eddie Parker** (Bill), **Frank McCarroll** (Joe), **Dick Dickinson** (Ed), **Milburn Morante** (Zeke), **Frank LaRue** (Jones), **Steve Clark** (Mason), **Henry Vroom, Victor Cox, Chuck Hannon, Ray Henderson** (henchmen), **George Morrell, Tex Cooper, Cactus Mack, Victor Adamson** (townsmen), **Carl Mathews, Jack Tornek, Ralph Bucko** (barflies), **Cal Shrum** and his Rhythm Rangers.

Director: **LAMBERT HILLYER**. Screenplay: **Adele Buffington** (writing as "Jess Bowers"). Photography: **Marcel Le Picard**. Film editor: **Dan Milner** (of *Phantom from 10,000 Leagues* fame). Set dresser: **Vin Taylor**. Music: **Frank Sanucci**. Assistant director: **Eddie Davis** (of *Color Me Dead* fame). Sound recording: **Glen Glenn**. Supervisor: **Charles J. Bigelow**. Producer: **Scott R. Dunlap**.

Copyright 13 September 1945 by Monogram Pictures Corp. No New York opening. U.S. release: 20 October 1945. No record of U.K. release. Never theatrically released in Australia. 6 reels. 53 minutes.

SYNOPSIS: Marshals Brown and Hatton put a stop to a stagecoach war between Holt and MacDonald.

COMMENT: Moderately entertaining Johnny Mack Brown western. The script (Jess Bowers) is the usual malarkey about a girl operating a stage line and being forced out of business by bandits raiding the gold shipments. Leader of the bandits, of course, is the local saloon keeper. Director Lambert Hillyer is an old hand at this sort of stuff. He keeps the story moving. The cast is good, but the action scenes are just fair. Photography is flat and the sets drab, but Sanucci's music score is mercifully less obtrusive than usual.

# the Lucky Texan

**John Wayne** (Jerry Mason), **Barbara Sheldon** (Betty Benson), **George "Gabby" Hayes** (Jake Benson), **Yakima Canutt** (Cole), **Lloyd Whitlock** (Harris), **Gordon D. Woods** (sheriff), **Edward Parker** (Al, the sheriff's son), **Earl Dwire** (banker), **Wally Wales, Tommy Coats** (henchmen), **Phil Dunham** (judge), **Tex Phelps** (prospector), **Artie Ortego** (deputy), **Tex Palmer, John Ince, George Morrell** (townsmen), **Jack Rockwell** (McGill), **Gordon De Main** (Banker Williams), **Julie Kingdon** (young girl).

Director: **ROBERT NORTH BRADBURY**. Original screenplay: **Robert North Bradbury**. Photography: **Archie Stout**. Film editor: **Carl Pierson**. Art director: **E.R. Hickson**. Stunts: **Yakima Canutt, Tommy Coats**. Sound recording: **Dave Stoner**. Producer: **Paul Malvern**. Executive producer: **Trem Carr**.

Copyright 15 January 1934 by Monogram Pictures Corp. A Lone Star Western. No New York opening. U.S. release: 6 January 1934. U.K. release through Pathé: 3 December 1934. 6 reels. 56 minutes.

SYNOPSIS: A blacksmith and his partner find gold in a creek bed.

COMMENT: George Hayes puts on his "Gabby" voice for this one. Even though he doesn't wear the "Gabby" costume and make-up, he does give us a cleverly done old lady impersonation by way of a bonus. But even of more interest than Gabby are two outstanding action chase sequences. Halfway through Wayne jumps for Parker from horseback — but misses. So he literally skates after him down a stormwater channel. The climax finds both our heroes in hot pursuit of the two villains; Wayne on horseback, Hayes in an old jalopy versus Whitlock and Canutt on a speeding rail handcar. The handcar is used not only for thrilling near-misses with the flivver, but as a camera mount for exciting running inserts and tracking shots.

Incidentally, in that otherwise excellent book on *John Wayne and the Movies* by Allen Eyles, the photo purporting to be from *The Lucky Texan* is wrongly captioned. The still actually shows Wayne, Hayes and Cecilia Parker in *Riders of Destiny*. Miss Parker is a petite blonde, but Miss Sheldon is smaller in stature and is neither as pretty nor as personable.

However, Barbara's role in *The Lucky Texan* rates as rather inconsequential. Not only does she make a late entrance, but she figures very little in either of the movie's two interconnected stories.

The movie suffers from the usual Lone Star defects of "B"-slow pacing and directorial whip pans (used for scene changes) that don't quite work, but Canutt has opportunities not only to act the villain but to double for Wayne in some thrilling stuntwork, while Wayne himself comes across in a most agreeable and sympathetic manner.

Despite its small budget and obviously hasty shooting schedule, *The Lucky Texan* (the title has little to do with the plot. Hayes is the one who is "lucky". Not only does he find the gold — admittedly assisted by the Texan — but escapes death twice) comes over as one of the most exciting and most interesting of the Lone Stars. Certainly it's tops in the all-important action department.

# Ma and Pa Kettle

**Marjorie Main** (Ma Kettle), **Percy Kilbride** (Pa Kettle), **Richard Long** (Tom Kettle), **Meg Randall** (Kim Parker), **Patricia Alphin** (secretary), **Esther Dale** (Mrs Birdie Hicks), **Barry Kelley** (Tomkins), **Harry Antrim** (Mayor Swiggins), **Isabel O'Madigan** (Mrs Hick's mother), **Ida Moore** (Emily), **Emory Parnell** (Bill Reed), **Boyd Davis** (Simpson), **O.Z. Whitehead** (Billings), **Ray Bennett** (Sam Rogers), **Alvin Hammer** (Alvin), **Lester Allen** (Geoduck), **Chief Yowlachie** (Crow-bar), **Rex Lease** (sheriff), **Dale Belding** (Danny Kettle), **Teddy Infuhr** (George Kettle), **George McDonald** (Henry Kettle), **Robin Winans** (Billy Kettle), **Gene Persson** (Ted Kettle), **Paul Dunn** (Donny Kettle), **Margaret Brown** (Ruthie Kettle), **Beverly Mook** (Eve Kettle), **Diane Florentine** (Sara Kettle), **Gloria Moore** (Rosie Kettle), **Melinda Plowman** (Susie Kettle), **Harry Tyler** (ticket agent), **Dewey Robinson** (bearded man), **Sam McDaniel** (waiter), **Ted Stanhope** (steward), **Harry Cheshire** (Fletcher), **Eddy C. Waller** (Green), **John Wald** (Dick Palmer), **Donna Leary** (Sally Kettle), **Elena Schreiner** (Nancy Kettle), **George Arglen** (Willie Kettle), **Nolan Leary** (the minister), **Wilbur Mack** (diner on train).

Director: **CHARLES LAMONT**. Screenplay: **Herbert Margolis, Louis Morheim, Al Lewis**. Based on characters from the 1945 book *The Egg and I* by **Betty MacDonald**. Photography: **Maury Gertsman**. Film editor: **Russell Schoengarth**. Music arranged and directed by **Milton Schwarzwald**. Art directors: **Bernard Herzbrun, Emrich Nicholson**. Set decorators: **Russell A. Gausman, Oliver Emert**. Costumes: **Rosemary Odell**. Make-up: **Bud Westmore**. Make-up man: **Jack Kevan**. Ma Kettle's make-up and costumes: **Marjorie Main**. Dialogue director: **Pat Betts**. Hair styles: **Carmen Dirigo**. Hairdresser: **Emmy Eckhardt**. Stills: **Bert Anderson**. Camera operator: **Harry Davis**. Grip: **Russ Franks**. Gaffer: **Johnny Brooks**. Production manager: **Howard Christie**. Assistant director: **William Holland**. Sound recording: **Leslie I. Carey, Richard De Weese**. Western Electric Sound System. Producer: **Leonard Goldstein**.

Copyright 15 March 1949 by Universal Pictures Co., Inc. New York opening at the Palace: 11 August 1949. U.S. release: 1 April 1949. U.K. release: No official release date, but prints were made available as from May 1950 to a few small chains and individual cinemas. Both Rank's Odeon chain and the Associated British chain declined to book the film. Australian release: 6 October 1949. 6,795 feet. 75 minutes.

SYNOPSIS: Just as the town council is about to condemn their rundown farm, the Kettles win a new, gadget-prone home in a tobacco slogan contest.

NOTES: Although the Kettles were introduced in *The Egg and I*, this is the first official film in the series. It was followed by *Ma and Pa Go To Town* (1950), *Ma and Pa Kettle Back on the Farm* (1951), *Ma and Pa Kettle at the Fair* (1952), *Ma and Pa Kettle on Vacation* (1953), *Ma and Pa Kettle at Home* (1954), *Ma and Pa Kettle at Waikiki* (1955), *The Kettles in the Ozarks* (1956) and finally *The Kettles on Old MacDonald's Farm* (1957). All the movies starred Marjorie Main. Percy Kilbride played Pa Kettle in all the movies except *The Kettles in the Ozarks* in which his character was written out of the script, and *The Kettles on Old MacDonald's Farm* in which he was replaced by Parker

Fennelly. All but *Ma and Pa Kettle at Home* and the two entries without Kilbride were produced by *Leonard Goldstein*.

Second to *Family Honeymoon* as Universal's top-grossing domestic release of 1949. Initial domestic film rentals gross: in excess of $2,850,000. Negative cost: less than $200,000. Whilst the film did comparable business for U-I in Australia, it's interesting to note it took close to zero at U.K. ticket windows. Universal blamed this failure on the prejudice of the theatre chains which refused to book the film. After a great deal of arm-twisting, Rank finally agreed to give a circuit release to *Ma and Pa Kettle Back on the Farm* — on the lower half of a double bill. Boxoffice results were not encouraging with many cinema managers reporting adverse and antipathetic audience reaction. To the puzzlement of Universal's home office executives, the Kettles never did win any following at all in the U.K. Rather the reverse. To say that Marjorie Main and Percy Kilbride were boxoffice poison would be a considerable understatement of the loathing in which they were held by all levels of the British picturegoing public.

COMMENT: Hard to believe that this inept offering started the regular series. The "jokes" are not only obvious and trite, but telegraphed well ahead, thanks to boringly flat direction. In fact production values are sorely limited. There seems to be a determination by everyone concerned to give the movie the look of Monogram grey, particularly in the photography and the sets. However, the players led by the determinedly gross Marjorie Main and the wistfully charismatic Percy Kilbride do what they can to extract a bit of humor from the ploddingly pedestrian script. Enthusiastic support is fortunately almost always on hand. In fact the screen is often so crowded with characters it could have been a challenge to identify who was who had not director Lamont taken such pains to keep the pace so uncomfortably slow. One odd bit of crediting is Patricia Alphin's. She receives no less than fifth billing, yet she is in the movie for all of ten seconds and has exactly seven words of totally unimportant dialogue. Mr Long and Miss Randall who directly precede Miss Alphin in the billing do however have quite a bit to do. Too much, some viewers will say. Besides the expected romantic cooing and misunderstandings, they also share a long scene with Ida Moore and her imaginary "Henry" — a scene which has absolutely nothing whatever to do with the main plot, but does provide an opportunity for Sam McDaniel's double takes. Mr Long strikes me as too sincere a hero, but former child actress Randall is nicely attractive.

Schwarzwald's sprightly music scoring is the film's most entertaining feature.

OTHER VIEWS: Although the Kettles here presented have been considerably divested of the gusto and eccentricities presented by Betty MacDonald in her best-selling book, something still remains here of their original vitality with Marjorie Main grandly sweeping the dining table clear of debris and dirty dishes with a destructively disdainful hand and Percy Kilbride bridling wrathfully against his carelessly self-inflicted sunburn. These attractive rough edges were smoothed out into complete blandness for subsequent entries.

And director Lamont even tries for a bit of style here in the opening scenes with a few long takes.

As for Betty MacDonald herself, although she died of cancer at 49 on 7 February 1958, she lived to see the fantastic success of the Kettles.

# the Man from Laramie

**James Stewart** (Will Lockhart), **Arthur Kennedy** (Vic Hansbro), **Donald Crisp** (Alec Waggoman), **Cathy O'Donnell** (Barbara Waggoman), **Alex Nicol** (Dave Waggoman), **Aline MacMahon** (Kate Canaday), **Wallace Ford** (Charley O'Leary), **Jack Elam** (Chris Boldt), **John War Eagle** (Frank Darrah), **James Millican** (Sheriff Tom Quigby), **Gregg Barton** (Fritz), **Boyd Stockman** (Spud Oxton), **Frank de Kova** (padre), **Frank Cordell, Jack Carry, William Catching, Frosty Royse** (mule drivers), **Eddy Waller** (Dr Selden).

Director: **ANTHONY MANN**. Screenplay: **Philip Yordan, Frank Burt**. Based on the story by **Thomas T. Flynn**, published in *The Saturday Evening Post*. Photographed in CinemaScope and Technicolor by **Charles Lang**. Film editor: **William Lyon**. Music composed by **George Duning**. Orchestrations: **Arthur Morton**. Title song by **Lester Lee** and **Ned Washington**. Music director: **Morris Stoloff**. Art director: **Cary Odell**. Set decorator: **James Crowe**. Make-up: **Clay Campbell**. Hair styles: **Helen Hunt**. Technicolor color consultant: **Henri Jaffa**. Stunts: **Chuck Roberson, Ted Mapes**. Assistant director: **William Holland**. Sound supervisor: **John Livadary**. Sound recording: **George Cooper**. RCA Sound System. Producer: **William Goetz**. A William Goetz Production.

Copyright 1955 by Columbia Pictures Corp. New York opening at the Capitol: 31 August 1955. U.S. release: 1 August 1955. U.K. release: September 1955. Australian release: 31 March 1956. 9,063 feet. 101 minutes.

SYNOPSIS: The story, unfortunately, is full of niggly little holes. The director keeps it moving at such a violent pace, few people will notice any oddities whilst the film is actually running. But when you think about it — and especially when you set out to write a synopsis such as this — you cross the barrier from believable fiction into artificial contrivance. Briefly, what the story is supposed to be — and certainly how it appears to a viewer in the first flush of a CinemaScope screening — is a tale of obsessive revenge/desire-for-justice. James Stewart has a typical role as the laconic but psychologically disturbed hero. He arrives on the scene, ostensibly as the leader and proprietor of a three-wagon train bringing supplies from Laramie, Wyoming, all the way across Colorado to a small town in New Mexico. It later turns out that he is a captain in the U.S. cavalry, who has taken leave of absence to investigate the massacre of a small cavalry patrol (which included the hero's young brother) by Apaches (whom someone has supplied with repeating rifles) on the loose in New Mexico.

It all seems like a crazy scheme, considering the length of the journey and its arduousness and danger. But okay, let's accept its madness as part of the hero's mental problem. But no sooner does the guy arrive in the town and establish his credentials, than he's off back to Laramie. But for a chance encounter with the villain, he'd have made a three or four month journey for nothing. Or are we to believe that he deliberately contrived to upset Mr Trigger-happy just to give himself an excuse to stay in the town? That he deliberately exposed himself, his men and his animals to maiming, death and destruction? And that later on, for the same reason, he deliberately crossed paths with the local drunk (maybe he did actually kill him himself) to have himself jailed and then released in custody? And what happened to that murder charge anyway? It's left completely unresolved at film's end. Because it turns out he's a cavalry captain, he's allowed to go around killing whoever he pleases? Or does the Indian witness relent and come to his defence? If so, why should he? That tame Indian is a completely enigmatic character from start to finish.

It's a sad reflection on the foresight of the U.S. cavalry command that a graceless man with such a quick temper and capacity for such ruthless violence and smouldering hate, would rise to the rank of corporal, let alone captain!

But if the hero is a flawed creation (and the heroine is no model of constancy or logicality either), the chief villain, played by Arthur Kennedy, is even more difficult to comprehend. On the surface, it should be simple to understand his motives, but he does crazy things, placing himself in jeopardy for no reason at all. He seems an intelligent man, obsessed with self-preservation, yet he enters into a partnership with his worst enemy! Unbelievable! But then he compounds this stupidity at least twice — maybe three or four times — over!

The Donald Crisp character is another who doesn't seem to know on which side his bread is buttered, but deliberately goes out of his way to make enemies, when his position is so delicate and untenable he needs all the help he can get. Are we supposed to believe that he only appears to be an intelligent and commanding leader of men, that he's actually a stupid bumbler who has built up this vast empire by a combination of chance and an opposition even more moronic?

Annoying isn't it that all these script inconsistencies could easily have been ironed out. (There are actually lots more, but fortunately you don't notice most of them while the film is actually running). Anyway, instead of hiring their customary scriptwriter, Borden Chase, Stewart convinced Mann and Goetz to hire Frank Burt, whose scripts for *Barbary Pirate*, *Chinatown at Midnight* (both 1949), *Fortunes of Captain Blood* (1950), *The Groom Wore Spurs* and *Stage to Tucson* (both 1951) had brought him such lasting fame and glory. I'm being sarcastic of course. Stewart's reason was that Burt had written the best scripts for Stewart's radio series, *The Six-Shooter*. "It wasn't a successful series," admitted Stewart, "but Frank Burt's stories far outshone the rest." Which proves again the old adage that actors are the world's worst judges of good script material.

NOTES: A top box-office success in the U.S.A./Canada, the film also took big money in Australia.

COMMENT: The last of the six collaborations between director Anthony Mann and actor James Stewart was also Columbia's fourth CinemaScope feature (after *The Violent Men*, *The Long Gray Line* and *Three for the Show*). Perhaps producer and director recognised weaknesses in the storyline and rightly thought these could be well disguised on the wide-wide screen. Certainly there are any number of spectacular and often dramatic vistas of rugged New Mexican landscapes. These often serve not just as atmospheric backdrops to the action, but as part and parcel of the action itself.

The action spots, which are many, are presented in a brutally realistic fashion. Coupled with sharp film editing and a lean camera style (the camera rarely moves, but when it does, it tracks or pans with great effectiveness and dynamism), the plot moves ahead with such pace and fluidity that few audiences will notice any inconsistencies in either the story or characters.

It is entirely the actors who are forced to carry the burden of weak and inconsistent motivations. Mostly, they manage to bring their characters to life either by blustering (Nicol, Kennedy) or simply by exercising their personal charisma (Stewart, Crisp). But, though we like her, Cathy O'Donnell often seems hard-pressed to make her reluctant storekeeper believable. Fortunately, while she often seems out of place, this is an appropriate reaction, but her behaviour still comes across as too strange and unpredictable to convey complete acceptance of her performance. She is not helped by over-emphatic make-up and prissy costuming which contrasts too sharply with Stewart's generally dishevelled and sloppy demeanor. (Stewart is a cavalry captain? He looks more like a perennially out-of-luck desert rat).

Fortunately the script is so action-packed, and so forcefully directed and staged on that expansive CinemaScope canvas (I believe all the many ruggedly impressive exteriors were shot on actual locations in New Mexico), that *The Man from Laramie*, despite all the extra weight in his saddle-bags (including a ridiculous title tune), is one cowpoke in the tradition of quiet, laconic strangers in town that stands proud above the rest.

OTHER VIEWS: Early "psychological" western that still impresses audiences as much in 2004 as it did on first release. True, we tend to notice the clichés of the "B"-western dialogue, the ludicrous stock characters and the sententious title song more than we did when psychological overtones were a novelty. True too, we tend to grate on the ripe hamming (especially by Alex Nicol, though the rest of the cast including even James Stewart are not exempt) and the embarrassing mis-casting of Cathy O'Donnell, more than the long tracking shot as Stewart advances on Nicol or the splendid dolly as Crisp charges at Stewart. Still, nothing can defeat from the grandeur of the early CinemaScope scenery and Mann is just the director to take full advantage of it.

— G.A.

*The Man from Laramie* proved to be the last collaboration between director Anthony Mann and actor James Stewart and a wholly fitting conclusion if there had to be one. In many respects, the director saw the movie as a summing up of their past work.

"I wanted to recapitulate, somehow, my five years of collaboration with Jimmy Stewart: *The Man from Laramie* distilled our relationship. I reprised themes and situations by pushing them to their paroxysms. So the band of cowboys surround Jimmy and rope him as they did before in *Bend of the River* . . . but here I shot him through the hand!

"There are some scenes that I thought very successful: the sequence on the salt flats, the one in the market place, the one where Arthur Kennedy returns with Alex Nicol's body. And I benefited from CinemaScope and from a perfectly harmonious crew: the shooting was easy and the film went very well. Do you know that Jimmy wound up back in first place in the Top Ten?"

Mann's skill in composing for CinemaScope is exhilarating and the entire film is visually the finest of their collaborations (by a short lead) as well as being as dramatically satisfying as any of them.

— Allen Eyles: *James Stewart.*

# the Mark of Zorro

**Tyrone Power** (Don Diego Vega), **Linda Darnell** (Lolita Quintero), **Basil Rathbone** (Captain Esteban Pasquale), **Gale Sondergaard** (Inez Quintero), **Eugene Pallette** (Fra Felipe), **J. Edward Bromberg** (Don Luis Quintero), **Montagu Love** (Don Alejandro Vega), **Janet Beecher** (Senora Isabella Vega), **Robert Lowery** (Rodrigo), **Chris-Pin Martin** (turnkey), **George Regas** (Sergeant Gonzales), **Belle Mitchell** (Maria), **John Bleifer** (Pedro), **Frank Puglia** (cafe proprietor), **Pedro De Cordoba** (Don Miguel), **Guy d'Ennery** (Don Jose), **Eugene Borden** (officer of the day), **Fred Malatesta, Fortunio Bonanova** (sentries), **Harry Worth, Gino Corrado, Lucio Vellegas** (caballeros), **Paul Sutton** (soldier), **Michael [Ted] North** (bit), **Ralph Byrd** (student/officer), **Franco Corsaro** (orderly), **Hector Sarno** (peon at inn), **Stanley Andrews** (commanding officer), **Victor Kilian** (boatman), **Raphael Curio** (manservant), **Charles Stevens** (Jose, a peon), **William Edmunds** (peon), **Jean Del Val** (sentry), **Frank Yaconelli** (servant), **Douglas Fowley** (student officer).

Director: **ROUBEN MAMOULIAN**. Assistant director: **Sidney Bowen**. Script: **John Tainton Foote**. Based on the 1919 novel *The Curse of Capistrano* by **Johnston McCulley**. Adaptation: **Garrett Fort, Bess Meredyth**. Director of photography: **Arthur Miller**. Editor: **Robert Bischoff**. Art directors: **Richard Day, Joseph C. Wright**. Set decorator: **Thomas Little**. Music: **Alfred Newman**. Costumes: **Travis Banton**. Sound: **W.D. Flick, Roger Heman**. Technical advisor: **Ernesto Romero**. Associate producer: **Raymond Griffith**. Producer: **Darryl F. Zanuck**.

Copyright 8 November 1940 by 20th Century-Fox Film Corporation. New York opening at the Roxy: 2 November 1940. U.S. release: November 1940. Australian release: 23 January 1941. 8,590 feet. 95 minutes.

SYNOPSIS: The film opens at the graduation ceremony of the Royal Spanish Military Academy in Madrid where handsome Don Diego Vega (Power) announces his intention of returning to his home in California. On his arrival in Los Angeles, he learns that his father (Montagu Love) has been deposed as Alcalde, and that the people are under the corrupt rule of Don Luis Quintero (J. Edward Bromberg), whose tyranny is enforced by cruel Captain Esteban Pasquale (Rathbone). Aware that his father disdains violence, Diego decides to take up the people's cause in disguise, and cloaks his outlaw activities as an effete dandy.

NOTES:

## Zorro Feature Films

| Title | Year | Country | Starring As Zorro |
|---|---|---|---|
| *The Mark of Zorro* | 1920 | USA | Douglas Fairbanks Sr |
| *Don Q., Son of Zorro* | 1925 | USA | Douglas Fairbanks Sr |
| *The Bold Caballero* | 1936 | USA | Robert Livingstone |
| *The Mark of Zorro* | 1940 | USA | Tyrone Power |
| *Il Sogno di Zorro* | 1952 | Italy | Walter Chiari |
| *Zorro the Avenger* | 1958 | USA | Guy Williams |

| Title | Year | Country | Starring As Zorro |
|---|---|---|---|
| *The Sign of Zorro* | 1958 | USA | Guy Williams |
| *El Zorro Escarlata* | 1957 | Mexico | Luis Aguilar |
| *El Zorro Escarlata* [sequel] | 1958 | Mexico | Luis Aguilar |
| *El Zorro Vengador* | 1961 | Mexico | Luis Aguilar |
| *Zorro Nella Valle dei Fantasmi* | 1961 | Mexico | Jeff Stone |
| *Zorro Alla Corte di Spagni* | 1962 | Italy | Giorgio Ardisson |
| *La Venganza del Zorro* | 1962 | Spain/Mexico | Frank Latimore |
| *Il Segno di Zorro* | 1962 | France/Italy | Sean Flynn |
| *L'Ombra di Zorro* | 1963 | Italy/Spain | Frank Latimore |
| *La Tre Spade di Zorro* | 1963 | Italy/Spain | Guy Stockwell |
| *Zorro E I Tre Moschiettieri* | 1963 | Italy | Gordon Scott |
| *Zorro Contro Maciste* | 1963 | Italy | Pierre Brice |
| *Il Giuramento di Zorro* | 1965 | Italy/Spain | Tony Russel |
| *La Montana Sin Ley* | 1965 | Spain | Jose Suarez |
| *Zorro il Ribelle* | 1966 | Italy | Howard Ross |
| *I Nippotti di Zorro* | 1968 | Italy | Dean Reed |
| *Zorro il Cavaliere della Vendetta* | 1968 | Italy/Spain | Charles Quiney |
| *El Zorro la Volpe* | 1968 | Italy | George Ardisson |
| *Zorro il Dominatore* | 1969 | Italy/Spain | Charles Quiney |
| *El Zorro Justiciero* | 1969 | Italy/Spain | Martin Moore |
| *Zorro Alla Corte D'Inghilterra* | 1969 | Italy | Spyros Focas |
| *Zorro Marchese di Navarro* | 1969 | Italy | Nadir Moretti |
| *Zorro la Maschera della Vendetta* | 1970 | Italy/Spain | Charles Quiney |
| *Les Aventures Galantes de Zorro* | 1972 | Belgium | Jean-Michel Dhermay |
| *The Erotic Adventures of Zorro* | 1972 | USA | Douglas Frey |
| *Il Figlio di Zorro* | 1973 | Italy/Spain | Robert Widmark |
| *Zorro* | 1974 | Italy/France | Alain Delon |
| *El Zorro* | 1974 | Mexico | Julio Aldama |
| *Il Sogno di Zorro* | 1975 | Italy | Franco Franchi |
| *The Mark of Zorro* | 1974 | USA | Frank Langella |
| *Zorro, the Gay Blade* | 1980 | USA | George Hamilton |

## Zorro Republic Serials

| Title | Year | Episodes | Starring |
|---|---|---|---|
| *Zorro Rides Again* | 1937 | 12 | John Carroll |
| *Zorro's Fighting Legion* | 1939 | 12 | Reed Hadley |
| *Zorro's Black Whip* | 1944 | 12 | Linda Sterling |
| *Son of Zorro* | 1947 | 13 | George Turner |
| *Ghost of Zorro* | 1949 | 12 | Clayton Moore |

## Zorro Television Series

| Title | Year Began | Episodes | Starring As Zorro |
|---|---|---|---|
| *Zorro* | 1957 | 78 | Guy Williams |
| *The New Adventures of Zorro* | 1981 | 13 | Animated Series |
| *Zorro and Son* | 1983 | 6 | Henry Darrow |
| *Zorro* | 1989 | 75 | Duncan Regehr |

Alfred Newman was nominated for an award from The Academy of Motion Picture Arts and Sciences for his Original Score, losing to *Pinocchio*. (He had to content himself with his prize for Best Score for *Tin Pan Alley*).

COMMENT: Such a masterpiece that one can only express surprise that critics didn't recognize it as such at the time of its original release. Mind you, the public liked it, though it didn't climb anywhere near the top of the year's revenue-raisers.

*The Mark of Zorro* is a perfect film from its stylish direction, its elegant camerawork, its witty script, its rousing score to its most ingratiating cast. Expansively produced, it's a film whose appeal is still undimmed. I've never found an audience that failed to be excited, thrilled, amused and vastly entertained by this *Zorro*.

Giving the performances of their lives: Tyrone Power, Basil Rathbone, J. Edward Bromberg. These are the roles for which Bromberg and Power will always be remembered, whilst Rathbone's Captain Esteban Pasquale shares equal eminence with his Sherlock Holmes. Gale Sondergaard, Eugene Pallette, Montagu Love and Linda Darnell also excel in tailor-made parts.

Technical credits, to which must be added the film's sumptuous sets and costumes, its incredibly smooth film editing and that marvellous 20th Century-Fox sound, are as stated, radiant in their perfection.

OTHER VIEWS: *The Mark of Zorro* was Twentieth Century-Fox's answer to Warner's *The Adventures of Robin Hood*. As if to emphasize the similarities between the two swashbuckling epics, the studio cast three actors from the earlier film in their picture — Basil Rathbone, Eugene Pallette, and Montagu Love — and ordered Alfred Newman to deliver a score reminiscent of the action themes composed by Erich Wolfgang Korngold.

Captain Esteban Pasquale must be counted as Rathbone's finest screen villain. The role was the ultimate progression from the black knight of *Robin Hood*. Both cunning *and a* man-of-action, Pasquale was a more dangerous adversary than Gisbourne could ever hope to be.

The soldier-of-fortune was seldom without his sword — always carrying it in his hand to accent his gestures. He explains early in the film to Diego: "Most men have objects that they play with... Churchmen have their beads... I toy with a sword."

The duel between the two men, although lacking the elaborate staging of Warner Brothers' *Robin Hood*, is an example of fine swordsmanship. Rathbone sustained two cuts on the forehead during the filming of this sequence.

— Michael B. Druxman: *Basil Rathbone*.

The year 1940 came to a glorious finish for Tyrone in one of the films for which he is best remembered. As Don Diego Vega, he played his first real swashbuckling screen role in *The Mark of Zorro* (Twentieth Century-Fox), directed by the esteemed craftsman, Rouben Mamoulian. Vega, the only son of the richest Spanish hidalgo in California of the 1820s, is a pampered fop from sunrise until sunset. But, at night, he covers his face with a black mask and rides his horse Tornado through the countryside, performing great deeds of daring in his goal to rid the land of its tyrannical military aide (Basil Rathbone) and corrupt Spanish overseer (J. Edward Bromberg).

From the pages of Johnston McCulley's story, *The Curse of Capistrano* (1919), written in six days, the property was first put to film in 1920 by United Artists with Douglas Fairbanks as Zorro. Critics such as Bosley Crowther of the *New York Times* stated that "Tyrone Power is no Douglas Fairbanks, and any resemblance which he may bear to his late predecessor in the title role is purely coincidental."

However, each film star had his own individual style, with Fairbanks excelling in acrobatic elan, while Tyrone, the more handsome of the two, was both romantic and dashing. Even the most casual re-viewing of *The Mark of Zorro* reveals aspects of Tyrone's acting that few critics of the day or screen historians of the present generation care to recall — that Power was adept with comedy lines. Throughout this dashing feature, an abiding tone of mock-seriousness courses like an elixir, a remedy utilized by director Mamoulian to insure that this resurrection of an old warhorse melodrama would be taken as entertainment and not as an historical relic.

— James Robert Parish & Don E. Stanke: *The Swashbucklers*.

# Men in Exile

**Dick Purcell** (James Carmody), **June Travis** (Sally Haines), **Alan Baxter** (Danny Haines), **Margaret Irving** (Mother Haines), **Victor Varconi** (Colonel Gomez), **Olin Howland** (Jones), **Veda Ann Borg** (Rita Crane), **Norman Willis** (Rocky Crane), **Carlos De Valdez** (General Alcatraz), **Alec Harford** (Limey), **John Alexander** (Ronald Winterspoon), **Demetris Emanuel, Sol Gorss, Julian Rivero** (Gomez's aides), **Cliff Saum** (jailer), **Leo White** (Flamingo waiter), **Paul Panzer** (Flamingo diner), **Jack Mower** (ship's captain), **George Lloyd** (Jake), **John Harron** (police radio man).

Director: **JOHN FARROW**. Screenplay: **Roy Chanslor**. Story: **Marie Baumer, Houston Branch**. Photography: **Arthur Todd**. Film editor: **Terry Morse**. Art director: **Carl Jules Weyl**. Music composed by **Howard Jackson**, directed by **Leo F. Forbstein**.

Dialogue director: **Jo Graham**. Unit manager: **Lee Hugunin**. Assistant director: **Carroll Sax**. Uncredited producer: **Bryan Foy**.

Copyright 19 February 1937 by Warner Bros. Pictures, Inc. A First National picture. No recorded New York opening. U.S. release: 4 April 1937. 6 reels. 58 minutes.

SYNOPSIS: Unjustly accused of murder, an American flees to the island of Caribo where he tries to avoid getting involved in gun-running for local revolutionaries.

VIEWER'S GUIDE: Alan Baxter's ultra-realistic portrayal of cowardice and treachery, plus a forceful firing squad sequence, may disturb children.

COMMENT: Definitely a minor work, but this Farrow film has its moments. Aside from the suspenseful firing squad episodes which are imaginatively staged and edited, the direction is fairly routine, though some of the action spots pack plenty of punch and Farrow has drawn some excellent performances, particularly from Alan Baxter as a double-crossing villain, the attractive June Travis as a spirited heroine, Veda Ann Borg as the two-timing Rita, Carlos De Valdez as a gentlemanly traitor, John Alexander as a put-upon waiter and Alec Harford as the loyal Limey. As the chief villain, blustering Norman Willis is okay (though we love the way he wears his hat), whilst Dick Purcell makes a reasonably serviceable adventurer. A pity someone more charismatic than Victor Varconi was not cast in the key role of Colonel Gomez and that Margaret Irving seems somewhat uncomfortable as Mother Haines, — she is obviously too young for the role. By second-string "B" levels, production values are considerably more than adequate. Todd's sharp cinematography is a major asset.

# Mexicali Rose

**Gene Autry** (Gene), **Smiley Burnette** (Frog), **Noah Beery** (Valdes), **Luana Walters** (Anita Loredo), **William Farnum** (Padre Dominic), **William Royle** (Carruthers), **LeRoy Mason** (Blythe), **Wally Albright** (Tommy), **Kathryn Frye** (Chalita), **Roy Barcroft** (McElroy), **Dick Botiller** (Manuel), **Vic Demourelle** (Hollister), **John Beach** (Brown), **Henry Otho** (alcalde), **Charles Stevens** (bandit), **Jack Ingram** (stockholder), **Ward Bond** (Mexican policeman), **Al Haskell, Merrill McCormack** (Valdez riders), **Fred "Snowflake" Toones** (cook), **Sherry Hall** (fiesta guest), **Al Taylor, Frankie Marvin** (henchmen), **Josef Swickard** (Gonzales), **Tom London** (Mexican police officer), **Jack Ingram** (investor), **Eddie Parker, Joe Dominguez,** and "Champion" the horse.

Director: **GEORGE SHERMAN**. Associate producer: **Harry Grey**. Screenplay: **Gerald Geraghty**. Story: **Luci Ward** and **Connie Lee**. Camera: **William Nobles**. Editor: **Tony Martinelli**. Music director: **Raoul Kraushaar**. Songs: "Mexicali Rose" by Tenney and Stone; "El Rancho Grande" by Costello, Morales, and Uranga; "You're the Only Star in My Blue Heaven" by Autry; "My Orchestra's Driving Me Crazy" by Burnette. Grip: **Nels Mathias**. Production manager: **Al Wilson**. RCA Sound System. Executive producer: **Herbert J. Yates**.

Copyright 27 March 1939 by Republic Pictures Corp. No recorded New York opening. U.S. release: 27 March 1939. U.K. release through British Lion. Australian release through British Empire Films: 28 October 1943 (sic, a mere four and half years plus one month and a day after its USA release). 6 reels. 58 minutes.

SYNOPSIS: Autry tackles oil swindlers in Mexico.

NOTES: Number 31 of Autry's 94 movies.

COMMENT: *Mexicali Rose* is not exactly loaded with action despite a script that seems to promise much but actually delivers little. There are the usual anachronisms of modern automobiles this time versus Mexican bandits led by Noah Beery in a tongue-spitting, scene-chewing impersonation of a ruffianly Robin Hood. Another actor in Beery's league is also on hand in the person of William Farnum whose eye-rolling seems to have found favor with the director and editor who use numerous reaction shots of his facial mugging. Luana Walters' heroine is not a particularly attractive person either. Even Autry himself is unflattering photographed at times. There's no stuntwork to speak of in this one. Even the climactic shoot-out is brief. There's only a tiny bit of location shooting too. Production values are well below the usual standard for an Autry pic. The plot is naive and old-hat and there is little excitement. The slapstick is strained. The only items of which the film has a fair quota are Mr Autry's songs and even these are presented and delivered for the most part in a desultory fashion.

# Montana

**Errol Flynn** (Morgan Lane), **Alexis Smith** (Maria Singleton), **S.Z. "Cuddles" Sakall** (Poppa Schultz), **Douglas Kennedy** (Rodney Ackroyd), **James Brown** (Tex Coyne), **Ian MacDonald** (Slim Reeves), **Charles Irwin** (MacKenzie), **Paul E. Burns** (Tecumseh Burke), **Tudor Owen** (Jock), **Lester Matthews** (George Forsythe), **Nacho Galindo** (Pedro), **Lane Chandler** (Jake Overby), **Monte Blue** (Charlie Penrose), **Billy Vincent** (Baker), **Warren Jackson** (Curley Bennett), **Forrest Taylor** (Clark), **Almira Sessions** (gaunt woman), **Gertrude Astor, Nita Talbot** (women), **Philo McCullough** (bystander), **Dorothy Adams** (Mrs Maynard), **Jack Mower, Creighton Hale** (ranchers), **Maude Prickett, Jessie Adams** (rancher's wives).

Directed by **RAY ENRIGHT**. Screenplay by **James R. Webb, Borden Chase,** and **Charles O'Neal**. Based on an original story by **Ernest Haycox**. Music by **David Buttolph**. Director of photography: **Karl Freund**. Color by Technicolor. Dialogue director: **Gene Lewis**. Film editor: **Frederick Richards**. Art director: **Charles H. Clarke**. Set decorator: **G. W. Berntsen**. Sound: **Francis J. Scheid**. Wardrobe: **Milo Anderson**. Flynn's wardrobe: **Marjorie Best**. Make-up: **Perc Westmore**. Orchestrations: **Leo Shuken** and **Sidney Cutner**. Assistant director: **Oren Haglund**. Color consultant: **William Fritzsche**. Unit manager: **Lou Baum**. Song "Reckon I'm in Love" by **Mack David, Al Hoffman,** and **Jerry Livingston**. Produced by **William Jacobs**.

Copyright 28 January 1950 (in notice: 1949) by Warner Bros Pictures, Inc. New York opening at the Strand: 3 February 1950. U.S. release: 28 January 1950. U.K. release: 24 July 1950. Australian release: 2 November 1951. 76 minutes.

SYNOPSIS: Flynn, relying almost completely on debonair charm to see him through the tedium, plays an Australian sheepherder determined to move in on the cattle territory of Montana. Alexis, as a wealthy cattle rancher opposed to any invasion of sheepherders, is attracted to Flynn before she realizes his true occupation. But once the truth is out, it's Errol and his sheepherders versus Alexis and the cattle barons. Fortunately, at the conclusion, Errol and Alexis, cattle and sheep — all get together.

— *The Films of Errol Flynn.*

COMMENT: A most exciting action western, splendidly directed from a taut script. Flynn is in fine form. And an excellent music score provides yet another bonus for Flynn fans.

OTHER VIEWS: An El Cheapo western if ever there was one, with a climax made up *entirely* of stock footage — and not particularly exciting stock footage at that — either used as is or very obviously projected on a back screen.

Still it's hard to put a good cast down — Flynn even gets the opportunity to sing a song. He's as charming as ever and Alexis Smith makes a colorful foil for his attentions. SZ Sakall dominates the first quarter-hour or so, then unaccountably disappears, while Douglas Kennedy makes an indifferent villain. Fortunately, Ian MacDonald makes an ugly enough henchman and Paul Burns is more than okay as Flynn's Walter Brennan type sidekick.

Enright's direction is competent if undistinguished, — at least he keeps the film moving. Karl Freund's photography (provided it isn't being used as a foreground to back projection) is as colorful as a postcard. But it lacks style. But then so does the rest of the film. The players give it a bit of class, but otherwise it's on its own. The script is no more than adequate. Maybe the plot and the characters were less familiar back in 1950 but I don't think so. Still at 76 minutes and by "B"-feature standards, it's a presentable enough offering.

— G.A.

After *They Died with Their Boots On*, Flynn's Westerns were considerably less than epic. The vigor, the splendor, the outstanding action sequences of the earlier films were only hinted at in subsequent efforts. *Montana*, the least impressive of the group, was a formula film (running a scant one hour and sixteen minutes), with a dull, undistinguished script. The scenery (Warners' Calabasas Ranch) was well photographed, the production was reasonably well mounted, but the people and situations were devoid of life and interest.

Flynn sang for the fourth time on the screen: a little ditty called "Reckon I'm in Love." This was a duet with Alexis, accompanied by what appears to be Flynn's guitar playing.

— *The Films of Errol Flynn.*

# Mountain Justice

**George Brent** (Paul Cameron), **Josephine Hutchinson** (Ruth Harkins), **Guy Kibbee** (Doc Barnard), **Mona Barrie** (Evelyn Wayne), **Robert Barrat** (Jeff Harkins), **Robert McWade** (Horace Bamber), **Margaret Hamilton** (Phoebe Lamb), **Fuzzy Knight** (Clem

Biggars), **Edward Pawley** (Tod Miller), **Elizabeth Risdon** (Meg Harkins), **Marcia Mae Jones** (Bethie Harkins), **Granville Bates** (Judge Crawley), **Russell Simpson** (Turnbull), **Sybil Harris** (Mrs Turnbull), **Guy Wilkerson** (Asaph Anderson), **Claire DuBrey** (young woman), **Gertrude Hoffman** (Granny Burnside), **Alice Lyndon** (Charity Topping), **Henry Hall** (Henniger), **Harry Davenport** (printer), **Jim Toney** (make-up man), **Earle Hodgins** (vendor), **Minerva Urecal** (Ella Crippen), **Herbert Heywood** (jury foreman), **Carl Stockdale** (Stout), **Walter Soderling** (Sheriff Willis), **Arthur Aylsworth** (justice of the peace), **Virginia Brissac** (Miss Hughes), **Heinie Conlin** (jury foreman), **Dennis Moore** (airplane pilot).

Director: **MICHAEL CURTIZ**. Original story and screenplay: **Norman Reilly Raine** and **Luci Ward**. Photography: **Ernest Haller**. Film editor: **George Amy**. Art director: **Max Parker**. Costumes: **Milo Anderson**. Music director: **Leo F. Forbstein**. Dialogue director: **Irving Rapper**. Technical advisor: **Mrs Elizabeth Hearst**. Production supervisor: **Lou Edelman**.

Copyright 6 November 1936 by Warner Bros. Pictures, Inc. New York release at the Rialto, 12 May 1937. U.S. release: 24 April 1937. 10 reels. 83 minutes.

SYNOPSIS: Patricide — obviously suggested by the Edith Maxwell case.

COMMENT: This engrossingly dramatic Warner Bros social documentary has been produced on an extremely lavish scale. Director Curtiz is in his element with the huge crowd scenes and has creatively and imaginatively handled the stunning courtroom sequences as well as the film's other tense moments.

Unfortunately, despite Curtiz's forceful efforts — aided by wonderfully skilful photography by Ernest Haller — the powerfully suspenseful atmosphere is a little undermined not only by some trite dialogue and stereotyped characterizations, but by some misguided efforts at comedy relief. Scriptwriters Norman Reilly Raine of *Tugboat Annie* fame and Luci Ward of innumerable "B" westerns are solely to blame.

In the Edith Maxwell part, Josephine Hutchinson plays with spirit yet dignity. A difficult role, but she handles it with perfect assurance and ease. Barrat is equally right as her brutal father. In a more conventional role, Brent comes across with reasonable force. Heading a great Warner Bros support cast, Marcia Mae Jones deserves a special mention as the heroine's understandably rebellious child-bride sister, whose flight is the catalyst for "murder".

# 'Neath the Arizona Skies

**John Wayne** (Chris Morrell), **Sheila Terry** (Clara Moore), **Jay Wilsey [Buffalo Bill, Jr]** (Jim Moore), **Shirley Ricketts [Shirley Jane Rickert]** (Nina), **George Hayes** (Matt Downing), **Yakima Canutt** (Sam Black), **Jack Rockwell** (Vic Byrd), **Phil Keefer** (Hodges), **Frank Hall Crane** (express agent), **Earl Dwire** (Nina's father), **Weston Edwards [Harry L. Fraser]** (man in the brush), **Artie Ortego** (Shorty), **Tex Phelps** (henchman who overhears Hodges), **Eddie Parker** (henchman who asks after Nina), **Herman Hack** (another henchman).

Director: **HARRY L. FRASER**. Original story and story: **B.R. "Burl" Tuttle**. Photography: **Archie Stout**. Film editor: **Charles Hunt**. Art director: **E.R. Hickson**. Music: **Paul Van Loan**. Stunts: **Yakima Canutt**. Sound recording: **Ralph Shugart**. Balsley and Phillips Sound System. Producer: **Paul Malvern**. A Lone Star Western.

Copyright 15 January 1935 by Monogram Pictures Corp. No New York opening. U.S. release: 5 December 1934. U.K. release through Pathé : 12 August 1935. 6 reels. 52 minutes.

SYNOPSIS: Wayne is the guardian of a little Indian girl, Shirley Jane Rickert, who is entitled to a royalty payment of $50,000 for an oil lease. Before she can get the money, however, Wayne needs to get a paper signed by her natural father, Earl Dwire. A gang of kidnappers led by Yakima Canutt also want the money. Matters are further complicated when a couple of bank robbers, Rockwell and Wilsey, cross paths.

COMMENT: This would be a dull Lone Star were it not for the surprise appearance of George Hayes, playing pretty close to his "Gabby" character. Although prominently featured in re-issue posters and advertising, Hayes isn't even mentioned in the credits. Maybe his part was added as an afterthought. However it says much for the quality for the rest of the movie, that Hayes is the highlight of interest. True the pace is fairly rapid and the plot has more twists than a snake on an ants' nest, but the action spots — and admittedly there are many — are poorly and unexcitingly staged. Mr. Fraser is not one of the better directors in this field. Not only are the action scenes lacking in vigor and punch, but the level of acting is far more amateurish than usual. Even Canutt has little color, whilst Wayne himself is wanting his usual assurance and sparkle. The heroine is somewhat dowdily costumed, though she has an attractive face, and as for Miss Rickert/Ricketts, it comes as no surprise to learn that she was a former member of the *Our Gang* series. She's one of those over-confident, over-forward but not particularly charismatic Hollywood kids which the studios seem to turn out by the cart-load. Still Buffalo Bill, Jr was mean and shifty enough as the villain, and Earl Dwire had one or two good moments as the never-do-well turned playful dad. (No-one could complain that Mr Dwire lacked variety in his various Lone Star roles). And maybe I imagined it, but "Sheriff" Jack Rockwell seemed uncomfortable in his unaccustomed role as a heavy.

As for the Arizona skies, we're still waiting. The locations are singularly uninteresting, even by Poverty Row's Hollywood Hills standards.

Yes, Mr Canutt does do a couple of stunts, including two leaps from a cliff, one on horseback, doubling himself; and one solo, doubling Wayne. Thanks to poor direction, both fail to impress.

# New Frontier

**John Wayne** (Stony Brooke), **Raymond Hatton** (Rusty Joslin), **Ray Corrigan** (Tucson Smith), **Phylis Isley [Jennifer Jones]** (Celia), **Eddy Waller** (Major Braddock), **Sammy McKim** (Stevie), **LeRoy Mason** (M.C. Gilbert), **Harrison Greene** (Bill Proctor), **Reginald Barlow** (Judge Lawson), **Burr Caruth** (Doc Hall), **Dave O'Brien** (Jason), **Hal Price** (sheriff), **Jack Ingram** (Harmon), **Bud Osborne** (Dickson), **Charles "Slim" Whitaker** (Turner), **Bob Burns, Chuck Baldra** (jailed ranchers), **Bob Reeves, Frank Ellis, Walt LaRue** (dance extras), **Jody Gilbert** (woman at dance), **Frankie Marvin**,

**Oscar Gahan, Fred Burns** (musicians), **Charles Murphy** (Zeke the mailman), **Herman Hack** (Jim the construction-wagon driver), **George Plues** (henchman), **Wilbur Mack** (Dodge), **Curley Dresden** (construction worker), **Cactus Mack** (fake Indian), **Jim Corey** (rancher), **George Chesebro, George Montgomery, Sam Flint, Bill Wolfe**.

Director: **GEORGE SHERMAN**. Screenplay: **Betty Burbridge, Luci Ward**. Based on characters created by **William Colt MacDonald**. Photography: **Reggie Lanning**. Film editor: **Tony Martinelli**. Music score: **William Lava**. Production manager: **Al Wilson**. Associate producer: **William Berke**. Executive producer: **Herbert J. Yates**.

Copyright 10 August 1939 by Republic Pictures Corp. No *New York Times* review. U.S. release: 7 September 1939. U.K. release through British Lion. Never released in Australia, either theatrically or on television. 6 reels. 56 minutes.

American TV title: *FRONTIER HORIZON*.

SYNOPSIS: Just as the good citizens are celebrating the 50th anniversary of the founding of New Hope (which occurred shortly after the end of the Civil War), word is brought that a neighboring city intends to flood the valley to ensure its water supply.

NOTES: Number 25 of the 52-picture *Three Mesquiteers* series, and Wayne's last "B" western.

The print under review is from the Republic Collection. Although the cassette blurb claims the print was "mastered from original film negatives", this is demonstrably untrue. It was in fact obviously duped from a 16mm television print, and not from the original 35mm negative. The grading is terrible, the lack of contrast so bad that many shots look almost completely washed out.

COMMENT: A John Wayne-Jennifer Jones picture? Yes indeed. Actually it was her first film and she appeared under her real name, Phylis Isley. She is billed after Wayne, Corrigan and Hatton and her role is fairly large, though she has few lines and only one close-up, and I think but three brief scenes with Wayne. The producers seem unsure what to do with her. In her introductory and longest scene, she has her hair long and dark. In her next scene and throughout the rest of the film she wears it short and light. We wonder if it's the same girl. She often stands in a shot while Eddie Waller does all or most of the talking. His is really the main role after Wayne. Both Corrigan and Hatton have so little to do, it's hardly fair to call this a **Three** Mesquiteers movie. Even Sammy McKim has a bigger part than Corrigan.

As with Miss Jones, the script bears every evidence of being changed or made up on the run. A couple of good guys unexpectedly change into villains and the plot leads into a series of climaxes, all of which unexpectedly fizzle out or come to nothing. Oddly, for a western, although there plenty of confrontations occur, there is no bloodshed at all. Not a drop. The villains are routed with no more than a dozen or so fists raised in anger, and the climax, instead of an expected Poverty Row duplication of *The Rains of Ranchipur* comes to nothing. All the lead-up with the dam waters being released raises expectations. We assume the farmsteads have been swept away before Wayne turns the water off. But the flood waters are neither shown wreaking havoc (no Lydecker special effects or miniatures in this movie) or even mentioned.

Aside from its cleverly contrived introduction when the audience is fooled into thinking a recreation of the Pony Express run is the actual McGuffin, the plot manages to whip up surprisingly little interest. Lackluster direction, dull locations and the paucity of action doesn't help. It's fortunate Miss Jones was cast in the film because the novelty of her presence is just about the only reason anyone would want to watch it from start to end. Even Wayne himself is less forceful than usual. Of course, fans of garrulously verbose Eddy Waller will be cheering themselves hoarse, but if Eddy's total fan following overflows a phone booth, I'd be very surprised.

Note the prominence given Wayne's name in the poster. Also that Phylis Isley is pictured pointing a rifle when in fact, true to her Jennifer Jones screen image, she does no such thing.

# the Night Riders

**John Wayne** (Stony Brooke), **Ray Corrigan** (Tucson Smith), **Max Terhune** (Lullaby Joslin), **Doreen McKay** (Soledad), **Ruth Rogers** (Susan Randall), **George Douglas** (Pierce Talbot/Don Luis De Serrano), **Tom Tyler** (Jackson), **Kermit Maynard** (Sheriff Pratt), **Sammy McKim** (Tim), **Walter Wills** (Hazelton), **Ethan Laidlaw** (Andrews), **Edward Peil, Sr** (Harper), **Tom London** (Wilson), **Jack Ingram** (Wilkins), **William Nestell** (Allen), **Cactus Mack, David Sharpe** (henchmen), **Lee Shumway, Hal Price, Bob Card, Hank Worden** (ranchers), **Roger Williams, Eva McKenzie** (townsfolk), **Olin Francis, Francis Walker, Bud Osborne** (enlisted men), **Jack Kirk** (bartender), **Glenn Strange** (blackjack player), **Georgia Summers** (woman with Susan), **David McKim** (messenger boy), **Francis Sayles** (President Garfield), **Horace Murphy** (Captain Beckett), **Frank O'Connor** (Washington operator), **Jane Keckley** (rancher's wife), **Allan Cavan** (judge), and **Hugh Prosser, George Montgomery.**

Director: **GEORGE SHERMAN**. Associate producer: **William Berke**. Screenplay: **Betty Burbridge, Stanley Roberts**. Based on characters created by **William Colt MacDonald**. Photography: **Jack Marta**. Film editor: **Les Orlebeck**. Musical score: **William Lava**. Assistant director: **Philip Ford**. RCA Sound System. Executive producer: **Herbert J. Yates**.

Copyright 12 April 1939 by Republic Pictures Corp. No recorded New York opening. U.S. release: 12 April 1939. U.K. release through British Lion. No Australian theatrical release. 6 reels. 58 minutes.

SYNOPSIS: Spanish land grant claimant successfully evicts the Mesquiteers from their 3M Ranch. They decide to prove the new land baron is a phony. In the meantime, disguised in flowing white capes, they rob the baron of his rent money and return it to the farmers awaiting eviction.

NOTES: Number 22 of the 52-picture series.

COMMENT: Shades of Sam Fuller's later *Baron of Arizona*, this entry ties a couple of interesting variants on the usual stock "B"-western land-grabbing theme. We enjoyed the heroes' caped crusaders (combining Robin Hood and Zorro). This movie was actually made right after Wayne's stint in *Stagecoach*. He plays the leader of the trio with his customary easy assurance. The plot device of linking the trio's fate with President Garfield's assassination is clever enough and we like Kermit Maynard's obliging sheriff.

Aside from what I've written above, however, *The Night Riders* has not a great deal to recommend it. Republic were obviously trying hard to produce a large-scale western on an extremely cramped budget. Stock shots; montages of newspaper headlines, posters, etc; closet-sized sets; meager crowds of extras; second-rate players abound. Worst of all, the direction lacks sweep. Even the few action scenes are put across in such a perfunctory fashion, they have little impact. And script opportunities to build up tension are often dissipated.

OTHER VIEWS: Wayne's easy charm stands him in good stead in this "Three Mesquiteers" entry. The script allows him some forceful moments as he and his buddies join the villain's army to hunt down — themselves! The writing, alas, is often more inventively plotted and sharper dialogued than what we actually see and hear on the screen, thanks to Sherman's lackluster direction and economy-conscious production values.

# On Our Selection

**Bert Bailey** (Dad Rudd), **Fred MacDonald** (Dave), **Alfreda Bevan** (mum), **John McGowan** (Maloney), **Molly Raynor** (Kate), **Richard Fair** (Sandy), **John Warwick** (Jim Carey), **Billy Driscoll** (uncle), **Lilias Adeson** (Lilly White), **Len Budrick** (Old Carey), **Bobbie Beaumont** (Sarah), **Ossie Wenban** (Joe), **Fred Kerry** (Cranky Jack), **Dorothy Dunckley** (Mrs White), **Fred Browne** (Billy Bearup), **Arthur Dodds** (reverend).

Director: **KEN G. HALL**. Screenplay: **Bert Bailey**. Based on the 1912 stage play by **Bert Bailey** and **Edmund Duggan**, which was in turn based on the novel by "Steele Rudd", pseudonym of **Arthur Hoey Davis**. Adaptation: **Ken G. Hall**. Photography: **Walter H.B. Sully**. Camera assistant: **Sid Whiteley**. Film editor: **George Malcolm**. Art director: **Jim Coleman**. Chief electrician: **George Gibson**. Technical supervisor: **Bert Cross**. Script girl: **Margery West**. Production manager: **John Souter**. Transport: **Banks Carrington**. Sound recording: **Arthur Smith**, assisted by **Clive Cross**. Cinesound-Smith Sound System. Producer: **Bert Bailey**. Executive producer: **Stuart F. Doyle**.

A Cinesound Production in association with Bailey and Grant. Australian release through British Empire Films: July 1932. Sydney opening at the Capitol.

U.K. release title: *Down on the Farm*.

SYNOPSIS: Dad Rudd, a typical Aussie outback battler, has to contend with drought, tight money, a grasping landlord, a wayward bull and an eager-to-help but slow-thinking and mishap-prone son.

NOTES: Eclipsed only by *Palmy Days* as the biggest ticket-seller in Australia in 1932. Counting revivals and re-issues up to 1980, *On Our Selection* has probably exceeded the Goldwyn picture's box-office takings four or five times over — though this comparison is a bit unfair to *Palmy Days* since that picture has never been circulated in Australia since its original release.

   Locations near Penrith, New South Wales.

VIEWERS' GUIDE: Okay for all.

COMMENT: This rural farce has some curiosity value as an example of primitive film-making, but it has little else to recommend it though it will probably still delight the yokel trade. The film editing is jerky, caused by the director's failure to shoot proper matching shots, there is no background music except under old silent-type titles, the continuity is abrupt, the acting over-ripe and directorial style almost non-existent except for a remarkably effective instance of double exposure. Location photography helps, though the technical quality is surprisingly variable.

# Owd Bob

**Will Fyffe** (Adam McAdam), **John Loder** (David Moore), **Margaret Lockwood** (Jeannie McAdam), **Graham Moffatt** (Tammas), **Moore Marriott** (Samuel), **Wilfrid Walter** (Thwaites), **Eliot Mason** (Mrs Winthrop), **Bromley Davenport** (magistrate), **H.F. Maltby** (Sergeant Musgrave), **Edmund Breon** (Lord Meredale), **Wally Patch, Alf Goddard** (bookies).

Director: **ROBERT STEVENSON**. Screenplay: **J.B. Williams, Michael Hogan**. Based on the novel by **Albert Ollivant**. Photography: **Jack Cox**. Film editor: **R.E. Dearing**. Cutting: **Alfred Roome**. Art director: **Alex Vetchinsky**. Music director: **Louis Levy**. Sound recording: **A. Cameron**. Producer: **Edward Black**.

Copyright 12 August 1938 by Gaumont British Picture Corporation of America. A Gainsborough Picture, presented by J. Arthur Rank, made by Gaumont British Picture Corp. Ltd. New York opening at the Continental: 12 April 1938. U.S. release through Gaumont British: 1 May 1938. U.K. release through General Film Distributors: January 1938. Australian release through G-B-D: 18 August 1938. 78 minutes.

U.S. release title: *TO THE VICTOR*.

SYNOPSIS: Which sheep-dog has suddenly turned killer? Suspicion turns to a newcomer to the district.

NOTES: Best British film of 1938 — Frank S. Nugent in *The New York Times*.
   Second to *Said O'Reilly to McNab* (also starring Will Fyffe) as G-B-D's most popular Australian release of 1938. (In New Zealand, the order was reversed).
   Fourth on New York's National Board of Review's list of the Ten Best Films of 1938. Will Fyffe was also included in Best Acting of the year.
   Second of four versions of the title novel (known as *Bob, Son of Battle* in the USA). The first starred J. Fisher White as Adam and was directed by Henry Edwards for Atlantic Union in 1924. 20th Century-Fox made *Thunder in the Valley* in 1947 with Edmund Gwenn in the McAdam role. Louis King directed. Fifty years later, the Ollivant novel was again remade, this time with James Cromwell, Colm Meaney and Jemima Rooper in the main roles, directed by Rodney Gibbons.

COMMENT: Hailed by contemporary critics as one of the greatest triumphs of British cinema during the 1930s, it's odd that this version of Ollivant's popular novel has been locked away for so long, whilst the entertaining though inferior Fox version has been widely circulated.

True, the black-and-white photography looks a little primitive alongside Fox's glossy Technicolor, but surely the somewhat drab gray tones are atmospherically most effective. And this after all is why Cox, a specialist in bleak lighting, was hired in the first place.

Even if we take current prejudices against Cox into account, *Owd Bob* creams *Bob, Son of Battle* in every other department.

Fyffe's is truly one of the all-time great performances of the cinema. By sheer charisma and presence, he turns what is seemingly a thankless role into a marvelous success. What other actor could play such an embittered, surly, selfishly mean, miserly old tyrant with such persuasive power that all members of the audience automatically take his side, not just against the other villagers (because that's par for the course in this type of film), but even against the agreeably clean-cut hero (nicely played here by John Loder) and the ultra-charming heroine (everyone's favorite, Margaret Lockwood)? Fyffe plays the role virtually straight, but he still manages to invest plenty of sly fun into the action. We love the twinkle in his rascally eye as he outwits his rivals at nearly every opportunity. The script hands him the dominating role and he seizes it, plays it and has fun with it as only a really great actor can.

Also playing straight for once is Moore Marriott. This time instead of stooging for Will Hay, he uses his partner Graham Moffatt to bring off a couple of pleasing jests, including a bell-ringing recital. The other support roles are likewise colorfully filled by people like Bromley Davenport as a horse doctor and H.F. Maltby as slow-movingly obese police sergeant.

We reserve a special paragraph for the dogs. The credits merely tell us that Owd Bob and Black Wull play themselves. But whatever and whoever and how many (and there are lots of others in prominent roles in any event), all are not only perfectly trained but will keep all dog-lovers fully entranced.

Stevenson has directed with a sure hand, making the most of his picturesque locations, and handling the action sequences (including a mighty pub brawl) with unusual vigor.

# the Painted Stallion

**Ray Corrigan** (Clark Stuart), **Hoot Gibson** (Walter Jamison), **Sammy McKim** (Kit Carson), **LeRoy Mason** (Alfredo Dupray), **Duncan Renaldo** (Zamorro), **Hal Taliaferro** (Jim Bowie), **Jack Perrin** (Davy Crockett), **Ed Platt** (Oscar), **Lou Fulton** (Elmer), **Julia Thayer** (The Rider), **Yakima Canutt** (Tom), **Maston Williams** (Macklin), **Duke Taylor** (Bill), **Loren Riebe** (Pedro), **George DeNormand** (Oldham), **Gordon DeMain** (governor), **Charles King** (Bull Smith), **Vinegar Roan** (Pete), **Henry Hale** (Juan), **Lafe McKee** (boat officer), **Frank Leyva** (captain of the guard), **Frankie Marvin** (clerk), **Curley Dresden** (Harris), **John Big Tree** (Indian chief), **Pascale Perry** (Joe), **Don Orlando** (Jose), **Edward Peil Sir** (marshal), **Horace Carpenter** (old timer), **Lee White** (Peters), **Joe Yrigoyen** (rancher), **Paul Lopez** (secretary), **Monte Montague** (Tanner), **Gregg Star Whitespear** (Topek), and **Ralph Bucko, Roy Bucko, Leo Dupee, Babe**

**DeFreest, Jose Dominguez, Jack Padjan, Al Haskell, Augie Gomez**, and "Minister" (the stallion).

Directors: **WILLIAM WITNEY, ALAN JAMES, RAY TAYLOR**. Screenplay: **Barry Shipman, Winston Miller**. Original story: **Morgan Cox, Ronald Davidson**. Suggested by the 1925 *Saturday Evening Post* serial *The Painted Stallion* by **Hal G. Evarts**. Photography: **William Nobles, Edgar Lyons**. Supervising film editor: **Murray Seldeen**. Film editors: **Helene Turner, Edward Todd**. Music supervisor: **Raoul Kraushaar**. Main title theme for all chapters except one composed by **William Lava**. Title theme for chapter One, "Get Zorro", composed by **Karl Hajos**. Songs: "Wagon Train" by **Gene Autry** and **Smiley Burnette**; "Oh Susanna" by **Stephen Foster**. "Minister" owned by **Frank Yrigoyen**, trained by **Leo Dupee**. Sound engineer: **Terry Kellum**. Associate producer: **J. Laurence Wickland**. Executive producer: **Herbert J. Yates**.

Copyright 18 June 1937 (chapters one through six) and 6 August 1937 (chapters seven through twelve) by Republic Pictures Corp. U.S. release: 5 June 1937. Each chapter has 2 reels, except number one which has 3. Chapter titles: *Trail to Empire, The Rider of the Stallion, The Death Leap, Avalanche, Volley of Death, Thundering Wheels, Trail Treachery, The Whistling Arrow, The Fatal Message, Ambush, Tunnel of Terror, Human Targets*.

SYNOPSIS: An American agent, Clark Stuart, is dispatched to Santa Fe to negotiate a trade agreement with the newly appointed Mexican governor. At the same time, the first American wagon train, led by Walter Jamison, leaves from Independence, Missouri, for Santa Fe, bearing goods for trade. The train is accompanied by Jim Bowie, famed inventor of the Bowie knife, and by the youthful Kit Carson.

The former governor of Santa Fe, Alfredo Duprey, anxious to regain his lucrative control of the territory, plots to sabotage the treaty by substituting one of his own men for Stuart before the new governor arrives.

Duprey's confederate, Zamorro and Zamorro's henchmen attempt to destroy the wagon train, first by stirring up an Indian attack and later by luring it into a mountain pass where the Indians use dynamite to send a landslide down. They also make several attempts to kill Stuart, but each attempt is foiled by a mysterious girl rider on a painted stallion who warns of danger to the Americans by shooting a whistling arrow.

NOTES: Alan James and Ray Taylor were the original directors. Witney accompanied them as film editor to the St George, Utah, locations. Because of bad weather, shooting fell behind schedule. Taylor was replaced by Witney, here making his directorial debut at the tender age of twenty-two.

Negative cost: $109,164, slightly above the budgeted estimate of $102,157. Shooting commenced on 10 February 1937 and wound up on 3 March 1937.

COMMENT: Such an exceptionally lively serial, it's hard to pick a favorite chapter. I would have to go for 7, even though the thrilling cliffhanger stunt is not shown complete until the reprise at the beginning of 8. The emphasis is on action, action, action. Rarely have all 12 chapters of a serial been so crammed with stunts that there is in fact little time for the story. I don't object to this. The dialogue — what we have of it — is pretty cliched anyway, and no-one is going to take the plot seriously. It's a great peg for the action and we like the whole device of the mystery rider and the whistling arrows. I'm not complaining either that the story moves in such a clipped, fast-paced fashion as to sometimes sacrifice smoothness and even clarity. All the players are personable, with Corrigan making a suitably rugged hero, Maston Williams a nice braggart of a henchman (cult favorite Charles King is killed off in an early chapter), whilst Gregg Star Whitespear makes an unusually enthusiastic Indian villain and DeMain a credible governor. Even young Sammy McKim is quite bearable as a junior Kit Carson. And there is one really outstanding performance: — Henry Hale as the pretender, Juan. (The only other films I have for Hale are Republic serials: *Robinson Crusoe of Clipper Island, Dick Tracy* and *SOS Coastguard*). This is another reason why 7 is my favorite episode. It's unusual of course to find a charismatic cameo in a serial, but *The Painted Stallion* has several other highly unusual features, including a cliffhanger in which the hero is actually shown making good his escape jump from the burning wagon *before* it plunges over the cliff. Not only are there no economy episodes in this one, not only are they all full of action — most set against impressive locations — but some chapters are strikingly individual. Thus 3 is the wipes chapter. If you like wipes — and who doesn't — 3 is the number for you. True, there are wipes in other eps, but nowhere do they come as thick and fast and various as in 3. Now if it's stunt falls that grab your fancy, 10 or 11 are the best bets. You like lots of pans, there's a chapter for you too. Personally I prefer running inserts — another reason I go for 7.

So many stunts so vigorously staged are not always as effective as they might be in the hands of a more experienced director. But frankly I prefer Witney's youthful enthusiasm, even if it occasionally misfires, to bland professionalism.

All told, most enjoyable — one of Republic's best!

OTHER VIEWS: Three rousing cheers! *The Painted Stallion* has just about everything the devoted serial fan is after, namely action, a vigorous pace and great production values. The action of course has to include loads of thrilling stuntwork, using real stuntmen not obvious miniatures and process screen; the fast pace should be achieved by clipping expository dialogue, comic relief, romance and other intrusions to the absolute bone; whilst production values must not only be extensive, with real locations, lots of costumed extras and expansive sets, but be of a consistently highly generous standard right through every episode. There's nothing worse than having to sit through an impoverished serial on which just about the whole budget has been blown on the first and second chapters. *The Painted Stallion* not only avoids all pitfalls, but its fast pace is made even more entertaining by a vast and varied array of trick wipes.

— G.A.

Corrigan is certainly a brave man. That's him right there in the burning presidio with flaming beams crashing around him. True, the beams are light cardboard or balsa wood — he kicks one that falls in front of him right out of his way — but I wouldn't like to be in his shoes... Whilst most of the action was especially staged for the film, there is a fair amount of striking and well-integrated stock footage, particularly in the three-reel introductory chapter which is virtually a miniature feature. Witney and James have directed not only at a crackerjack pace but with such close eyes for detail that the serial needs to be seen at least twice to pick up the many realistic little background touches with which some scenes are enriched. Episode 7 with the substitute governor Juan in his full regalia standing in the background as he awaits the coach and then being forced to double up with one of the bandits as they're put to flight, is an excellent example of this admirably minute attention to details... The editing with its delightfully extravagant optical wipes and its skilfully hair's breadth proximity to jump cutting is so fast-paced few viewers will notice the deft insertion of occasional stock footage or the repetition in different guises of three or four shots from earlier episodes.

— C.F.

# Paradise Canyon

**John Wayne** (John Wyatt), **Earle Hodgins** (Dr Carter), **Marion Burns** (Linda Carter), **Yakima Canutt** (Curly Joe Gale), **Reed Howes** (Trigger), **Perry Murdock** (Ike), **Gordon Clifford** (Mike), **Gino Corrardo** (captain of rurales), **Tex Palmer** (Curly gang member), **Herman Hack** (deputy), **Earl Dwire** (Arizona sheriff), **Bob Burns** (New Mexico sheriff), **Henry Hall** (Captain Peters), **James Sheridan** (Pete), **Fred Parker** (skeptic), **George Morrell** (townsman), **John F. Goodrich** (cowboy), **Horace B. Carpenter** (blacksmith), **Jose Dominguez** (Miguel), **Chuck Baldra** (Slim).

Director: **CARL L. PIERSON**. Screenplay: **Lindsley Parsons, Robert Emmett Tansey**. Original screen story: **Lindsley Parsons**. Photography: **Archie Stout**. Film editor: **Gerald "Jerry" Roberts**. Songs: "When We Were Young and Foolish" (Texas Two); "Snap Those Old Suspenders Once Again" (Texas Two). Art director: **E.R. Hickson**. Stunts: **Yakima Canutt**. Sound recording: **Dave S. Stoner**. Producer: **Paul Malvern**.

Not copyrighted. A Lone Star Western, released through Monogram in the U.S.A.: 20 July 1935. No New York opening. U.K. release through Exclusive: November 1936 (sic). 52 minutes.

Alternative title: *PARADISE RANCH*.

SYNOPSIS: On the trail of counterfeiters, a government agent joins a medicine show.

NOTES: This was Wayne's last official Lone Star. In his next film *Westward Ho* — made for Republic — he continued to play the character "John Wyatt".

COMMENT: The last and least interesting of Wayne's Lone Star westerns. True, it has a bit of action but all of it is thoroughly undermined by unimaginative staging and poor direction. A dive by horse and rider over a cliff should have been a highlight, but it is shot from such a pedestrian angle that all the impact of the stunt is lost. There are no running inserts at all, with every chase filmed from uninteresting fixed-angle positions. Even the background scenery is drab and there is no music whatever to generate excitement. The opening chase after the medicine show wagon is ho-hum bland the first time around. But then it is repeated with but a slight variation. The constant cutting between weak sound effects of horses' hooves pounding along and the fuzzy motor roaring is nothing short of irritating. And yet it's given a second run! Incredible!

Yakima Canutt has a major role. He's the chief heavy in fact. But good to see him though it is, he doesn't do any stuntwork to speak of. In fact his fist fights with Wayne are among the weakest and phoniest we've ever seen.

The real star of the film is not Wayne at all. Here he takes a back seat to the voluble, endlessly verbose, uninterruptedly garrulous Earle Hodgins. No wonder Wayne seems somewhat reticent and even lackluster. Miss Burns is a moderately attractive heroine, but the rest of the players are a write-off, particularly Gino Corrado, a most unconvincing Italian-accented Mexican rurale captain, who sports the most ridiculous prop hat imaginable.

I was wrong when I said no music. There are in fact two songs, sung by the Texas Two. It says much for the excitements of the rest of the movie when I say with confidence that these two songs are the most entertaining parts of the whole film.

If *Paradise Canyon* is fair sample of Mr Pierson's work, he is most definitely a director to avoid at all costs.

# Prairie Moon

**Gene Autry** (himself), **Smiley Burnette** (Frog Millhouse), **Shirley Deane** (Peggy Shaw), **William Pawley** (Legs Barton), **Stanley Andrews** (Frank Welch), **Jack Rockwell** (sheriff), **Glenn Strange** (rustler), **Tommy Ryan** (Brains), **Walter Tetley** (Nails), **David Gorcey** (Slick), **Tom London** (Steve), **Warner Richmond** (Mullins), **Bud Osborne** (Pete), **Peter Potter** (band leader), **Ray Bennet** (Hartley), **Hal Price** (policeman), and **Merrill McCormack, Lew Meehan, Jack Kirk**, and "Champion".

Director: **RALPH STAUB**. Original screenplay: **Betty Burbridge, Stanley Roberts**. Photography: **William Nobles**. Film editor: **Lester Orlebeck**. Music director: **Raoul Kraushaar**. Songs: "Girl in the Middle of My Heart" (Autry), "Trigger Joe" (Burnette), "Welcome Strangers" — all by **Eddie Cherkose** and **W. Kent**; "Rhythm of the Hoofbeats" (Autry) by **Johnny Marvin**; "The West a Nest and You" (Autry) by **Yoell** and **Hill**. Production manager: **Al Wilson**. RCA Sound System. Associate producer: **Harry Grey**. Executive producer: **Herbert J. Yates**.

Copyright 7 October 1938 by Republic Pictures Corp. No recorded New York opening. U.S. release dates: 25 September, 8 October, 19 October 1938. U.K. release through British Lion. Never theatrically released in Australia. 6 reels. 58 minutes.

SYNOPSIS: Three tough city kids are left a ranch when their father dies. Autry is the foreman of the ranch and assumes custody of the budding junior hoodlums. The plot utilizes a background of cattle rustling for Autry to teach the neophyte toughs the difference between right and wrong.

NOTES: Number 27 of Autry's 94 movies.

COMMENT: The title has nothing whatever to do with the plot. Dying criminal asks Gene Autry to look after his three boys. The lads, however, fall in with the local cattle rustler... The credit of direction by Ralph Staub doesn't augur any too well (he also directed another Autry vehicle *Western Jamboree*) though one must admit that the direction here is competent, though the pace is rather slow and Staub is careful not to break into or break up any of the musical numbers including quite a long all-music stretch at the local square dance. There are a few running inserts and some tracking shots though many of the angles, even in the action sequences (which include some terrific stunt work and Gene galloping after a runaway carriage, a standard feature of just about all his films) are stationary, or panning shots from fixed camera positions. Also Stanley Andrews does not make a particularly colorful villain, while ace villain William Pawley is restricted to a small and unimportant role as his deputy-stooge. Still, nice to see Tom London and Bud Osborne as a couple of bushwackers and Jack Rockwell as the sheriff. The boys are given exaggerated gangster clichés by way of dialogue — probably the scriptwriters were deliberately aiming at parody, but unfortunately the lads under Mr Staub's heavy-handed direction play it perfectly straight. The heroine has but a small and unimportant part — she exists mainly to feed lines to Autry though she also serves as the butt of some of the comedy. Mr Burnette has a sizable role with much elemental slapstick. Production values are better-than-average by "B" western standards, the photography is not as flat as in many of the Autry westerns and there is some lively background music under the location-filled action scenes.

# Public Cowboy Number One

**Gene Autry** (Gene Autry), **Smiley Burnette** (Frog Millhouse), **Ann Rutherford** (Helen Morgan), **William Farnum** (Sheriff Matt Doniphon), **James C. Morton** (Eustace Quackenbush), **Frank LaRue** (Justice), **Maston Williams** (Thad Slaughter), **Arthur Loft** (Jack Shannon), **Frankie Marvin** (Stubby), **House Peters, Jr** (Jim Shannon), **Milburn Morante** (Ezra), **King Mojave** (Steve), **Hal Price** (Bidwell), **Jack Ingram** (Larry), **Ray Bennett** (Collins, pilot), **Frank Ellis, George Plumes** (townsmen), **James Mason** (henchman), **Douglas Evans** (radio announcer), **Bob Burns** (extra), and "Champion".

Director: **JOSEPH KANE**. Supervising film editor: **Murray Seldeen**. Screenplay by **Oliver Drake** based on a story by **Bernard McConville**. Camera: **Jack Marta**. Editors: **Lester Orlebeck** and **George Reid**. Songs: "Wanderers of the Waste Land", "The West Ain't What It Used to Be", "I Picked up the Trail", "Heebie Jeebie Blues", "Defective Detective from Brooklyn" and "Old Buckaroo". Songs by: **Felix Bernard, Paul Francis Webster, Oliver Drake** and **Fleming Allen**. "Old Buckaroo" by **Johnny Marvin** and **Gene Autry**. Music director: **Raoul Kraushaar**. Sound recording: **Terry Kellum**. RCA Sound System. Associate producer: **Solomon C. Siegel**. Executive producer: **Herbert J. Yates**.

Copyright 23 August 1937 by Republic Pictures Corp. No recorded New York opening. U.S. release: 23 August 1937. U.K. release through British Lion. Australian release through British Empire Films: 18 May 1939. 6 reels. 60 minutes.

SYNOPSIS: The movie opens with a sequence showing big city crooks bringing modern cattle rustling techniques to the prairies. In a scene that must have seemed then like a sophisticated James Bond caper, we see rustlers operating a mobile slaughter house. A plane spots the herd and radios its location to trucks hauling men and horses. Riders quickly round up the cattle and butchers clout them over the head as they come through a chute. They remove their hides, quarter them and load the beef aboard refrigerated trucks for shipping to a packing house. Then, it's a quick fadeout before Sheriff Matt Doniphon (William Farnum) and Gene Autry, his first deputy, come to the scene.

The slick operation has brought mounting headaches to the sheriff. The raids, combined with a rancher's killing, have brought a storm of protests. Headlines in the *Prairie County Courier* blare: "Rustlers Strike Again. Another Herd Vanishes Overnight." "Reign of Terror Sweeps Prairie County." "Sheriff Doniphon No Match for Modern Rustlers."

Newspaper editor Helen Morgan (Ann Rutherford) thinks the sheriff's oldtime methods are outmoded. She is campaigning to have him ousted.

NOTES: Autry's 20th of his 94 movies.

COMMENT: Kane's 21st film as a director, but he was still young enough here to experiment a bit with the camera, what with whip pans, running inserts, diagonal angles, dollying-back shots, even a combination whip pan and running insert. True a lot of his direction is expectedly routine and some of it is even a bit rough around the edges, but overall it has a vigor lacking in his later more polished (if still thoroughly routine) efforts.

Fortunately the accent is firmly on action in this *Public Cowboy*, though Gene does get to sing four or five songs, including happily "The Old Buckaroo". The budget is high with lots of extras, plus location shooting. Our only complaint is that the long-anticipated big action climax starts off big enough but ends rather tamely.

Autry is as personable and ingratiating as ever, whilst Burnette provides amusing support. Miss Rutherford is much more appealing here than in her childish impressions over at M-G-M's Andy Hardy stables. Silent star William Farnum has a meaty role. Arthur Loft is okay as the villain, James C. Morton equally acceptable as an additional comedy relief.

# Pursued

**Teresa Wright** (Thorley Callum), **Robert Mitchum** (Jeb Rand), **Dame Judith Anderson** (Medora Callum), **Dean Jagger** (Grant Callum), **Alan Hale** (Jake Dingle), **Harry Carey, Jr** (Prentice McComber), **John Rodney** (Adam Callum), **Clifton Young** (the sergeant), **Ernest Severn** (Jeb at age 11), **Charles Bates** (Adam at age 11), **Peggy Miller** (Thorley at age 10), **Norman Jolley, Lane Chandler, Elmer Ellingwood, Jack Montgomery, Ian MacDonald** (the Callums), **Ray Teal** (army captain), **Ian Wolfe** (coroner), **Kathy Jeanne Johnson** (Thor at age 3), **Mickey Little** (Jeb at age 4), **Scotty Hugenberg** (Adam at age 4), **Eddy Waller** (storekeeper), **Russ Clark** (drill master), **Jack Davis** (doctor), **Crane Whitley** (general), **Carl Harbaugh** (bartender), **Lester Dorr** (dealer), **Bill Sundholm, Paul Scardon** (jurymen), **Harry Lamont** (ticket taker), **Erville Alderson** (undertaker), **Sherman Saunders** (square dance caller), **Al Kunde** (minister), **Ben Corbett** (idler), **Charles Miller** (coachman), **Tom Fadden** (preacher), **Virginia Brissac** (preacher's wife), **Ervin Richardson** (Rand), **Louise Volding** (Mrs Callum), **Ed Coffey** (man at hanging), **Mae Marsh** (townswoman).

Director: **RAOUL WALSH**. Original screenplay: **Niven Busch**. Photography: **James Wong Howe**. Film editor: **Christian Nyby**. Music composed by **Max Steiner**, orchestrated by **Murray Cutter**, directed by **Leo F. Forbstein**. Art director: **Ted Smith**. Set decorator: **Jack McConaghy**. Wardrobe: **Leah Rhodes**. Special effects directed by **William McGann**, photographed by **Willard Van Enger**. Make-up: **Perc Westmore**. Dialogue director: **Maurice Murphy**. Assistant director: **Russell Saunders**. Sound recording: **Francis J. Scheid**. RCA Sound System. Producer: **Milton Sperling**. A United States Picture for Warner Bros. Executive producer: **Niven Busch**

Copyright 8 March 1947 by Hemisphere Films, Inc. Presented by Warner Bros. Pictures, Inc. New York opening at the Strand: 7 March 1947. U.S. release: 2 March 1947. U.K. release: 10 November 1947. Australian release: 24 June 1948. 9,020 feet. 102 minutes.

SYNOPSIS: In turn of the century New Mexico, an avenger seeks to kill the last of the Rands.

NOTES: Film debut of John Rodney. He followed up his impressive performance here with an unimportant part in *Key Largo*; and that was followed by *Fighter Squadron* (1948). Which is all I have for his career.
   Locations in Monument Valley.

COMMENT: Fascinating variant on *Wuthering Heights*, superbly photographed, drivingly scored and forcefully directed, with Judith Anderson and surprisingly Dean Jagger and newcomer John Rodney giving forceful portrayals. Mitchum and Teresa Wright are also well cast and directed, with excellent cameos by Alan Hale and Harry Carey Jr. Walsh makes marvelous use both of his broadly scenic natural locations (in awesomely mountainous and rimrock country) and his realistic backlot sets. The action set-pieces are superlatively staged. Impossible to forget such sequences as the rifle ambush from the ridge and the shoot-out with Harry Carey Jr (one of his most unforgettable portraits). Jagger is grippingly malicious as the vengeful Grant Callum, while Judith Anderson's strong portrait is likewise unforgettable. One of Steiner's most appropriately aggressive scores.
   One of the first of the so-called psychological westerns — and one of the most suspensefully written and directed and spellbindingly produced.

# Rawhide

**Smith Ballew** (Larry Kimball), **Lou Gehrig** (himself), **Evalyn Knapp** (Peggy Gehrig), **Arthur Loft** (Ed Saunders), **Carl Stockdale** (Bascomb), **Si Jenks** (Pop Mason), **Cy Kendall** (Sheriff Kale), **Lafe McKee** (McDonnell), **Dick Curtis** (Butch), **Cecil Kellogg** (Gillam), **Slim Whitaker** (Biff), **Tom Foreman** (Rudy), **Cliff Parkinson** (Pete), **Harry Tenbrook** (Rusty), **Lee Shumway** (Johnson), **Ed Cassidy** (Fuller), **Al Hill**.

Director: **RAY TAYLOR**. Screenplay: **Jack Natteford, Dan Jarrett**. Original story: **Dan Jarrett**. Photography: **Allen Q. Thompson**. Film editor: **Robert C. Crandall**. Music supervisor: **Michael Breen**. Songs: "When a Cowboy Goes to Town" by **Albert von Tilzer** and **Eddie Grant**; "A Cowboy's Life" by **Charles Rosoff** and **Eddie Cherkose**; "Drifting" by **Albert von Tilzer** and **Harry MacPherson**; "That Old

Washboard Band" by **Norman Phelps** and **Willie Phelps**. Art director: **Lewis J. Rachmil**. Lou Gehrig appears by arrangement with **Christy Walsh**. Assistant director: **V. O. Smith**. Sound recording: **Tom Carmen**. RCA Sound System. Producer: **Sol Lesser**. Print under review presented by **Gordon W. Hedwig**.

Copyright 8 April 1938 by Principal Productions, Inc. New York opening at the Globe: 24 April 1938. Released through 20th Century-Fox: 8 April 1938. Australian release: 16 June 1938. 6 reels. 59 minutes.

SYNOPSIS: Baseball star buys a ranch.

COMMENT: In his first and only Hollywood feature, baseball legend Lou Gehrig (later to be immortalized by Gary Cooper in *Pride of the Yankees*) understudies the now-forgotten Smith Ballew, a popular singer of the time, who made five "B" westerns for Fox (this is the fourth) in the late 1930s. Although Ballew displays a pleasant voice and personality in the main role, all eyes are on Gehrig in support., He handles himself with a professional finesse (all sports people are actors after all), exhibiting enough individual charisma to lend credence to the assumption that he would have successfully made the transition from sports star to popular character actor had he lived. Although he's allowed only two opportunities to show off his baseball prowess, it's hard to take a great deal of interest in the other players. True, Miss Knapp is an attractive enough heroine, whilst villain Loft does a lot of gabbing and henchman Curtis makes with the scowls. And it's good to see Cy Kendall as the crooked sheriff and Lafe McKee the upright McDonnell. But neither the other actors nor the play (routine in its plot but allowing for a fair amount of location action — some obviously stock) are the thing in this *Rawhide*.

# Red River

**John Wayne** (Tom Dunson), **Montgomery Clift** (Matthew Garth), **Joanne Dru** (Tess Millay), **Walter Brennan** (Groot Nadine), **Coleen Gray** (Fen), **John Ireland** (Cherry Valance), **Noah Beery, Jr** (Buster McGee), **Harry Carey, Sr** (Millville), **Harry Carey, Jr** (Dan Latimer), **Paul Fix** (Teeler Yacy), **Mickey Kuhn** (Matt as a boy), **Chief Yowlachie** (Quo), **Ivan Parry** (Bunk Kenneally), **Ray Hyke** (Walt Jergens), **Hank Worden** (Simms), **Dan White** (Laredo), **Paul Fiero** (Fernandez), **William Self** (wounded wrangler), **Hal Taliaferro** (Old Leather), **Tom Tyler** (a quitter), **Lane Chandler** (colonel), **Glenn Strange** (Naylor), **Shelley Winters** (dance-hall girl), **Lee Phelps, George Lloyd** (gamblers).

Director: **HOWARD HAWKS**. Second unit director: **Arthur Rosson**. Screenplay: **Borden Chase, Charles Schnee**, from the *Saturday Evening Post* story *Blazing Guns on the Chisholm Trail*, by **Borden Chase**. Cinematographer: **Russell Harlan**. Art director: **John Datu Arensma**. Film editor: **Christian Nyby**. Special effects: **Don Steward**. Special photographic effects: **Allan Thompson**. Music composed and directed by **Dimitri Tiomkin**. Song, "Settle Down", by **Dimitri Tiomkin**. Make-up: **Lee Greenway**. Production manager: **Norman Cook**. Assistant director: **William McGarry**. Sound recording: **Richard DeWeese**. Music recording: **Vinton Vernon**. Western Electric Sound System. Producer: **Howard Hawks**. Executive producer: **Charles K. Feldman**.

Copyright 17 September 1948 by Monterey Productions. Released through United Artists. New York opening at the Capitol: 30 September 1948. U.S. release: 17 September 1948. U.K. release: 17 January 1949. Australian release: 28 April 1949. 11,701 feet. 130 minutes.

SYNOPSIS: A big-time Texas rancher falls out with his adopted son on their first cattle drive along the Chisholm Trail.

NOTES: The full 130-minutes version was shown only in Australia. Elsewhere the film was cut by five minutes. Needless to say, it is the cut version that now plays on worldwide TV (including Australia).

Nominated for Academy Awards for Best Story, Borden Chase (who lost to *The Search*); and Best Film Editing, Christian Nyby (who lost to *The Naked City*).

Negative cost: approximately $2.5 million. Initial domestic gross: approximately $4 million.

Film debut of Montgomery Clift.

Location scenes: Elgin, Arizona.

COMMENT: Despite its so-called "classic" status, *Red River* doesn't hold up too well. The cattle stampede is poorly and clumsily motivated (it's obvious that Harry Carey Jr is a goner because he has this scene right before in which he tells John Wayne how he is going to spend the money he will earn buying a nice piece of land), no chuck wagon would be loaded up with so many rattly pots and pans and nobody bothers to go to the cowhand's assistance, they just sit there and wait for the cattle to get thoroughly spooked. And then the stampede itself has obviously been culled from stock footage which lessens its effectiveness considerably. Later on there are some spectacular scenes with the cattle genuinely fording a genuine river with genuine actors from this film and then crossing the railroad to enter the town of Abilene but the long-awaited climax (with Wayne's double doing a header into the chuck wagon) is a fizzer with the John Ireland character disposed of in seconds and then the fight abruptly broken up just as it has got started. Altogether the proportion of talk to action is disproportionately high. There's far too much empty talk and Walter Brennan giving another of his garrulous character studies is by far the worst offender. Oddly enough, John Wayne, the epitome of the strong, silent, action-speaks-louder type, is almost as talkative, while the scriptwriters turn Joanne Dru into a positive chatterbox. Even Montgomery Clift tends to have too much to say. John Ireland handles himself and his dialogue well but as his part doesn't amount to anything... Photographer Harold Rosson has a field day with his real locations, though studio inserts against a process screen are very obvious and Tiomkin has contributed an exciting, choral score. With Hank Worden and the two Harry Careys in the cast, not to mention Wayne himself, it's almost a John Ford picture, but director Howard Hawks with his monotonous eye-level compositions is a long way from the visual richness and nostalgic fervor of the Old West of the master. Still at half the length and with half our expectations, it would be fairly entertaining. And the photography, impressive though it sometimes is, cannot compete with Russell Harlan's work on some of the Hoppy pictures.

OTHER VIEWS: Pretty good, though it has its faults. Offsetting the sweep and vigor of the 2nd unit work are Hawks' own dull, eye-level handling of the studio scenes and Walter Brennan's garrulously over-familiar study of a crusty old side-kick. And the climax itself, despite the effectively casual dismissal of John Ireland, is a mite disappointing after that beautifully elaborate build-up.

— C.F.

Most people are going to enjoy this film. The story builds up well with some wonderful action set-pieces and montages, even though it could certainly benefit from further trimming. Coleen Gray making too much of her one scene would be twice as effective at half the length; and as for Joanne Dru, she doesn't belong in the film at all. True, she makes an extremely late entrance, but the story got along quite effectively without her. All she does is slow the pace and dissipate most of the tension. Mind you, the plot has some gaping holes. For instance, Wayne claims he's too poor to buy some sacks of flour and few pounds of beans, yet he has no trouble engaging a band of badmen and buying them ammunition! And what a neat co-incidence that one of the pursuing Indians was wearing that charm bracelet that belonged — of course — to Wayne's mother! Wayne is his usual ruggedly roughshod self, Clift is less neurotic than usual, Brennan minus more teeth is more talkative than ever and even has an off-camera commentary as well! A fascinating assembly of support players includes the Careys, father and son (though the two never meet), Tom Tyler (briefly glimpsed), Paul Fix as a whinger saved from a hanging and Chief Yowlachie surprisingly amusing as a comic relief assistant cook and bottlewasher!

— G.A.

# Ride 'Em Cowboy

**Bud Abbott** (Duke), **Lou Costello** (Willoughby), **Anne Gwynne** (Anne Shaw), **Samuel S. Hinds** (Sam Shaw), **Dick Foran** (Robert "Bronco Bob" Mitchell), **Richard Lane** (Peter Conway), **Judd McMichael** (Tom), **Ted McMichael** (Dick), **Joe McMichael** (Harry), **Mary Lou Cook** (Dotty Davis), **Johnny Mack Brown** (Alabam), **Ella Fitzgerald** (Ruby), **Douglass Dumbrille** (Jake Rainwater), **Jody Gilbert** (Moonbeam), **Morris Ankrum** (Ace Anderson), **Charles Lane** (Martin Manning), **Russell Hicks, Tom Hanlon** (announcers), **Wade Boteler** (rodeo manager), **James Flavin** (railroad detective), **Boyd Davis** (doctor), **Eddie Dunn** (2nd detective), **Isabel Randolph** (lady), **James Seay** (ranger captain), **Harold Daniels** (reporter), **Ralph Peters** (1st henchman), **Linda Brent** (Sunbeam), **Lee Sunrise** (2nd Indian girl), **Chief Yowlachie** (Chief Tomahawk), **Harry Monty** (midget), **Sherman E. Sanders** (square dance caller), **Carmela Cansino** (1st Indian girl), **The Hi-Hatters, The Buckaroos Band, The Ranger Chorus of Forty, The Congoroos with Dorothy Dandridge** (themselves), **Harry Cording** (poker tough), **Bob Blake**.

Director: **ARTHUR LUBIN**. Screenplay: **True Boardman, John Grant**. Adapted by **Harold Shumate** from an original story by **Edmund L. Hartmann**. Photography: **John W. Boyle**. Film editor: **Philip Cahn**. Art directors: **Jack Otterson, Ralph M. DeLacy**. Set decorator: **Russell A. Gausman**. Gowns: **Vera West**. Dialogue director: **Joan**

**Hathaway**. Songs: "A-Tisket A-Tasket" (Fitzgerald) by **Ella Fitzgerald, Al Feldman**; "I'll Remember April" (Foran, chorus) by **Don Raye, Gene De Paul, Patricia Johnston**; "Give Me My Saddle" (Foran), "Beside the Rio Tonto Shore" (McMichael Brothers, Cook), "Wake Up Jacob" (McMichael Brothers, Cook), "Rockin' and Reelin'" (McMichael Brothers, Cook, Fitzgerald), "Ride 'Em Cowboy" (Foran, McMichael Brothers, Cook, chorus), "Cow Boogie" — all by **Don Raye** and **Gene De Paul**. Musical numbers staged by **Nick Castle**. Music supervisor: **Ted Cain**. Music director: **Charles Previn**. Music score: **Frank Skinner**. Still photos: **Roman Freulich**. Assistant director: **Gil Valle**. Sound supervisor: **Bernard B. Brown**. Sound technician: **Hal Bumbaugh**. Western Electric Sound System. Associate producer: **Alex Gottlieb**.

Copyright 4 December 1941 by Universal Pictures Co., Inc. New York opening at Loew's Criterion: 4 March 1942. U.S. release: 13 February 1942. Australian release: 24 September 1942. 7,859 feet. 87 minutes.

SYNOPSIS: An author of dime-novel westerns who pretends to be a real cowboy is in danger of being exposed as a fake. So he books himself into a dude ranch in Arizona to learn about the real thing. A pretty cowgirl whom he bumps into at a rodeo has something to do with this decision. On arrival at the Lazy S, however, he discovers he has a rival for the lady's affections. Matters are further complicated by the town gambler who kidnaps the ranch foreman in order to prevent him competing in the local rodeo.

COMMENT: As can be seen from the above Synopsis, there is enough material even in this bald outline of the straight story to sustain interest, especially when that story is fleshed out with so many musical numbers. Some of these are very elaborately staged too, especially the rousing title tune and the memorable romantic ballad "I'll Remember April". There would seem little room for Abbott and Costello — but there you would be wrong. The comedians get up to all their usual tricks of elemental slapstick and verbal punning, even though their plot runs parallel to the main action. Except for a brief meeting at the climax, their lines rarely cross. In fact, aside from this brief bit, I don't think the comics have a single scene with the hero. (I've seen a publicity still from the "Crazy House" sequence with Foran and Gwynne sharing the scene with Costello, but this snip is not in the actual film).

All the same, this is one of the better Abbott and Costello vehicles. For once, the songs are rather good and they are presented in a smooth, polished fashion by director Arthur Lubin and cinematographer John Boyle. The boys are in their usual form, whether playing poker ("Ante up!" — "What?" — "Where's your ante?" — "She's with my uncle." — "No! Feed the kitty!" — "Here, puss, puss.") or milking cows ("Put the bucket under the udder." — "The other what?") and there is a good triple climax with the boys pursued by Indians, and those stalwarts of the western "B", Foran and Brown, chased by Hopalong Cassidy villain Morris Ankrum. The business with Dumbrille as a wooden Indian and the following dream sequence are pretty tedious and unimaginative (except for one good joke: *"Do you want your palm red?"*). Miss Gwynne is a most fetching heroine.

OTHER VIEWS: Beautifully photographed and directed with some element of visual style — particularly in its spectacular action climax which incorporates some good stunts excitingly filmed with running inserts on actual locations (though process screen inserts and equally obvious undercranking don't help). Dick Foran gets to sing a couple of songs, including the beautiful melody "I'll Remember April", as well as joining a jostling parade for the rousing title tune (reminds us of *Rio Rita*). Anne Gwynne makes an attractively personable heroine and is effectively doubled for her stunts. The agreeable Johnny Mack Brown is also on hand. Helping out with the singing chores are the wonderful Ella Fitzgerald and the so-called Merry Macs. The support players headed by Richard Lane, Douglass Dumbrille and Samuel S. Hinds include a number of our firm favorites. The movie is colorful, very slickly produced and often most effectively staged. The script on which the musical numbers are pegged is pleasantly light, the songs themselves are appealing, the players ingratiating. The only thing mostly missing is fun. Abbott and Costello are a couple of damp squibs. Their material is a wet blanket of tired slapstick and verbal bullying. Not only are their puns weak and unfunny, but their gauche, unstylish slapstick fails to strike even the mildest of sparks. Worse, obvious doubles and stuntmen substitute for the oafish comics whenever there's any real work to be done, as in the bronco-busting sequence.

— G.A.

# Riders of Black River

**Charles Starrett** (Wade Patterson), **Iris Meredith** (Linda Holden), **Dick Curtis** (Blaze Carewe), **Stanley Brown** (Terry Holden), **Bob Nolan** (Bob), **Francis Sayles** (Doc Greene), **Edmund Cobb** (Colt Foster), **Forrest Taylor** (Sheriff Dave Patterson), **George Chesebro** (ranch hand), **Carl Olin Francis** (Whit Kane), **Lew Meehan** (rustler), **Maston Williams** (Ed Gills), **Carl Sepulveda** (Rip), **Ethan Allen** (Joel Matthews), **The Sons of the Pioneers** including **Pat Brady, Hugh Farr, Karl Farr, Lloyd Perryman, Tim Spencer** (themselves), **Alfred P. James** (storekeeper), **Buck Connors** (Winters) and **Clem Horton**.

Director: **NORMAN DEMING**. Screenplay: **Bennett R. Cohen**. Based on the 1935 screenplay *The Revenge Rider* by **Ford Beebe**. Photography: **George Meehan**. Film editor: **William Lyon**. Incidental music: **Lew Porter**. Songs by **Bob Nolan** and **Tim Spencer**. Assistant director: **Milton Carter**. Producer: **Harry L. Decker**. Executive producer: **Irving Briskin**.

Copyright 31 August 1939 by Columbia Pictures Corp. No recorded New York opening. U.S. release: 23 August 1939. 6 reels. 59 minutes.

SYNOPSIS: An ex-Texas Ranger defeats rustlers on his girlfriend's ranch.

NOTES: A remake of *The Revenge Rider* (1935) which starred Tim McCoy.

COMMENT: A very interesting and agreeable western. The Sons of the Pioneers are always welcome and here they are in top-notch form. Their songs are very pleasing and they also contribute to the action as well as providing some gentle comic relief — full marks to the scriptwriter and director for exploiting their talents so well. It is interesting that the director uses these songs exclusively throughout the film and does not employ any other music at all. In fact, there is no background music as such, not even under the front and end titles. Instead, there is a startlingly effective use of sound effects: the rustle of a piece of paper, the click of a latch, the whittling of a piece of wood, fingers drumming on a table, a group of hoofbeats moving off followed by those of a lone rider. In conjunction with this, the director frequently has the characters doing bits of business, and he uses close-ups most effectively. The action scenes are well-staged, and surprisingly, no doubles are used, even in the climactic fist fight in a burning cabin. Charles Starrett and Iris Meredith turn in their usual capable portrayals, Dick Curtis makes splendid work of the villain (with delightfully dour-faced Eddie Cobb along in his usual type-casting as a loyal henchman), while Stanley Brown gives an excellent impersonation of a wavering gang member. George Meehan's photography (with an assist from the laboratory) has a bright, dusty haze that is atmospherically in character. The screenplay has interesting dialogue and entertaining plot twists, though it is a bit short of on-camera action. All in all, a commendable effort.

# Riders of Destiny

**John Wayne** (Singin' Sandy Saunders), **Cecilia Parker** (Fay Denton), **George "Gabby" Hayes** (Sheriff Denton), **Forrest Taylor** (James Kincaid), **Al "Fuzzy" St John** (Bert), **Heinie Conklin** (Pete, stage driver), **Earl Dwire** (Slip Morgan), **Lafe McKee** (Sheriff Bill Baxter), **Fern Emmett** (farm woman), **Addie Foster** (wife), **Yakima Canutt** (henchman), **Silver Tip Baker, Hal Price** (townsmen), **Si Jenks** (farm man), **Horace B.Carpenter, William Dyer, Bert Lindley** (ranchers), **Yakima Canutt** (stunt double for John Wayne), and "Duke" (the devil horse).

Director: **ROBERT N. BRADBURY**. Original story and screenplay: **Robert N. Bradbury**. Photography: **Archie Stout**. Film editor: **Carl Pierson**. Art director: **E.R. Hickson**. Sound recording: **Glenn Rominger, John A. Stransky Jr**. Balsley & Phillips Sound System. Producer: **Paul Malvern**. A Lone Star Western.

Copyright 22 January 1934 by Monogram Pictures Corp. Presented by Lone Star Productions. No New York opening. U.S. release: 10 October 1933 (sic). U.K. release through Pathe: 16 July 1934. 6 reels. 58 minutes.

SYNOPSIS: Undercover government agent helps ranchers get their rightful water rights.

NOTES: Wayne's first of sixteen Lone Star westerns. Negative costs rarely exceeded $12,000 on a shooting schedule of less than a week.

COMMENT: The first of the Lone Stars starts off on a distinctly wrong track by attempting to pass John Wayne off as a singing troubadour. Mouthing to the somewhat inappropriate voice of Smith Ballew, Wayne "sings" two songs. We like the one about "There'll be blood a-runnin' in town before night. There'll be guns a-blazin; and singin' with lead. Tonight you'll be drinkin' your drinks with the dead." Wayne seems definitely uncomfortable in this warbling role, but fortunately is obviously much more at ease in the action spots, especially when doubled by Yakima Canutt. In addition to doubling Wayne and general stunting (he performs a fine quota of spectacular falls and leaps), Canutt has a minor genuine on-screen role as one of the villain's henchmen, though he disappears from view at an early stage. G."G". Hayes, on the other hand, has a major part, doing a variant on his famous "Gabby" characterization. Heroine Cecilia Parker is a lovely girl, but though appealingly photographed, her acting is so amateurish it's a miracle she survived to be re-born as Andy Hardy's sister. Normally respectable Forrest Taylor has an off-beat role as the heavy, with Heinie Conklin of all people as a pratfalling henchman. Wayne himself is reasonably personable. There's enough action to satisfy the fans ("Make it fast, Slippery. This is your last draw!"), and for once the background locations are not drably uninteresting. Bradbury's direction is competent, though his fondness for whip pans as a scene-changing device will make the movie seem even more dated and old-hat to 1994 viewers.

# Riding Shotgun

**Randolph Scott** (Larry Delong), **Wayne Morris** (Tub Murphy), **Joan Weldon** (Orissa Flynn), **Joe Sawyer** (Tom Biggert), **James Millican** (Dan Marady), **Charles Buchinsky [Charles Bronson]** (Pinto), **James Bell** (Doc Winkler), **Fritz Feld** (Fritz) **Richard Garrick** (Walters), **Victor Perrin** (Bar-M rider), **John Baer** (Hughes), **William Johnstone** (Colonel Flynn), **Kem Dibbs** (Ben), **Alvin Freeman** (Johnny), **Ned Young** (Manning), **Paul Picerni** (Bob Purdee), **Jay Lawrence** (Lewellyn), **Jack Woody** (Hardpan), **Richard Benjamin** (Blackie), **Boyd Red Morgan** (Red), **Mary Lou Holloway** (Cynthia Biggert), **Lonnie Pierce** (Ellie), **Dub Taylor** (Eddie), **Evan Lowe, Holly Brooke** (dance hall girls), **Allegra Varron** (Mrs Fritz), **Frank Ferguson** (helpful townsman), **Edward Coch Jr** (Pablo), **Frosty Royse** (outlaw), **Jimmy Mobley** (Petey), **Ruth Whitney** (Petey's mother), **Joe Brockman, Clem Fuller, Bud Osborne** (townsmen), **Budd Buster, Dick Dickinson, Buddy Roosevelt** (men), **Harry Hines** (Cooky), **Morgan Brown, Bob Stephenson** (card players), **Mira McKinney** (townswoman), **Merry Townsend** (younger woman), **Phil Chambers** (Abel), **Maura Murphy** (Mrs Purdee), **George Ross** (Lam), **Ray Bennett** (man), **Jack Kenney** (Sam), **Opan Evard**.

Director: **ANDRE DE TOTH**. Screenplay: **TOM BLACKBURN**. Based upon the story "Riding Solo" by **Kenneth Perkins**. Photographed in WarnerColor by **Bert Glennon**. Film editor: **Rudi Fehr**. Art director: **Edward Carrere**. Set decorator: **Benjamin S. Bone**. Make-up: **Gordon Bau**. Music: **David Buttolph**, orchestrated by **Maurice de Packh**. Assistant director: **James McMahon**. Sound recording: **C.A. Riggs**. RCA Sound System. Producer: **Ted Sherdeman**.

Copyright 1954 by Warner Bros. Pictures, Inc. New York opening at the Holiday: 1 April 1954. U.S. release: 10 April 1954. U.K. release (on the lower half of a double bill): 29 November 1954. Australian release: 3 June 1955. Sydney opening at the Palace (ran two weeks). 6,701 feet. 74 minutes.

SYNOPSIS: Shotgun guard finally crosses paths with the killer he is hunting.

COMMENT: From its very opening shot as the camera pans from right to left with Scott riding shotgun on the stagecoach and Millican enters from the right literally crossing the path towards the camera as Scott says these very words on the sound track, we know we are in for an extremely stylish and exciting western. Not only is de Toth a master of the panning shot, but every scene is beautifully, electrically composed. To add to de Toth's and Glennon's exercises of skill, *Riding Shotgun* was made at a time when many cinemas were experimenting with widescreen projection. *Riding Shotgun* is one of a mere handful of movies that look dramatic in either format. Most directors and cameramen compose for widescreen by simply leaving a lot of waste space at the top of the frame. Some even carelessly bung the microphone boom or its shadow into this space, not realizing that in theatres unequipped for widescreen, audiences will have their illusions momentarily shattered. De Toth and Glennon not only don't fall into this error, but compose every shot with both scrupulous care and flair.

And what a wonderful group of players they have at their disposal for this tautly exciting script! Richard Garrick gives the best performance of his career as an excitable, meddling old town leader, while many critics say the same for Wayne Morris who has a character role as a gluttonous deputy. Ditto Fritz Feld who abandons his mouth-popping trademark to play a slovenly, money-grubbing old innkeeper whose pride and joy is a small panelled mirror that hangs over his scungy bar. James Millican is also most impressive as the ruthless heavy, while the charming Joan Weldon has likewise an indelible role. And not to forget Scott himself who is perfect as the harassed gunman whose story no-one believes.

The script's tension is partly derived from its insistence on the Greek unities of one story, one setting and one period of steadily progressing time. No flashbacks are used, Scott filling us in with an effective behind-the-camera commentary as the story builds to its inevitable climactic showdown. The action spots are as vigorously directed as the dialogue scenes, with some excellent stuntwork.

Incidentally, Charles Bronson fans will have no trouble identifying their hero in this one, as he has a meaty part, including a pre-fade-out encounter with Scott and Jimmy Mobley.

The script has a fair amount of humor and even a few satiric thrusts which adds to rather than undermines the overall suspense.

Although the movie has now taken its place as a cult western and is now widely regarded as one of the best of Scott's movies, it was not so judged in its time. With the exception of the Sydney critics who for once were surprisingly perceptive in recognizing the film's unusually dramatic and outstanding entertainment qualities, most comments ranged from lukewarm to dismissive. Public response was similarly indifferent. In the United Kingdom, *Riding Shotgun* played on the lower half of a double bill.

Amazing! Here was a whole group of players — Morris, Weldon, Millican, Feld, Garrick, Baer — giving the performances of their lives, plus others at their best or near-best, in a tightly-written, neatly directed, imaginatively photographed, super suspenseful story, yet very few people recognized those facts back in 1954. I am glad at least that I was one of those few pioneers. Forty years later, my enthusiasm for *Riding Shotgun* is undimmed.

# Rio Rita

**Bud Abbott** (Doc), **Lou Costello** (Wishy), **Kathryn Grayson** (Rita Winslow), **John Carroll** (Ricardo Montera), **Patricia Dane** (Lucille Brunswick), **Tom Conway** (Maurice Craindall), **Peter Whitney** (Jake), **Arthur Space** (Trask), **Joan Valerie** (Dotty), **Dick**

**Rich** (Gus), **Barry Nelson** (Harry Gantley), **Eva Puig** (Marianna), **Mitchell Lewis** (Julio), **Eros Volusia** (dancer), **Julian Rivero** (Mexican gent), **Douglass Newland** (control man), **Lee Murray** (little Mexican), **Inez Cooper** (Pulque), **Frank Perry** (chef), **Violet Kane** (girl 3), **Barbara Simmons** (girl 4), **Marjorie Dean** (girl 5), **Roberta Anderson** (girl 6), **Barbara Coleman** (girl 7).

Director: **S. SYLVAN SIMON**. Screenplay: **Richard Connell, Gladys Lehman**. Special comedy material for Abbott & Costello: **John Grant**. Based on the Broadway musical (opened 2 February 1927, produced by Florenz Ziegfeld) by **Guy Bolton** and **Fred Thompson**. Photography: **George Folsey**. Film editor: **Ben Lewis**. Songs: "Long Before You Came Along" (Grayson, Carroll) by **E.Y. Harburg** (lyrics) and **Harold Arlen** (music); "The Ranger's Song" (sic) (Carroll, Grayson and male chorus) by **Joseph McCarthy** (lyrics) and **Harry Tierney** (music); "Rio Rita" (Carroll) by **Joseph McCarthy** (lyrics) and **Harry Tierney** (music); "Brazilian Dance" (Volusia) by **Nilo Barnett**; "Ora O Conga" (Grayson) by **Lacerdo**. Music director: **Herbert Stothart**. Music orchestrations: **Murray Cutter, Leo Arnaud, Paul Marquard**. Art directors: **Cedric Gibbons, Eddie Imazu**. Set decorator: **Edwin B. Willis**. Gowns: **Kalloch**. Men's wardrobe: **Gile Steele**. Special effects: **Warren Newcombe**. Sound supervisor: **Douglas Shearer**. Western Electric Sound System. Producer: **Pandro S. Berman**.

Copyright 24 March 1942 by Loew's Inc. A Metro-Goldwyn-Mayer picture. New York opening at the Capitol: 7 May 1942. U.S. release: 11 March 1942. Australian release: 31 December 1942. 9 reels. 8,187 feet. 91 minutes.

SYNOPSIS: Nazi 5th columnists attempt to send coded messages on radio broadcasts originating from a dude ranch in Texas.

COMMENT: Abbott and Costello's first film for MGM is nothing if not handsomely photographed. And the boys themselves are in fine form. Their usual gag writer has provided some clever routines involving typical puns, misunderstandings and comebacks, plus a number of slapstick knockabouts which actually come across satisfactorily thanks to deft special effects. The boys also have help from a director with a bit of imagination and sense of camera fluidity. Above all, they are surrounded by a particularly able support cast. True, the principals are not so graciously served by both script and sound recording (though the songs themselves are pleasant enough, and Miss Grayson is attractively photographed), but Tom Conway is menacingly suave, Peter Whitney makes an admirable stooge, whilst stunningly costumed Patricia Dane turns in such an exotically glamorous performance her presence alone elevates *Rio Rita* to a must-see category. She is a great foil for the boys too and is able to stand up to them with both convincing aloofness and involving patronage. Altogether perfect, it's a pity Abbott & Costello failed to realize what a gifted, heaven-sent asset she was to both them and the film and that they didn't employ her subsequently (as the Marx Brothers did with Margaret Dumont).

OTHER VIEWS: I saw a program on Cinematography on television the other night and was amazed that the first photographer one of the interviewees listed as a prime example of artistic craftsmanship was George J. Folsey. He was right up there with Arthur Miller, Charles Lang, William Daniels and James Wong Howe, despite the fact that he never won any prestigious awards (though nominated quite a few times) and that his is hardly a well-known name even among dedicated film buffs. This feast for the eyes is a good example of Folsey's work, even though he was unable or unwilling to disguise some obvious backdrops and glass shots... Despite their hokey words (in a stage show I saw the songs were deliciously sent up, but here of course they are played perfectly straight by the humorlessly wooden Carroll — effecting a phoney accent — and the inexperienced if lovingly photographed Grayson — this was only her second movie after all), the old tunes still thrill the ears. It's an ingenious script device that brings in the Ranger's Song and reprises it for the climax. The staging is rather elaborate too, with pans across both sides of the screen and an editor's nightmare of studio process and real outdoor shots. Mind you, it doesn't quite work, principally because Carroll is so deadly dull... Abbott and Costello indulge us with some typical amusing routines ranging from smart one-liners and clever puns to well-rehearsed slapstick falls and chases. They are obviously both enjoying their work.

# Robbery Under Arms

**Peter Finch** (Captain Starlight), **Ronald Lewis** (Dick Marston), **Maureen Swanson** (Kate Morrison), **David McCallum** (Jim Marston), **Vincent Ball** (George Storefield), **Jill Ireland** (Jean), **Dudy Nimmo** (Eileen), **Jean Anderson** (Ma), **Ursula Finlay** (Grace Storefield), **Johnny Cadell** (Warrigal), **Larry Taylor** (Burke), **Russell Napier** (Green), **Laurence Naismith** (Ben Marston), **Yvonne Buckingham** (saloon girl), **George Cormack** (minister), **Doris Goddard** (Madam Franciana), **Colin Ballantyne** (Runnimal), **S. Scrutton** (auctioneer), **Robert Reardon** (Mullockson), **Sergeant Holmes** (James), **John Hargreaves** (clerk), **Rita Ponsford** (lady in coach), **Billy Pepper** (blacktracker), **Pat Hagan** (Barker), **Ivor Bromley** (Falkland), **Laurie Pumpa** (Moran), **Philippa Morgan** (child's mother), **Edna Morris** (aunt), **Max Wagner** (Goring), **Bartlett Mullins** (Paddy).

Director: **JACK LEE**. Screenplay: **W.P. Lipscomb, Alexander Baron**. Additional scenes: **Richard Mason**. Based on the 1888 novel by **Rolf Boldrewood** (pseudonym of **Thomas Alexander Browne**). Photographed in Eastman Color by **Harry Waxman**. Film editor: **Manuel del Campo**. Art director: **Alex Vetchinsky**. Costumes: **Olga Lehmann**. Make-up: **Robert Lawrence**. Hair styles: **Stella Rivers**. Camera operator: **James Bawden**. Music composed and conducted by **Matyas Seiber**. Set continuity **Marjorie Lavelly**. Location manager: **Ron Whelan**. Locations in the Flinders Ranges, South Australia, and near Bourke, New South Wales. Production manager: **Jack Hanbury**. Production controller for Pinewood Studios: **Arthur Alcott**. Assistant director: **Bert Batt**. Sound editor: **Harry Miller**. Sound recording: **Geoff Daniels, William Daniels**. Producer: **Joseph Janni**. Executive producer: **Earl St John**.

Copyright 1957 by Rank Film Productions Ltd. Made at Pinewood Studios, England and on location in Australia. Presented by J. Arthur Rank. U.S. release through Rank Film Distributors of America: May 1958. No New York opening. U.K. release Rank Film Distributors: 3 November 1957. Australian release through British Empire Films: 12 December 1957. Running times: 104 minutes (Aust), 99 minutes (UK), 83 minutes (USA).

SYNOPSIS: A couple of cattle rustlers attempt to go straight on the goldfields. Their claim is moderately successful, but unfortunately their past catches up with them.

NOTES: Second to *Witness for the Prosecution* as the most popular film released in Australia in 1958.

COMMENT: Although it was a huge commercial success in Australia, *Robbery under Arms* proved nowhere near as powerful as *The Shiralee* at the British boxoffice. U.K. picturegoers seemed to feel that what they were being offered here was little more than a transplanted Western with all the usual stage hold-ups, bank robberies, shoot-outs, attempted lynchings, cattle rustling and extended chases through rugged terrains characteristic of the genre. It is hard to argue against such an assessment. True, the movie is ingratiatingly acted by Finch and company and has been produced on a grand scale. But aside from the scenery and the setting, there is little to differentiate this movie from any of the equally big-budget Hollywood equivalents.

*Robbery under Arms* is very entertaining, has plenty of action, involving characters, fascinating backgrounds and (after a beginning that is a little, just a little on the slow side) moves with suspenseful rapidity. Production values are unstinting and technical credits highly proficient. Jack Lee is not exactly a highly imaginative director but his staging for the most part is skilful and highly competent. He has drawn realistic performances from his players, made impressive use of his locations, and knitted such other elements as photography, music, costumes and sets into a satisfying whole

# Robin Hood of Texas

**Gene Autry** (himself), **Lynne Roberts** (Virginia), **Sterling Holloway** (Droopy), **Adele Mara** (Julie Reeves), **James Cardwell** (Duke Mantel), **John Kellogg** (Nick Castillo), **Ray Walker** (Lacey), **Michael Branden** (Jim Preston), **Paul Bryar** (Ace Foley), **James Flavin** (Captain Danforth), **Dorothy Vaughan** (Mrs O'Brien), **Stanley Andrews** (Hamby), **Alan Bridge** (sheriff), **Bert Dodson, Fred S. Martin, Jerry Scoggins** (Cass County Boys), **Edmund Cobb** (deliveryman), **Hank Patterson** (taxi-driver), **Lester Dorr** (photographer), **Willian Norton Bailey** (motorist), **Irene Mack, Opal Taylor, Eve Novak, Norma Brown, Frankie Marvin, Billy Wilkerson** (guests), **Duke Greene** (Blinky Charleston), and **Ken Terrell, Joe Yrigoyen, Duke Greene** (stuntmen), "Champion Jr" the horse.

Director: **LESLEY SELANDER**. Original screenplay: **John K. Butler, Earle Snell**. Photography: **William Bradford**. Film editor: **Harry Keller**. Art director: **Paul Youngblood**. Set decorators: **John McCarthy Jr, Charles Thompson**. Costumes: **Adele Palmer**. Make-up: **Bob Mark**. Special effects: **Howard Lydecker, Theodore Lydecker**. Music director: **Morton Scott**. Music orchestrations: **Nathan Scott**. Songs: "Goin' Back to Texas", "You're the Moment of a Lifetime", "Merry-Go-Round-Up" (all Autry, backed up by the Cass County Boys), by **Gene Autry, Carson J. Robison, Sergio DeKarlo, Kay Charles**. Assistant director: **Joe Dill**. Sound recording: **Fred Stahl**. RCA Sound System. Associate producer: **Sidney Picker**. Executive producer: **Herbert J. Yates.**

Copyright 15 July 1947 by Republic Pictures Corp. No New York opening. U.S. release: 15 July 1947. U.K. release through British Lion: August 1949 (sic). Australian release through British Empire Films: 1 June 1950. 6,432 feet. 71 minutes.

SYNOPSIS: Autry versus bank robbers.

NOTES: Last of the 57 movies Gene Autry made for Republic.

VIEWER'S GUIDE: This film was given an "A" certificate by the British Board of Film Censors (presumably because of excessive violence). Children were not admitted to cinemas unless accompanied by a responsible adult.

COMMENT: This feeble-minded script has nothing whatever to do with Robin Hood or any modern equivalents of same. It's another contemporary western for the kids with Autry chasing bank bandits in a roadster, though at the climax it must be admitted his double does chase a speeding buckboard on horseback. Much use is made of the process screen in the film's few action spots. Otherwise, there's a bit of desultory singing and lots and lots of brainless talking. The predictable plot wouldn't interest a two-year-old. Autry and the rest of the cast go through their paces in a listless, mechanical manner while Sterling Holloway provides some stereotyped comic relief. Direction is disinterestedly routine, photography flat and other credits merely adequate — well within the limits of the film's obvious "B" budget.

# Robin Hood of the Range

**Charles Starrett** (Steve Marlowe), **Arthur Hunnicutt** (Arkansas), **Kay Harris** (Julie Marlowe), **Kenneth MacDonald** (Henry Marlowe), **Douglass Drake** (Ned Harding), **Hal Price** (sheriff), **Edward Piel, Sr** (Grady), **Frank LaRue** (Carter), **Bud Osborne** (Thompson), **Stanley Brown** (Santana), **Frank McCarroll, Ray Jones, Johnny Bond, Merrill McCormack, The Jimmy Wakely Trio.**

Director: **WILLIAM BERKE**. Original story and screenplay: **Betty Burbridge**. Photography: **Benjamin H. Kline**. Film editor: **Jerome Thoms**. Art directors: **Lionel Banks, Perry Smith**. Set decorator: **James Crowe**. Songs by **Gene Autry, Jimmy Wakely, Dick Heinhart, Johnny Bond**. Producer: **Jack Fier**.

Copyright 29 July 1943 by Columbia Pictures Corp. No New York opening. U.S. release: 29 July 1943. Australian release: 2 November 1944. 6 reels. 5,185 feet. 57 minutes.

SYNOPSIS: Homesteaders battle the railroad company.

NOTES: Starrett's 58th western. Although Starrett starred in *The Durango Kid* back in 1940, the follow-up movie (and the start of the series) did not eventuate until *The Return of the Durango Kid* in 1945.

COMMENT: If you're used to Starrett as the Durango Kid, this movie is a bit of a revelation. The budget, though still firmly in the "B" range, is noticeably higher, and Mr Berke's direction is a cut above such Durango stalwarts as Ray Nazarro and Derwin Abrahams. There's some marvelous photography in this one too, including a number of beautiful outdoor shots and a scene where the camera tracks from the exterior to the interior of a bar, pans to the left, and then reverses. Betty Burbridge's script, however, with its batman-like bandit, its stilted dialogue and its lack of a romantic interest (the heroine is the hero's **sister**) is strictly for six-year-olds. However, there are some pleasant songs.

# Rolling Home

**Jean Porter** (Francis Crawford), **Russell Hayden** (Reverend David Owens), **Raymond Hatton** (Pop Miller), **Pamela Blake** (Pamela Crawford), **Jo Anne Marlowe** (Sandy Crawford), **James Conlin** (Grandpa Crawford), **Robert Dee "Buzz" Henry** (Gary Miller), **Jonathan Hale** (chairman of church board), **Jimmy Dodd** (cowhand), **Harry Carey Jr** (rodeo rider), **Milton Parsons** (Charlie Caine), **Andre Charlot** (doctor), **William Farnum** (rodeo official), **George Tyne** (chauffeur), **Elmo Lincoln** (rodeo rider).

Director: **WILLIAM BERKE**. Screenplay: **Edwin V. Westrate**. Original screen story: **William Berke**. Photography: **Benjamin Kline**. Film editor: **Arthur A. Brooks**. Music score: **Darrell Calker**. Music director: **David Chudnow**. Production manager: **Seymour Roth**. Gowns: **Jeanne Feintuch**. Make-up: **Robert Cowan**. Sound recording: **Hugh McDowell**. RCA Sound System. Song, "The End of the Trail", by **Jimmie Dodds**. Associate producer: **Samuel L. Decker**. Producer: **William Berke**. Executive producer: **Robert L. Lippert**.

Copyright 15 November 1946 by Screen Guild Productions. An Affiliated Productions, Inc. photoplay, released in the U.S. through Screen Guild: 1 November 1946. No New York opening. U.K. release through Exclusive: floating from September 1949 (sic). No Australian release. 7 reels. 71 minutes. Cut to 63 minutes in the U.K.

SYNOPSIS: A very artless story of a parson's fight to raise money for his church. The clergyman, David Owens, is adequately played by Russell Hayden. He looks after an injured horse owned by an old-timer, Pop Miller, and his grandson Gary. Pop learns that David needs funds for his church and also that a Mrs Crawford is in love with him, while he favors a pretty local girl. In the circumstances Mrs Crawford won't help the fund.

VIEWER'S GUIDE: Suitable for all.

COMMENT: I'm not a Raymond Hatton fan. So a film that offers the garrulous Raymond as a third lead — and is directed by William Berke to boot — is hardly likely to inspire my confidence.

However *Rolling Home* is more entertaining than I expected. True, Raymond Hatton certainly rates as aggressively hammy — even more so than usual — but he is removed from the scene halfway through. True too that the ham stakes are then taken over by Jimmy Conlin, who seems unswervingly determined to make an impression, no matter how thin his material. Needless to say, director Berke indulges these two scene-chewers with lots of close-ups.

Another early strike against the film occurs when we discover that Russell Hayden is playing a parson. The presence of Pop's grandson is also not guaranteed to lift our entertainment expectations. Fortunately though, the grandson is played by a quite presentable youngster named "Buzz" Henry. And also by good script fortune, Mr Hayden's ministerial duties do not preclude him from racing and fighting.

And wonder of wonders, Mr Berke lifts his game quite a notch with fairly frequent tracking shots yet, a couple of pans and even two or three attempts to use the dolly. Clumsy attempts, but the thought was there. However, there are plenty of typical Berke effects as well, like ruthlessly mundane camera set-ups, jerky continuity, poorly-matched close-ups (including a confrontation scene between Hayden and Hale which was originally filmed in a two-shot but is now intercut between close-ups obviously blown up in the lab), dull backgrounds, copious quantities of ancient stock footage, and — worst of all — truncated, economically staged and disappointingly ineffective action scenes. It's in these clumsily inept action spots that the budget limitations of the movie are so dramatically defined.

On the credit side, however, it must be admitted that *Rolling Home* does have a certain rustic charm. It's rare for a mainstream Hollywood plot to concern itself with such matters as a new parson's fight with his money-tight church board. And there are a couple of other plot surprises and innovations as well.

*Rolling Home* also benefits from its interesting cast. The lead Jean Parker (the heroine of *Sequoia* and *Texas Rangers*), here plays a villain — and she acts it out most convincingly too.

We've already commended young "Buzz" Henry. Hayden, Blake and Marlowe are adequate enough, though Marlowe is maybe too Hollywood a sprat. But it's fascinating to see people like Jimmy Dodd, Harry Carey Jr, Andre Charlot (his voice seems to be dubbed — or maybe that's his real accent), Milton Parsons, William Farnum and Elmo Lincoln in such small roles.

Whether you agree that this movie's acting virtues overcome its many faults, you must admit *Rolling Home* is a definite curiosity.

OTHER VIEWS: It's certainly odd to find the demure Jean Parker — still looking mighty youthful and appealingly svelte — essaying a forceful character role as a small-town meanie. It's as if Audrey Hepburn has suddenly decided to play the wicked step-mother in *Cinderella*. Without the character's usual heavy make-up. But with **her** usual grace and finesse.

— G.A.

# Romance of a Horse Thief

**Yul Brynner** (Stoloff), **Eli Wallach** (Kifke), **Jane Birkin** (Naomi), **Oliver Tobias** (Zanvill Kradnik), **Lainie Kazan** (Estusha), **David Opatoshu** (Schloime Kradnik), **Serge Gainsbourg** (Sigmund), **Henri Sera** (Mendel), **Linda Veras** (Countess Grabowsky), **Branko Plesa** (Lieutenant Vishinsky), **Vladimir Bacic** (Gruber), **Alenka Rancic** (Sura), **Branko Spoljar** (Strugatch), **Dina Rutic** (Cheitche), **Marilu Tolo** (Manka), **Maria Mizar** (Schoolteacher), **Mile Sosa** (Grisha), **Aljosa Vuckovic** (tailor), **Mort Shuman** (piano player), **Vida Jerman, Vera Stanojevic, Mira Blaskovic, Nada Cibic** (girls), **Eugen Werber** (tailor).

Director: **ABRAHAM POLONSKY**. Screenplay: **David Opatoshu**. Based on a novel by **Joseph Opatoshu**. Photographed in Technicolor by **Piero Portalupi**. Film editor: **Kevin Connor**. Art directors: **Otto Pischinger, Vlastimir Gavrik**. Costumes: **Ruth Myers**. Music: **Mort Shuman**. Music editor: **Robin Clarke**. Music mixer: **Eric Tomlinson**. Wardrobe master: **Ray Beck**. Make-up: **Sergio Angeloni**. Hairdresser: **Anna Graziosa**. Set decorator: **Herta Pischinger**. Camera operator: **Cesare Allione**. Construction manager: **Tania Frankol**. Location manager: **Dusan Eregovic**. Dubbing mixer: **Doug Turner**. Dubbing editors: **Peter Keen, John Ireland**. Sound recording: **Michael Sale**. Music supervisor: **Carl Prager**. Production executive: **Peter E. Strauss**. Song "La Noyee" composed by **Serge Gainsbourg**. Titles: **Julia Aldridge, Rex Neville**. Production managers: **Georg Reuther, Donko Buljan**. Set continuity: **Ann Edwards**. 2nd unit director: **Henry Polonsky**. Assistant to the producer: **Jane Oscroft**. Unit manager: **Wolfram Kortz**. Assistant director: **Svetolik Maricic**. Producer: **Gene Gutowski**. Executive producer: **Emanuel L. Wolf**.

Copyright 1971 by Allied Artists (Los Angeles) and Jadran Film (Zagreb). A United States-Yugoslavian co-production, released in the U.S.A. through Allied Artists: July 1971. New York opening at Loew's Tower East: 18 August 1971. Never theatrically released in the U.K. but made available to 16mm non-theatrical users through Kingston (from whom our *Hollywood Classics* review print was obtained) as from August 1977 (sic). Released in Australia through Paramount. 101 minutes.

SYNOPSIS: Malava, a Polish village near the German border in 1904. Having just won his daughter a dowry by selling Herr Gruber of Germany a horse from his own stables, the Jewish horse-trader Shloime Kradnik, his son Zanvill, and his old associate Kifke, are desolated when the local Cossack commander, Captain Stoloff, commandeers this horse along with all others in the village for service in the Russo-Japanese war. Covetously eyeing the splendid but closely guarded white stallions belonging to Countess Grabowsky, Zanvill is gratified to be taken aside by the Countess and given a stallion in reward for his services. Selling it to the delighted Gruber, Zanvill optimistically promises ten more of the same, and with the advance payment provides his sister Cheitche with the dowry for her marriage to Mendel, a future Rabbi. Meanwhile, in love with Naomi, who has returned from Paris as a fervent revolutionary disciple of the dilettante Frenchman, Sigmund, whom she has in tow as a fiance, Zanvill wins her favor by contriving to shower the village square with inflammatory leaflets, breaking up a patriotic celebration organised by Stoloff. Stoloff, however, has announced the immediate mobilisation of all young men for service in the Tsarist armies. Planning to emigrate to America, Zanvill and Mendel escape to Germany, taking Gruber three horses hitherto hidden in the brothel and spirited away under Stoloff's nose with the aid of Kifke, who leaves them at the border, unable to abandon his old flame Estucha, the brothel madam. But when Sigmund, expelled for (reluctantly) distributing leaflets, contacts them at Gruber's with the news that Naomi awaits execution for the same crime, Zanvill and Mendel return. In an elaborate plot, with Shloime, Zanvill and Kifke masquerading as Cossack veterinarians while Estucha keeps Stoloff busy, the Cossacks are persuaded that their horses are plagued by anthrax.

NOTES: Last of the three films directed by Abraham Polonsky, one of the most famous of Hollywood's blacklisted writers. His other (and far more critically acclaimed) directorial assignments: *Force of Evil* (1948), and *Tell Them Willie Boy Is Here* (1969).

And yes, I know this is not a western. It's an eastern. But I'm not going to run separate books for gauchos and Cossacks, charros and caballeros, bushrangers and bronc-busters, so here it will have to stay.

VIEWER'S GUIDE: Adults.

COMMENT: I have just read Tom Milne's extraordinary review in the *Monthly Film Bulletin*. The opening sentence neatly sums up his whole approach: It is perhaps not altogether surprising that *Romance of a Horse Thief* should have had such a stormy critical passage, since Polonsky hasn't chosen an exactly easy path for himself with a narrative whose fantasy can so easily be taken as botched realism, and where the comedy isn't meant to be funny so much as tenderly evocative of an idealized world that never existed except in memory.

While watching the film it never occurred to me that it was meant to be taken as a fantasy. True, it is a remembrance of things past, true it is sometimes a romanticised memory, but for all its often mellow images it is primarily realistic. Perhaps too real. The opening sequence in which Gruber drives his irritatingly noisy little car into the teeming squalor of Malava is no fantasy. You can almost smell the God-forsaken place. This is not an untypical sequence. True the accent is on comedy as the likeably rascally thieves outwit the Cossacks, but the sets seem so real you could be a part of them. In fact Polonsky's aim it seems to me is to break down the barrier between the picture and the audience. You walk these muddy streets, you are intimidated by these Russians, you hide out in a bordello.

Polonsky's real approach depends for complete success not only on great camerawork and lavishly realistic sets -- which the movie definitely delivers -- but also on an involving script and charismatic acting. It's in these two departments that *Romance* is less successful in my opinion. Brynner is the one charismatic player. The movie is at its most engaging when he's on screen, even when his material is slight and/or trivial and/or not particularly important (for instance his running joke about his ill-fitting uniform). Jane Birkin is also beguilingly right as the she-knows-she's-pretty-but-she's-determined-to-be-serious-minded heroine. Unfortunately, the rest of the players are not in this league, the acting ranging from the moderately appealing to the indifferent (Oliver Tobias and oddly screenwriter Opatoshu himself) to the downright hammy (Serge Gainsbourg, Vladimir Bacic). As for Opatoshu's script (from his father's novel) it has both a deliberate inwardness and xenophobia which lessens its appeal to non-Jewish audiences plus an approving indulgence of behavior which many people would find neither quaintly charming nor even moral; yet at the same time it contrives to make light of and treat lightly, even comically, serious social questions (perhaps this is the element of fantasy that Milne so appreciates). In other words it's never fully involving. The treatment seems superficial. The intent of the movie seems to be to provide a light sketch of Polish Jewish urban village life at the turn of the century. In this aim the movie is signally successful. But is it enough to keep an audience on its toes for 100 minutes? Especially a Gentile audience which is likely to object to or resent being made the villains and fools of this exercise.

OTHER VIEWS: We love all the scenes with Yul Brynner. He has a characteristic role which he plays as if to the Cossack captain born. Unfortunately, with the exception of the charming Jane Birkin, the other players are much less successful at gaining audience sympathy and confidence. The sad fact is that despite his lead billing, Brynner's role is actually a supporting one. Never mind, he does have at least one unforgettable moment when at the Czar's birthday celebrations he presents his father's watch to the local winner of the riding contest. Newcomer Oliver Tobias, a rather callow youth, whose riding skills are obviously doubled, is that rather unlikely winner. Beautifully photographed and expensively mounted though the picture itself is, it fails — whether through indifferent acting, slack direction or a none too well-focused script — to completely grip an audience's attention. As entertainment, despite its virtues of color, exotic if slummy setting, Birkin and Brynner, *Romance of a Horse Thief* must be counted a near miss.

— G.A.

Poland, 1904. A memorable recreation. Some may claim that at times it is a little too fanciful and exaggerated to be wholly convincing (and certainly Jane Birkin's very patent Englishness doesn't fit well into her role as the belle of the town), but Portalupi's glowing, impressionistic photography, Shuman's lively, gypsy-like music score, and skilful performances by Eli Wallach, Lainie Kazan and Serge Gainsbourg are knitted into a pleasing and attractive whole by Abraham Polonsky whose staging, use of sets and locations and general mise-en-scene recreation of the period make the picture a constant joy to behold. Produced on an extremely lavish budget with wondrous location photography, this *Romance* is a movie to enjoy again and again. The script has not only wit and vivacity, but provides some truly memorable characters.

— Pius Verity.

# Rough Riders' Round-Up

**Roy Rogers** (Roy Rogers), **Mary Hart** (aka Lynne Roberts) (Dorothy Blair), **Raymond Hatton** (Rusty), **Eddie Acuff** (Tommy), **William Pawley** (Arizona Jack), **Dorothy Sebastian** (Rose), **George Meeker** (Lanning), **Jack Rockwell** (Commander Harrison), **Guy Usher** (Blair), **George Chesebro** (Mosby), **Glenn Strange** (Boggs), **Duncan Renaldo** (alcalde), **Hank Bell** (helpful ranger), **Fred Kelsey** (agitator), **Dorothy Christy** (bargirl), **Augie Gomez** (cantina proprietor), **Jack Kirk** (Jim Horn), **Fred Burns, George Plues** (stage drivers), **John Merton** (messenger), **George Montgomery** (Joe), **Al Haskell, Jim Corey, George DeNormand, Merrill McCormick, Bill Nestell, Bud Osborne, Bob Reeves, Blackjack Ward** (henchmen), **Frank Ellis** (waiter), **Chris-Pin Martin** (Ramon), **Frank McCarroll** (rough rider), **Art Dillard, Dan White, Art Mix, Tom Smith** (ranger patrolmen), **Allan Cavan** (officer), **Oscar Gahan** (musician), **I. Stanford Jolley, Pascale Perry** (cantina barflies), **Fred Parker** (clerk), **Jay Wilsey, Chick Hannon** (barflies), **Soledad Jimenez** (old squaw), **Murdock MacQuarrie** (spectator), **Nellie Walker** (stunt double for Mary Hart), and "Trigger".

Director: **JOSEPH KANE**. Original screenplay: **Jack Natteford**. Photography: **Jack Marta**. Film editor: **Lester Orlebeck**. Music director: **Cy Feuer**. Songs: "Ridin' down the Trail" (Rogers), "When Johnny Comes Marching Home" (Rogers, chorus), "Here on the Range with You" (Rogers). Stunts: **George DeNormand**. Production manager: **Al Wilson**. RCA Sound System. Associate producer: **Joseph Kane**. Executive producer: **Herbert Yates**.

Copyright 13 March 1939 by Republic Pictures Corp. No New York opening. U.S. release: 13 March 1939. 6 reels. 55 minutes.

SYNOPSIS: See review.

NOTES: Rogers' seventh starring western.

COMMENT: An unusually complicated story-line finds Rogers, Hatton and Acuff joining the Arizona Border Patrol after a stint in Teddy Roosevelt's Rough Riders. The territory is being terrorised by a gang of bandits led by a mysterious "Arizona Jack" who hides out across the Mexican border between raids. What seems at first a standard goodies-versus-outlaws chase (compounded by vengeance, though this aspect is soft-pedalled) is made more complex by the runaway daughter of a rich mine-owner who wants to marry her father's manager. Unfortunately for her, the manager...

It can be seen that Rogers' role is less central than in most of his vehicles. Indeed it's the girl who has the main part — and that makes this a very unusual "B" western indeed. Rogers still finds time to sing a couple of pleasant songs plus a chorus of two of "Johnny Comes Marching Home", but all the numbers are staged in odd circumstances. What's more the musical interludes are not built up as ends in themselves, but are treated in a much more realistic and casual fashion. Compared to their obligatory central staging in his later westerns, here the songs are almost peripheral to the main action. Rogers' personality is more likeably subdued here too, allowing the other players to make much more of an impression. Of course if you're a rabid Rogers fan, you may find the amount of screen time devoted to the other characters — Miss Hart, Pawley, Meeker, Miss Sebastian, even Rockwell — unappealing, though I enjoyed their performances. (It was also good to see George Chesebro up to his usual villainy. Glenn Strange can easily be recognized as one of the bandits, while the more eagle-eyed will pick George Montgomery in a triple-threat role as a rough-rider, a bandit and a double for Rogers).

Kane omits this picture from his filmography, though it's certainly nothing to be ashamed of. The director makes good use of his locations, his players and a surprisingly expansive budget. There's more than enough chase, fisticuffs and shoot-out action to satisfy the fans, though the final rounding-up of the bandits is disappointingly short.

OTHER VIEWS: Herbert J. Yates had the bright idea of re-naming Miss Roberts as Mary Hart so that he could bill "Rogers and Hart" as the new sweethearts of the west. To this end, he probably ordered his scripters and directors to focus more — or at least just as much — on Hart as Rogers. In this one, during one of Roy's obligatory songs, there are actually more reaction shots of Hart than close-ups of Rogers himself. In another number, her entrance actually displaces Rogers completely, his introductory chorus limited to a muted warble off-camera! In other respects, this is pretty much a routine but enjoyable offering, with Raymond Hatton stealing a number of Rogers' scenes, and a great deal of attention paid to the more colorful villains.

# Round-Up Time in Texas

**Gene Autry** (Gene), **Smiley Burnette** (Frog), **Maxine Doyle** (Gwen), **The Cabin Kids** (themselves), **LeRoy Mason** (Cardigan), **Earle Hodgins** (Barkey), **Dick Wessel**

(Johnson), **Buddy Williams** (Bosuto), **Elmer Fain** (chief's son), **Cornie Anderson** (Namba), **Frankie Marvin** (second Cape cop), **Ken Cooper** (Tex), **Al Ferguson** (captain), **Slim Whitaker** (corporal), **Carleton Young** (diamond news man), **Jack C. Smith** (henchman), **Jim Corey** (Bill), **Jack Kirk** (cook), **George Morrell** (dealer), **Charles Murphy** ("Gate open!"), **Al Taylor** (ranch hand), **Billy Franey** (man with cigar), and **Al Knight**, "Champion" the horse.

Director: **JOSEPH KANE**. Original screenplay: **Oliver Drake**. Photography: **William Nobles**. Film editor: **Lester Orlebeck**. Supervising film editor: **Murray Seldeen**. Music director: **Harry Grey**. Songs: "Old Chisholm Trail", "Prairie Rose", "Dry Dry Dry", "Moon of Desire", "Noah's Ark". Composers and lyricists: **Gene Autry, Smiley Burnette, Sam Stept, Sidney Mitchell, Ned Washington, Sam Lewis, Joe Young, Harry Akst, Andy Razof, Vincent & Howard**. Sound recording: **Harry Jones**. Associate producer: **Armand Schaefer**. Producer: **Nat Levine**.

Copyright 8 February 1937 by Republic Pictures Corp. No recorded New York opening. U.S. release: 28 February 1937 and 22 April 1937. U.K. release through British Lion. No Australian theatrical release. 7 reels. 63 minutes. (Also listed at 58 minutes).

SYNOPSIS: Texas? See review below.

NOTES: Autry's 16th of his 94 movies.

COMMENT: *Round-Up Time in Texas* refers to the song sung by Autry and his saddle-pals immediately the film opens. After this initial burst of melody, the scene abruptly shifts to Dunbar (sic), South Africa where it remains for the rest of the film.

Despite the novelty of the setting (which is used to introduce a few ancient wild animal clips including one in which an obviously process screen lion makes for the camera) and the fact that Gene has a brother, Tex Autry, (actually he doesn't figure overmuch in the story) this is a rather tame and dreary affair.

You can trust Gene to sing a song at the drop of a hat and you can rely on Smiley to perpetrate a lot of foolery — in this case, escaping from the clutches of a music-loving native chief.

There's also a what's a nice girl like you doing in a place like this heroine (this thought is never expressed but it is obvious nonetheless) played in an extremely colorless fashion by Maxine Doyle.

The villain, alas, is also none too interestingly played (LeRoy Mason) and though Earl Hodgins contributes a characteristically breezy study (complete with phoney Cockney accent), acting generally is unengaging.

Autry's eyes have been circled with black rings, probably to give him a more rugged appearance, which is unsuccessful in view of the fact there is virtually no action in the film at all — for a time it looks as though Autry's double isn't even going to do his customary stunt of riding after a runaway wagon — but would you believe this familiar little act forms the larger part of the action climax!

Kane's direction seems quite ordinary and uninterestingly pedestrian, the photography is flat. Other credits are likewise undistinguished and production values rate no more than average by "B" western standards.

# Rovin' Tumbleweeds

**Gene Autry** (himself), **Smiley Burnette** (Frog Millhouse), **Mary Carlisle** (Mary), **Douglass Dumbrille** (Holloway), **William Farnum** (Senator Nolan), **Lee "Lasses" White** (storekeeper), **Ralph Peters** (Satchel), **Gordon Hart** (Fuller), **Vic Potel** (Zeke), **Jack Ingram** (man blocking entry to Rand County), **Sammy McKim** (Eddie), **Reginald Barlow** (Higgins), **Eddie Kane** (congressman at Ways & Means committee), **Guy Usher** (Craig), **Forrest Taylor** (man with Frog at railroad station), **Frank Ellis** (man with sheriff at eviction), **Horace Murphy** (jailer), **David Sharpe** (reporter), **Jack Kirk** (jailbird), **Rose Plummer, Jane Keckley** (ranchers' wives), **Robert "Bob" Burns** (migrant), **Fred Burns** (rancher), **Art Mix** (brawler), **Edward Cassidy** (sheriff), **Tom Chatterton** (speaker of the house), **Horace B. Carpenter** (radio listener), **Fred "Snowflake" Toones** (porter), **Crauford Kent** (Hutton), **Maurice Costello** (member of the ways and means committee), **Charles K. French** (committee member), **Lee Shumway** (congressman), **Bud Osborne** (jobs announcer), **Harry Semels** (vendor), **Chuck Morrison** (packing plant man), **Nora Lou Martin and Bud Jackson, Larry Shore, Harold Pullian, Howard Russell** {Pals of the Golden West} (themselves), **Eddie Dean** (cowhand singer), **Tex Terry** (rancher), **Joe Yrigoyen** (stunt double for Gene Autry), and "Champion".

Director: **GEORGE SHERMAN**. Original screenplay: **Betty Burbridge, Dorrell McGowan, Stuart McGowan**. Photography: **William Nobles**. Film editor: **Tony Martinelli**. Music director: **Raoul Kraushaar**. Songs: "Back in the Saddle Again" by **Gene Autry** and **Ray Whitley**; "Old Peaceful River"; "Rocky Mountain Express"; "Away Up Yonder" by **Fred Rose** and **Johnny Marvin**. Production manager: **Al Wilson**. Assistant director: **Harry Knight**. Associate producer: **William Berke**. Executive producer: **Herbert J. Yates**.

Copyright 16 November 1939 by Republic Pictures Corp. No recorded New York opening. U.S. release: 16 November 1939. U.K. release through British Lion. No Australian theatrical release. 7 reels. 62 minutes.

Shooting title: *Washington Cowboy*.

SYNOPSIS: "One of his worst duds on record" is the way one critic referred to this tumbleweed saga. The working, prerelease title on the film was *Washington Cowboy*, a moniker more suited to what actually occurs in the story.

A crooked Washington politician is stalling a flood control bill long enough to set himself up for a huge land sale profit when the bill goes through. The poor, common people who are affected by the scheme finally rise up and elect radio singer Gene Autry to Congress.

— David Rothel in *The Singing Cowboys*.

NOTES: Number 36 of Autry's 94 movies.

COMMENT: The original title was accurate, but the release title has absolutely nothing to do with this plot variant of *Mr Smith Goes to Washington*. Like Sherman's vastly superior *Colorado Sunset* this is a political western. But whereas the politics were an entertaining and action-full ingredient of *Sunset* here they are banal and inept. In fact the best sections of this movie are those set strictly in the west. Though the customary sequence in which Autry gallops after a runaway horse is exceptionally weak, there's nonetheless some good action (set off by nice pictorial shots) at beginning and end. Sherman is at his best in a sequence with wagons racing across the terrain (though there are even more exciting examples of this type of work in his *Colorado Sunset* and *Pillars of the Sky*).

Alas, as soon as Congressman Autry hits Washington, our interest takes a nosedive. A totally irrelevant and unlikely rodeo episode, made up entirely of ancient stock footage, is introduced. Then there's a dime-novel plot twist that will have most viewers rubbing their eyes in disbelief. The one politico that Autry had won over is run over by an automobile and killed (off camera, of course). This development is then topped for unintentional ludicrousness with the sudden fade-out change-of-heart by the yarn's chief villain (played here in a characteristic but unhappily undistinguished — his material is so weak — manner by Douglass Dumbrille).

Fortunately, Autry and Burnette are their usual amiable selves. William Farnum is embarrassingly enthusiastic in a role written with singular ineptitude, even by the cliched standards of dialogue and characterization in evidence in this *Washington*. As for Mary Carlisle who made such a strong impression as Bing Crosby's leading lady in no less than three of his movies, her career seems to be slipping. The writers give her such thin and sparse material she can't help but make a colorless heroine.

Yes, there are songs, including one of Autry's most famous — he uses it as the title of his autobiography — and some mild comedy relief.

In all, *Rovin' Tumbleweeds* is a disappointing effort, especially when judged by Autry's usual high standards. Production values are no more than average "B". Technically, whilst the photography is a bit less flat, the direction is a lot less imaginative. True, the movie does offer some fair entertainment qualities, but we are inclined to agree with those critics who put it down as a failure.

# Sagebrush Trail

**John Wayne** (John Brant), **Nancy Shubert** (Sally Blake), **Lane Chandler** (Bob Jones), **Yakima Canutt** (Ed Walsh), **Bob Burns** [Robert E. Burns] (Sheriff Parker), **Wally Wales** (deputy sheriff), **Art Mix** (henchman), **Hank Bell** (outlaw with chair) **Earl Dwire** (Blind Pete), **Henry Hall** (Blake), **Slim Whitaker, Robert Walker, Tex Phelps, Blackjack Ward** (henchmen), **Ted Adams** (Taggart), **Silver Tip Baker** (townsman), **Hal Price** (train driver), **William Dyer** (Blind Pete), **Julie Kingdon** (town girl), **Archie Ricks** (stage driver), **Yakima Canutt** (stunt double for John Wayne).

Director: **ARMAND SCHAEFER**. Screenplay: **Lindsley Parsons**. Story: **Lindsley Parsons** and **Will Beale**. Photography: **Archie Stout**. Film editor: **Carl Pierson**. Art director: **E.R. Hickson**. Sound recording: **John A. Stransky, Jr**. Balsley & Phillips Sound System. Producer: **Paul Malvern**. Executive producer: **Trem Carr**.

A Lone Star Western, copyright 1 December 1933 by Monogram Pictures Corp. No New York opening. U.S. release: 15 December 1933. U.K. release: 4 March 1935 (sic). 6 reels. 54 minutes.

SYNOPSIS: Unjustly convicted murderer escapes from prison to hunt down vital missing witness.

NOTES: The second of Wayne's 16 Lone Star Westerns. Negative cost: a measly $10,900, comprising only 3 days of location work and but a single day of studio interiors.

COMMENT: Although it doesn't hold a candle to Wayne's Republic westerns in any department, this is still a most entertaining Lone Star Western. Nice to see Lane Chandler in a featured role, for once, and acquitting himself with honor too. Wayne is great as always, even here showing the sort of charisma and star power that would later delight so many millions of fans. The rest of the players are not much, though Yakima Canutt has a sizable on-camera role as leader of the outlaw band. Despite limited production values and obvious technical deficiencies, plus some clichéd and rather clumsily delivered dialogue, one can still enjoy the reasonably picturesque locations and the action spots, complete with stuntwork and fast panning, which are nothing if not most enthusiastically staged.

# San Antonio

**Errol Flynn** (Clay Hardin, an exiled cattleman), **John Litel** (Charlie Bell, a long-time friend), **Alexis Smith** (Jeane Starr, an entertainer), **S.Z. "Cuddles" Sakall** (Sacha Bozic, manager), **Florence Bates** (Henrietta, companion), **Paul Kelly** (Roy Stuart, large-scale cattle rustler and co-owner of the Bella Union), **Victor Francen** (Legare, co-owner of the Bella Union), **Robert Shayne** (Captain Morgan), **Robert Barrat** (Colonel Johnson), **Tom Tyler** (Lafe McWilliams), **John Alvin** (Pony Smith), **Monte Blue** (Cleve Andrews), **Pedro De Cordoba** (Ricardo Torreon), **Chris-Pi, Martin** (Hymie Rosas, hired stage driver), **Charles Stevens** (Sojer Harris, a Stuart henchman), **Poodles Hanneford** (San Antonio stage driver), **Robert Dudley** (telegraph clerk), **Doodles Weaver** (square dance caller), **Ray Spiker** (Rebel White), **Al Hill** (Hap Winters), **Wallis Clark** (Tip Brice), **Dan White** (Joey Sims), **Harry Cording** (hawker), **Fred Kelsey** (bartender, Bella Union), **Chalky Williams** (poker player), **Bill Steele** (Roper), **Arnold Kent** (comic dancer), **Howard Hill, Allen E. Smith** (Clay's henchmen), **Don McGuire, John Compton** (cowboys), **Eddie Acuff** (gawking cowboy), **Si Jenks** (station boss), **Denver Dixon** (barfly), **Snub Pollard** (dance extra), **Dan Seymour** (Laredo border guard), **Brandon Hurst** (gambler), **Harry Semels** (Mexican), **Francis Ford** (old-timer greeting coach), **William Gould, Jack Mower** (cowmen in square), **Harry Seymour** (waiter), **Brad King, Johnny Miles, Lane Chandler, Hal Taliaferro** (cowboys), **Norman Willis** (Jay Witherspoon), **Eddy Waller, Henry Hall, James Flavin** (cattlemen), **Cliff Lyons** (double for Errol Flynn).

Director: **DAVID BUTLER**. Uncredited direction: **Raoul Walsh, Robert Florey**. Original screenplay by **Alan LeMay** and **W.R. Burnett**. Uncredited additional dialogue: **Robert Buckner**. Photographed in Technicolor by **Bert Glennon**. Film editor: **Irene**

**Morra**. Art director: **Ted Smith**. Set decorator: **Jack McConaghy**. Costumes: **Milo Anderson**. Make-up: **Perc Westmore**. Special photographic effects: **Willard Van Enger**. Music composed by **Max Steiner**, orchestrated by **Hugo Friedhofer**, directed by **Leo F. Forbstein**. Songs: "Some Sunday Morning" (Smith and male quartette) by **Ted Koehler** (lyrics), **Ray Heindorf** and **M.K. Jerome** (music); "Somewhere in Monterey" (Smith and male quartette) by **Charles Kisco** and **Jack Scholl**; "Put Your Little Foot Right Out" (Weaver) by **Larry Spier**. Dance director: **LeRoy Prinz**. Technicolor color consultants: **Natalie Kalmus** and **Leonard Doss**. Dialogue director: **Frederick De Cordova**. Assistant director: **William Kissel**. Sound recording: **Everett A. Brown**. RCA Sound a System. Producer: **Robert Buckner**.

Copyright 5 January 1946 by Warner Bros. Pictures, Inc. A Warner Bros.-First National picture. New York opening at the Strand, 28 December 1945 (ran 4 weeks). U.S. release: 29 December 1945. U.K. release: 1 July 1946. Australian release: 24 October 1946. 111 minutes.

SYNOPSIS: Former cattle rancher and local hero finally gets the goods on big-time rustler.

COMMENT: I love this movie. Contemporary reviews were luke-warm at best, but it has everything I like about the classic big-scale western. First of all, it's most lavishly produced- which no-one can deny, despite the use of a few stock shots under the opening narration. Secondly, it stars Errol Flynn at his cavalier best. Few other heroes can stand up to the villain with quite the tongue-in-cheek bravado, the calculated insouciance, the devil-may-care yet firmly right-thinking charm that Flynn always seems to project with such consummate ease and artistry. Thirdly, our boy is almost evenly matched by a first-rate pair of truly hard-hearted villains: Victor Francen, all purring viciousness; and Paul Kelly, the master of cowardly opportunism. Fourthly — and it's downright boorish of me to place her so far down the pecking order — is the radiant Alexis Smith, whose sweeping presence, gorgeous costumes and sparkling performance will keep even the most misogynist western fan happy. We could go on from here to list the virtues of all the support cast, but space prevents all but three. It would be churlish indeed to pass over the delightful Florence Bates. S.Z. Sakall is equally winning in a more dramatic role than usual. Last but by no means least, Tom Tyler. Tom always seemed a bit uncomfortable as Captain Marvel. It's great to see him back on firmer ground as the snarlingest, meanest-faced bushwacker this side of the Rio Grande.

Another thing I really like about *San Antonio* is the way it's directed. One of the big differences between English and American films is that the vast majority of English directors are competent but frightfully dull, whereas their Hollywood colleagues tend to be much more daring and adventurous. *San Antonio* is an excellent example of the Hollywood willingness to push the medium to its limits. What does it matter if some of the angles don't match when the film is directed with such gusto and vitality? The director never loses an opportunity to take full advantage of the film's lavish budget. The camera glides through jostling crowds , pulls back from the stage of the cavernously ornate Bella Union, and frames some eye-catching vistas of both real locations and Hollywood sets. (Raoul Walsh is reported to have made a "substantial contribution" to the film, but which scenes are his are impossible to identify).

The script has been widely condemned as routine and derivative. Both these observations are misleading. True, the basic bedrock plot is predictable, but most moviegoers — including me — would be very upset if the hero didn't thwart the villains and get the girl. Aside from this important premise, however, there are plenty of unexpected twists and turns. What's more, the script takes in some really interesting characters, not the least of which are Alexis Smith's unusually spirited heroine and Victor Francen's memorably double-dealing bad guy. Furthermore, the no-expense-spared budget has allowed the screenwriters plenty of scope for enough extravagantly staged action and breathtaking stunts to enliven at least three or four normal-sized movies.

Technical credits are superb. Max Steiner's rousing score, Bert Glennon's atmospheric photography and Milo Anderson's gorgeous costumes deserve special applause. Ted Smith and Jack McConaghy were nominated for an Academy Award in the Color Art direction category (losing to *Frenchman's Creek*), while "Some Sunday Morning" was nominated for Best Song (losing to "It Might As Well Be Spring" from *State Fair*).

OTHER VIEWS: Fascinating! What happened was that both Flynn and Smith took ill in the middle of shooting. And when she recovered, Smith was not available for *San Antonio* anyway, but was required back on the set of *The Horn Blows At Midnight*. As a result, the direction of *San Antonio* is to say the least peculiar. The movie is a patchwork quilt of the great and the mediocre, the inventively expedient and the downright banal. Producer Buckner doubtless took a hand in trying to doctor the script around his ailing stars, but his material is pretty pedestrian. Fortunately most of this hokey additional talk occurs at the beginning. John Litel's part has been built up, but he is not the sort of charismatic actor who can stand up with radiance in the limelight. On the other hand, it seems that Victor Francen, Paul Kelly and Tom Tyler's roles have also been considerably strengthened — and this is certainly good news. Flynn's shoot-out with Tyler is very imaginatively handled with Flynn's back to the camera. The actor spins around to gun down Tyler. This enables the producer to cut in a rear view of Flynn's double in the following saloon scenes with Alexis Smith. When Flynn actually faces the camera, he looks tired and unwell. By wonderful chance (or perhaps the script was re-written) this ties in vividly with his role. However, I thought that Smith's performance lacked color and I can only marvel why she wasn't replaced. She doesn't even do her own singing. Maybe too much footage had already been shot. As for S.Z. Sakall, well he does have at least one genuinely funny scene, though he is often forced to ham up rather threadbone dialogue and "business"... All manner of funny editing cuts reveal how the film was laboriously pieced together from camera takes lensed over a long period of time. Close-up inserts, for example, are very clumsily hacked into the climax, undermining its rhythm and pace. The direction too often seems peculiarly odd. Many scenes with promising potential misfire because of wrong camera placements as well as rough editing. Yet other scenes work brilliantly. All the Bella Union sequences, the staging of "Some Sunday Morning", the grand shoot-out, are most exciting. In fact some of the action spots are equal to the most spectacular and vigorously staged in any Warner Bros western. Maybe a second unit shot some of the action... Color photography is also of variable quality. Ditto the sets. Most are great, but the Alamo is unconvincing, despite its deft use as background for the climactic confrontation. Max Steiner's music score is likewise inconsistent, varying from the cheeringly stirring to the ploddingly pedestrian. Smith's costumes, however, are always stunning.

# the Searchers

**John Wayne** (Ethan Edwards), **Jeffrey Hunter** (Martin Pawley), **Vera Miles** (Laurie Jorgensen), **Ward Bond** (Captain Rev. Samuel Clayton), **Natalie Wood** (Debbie Edwards), **John Qualen** (Lars Jorgensen), **Olive Carey** (Mrs Jorgensen), **Henry Brandon** (Chief Scar), **Ken Curtis** (Charlie McCorry), **Harry Carey, Jr** (Brad Jorgensen), **Antonio Moreno** (Emilio Figueroa), **Hank Worden** (Mose Harper), **Lana Wood** (Debbie as a child), **Walter Coy** (Aaron Edwards), **Dorothy Jordan** (Martha Edwards), **Pippa Scott** (Lucy Edwards), **Pat Wayne** (Lieutenant Greenhill), **Beulah Archuletta** (Look), **Jack Pennick** (private), **Peter Mamakos** (Futterman), **Bill Steele** (Nesby), **Cliff Lyons** (Colonel Greenhill), **Chuck Roberson** (man at wedding), **Ruth Clifford** (deranged woman at fort), **Mae Marsh** (woman at fort), **Dan Borzage** (accordionist at funeral), **Billy Cartledge, Chuck Hayward, Slim Hightower, Fred Kennedy, Frank McGrath, Dale Van Sickel, Henry Wills, Terry Wilson** (stuntmen), **Away Luna, Billy Yellow, Bob Many Mules, Exactly Sonnie Betsuie, Feather Hat, Jr, Harry Black Horse, Jack Tin Horn, Many Mules Son, Percy Shooting Star, Pete Grey Eyes, Pipe Line Begishe, Smile White Sheep** (Comanches).

Director: **JOHN FORD**. Screenplay: **Frank S. Nugent**. Based on the 1954 novel by **Alan LeMay**. Photographed in VistaVision and Technicolor by **Winton C. Hoch**. 2nd unit photography: **Alfred Gilks**. Film editor: **Jack Murray**. Music: **Max Steiner**. Title song by **Stan Jones**, sung by the **Sons of the Pioneers**. Art directors: **Frank Hotaling, James Basevi**. Set decorator: **Victor Gangelin**. Wardrobe: **Frank Beetson** (men's), **Ann Peck** (women's). Special effects: **George Brown**. Production supervisor: **Lowell J. Farrell**. Assistant director: **Wingate Smith**. Technicolor color consultant: **James Gooch**. Make-up: **Web Overlander**. Hair styles: **Fae Smith**. Property master: **Dudley Holmes**. Script supervisor: **Robert Gary**. Music orchestrations: **Murray Cutter**. Sound recording: **Hugh McDowell, Howard Wilson**. RCA Sound System. Associate producer: **Patrick Wayne**. Producer: **John Ford**. Executive producer: **Merian C. Cooper**. A John Ford Production. Presented by **C.V. Whitney**.

Copyright 1956 by C.V. Whitney Pictures. Released through Warner Bros. Pictures. New York opening at the Criterion: 30 May 1956. U.S. release: 13 March 1956. U.K. release: 25 September 1956. Australian opening at the Sydney Regent: 16 May 1957 (sic). 119 minutes.

SYNOPSIS: Moving always grandly through the deserts and towering outcrops of Monument Valley, *The Searchers* is, no doubt about it, an exceptionally handsome film. From the start, the set-ups are emphatically composed, with strong, monumental grouping and movement within the frame. The opening sets the style. After the titles, which are accompanied by a rhetorical-romantic Stan Jones ballad ('What makes a man to wander, what makes a man to roam? . . .'), the screen goes black. A door opens out of the darkness, on to a sunlit desert. A woman walks from behind camera, to stand for a moment, silhouetted against the bright landscape. She moves forward on to a porch, the camera tracking with her to lose the black surround, into the open air. Cut round: the woman, in mid-close-up, raises her left hand against her forehead, shielding her eyes from the sun. Cut round: a man approaches on horseback, framed between huge outcrops of red rock in the distance. Cut again to the reverse: a man steps down from the porch, crosses behind the woman and comes forward of her into close-up. Wordlessly they gaze out at the rider. A shot down the porch groups a little girl with a dog at her heels and an older girl, her full skirt blowing in the wind. A young boy, carrying wood, crosses foreground to stand with the others, looking out. The rider approaches, dismounts, walks forward: a black, broad-brimmed hat shadows his eyes ominously. The woman comes to greet him. A long shot shows the homestead, the family group, the woman embracing the traveler. He is led into the house. Ford's opening sequences are usually composed with firmness and clarity, stating the main theme early, but without loss of spontaneity. Here the effect is more studied than defined. The balance tips from style into formality.

The interior scenes which follow introduce the characters and suggest their relationships. The rider is Ethan Edwards, arriving at his brother's home after a long absence fighting in the Civil War and straying mysteriously in the years since (an initial title has told us that the year is 1868 and the place Texas.) Aaron Edwards is less welcoming to his brother than his wife Martha. Living with the Edwards and their three children is their adopted son Martin Pawley, a boy of eighteen or so, one-eighth (he claims) Cherokee. Ethan's prejudice is clear from his harsh, insulting way with the boy — compared with the fondness and generosity he shows to his nephew and nieces. We sense bitterness, and isolation.

The development of *The Searchers* is precipitated by tragedy. The little community of homesteaders is disturbed by reports of Comanche marauders. Led by the Reverend Clayton, preacher and ranger, a posse of farmers rides out in pursuit. The posse is tricked: the Indians are not out to rustle cattle but to destroy the homesteads. Ethan and Martin return to find the Pawleys' farm a burned-out ruin.

— Lindsay Anderson in *About John Ford*.

NOTES: Shooting from mid-June to mid-August 1955. Location scenes in Utah, studio interiors at RKO-Pathé.

Although not nominated for any peer awards, the film came in number 10 at the U.S. boxoffice for the year. It did even better in the U.K. reaching 7th position in 1956's top money-making pictures. By contrast in Australia, the movie did only so-so business, not even selling enough tickets to be included in 1957's top fifty.

COMMENT: *The Searchers* should have made a fine film but somewhere along the way someone got the bright idea of adding a lot of rambunctious, unconvincingly loud-mouthed humor to relieve its dark and brooding yet involving storyline. Only Wayne manages to preserve dignity and credibility amidst all these hammy goings-on in which Ward Bond rants and raves and John Qualen opens the floodgates of his ridiculous "by golly" stage Norwegian. The film is further handicapped by the casting of the unconvincingly amateurish Jeff Hunter in a key role. Pat Wayne is also a dead loss as a supposedly humorous green lieutenant and Henry Brandon does little with the Scar. Nonetheless a Max Steiner score and superb location filming (by Hoch and Gilks) in Monument Valley give the film a pictorial richness and atmosphere that is often quite striking, restoring the mood of drama and vengeance the "humor" tries so valiantly to obliterate.

A mixed film, out of which oddly enough only Wayne (and the camerawork) emerge with real credit.

P.S. The passage of years has not softened my original view printed above. If anything John Qualen's merciless caricature has become even more obnoxious. Likewise strained is my tolerance for Vera Miles. True, she has both a ridiculous and superfluous part to play, but she gives it not the slightest dram of interest or credibility. Ward Bond's outrageously hammy performance seems more disillusioningly loud-mouthed than ever. *The Searchers* does have the makings of a fine picture. The dramatic scenes and the action episodes are all most vividly and forcefully presented, with Ford making powerful use of his ruggedly picturesque Utah locations. By focusing our attention exclusively to Wayne and excising as much of the comedy knockabout as possible, including just about all of Qualen, Miles and Curtis, as much of Bond and Hunter as will not be detrimental to continuity, plus all of Archuletta, and we could be left with a grimly purposeful, ultimately triumphant, orphic odyssey.

OTHER VIEWS: Handsomely photographed, lavishly mounted *The Searchers* is an excitingly dynamic western so long as the camera keeps Wayne — giving one of his finest performances here — center stage. Ethan is a complex, yet purposeful character, a real human being. Not altogether likeable certainly, but always colorful. When the story shifts to the other searchers and those left behind, interest lapses. In the first place, they're all caricatures or stage figures. In the second place the actors make the mistake of trying to breathe life into these cardboard cut-outs by strident over-acting which destroys all our belief in what's going on. Fortunately, when the story moves back to Wayne, his is such an engrossing study, he's able to re-kindle our absorption and sympathy. A pity the film editor didn't take his scissors to everything not germane to the main (that's Wayne) plot.

— G.A.

# Seminole Uprising

**George Montgomery** (Lieutenant Cam Elliott), **Karin Booth** (Susan Hannah), **William Fawcett** (Cubby Crouch, Scout), **Steve Ritch** (Black Cat, Seminole chief), **Ed Hinton** (Captain Phillip Dudley), **John Pickard** (Sergeant Chris Zanoba), **Jim Maloney** (Tony Zanoba), **Rory Mallinson** (Toby Wilson), **Howard Wright** (Colonel Hannah), **Russ Conklin** (High Cloud), **Jonni Paris** (Malawa), **Joanne Rio** (Tasson Li), **Richard Cutting** (Colonel Robert E. Lee), **Paul McGuire** (Spence), **Kenneth MacDonald** (Dinker), **Rube Schaffer** (Wood), **Edward Coch** (Marsh).

Narrated by **William Fawcett**.

Director: **EARL BELLAMY**. Screenplay: **Robert E. Kent**. Based on the 1952 novel *Bugle's Wake* by "Curt Brandon", pseudonym of **Curtis Bishop**. Photographed in Technicolor by **Henry Freulich**. Film editor: **Jerome Thoms**. Music director: **Mischa Bakaleinikoff**. Art director: **Paul Palmentola**. Set decorator: **Sidney Clifford**. Technicolor color consultant: **Francis Cugat**. Unit manager: **Leon Chooluck**. Special effects: **Jack Erickson**. Assistant director: **Jack Corrick**. Sound supervisor: **John**

**Livadary**. Sound recording: **Josh Westmoreland**. Western Electric Sound System. Producer: **Sam Katzman**. An Eros Films Productions.

Copyright 1955 by Columbia Pictures Corp. No New York opening. U.S. release: 2 May 1955. U.K. release through Eros Film Distributors: April 1956. Australian release: 1 June 1956. Running times: 74 minutes (USA), 71 minutes (UK), 68 minutes (Aust).

SYNOPSIS: In the days before the Civil War, a cavalry lieutenant is assigned by Colonel Robert E. Lee to put down an Indian uprising in Texas led by a band of Florida's Seminoles.

COMMENT: Although the scriptwriter manages to work up some interest in the story in the opening and middle sections of the film, the climax is undermined by obvious intercutting between the unit's footage and some spectacular (but poorly matched) stock material. And after this, although the main tensions are perfunctorily resolved, it all ends rather abruptly with several issues still up in the air.

All the same, by producer Sam Katzman's very humble standards, this is one of his better entries. It's hard to think of Earl Bellamy as a class director, but he has not only used his extras effectively with running inserts yet and given some zing to the action spots (a good fire scene) and real locations, but he has drawn forceful performances from hero George Montgomery, Howard Wright who commands authority as Colonel Hannah, and Steve Ritch who lends plausibility and dignity to Black Cat. Our heroine Karin Booth is spirited and charming, and the story is narrated by William Fawcett of all people, who has his biggest role ever here as Montgomery's scout, a sort of Z-grade Walter Brennan.

There's certainly plenty of action. And the budget looks pretty fair. But I'd love to know from which movie Katzman stole all that awesome rock action at the climax.

OTHER VIEWS: The climax is tricked out with a load of spectacular footage from an "A" western I didn't recognize but whose forceful quality couldn't be dimmed even by ill-judged and meat-axed intercutting with *Seminole Uprising*'s Hollywood Hills locations. The cast is second-rate but serviceable. The story is a bit more interesting than usual for a Katzman "B" too.

—J.H.R. in Photoplayer.

# Seventh Cavalry

**Randolph Scott** (Captain Tom Benson), **Barbara Hale** (Martha Kellogg), **Jay C. Flippen** (Sergeant Bates), **Jeanette Nolan** (Mrs Reynolds), **Frank Faylen** (Krugger), **Leo Gordon** (Vogel), **Denver Pyle** (Dixon), **Harry Carey, Jr** (Corporal Morrison), **Michael Pate** (Captain Benteen), **Donald Curtis** (Lieutenant Bob Fitch) **Frank Wilcox** (Major Reno), **Pat Hogan** (Young Hawk), **Russell Hicks** (Colonel Kellogg), **Peter Ortiz** (Pollock), **William Leslie, Jack Parker, Edward F. Stidder, Al Wyatt**.

Director: **JOSEPH H. LEWIS**. Screenplay: **Peter Packer**. Story: **Glendon F. Swarthout**. Photographed in Eastman Color (print by Technicolor) by **Ray Rennahan**. Film editor: **Gene Havlick**. Art director: **George Brooks**. Set decorator: **Frank Tuttle**. Music conducted by **Mischa Bakaleinikoff**. Assistant to the producer: **David Breen**. Technicolor color consultant: **Henri Jaffa**. Assistant director: **Abner E. Singer**. RCA

Sound System. Associate producer: **Randolph Scott**. Producer: **Harry Joe Brown**. A Scott-Brown Production for Columbia.

Copyright 1956 by Producers-Actors Corporation. No New York opening. U.S. release: December 1956. U.K. release: 14 October 1956 (sic). Australian release: 29 March 1957. Sydney opening at the Victory. 6,757 feet. 75 minutes.

SYNOPSIS: Captain Tom Benson, a protege of General Custer, is accused of absenting himself without leave prior to the Little Big Horn massacre.

COMMENT: Although action fans may be a bit disappointed, this is a grandly staged, inventively directed, well acted and tautly scripted historical piece, filmed against some impressively picturesque natural locations. Of its very nature, the main thrust of the script is to eschew action (though Leo Gordon has opportunities to uncover his usual villainy, and even has an extended punch-up with Randy in which he uses no doubles -- whereas Randy does) as it deals rather interestingly with the aftermath of Little Big Horn rather than the battle itself. Mind you, there is still plenty of suspense right from the *Beau Geste* opening though the court of enquiry to the impressive line-up of war-painted Indian braves filling the screen from one end to the other. The script also provides some interesting conflicts between the Scott character and his fellow officers, as well as his men — *Dirty Dozen* "volunteers".

Scott as usual is excellent in the lead, and receives convincing support right down the line from Russell Hicks' prejudiced colonel through Jay C. Flippen's prevaricating sergeant to Frank Faylen's diamond-in-the-rough trooper. Michael Pate, as a biased adjutant, is effective too.

Lewis' direction is remarkably astute, a text-book model in fact for everything that strong, vigorous direction should be. Lewis for the most part keeps the film editor at bay by using long takes (though Havlick does interrupt a 360 degree pan by repeating a close-up of Scott) and is not afraid to ask his producer star to keep his back to the camera in scenes where the support player is dominant.

All in all, a top western.

OTHER VIEWS: The story has a neat twist, is powerfully constructed and filled with tautly antagonistic characters... Stunning color photography, impressive outdoor locations, enough action and spectacle to satisfy all but the most bloodthirsty fans.

# Shootout at Medicine Bend

**Randolph Scott** (Captain Devlin), **James Craig** (Clark), **Angie Dickinson** (Priscilla King), **Dani Crayne** (Nell), **James Garner** (Sergeant Maitland), **Gordon Jones** (Private Clegg), **Trevor Bardette** (sheriff), **Don Beddoe** (mayor), **Myron Healey** (Ray Sanders), **John Alderson** (Clyde Walters), **Harry Harvey Sr** (King), **Robert Warwick** (Brother Abraham), **Philip Van Zandt** (sandwich board man), **Syd Saylor** (Dutchie, the bartender), **Ann Doran** (Mrs Devlin), **Harry Lauter** (Briggs), **Lane Bradford** (ranch hand), and **Howard Negley, Marshall Bradford, Daryn Hinton, Dickie Bellis, Edward Hinton, Francis Morris, Robert Lynn, Sam Flint, Guy Wilkerson, Harry Rowland, Marjorie Bennett, Jesslyn Fax, Marjorie Stapp, Nancy Kulp, George Meader, Rory**

Mallinson, Dee Carroll, Gerald Charlebois, Dale Van Sickel, Gil Perkins, George Russ, Carol Henry, George Pembroke, Tom Monroe, John Roy, Buddy Roosevelt, George Bell.

Director: **RICHARD L. BARE**. Screenplay: **John Tucker Battle, D.D. Beauchamp**. Photography: **Carl Guthrie**. Film editor: **Clarence Kolster**. Art director: **Stanley Fleischer**. Set decorator: **Ben Bone**. Costumes: **Marjorie Best**. Music composed by **Roy Webb**, orchestrated by **Maurice de Packh**. Song, "Kiss Me Quick" (Crayne) by **Ray Heindorf** (music) and **Wayne Shanklin** (lyrics). Make-up: **Gordon Bau**. Dialogue director: **Henry Staudigl**. Assistant director: **William Kissell**. Sound recording: **Francis E. Stahl**. RCA Sound System. Producer: **Richard Whorf**.

Copyright 1957 by Warner Bros. Pictures, Inc. No New York opening. U.S. release: May 1957. U.K. release: 29 December 1957. Australian release: 7 November 1957. Running times: 87 minutes (USA), 7,807 feet, 86½ minutes (UK), 92 minutes (Australia).

SYNOPSIS: Shortly after the end of the Civil War, an unscrupulous merchant who has both the mayor and the sheriff in his pocket, attempts to gain a monopoly of supplying stores and supplies at Medicine Bend.

NOTES: Although well-produced, Scott's second last film under his Warner Bros contract was churlishly handled by the studio in post-production and publicity. The movie was deliberately over-lit by cinematographer Carl Guthrie who had been assured that all prints of the film would be washed in a sepia bath. This would restore tone and contrast, making the images that look washed-out and over-exposed in ordinary black-and-white take on sharpness, contrast and color. Without over-lighting, many of the shots would look too dark when printed in sepia. However, the studio decided to save money by releasing prints in black-and-white only. Economy was also exercised on posters and lobby cards — the latter, overprinted in a deep red, are probably the least attractive cards the studio ever issued.

COMMENT: An ingenious little western with a novel plot idea which allows for both action and comedy, plus a touch of romance. Randolph Scott, reaching the end of his career here still delivers the goods in his battle against those delightfully unscrupulous villains, James Craig and Myron Healey. While it's a late appearance for Scott, it's an early one for Angie Dickinson (her 9th actually) — though her fans are going to be mighty disappointed by her prim and modest demeanor and attire (Dani Crayne plays the saloon singer and plays it very nicely) — and an even earlier one for James Garner (his 3rd). He is just as uninspiring (both physically and histrionically) as ever. However, the rest of the support cast is very able. There's a fair bit of action with Scott doubling as a sort of masked avenger. Interest does flag a bit towards the end but it is revived with a bang by a splendid climax in which Scott and Craig demolish practically the entire contents of a well-stocked general store. Bare's direction is efficient without being in any way distinguished. The film is helped in its early stages by a bit of location shooting and production values generally are first rate — with a special mention for the lavishly stocked sets. There are a goodly number of extras milling about. Photography and other production credits are adequate.

OTHER VIEWS: An agreeable western, with plenty of action, racy dialogue, colorful villains and crisp direction. An attempt has been made to make the characters a little more 3-dimensional than the usual stereotypes and the players rise to the occasion. James Craig is much more believable as the heavy than as the hero he usually plays. Mr Scott gives an equally strong portrayal, though his manner is appropriately restrained. The support players fit into their roles with both ease and enthusiasm, though Miss Dickinson's admirers will be disappointed by the comparative smallness and unglamorousness of her part — Dani Crayne has the glamour spot as well as well as the bigger part! Production values are well up to "A" standard and there is a fine fight climax in which Scott and Craig wreck a store. Credits are first-class.

# Silly Billies

**Bert Wheeler** (Roy Banks), **Robert Woolsey** (Doc Pennington, painless dentist), **Dorothy Lee** (Mary Blake), **Delmar Watson** (Morton), **Dick Alexander** (John Little), **Harry Woods** (Hank Bewley, scout), **Ethan Laidlaw** (Trigger), **Chief Thundercloud** (Chief Clyclone).

Director: **FRED GUIOL**. Screenplay: **Al Boasberg, Jack Townley**. Story: **Fred Guiol, Thomas Lennon**. Photography: **Nicholas Musuraca, J. Roy Hunt**. Film editor: **John Lockert**. Song, "Tumble on Tumbleweed" (chorus and just about the whole cast) by **Jack Scholl, Dave Dryer**. Music director: **Roy Webb**. Art directors: **Albert S. D'Agostino, Feild Gray**. Special photographic effects: **Vernon L Walker**. Sound recording: **John E. Tribby**. RCA Sound System. Associate producer: **Lee Marcus**.

Copyright 20 March 1936 by RKO Radio Pictures, Inc. New York opening at the Rialto: 5 April 1936. Australian release: 6 May 1936. 7 reels. 65 minutes.

SYNOPSIS: A dentist seeks pickings out West.

COMMENT: Let's have a contest. Who is the most obnoxious child actor Hollywood ever produced? Is it Delmar Watson or his younger brother, Bobs? On the strength of *On Borrowed Time*, Bobs would certainly get my vote, but Delmar certainly runs him a close second. His presence in this film is enough to cast a suspicious cloud over its entertainment prospects. Otherwise, aside from a needlessly elongated and unmercifully attenuated scene in which Richard Alexander sells our heroes an office building (filmed for the most part in understandably disinterested long takes), *Silly Billies* isn't too bad. Certainly it doesn't deserve its poor reputation. True, there's not a great deal of comedic suspense, but that's not entirely the fault of this movie, as its plot was partly re-used in *The Paleface*. And while the conclusion is foregone, it does still have a few neat twists and surprises. What's more, it was lensed on a pretty expensive budget, not the meagre resources some present-day reviewers would have us believe. There's lots of location photography (doubtless the work of J. Roy Hunt), with plenty of action, stunts and extras. The scene in which our heroes try to wake the deserted town is genuinely amusing, as well as inventively staged and directed. In fact Mr Guiol often has a fine old time with his extensive exterior sets and milling crowds of extras. I love the song too. And the perky heroine.

In all, although Wheeler and Woolsey are not quite as lively as in their next effort, *Mummy's Boys* (also directed by Guiol), they still manage enough of their characteristic turns and humor to make this an enjoyably action-filled comedy. Wheeler is an appropriately sad-faced, chucklesomely glum, romantic suitor, while Woolsey's Philip Painless Pennington of a dentist rivals the boisterous incompetence of Bob Hope's Painless Potter in *The Paleface*. And Woolsey has the advantage of his trademark cigar and warcry whoop.

# Silver Dollar

**Edward G. Robinson** (Yates Martin), **Bebe Daniels** (Lily Owens), **Aline MacMahon** (Sarah Martin), **Jobyna Howland** (Poker Annie), **De Witt Jennings** (mine foreman), **Robert Warwick** (Colonel Stanton), **Russell Simpson** (Hamlin), **Harry Holman** (Adams), **Charles Middleton** (Jenkins), **John Marston** (Gelsey), **Marjorie Gateson** (Mrs Adams), **Emmett Corrigan** (President Chester A. Arthur), **Wade Boteler, William Le Maire, David Durand** (miners), **Lee Kohlmar** (Rische), **Theresa Conover** (Mrs Hamlin), **Leon Ames** (secretary), **Virginia Edwards** (Emma Abbott), **Christian Rub** (Hook), **Walter Rogers** (General Grant), **Niles Welch** (William Jennings Bryan), **Bonita Granville** (little girl in store), **Herman Bing** (pawnbroker), **Walter Long** ("sick" miner), **Charles Coleman** (butler), **Willard Robertson** (secretary), and **Wilfred Lucas, Alice Wetherfield, Frederick Burton.**

Director: **ALFRED E. GREEN**. Screenplay: **Carl Erickson, Harvey Thew**. Based on the 1932 biography *Silver Dollar: The Story of the Tabors* by **David Karsner**. Photography: **James Van Trees**. Film editor: **George Marks**. Art director: **Robert Haas**. Costumes: **Orry-Kelly**. No producer credited.

Copyright 24 March 1933 by First National Pictures, Inc. A Warner Bros-First National Picture. New York opening at the Strand: 22 December 1932. U.K. release: 3 June 1933. 84 minutes.

SYNOPSIS: Yates Martin, a Kansas farmer, gets caught up in the Colorado gold rush, and with his wife, Sarah, opens a general store in one of the boom towns. However, Yates goes broke extending credit to the miners who pay him in shares to their mines. The Martins are about to return to Kansas and farming when two miners come in with silver bags. Martin becomes the richest of them all. Soon Martin becomes a leading town figure, and enters politics, being elected in turn mayor, postmaster, sheriff and eventually lieutenant governor. He has so much money he is literally throwing it away. He buys a mansion in Denver, erects a big opera house, donates land for a post office, and is the first to give to charity on any occasion.

Martin meets Lily, a beautiful woman who delights in diamonds and pearls, and adores the limelight — a complete contrast to his wife. Martin leaves Sarah for Lily. The resulting scandal almost ruins his chance for running for the U.S. Senate, but he manages to win a vacant seat. He weds Lily in Washington with the President and Senators attending the nuptials. Returning to Denver, Martin continues his reckless spending.

NOTES: Number 22 at the Australian box-office for 1933, which is actually even better than it sounds, as this picture sold only about twenty thousand tickets less than the number 4 placegetter *Kid from Spain*.

One of Mordaunt Hall's selections for his supplementary list of "Fifty Notable Films of 1932" for *The New York Times*.

VIEWERS' GUIDE: Adults.

COMMENT: Not just another rags to riches to rags story but a superbly staged chronicle of the rise and fall of Haw Tabor, the Colorado silver mining tycoon and aspiring U.S. Senator, brilliantly and engrossingly brought to life by Ed G.

The other figures of Tabor's life are well enacted too: Aline MacMahon almost too realistic as Tabor's nagging wife, Bebe Daniels (who doesn't come on till half-way through) as the gold-digger who surprisingly sticks by him.

Production values are exceptionally lavish (marvelous sets by Robert Haas).

Peppy direction.

OTHER VIEWS: Robinson turns in one of his greatest performances.
— *Motion Picture Guide*.

# Singin' in the Corn

**Judy Canova** (Judy McCoy), **Allen Jenkins** (Glen Cummings), **Guinn "Big Boy" Williams** (Hank), **Charles Halton** (Obediah Davis), **Alan Bridge** (Honest John Richards), **Robert Dudley** (Gramp McCoy), **Nick Thompson** (Indian chief), **Frances Rey** (Ramona), **George Chesebro** (Texas), **Ethan Laidlaw** (Silk Stevens), **Frank Lackteen** (medicine man), **The Singing Indian Braves** (themselves), **Guy Beach** (judge), **Jay Silverheels, Rodd Redwing** (braves), **Dick Stanley, Charles Randolp** (Indians), **Si Jenks** (old man), **Pat O'Malley** (O'Rourke), **Chester Conklin** (Austin driver), **Mary Gordon** (Mrs O'Rourke).

Director: **DEL LORD**. Screenplay: **Isabel Dawn, Monte Brice**. Additional dialogue: **Elwood Ullman**. Screen story: **Richard Weil**. Photography: **George Meehan**. Film editor: **Aaron Stell**. Art director: **Sturges Carne**. Set decorator: **Bill Calvert**. Music director: **George Duning**. Songs (all Canova): "I'm a Gal of Property", "Pepita Chiquita", "An Old Love Is a True Love" — all by **Doris Fisher** and **Allan Roberts**: "Ma, He's Making Eyes at Me", lyrics by **Sidney Clare**, music by **Con Conrad**. Producer: **Ted Richmond**.

Copyright 26 December 1946 by Columbia Pictures Corp. No recorded New York opening. U.S. release: 26 December 1946. U.K. release: June 1947. Australian release: 7 August 1947. 5,904 feet. 65½ minutes.

U.K. release title: *GIVE AND TAKE*.

SYNOPSIS: A carnival girl inherits a ghost town.

COMMENT: In this off-beat little item director Del Lord even exhibits a few traces of style (the long shot and angle shots of the hotel). He has a much larger budget than usual to play around with and the ghost town (presumably a standing set on Columbia's back lot) is quite impressive. The script has the usual number of weak puns ("They certainly played with spirit!"), but it has enough off-beat elements to make it passably appealing (in fact, it was later re-made as an Elvis Presley vehicle, *Tickle Me*). We liked Miss Canova's crack about the invisible band. The pace is brisk and there is an agreeable chase climax. Miss Canova's vehicles were generally not much, but this is certainly one of her better ones.

# Six-Gun Law

**Charles Starrett** (Steve Norris), **Smiley Burnette** (himself), **Nancy Saunders** (June Wallace), **Paul Campbell** (Jim Wallace), **Hugh Prosser** (Boss Decker), **George Chesebro** (Bret Wallace), **Billy Dix** (Crowl), **Bob Wilke** (Larson), **Bob Cason** (Ben), **Ethan Laidlaw** (Sheriff Brackett), **Pierce Lyden** (Jack Reed), **Bud Osborne** (Barton), **Budd Buster** (Bank Clerk Duffy), **Jock Mahoney** (stunt double for Charles Starrett), **Curly Clements and his Rodeo Rangers**.

Narrated by **Charles Starrett**.

Director: **RAY NAZARRO**. Original screenplay: **Barry Shipman**. Photography: **George F. Kelley**. Film editor: **Henry DeMond**. Art director: **Charles Clague**. Set decorator: **David Montrose**. Hair styles: **Helen Hunt**. Assistant director: **Gilbert Kay**. Camera operator: **Gert Anderson**. Grip: **Al Becker**. Stills: **Don Christie**. Set continuity: **Wyonna O'Brien**. Sound recording: **Lambert Day**. Sound engineer: **Frank Goodwin**. Western Electric Sound System. Producer: **Colbert Clark**.

Copyright 26 November 1947 by Columbia Pictures Corp. No New York opening. U.S. release: 9 January 1948. No record of any U.K. theatrical release. Australian release: 25 August 1949. 4,981 feet. 55 minutes.

SYNOPSIS: Framed into believing he has killed the local sheriff, a rancher is forced to fill the post himself.

NOTES: Charles Starrett's 95th western.

COMMENT: There's plenty of action in this entertaining Durango Kid western, including a spectacular stagecoach chase with running inserts and thrilling stunt-work (performed by Jock Mahoney, easily recognizable in Durango's garb). This footage is so good it was used again 3 or 4 years later in another entry in this series. For once, the title has something to do with the script which casts Starrett in the meaty role of an unwillingly crooked sheriff. Hugh Prosser and Robert Wilke make a fine pair of villains. Nancy Saunders is an attractive heroine, though she has very little footage. George Chesebro is on the right side of the law, for a change. Smiley Burnette doesn't figure much in the early stages of the film, but he comes into his own later on with his camera used in a thrilling development of the plot. The musical interludes are pleasant, with Mr Curly Clements performing some mean tricks on a fiddle. The script uses narration effectively to maintain interest. Ray Nazarro's direction is capable and the location photography is often quite attractive.

# Sons of the Pioneers

**Roy Rogers** (Roy Rogers), **Pat Brady** (himself), **George "Gabby" Hayes** (Gabby Whittaker), **Maris Wrixon** (Louis Harper), **Forrest Taylor** (Jim Bixby), **Minerva Urecal** (Mrs Bixby), **Bradley Page** (Frank Bennett), **Bob Nolan** (Louise's foreman), **Hal Taliaferro** (Briggs), **Chester Conklin** (old timer), **Fred Burns** (rancher), **Fern Emmett** (landlady), **Jack O'Shea** (Pete), **Frank Ellis, Art Mix** (cowhands at dance), **Tom London** (Joe), **Bob Woodward, Ken Cooper** (Tom), **Karl Hackett** (Dr Thompson), **Horace B. Carpenter** (rancher), **Pascale Perry, Tex Harper** (cowhands), **Tommy Coats, Bud Osborne** (henchmen), **Herbert Rawlinson, Duke Taylor, Lew Murphy** (townsmen), "Trigger" the horse, and **Bob Nolan, Lloyd Perryman, Tim Spencer, Carl Farr, Pat Brady** (The Sons of the Pioneers), **Joe Yrigoyen** (stunt double for Len Slye).

Director: **JOSEPH KANE**. Screenplay: **M. Coates Webster, Mauri Grashin, Robert T. Shannon**. Original story: **Mauri Grashin, Robert T. Shannon**. Photography: **Bud Thackery**. Film editor: **Edward Schroeder**. Songs: "The West Is in My Soul" (Rogers, Pioneers), "There's Gloom Around the Ranch-House Tonight" (Hayes, Brady, Rogers), "Easy-A, Easy-O" (Rogers, Pioneers) by **Bob Nolan** and **Tim Spencer**. Music director: **Cy Feuer**. Art director: **Russell Kimball**. Set decorator: **Otto Siegel**. Assistant director: **Art Siteman**. Stunts: **Tommy Coats, Duke Taylor, Bob Woodward, Nellie Walker**. RCA Sound System. Associate producer: **Joseph Kane**. Executive producer: **Herbert J. Yates**.

Copyright 2 July 1942 by Republic Pictures Corp. No recorded New York opening. U.S. release: 2 July 1942. Never theatrically released in Australia or broadcast on television. 6 reels. 61 minutes.

SYNOPSIS: Zorro/Destry revisited.

COMMENT: Our hats are off to the boys at Roadshow Video. No hard-headed theatermen these, with their eyes firmly fixed on profits. One of their first offerings in their new Republic Collection is a Roy Rogers movie originally judged so lacking in commercial appeal in some territories that it wasn't even released . Of course it's possible the original distributors were wrong. But now that we've had a chance to view the movie at long last — for which our heartfelt thanks — we're tempted to agree that it's not one of Roy's finest.

Mind you, it's attractively cast. Rogers himself is at his charming best, even though he's handed only three choruses, and he's appealingly supported by Hayes doing his juggling act (a nice bit of business this), and Maris Wrixon acting perky and looking beautiful. Bradley Page is okay as the heavy, Hal Taliaferro is more impressive as his henchman, and Chester Conklin has a few close-ups to try out one or two of his comic expressions. Although unbilled, Pat Brady has a lead role as Gabby's sidekick, while Bob Nolan is oddly though not disturbingly cast as the heroine's ranch foreman.

The problems are not entirely with the script either. It builds up to a double-action climax and has a few chases and stunts along the way. The trouble is that the climax is resolved too quickly, the chases are all filmed from static camera positions, and one of the stunts is so weak I could do it myself (and I'm no athlete). A lot of the action takes place at night. While the darkened studio interiors look good, the day-for-night exteriors look very shoddy indeed. The washed out, TV-graded dupe of a 16mm print under review doesn't help. (This video was allegedly mastered from "original film negative". I don't know about you, but I call original film negative the master negative from which the 1942 35mm theatrical prints were struck. Instead this video print was made from a 16mm dupe negative, deliberately over-exposed for TV use. A dupe negative — and a lousy one at that — is not original film negative, boys).

In short a minor western outing indeed, made on a limited budget, hastily directed and at times even clumsily edited. This one's mainly for Maris Wrixon fans.

Incidentally, the title has nothing to do with the plot. And as for The Sons of the Pioneers as a singing group, they figure very briefly only at the beginning and end of the picture.

# the Spoilers

**Marlene Dietrich** (Cherry Malotte), **Randolph Scott** (Alexander McNamara), **John Wayne** (Roy Glennister), **Margaret Lindsay** (Helen Chester), **Harry Carey** (Al Dextry), **Richard Barthelmess** (Bronco Kid Farrell), **George Cleveland** (Banty), **Samuel S. Hinds** (Judge Stillman), **Russell Simpson** (Flapjack Simms), **William Farnum** (Wheaton), **Marietta Canty** (Idabelle), **Jack Norton** (Skinner), **Ray Bennett** (Clark), **Forrest Taylor** (Bennett), **Charles McMurphy, Art Miles, William Haade** (deputies), **Charles Halton** (Jonathan Struve), **Bud Osborne** (marshall), **Drew Demarest** (Galloway), **Robert W. Service** (poet), **Robert Homans** (sea captain), **Irving Bacon** (hotel proprietor), **Robert McKenzie** (restaurateur), **Chester Clute** (Montrose), **Harry Woods** (complaining miner), **William Gould** (Marshal Thompson), **Willie Fung** (jailed Chinaman), **Lloyd Ingraham** (Kelly), **Si Jenks** (man seeking room).

Director: **RAY ENRIGHT**. Screenplay: **Lawrence Hazard, Tom Reed**. Based on the 1906 novel by **Rex Beach**. Photography: **Milton Krasner**. Film editor: **Clarence Kolster**. Music composed by **Hans J. Salter**, directed by **Charles Previn**. Songs: "Little Joe, the Wrangler", by **Frederick Hollander** (music) and **Frank Loesser** (lyrics); "Kathleen" (male quartette). Art directors: **Jack Otterson, John B. Goodman**. Set decorators: **Russell A. Gausman, Edward R. Robinson**. Costumes: **Vera West**. Stunts: **Eddie Parker, Alan Pomeroy**. Dialogue director: **Gene Lewis**. Special photographic effects: **John P. Fulton**. Assistant director: **Vernon Keays**. Sound director: **Bernard B. Brown**. Sound technician: **Robert Pritchard**. Western Electric Sound System. Associate producer: **Lee Marcus**. Producer: **Frank Lloyd**. A **Charles K. Feldman** Group Production for Frank Lloyd Productions, Inc.

Copyright 15 April 1942 by Universal Pictures Co., Inc. New York opening at the Capitol: 21 May 1942. U.S. release: 8 May 1942. U.K. release through General Film Distributors: 13 July 1942. Australian release: 17 June 1943. 7,914 feet. 87 minutes.

SYNOPSIS: A bogus gold commissioner and a crooked judge gain control of an Alaskan gold mine.

NOTES: Fourth of five versions of *The Spoilers*. The others were made in 1914, 1923, 1930 and 1955. William Farnum, who plays the lawyer Wheaton in this one, starred as Glennister in the 1914 movie, while Lloyd Ingraham who plays a minor role here was

Judge Stillman in the 1930 Gary Cooper-William Boyd version. Other Roy Glennisters were Milton Stills in 1923 and Jeff Chandler in 1955. McNamara was played by Tom Santschi, Noah Beery, William "Stage" Boyd, Randolph Scott and finally Rory Calhoun. The 1923 film was directed by Lambert Hillyer, while Edwin Carewe took control in 1930. Jesse Hibbs handled the 1955 film. This one was nominated for an award from The Academy of Motion Picture Arts and Sciences for its black-and-white Art Direction, but lost to *This Above All.*

COMMENT: Good to see this one again. True, the climactic fist fight in which Wayne and Scott are helped out by doubles Eddie Parker and Alan Pomeroy now seems somewhat less exciting. But it's hard to dim the allure of Miss Dietrich at her zenith (even if the script oddly fails to provide her with a single song, despite ample opportunities for same), whilst Scott is especially convincing as the villain. (Was this the only time he played a heavy?)

Wayne of course is Wayne, but he is helped out by Harry Carey and a grand support cast. We could go through the list of players, commending people right, left and center, but we'll limit ourselves to a special pat on the back for Richard Barthelmess.

The script packs in plenty of humor. The approach is often light-hearted with in-jokes ("Lee Marcus just checked out") including a guest appearance by Robert W. Service. The direction by Ray Enright is surprisingly fluid, and production values are nothing short of lavish.

OTHER VIEWS: This *Spoilers* holds up rather well. The pace is fast, packing in plenty of action and even a few intentional laughs. Spectacularly filmed on an extremely lavish budget, with remarkably authentic-looking sets that were justly nominated for a prestigious Award, this version also features an outstanding cast. Not only are the principals exciting, but many of the character players including favorites like Russell Simpson, Jack Norton, William Haade and Charles Halton are given some great opportunities to shine. Good to see Samuel S. Hinds excelling himself on the wrong side of the law for once. Ditto Margaret Lindsay. Of course Richard Barthelmess is always interesting, and we love Harry Carey too. Directed with marvelous pace and a fluid camera style by Ray Enright, of all people, but he was doubtless heavily strong-armed by producer Frank *Mutiny on the Bounty* Lloyd. The three stars deserve cheers. Three cheers for the stars. Three cheers for the support players. Three cheers for the writers and all the technical personnel. Five stars for the movie.

# Spy Smasher

**Kane Richmond** (Alan Armstrong/Jack Armstrong), **James Dale** (lookalike stand-in for both Alan and Jack), **David Sharpe, Carey Loftin, Bud Wolfe, John Daheim** (stunt doubles for Spy Smasher), **Marguerite Chapman** (Eve Corby), **Sam Flint** (Admiral Corby), **Hans Schumm** (The Mask), **Tristram Coffin** (Drake), **Franco Corsaro** (Pierre Durand), **Hans von Morhart** (Gerhardt), **Georges Renavent** (Governor LeConte), **Robert O. Davis [Rudolph Anders]** (Von Kahr), **Henry Zynda** (Ritter Lazar), **Paul Bryar** (Lawlor), **Tom London** (Crane), **Richard Bond** (Hayes), **Crane Whitley** (Hauser), **John James** (Steve), **Yakima Canutt** (armored car driver), **Max Waizman** (auto clerk), **Howard Hughes, Charley Phillips** (bank heavies), **Martin Faust**

(blacksmith), **Tom Steele, Eddie Jauregui, John Daheim, Bob Jamison, Walter Low** (brick heavies), **Jerry Jerome** (Burns), **Jack Arnold** (camera clerk), **Martin Garralaga** (captain), **Robert J. Wilke** (chief operative), **Buddy Roosevelt** (commandant), **Bud Wolfe** (Craig/policeman), **William Forrest** (Gerald Douglas), **Nick Vehr** (dungeon guard), **Duke Taylor** (Fritz/storm trooper), **Sid Troy** (gold heavy), **Lee Phelps** (guard), **Lowden Adams** (headwaiter), **George Sherwood** (jailer), **Ken Terrell** (Jerry/storm trooper/policeman), **Louis Tomei** (Joe), **Carey Loftin** (launch heavy), **Jimmy Fawcett** (Lewis/policeman), **Leonard St Leo** (lieutenant), **Ray Parsons** (Livingston), **Duke Green** (lumber heavy), **Charles Regan** (manager), **Bert LeBaron** (mechanic), **Bill Wilkus, Loren Riebe** (pipe heavies), **Dudley Dickerson** (porter), **Carleton Young** (power clerk/Taylor), **Cy Slocum** (private), **John Peters** (quartermaster), **Al Seymour** (Sloan), **David Sharpe** (sniper), **Roy Brent, Ray Hanson, Ray Jones** (soldiers), **Tommy Coats** (squad leader), **Hugh Prosser** (squadron leader), **Frank Alten** (storm trooper captain), **George J. Lewis** (Stuart), **Arvon Dale** (Thornton), **Robert Stevenson** (torpedo chief), **Gil Perkins** (valve sailor), **Pat Moran** (waiter), **John Buckley** (Walker), **Jack O'Shea**.

Director: **WILLIAM WITNEY**. Screenplay: **Ronald Davidson, Norman S. Hall, William Lively, Joseph O'Donnell, Joseph Poland**. Story: **Harrison Carter**. Based on the comic strip character "Spy Smasher" created by **Ralph Daigh** and **Charles Clarence Beck** under the editorial supervision of **William Parker** of Fawcett Publications, Inc. Photography: **Reggie Lanning**. Film editors: **Tony Martinelli, Edward Todd**. Music score by **Mort Glickman, Arnold Schwarzwald, Paul Sawtell**. First Movement of the Fifth Symphony by **Ludwig van Beethoven** arranged by **Mort Glickman, Cy Feuer, Raoul Kraushaar**. Music director: **Mort Glickman**. Special effects: **Howard Lydecker**. Unit manager: **Mack d'Agostino**. RCA Sound System. Associate producer: **W.J. O'Sullivan**. Executive producer: **Herbert J. Yates**.

Copyright 4 April 1942 by Republic Pictures Corp. U.S. release: 4 April 1942. Approx. 207 minutes in all. First chapter has 3 reels, following eleven chapters 2 reels each. Chapter titles: *America Beware, Human Target, Iron Coffin, Stratosphere Invaders, Descending Doom, the Invisible Witness, Secret Weapon, Sea Raiders, Highway Racketeers, 2700° Fahrenheit, Hero's Death, V...-*.

SYNOPSIS: Twin brothers battle Nazis and their agents.

NOTES: William Witney who had directed the action sequences in such previous Republic serials as *Zorro Rides Again, The Lone Ranger, Fighting Devil Dogs* and *Dick Tracy Returns*, took over the solo reins here for the first time. [Admittedly, *Spy Smasher* is not a western, but I include it here to honor the man I believe deserves the title, "King of the Serials," William Witney].

Shooting commenced 22 December 1941 and finished 29 January 1942. Negative cost: $156,431 which was less than $3,000 over budget. Locations, all in Southern California, included Lake Elsinore, the Los Angeles Brick & Clay Products factory at Alberhill, the Van Nuys police station, Iverson's ranch, the Consumers Rock & Gravel Company in North Hollywood, and even Republic's miniature shop and transportation garage, as well as an empty sound stage and backlot replicas of a Spanish fort and New York Square.

COMMENT: Witney's first solo serial is also undoubtedly his best. Every episode, but one, is absolutely full of action. In fact some of the middle action is often more exciting than the actual cliffhanger. Spy Smasher is nothing if not athletic. But these doubles are not alone for thrilling stuntwork and their ability to tumble over and smash up breakaway furniture. The heavies are a pretty gymnastic lot too.

Witney has stylishly used a number of most effective natural locations, yet at the same time has drawn reasonably convincing performances from his large roster of players. The pace hardly ever lets up. What's more, the serial always looks good. It's hard to believe the budget was no more than Republic serial average. Witney has made such ingenious use of Republic's own facilities as well as some fascinating real locales.

Richmond gives a creditable account of his dual role, whilst Marguerite Chapman makes a most attractive heroine. This alas was her only Republic serial. Our only regret is that she doesn't have more footage.

Howard Lydecker has contributed some wonderful special effects work, Lanning's photography is first-class, and other credits are likewise super-proficient.

One of the most creditable features of *Spy Smasher*, aside from its continuously effective, fast-paced action, is its frequent changes of setting and scene. This has caused continuity problems for the feature length cut-down, *Spy Smasher Returns*. For the first half-hour particularly, story continuity in this re-edited version is especially jerky and abrupt. Still it does retain the best of the action sequences.

Episode 1 is virtually a miniature movie. The characters are introduced with a minimum of talk and a maximum of exciting action. The cliffhanger is an absolute stand-out. Unfortunately it is resolved by a cheat in Episode 2. Not that anyone will notice for this ep too is absolutely crammed with chases and stunts. Only the hanger is weak. For some reason, this weakest of weak piece of action is not only copiously repeated at the beginning of Chapter 3, but is resolved in a needlessly complicated fashion. However the director and scriptwriters make amends with even more chock-a-block action including a suspenseful cliffhanger in the middle. The actual end hanger is reasonably exciting. And what we particularly like about Chapters 2 and 3 is the welcome change of setting. Chapter 4 introduces the ingenious Flying Wing. Lydecker has excelled himself with his fascinating miniatures and realistic explosions.

Number 6 is the economy episode in which the characters mostly stand around and talk in the studio interiors. Though it does have two attractive fight scenes including a fine donnybrook of a climax which oddly is not repeated at the start of Chapter 7. Slow dialogue delivery is not helped by incessant if low-volume background music. At least the attractive Marguerite Chapman figures briefly.

Episode 7 puts *Spy Smasher* firmly back on track. Not only does it feature another vigorous punch-up in the middle but this time it's followed by a car chase (admittedly slightly undermined by obvious studio process screen cut-ins). It ends up with another all-in brawl, this time at a fascinating tower locale. It's good to have this punch-a-second, rough-and-tumble repeated in full at the opening of Chapter 8, an ep which not only features daredevil stunt-work and a breathtaking Lydecker explosion but yet another vigorous fight in a fine factory setting. Faster dialogue delivery adds further zest to the pace. And it all comes to a pretty good climax, which is run through again at the start of treat number 9. The dialogue slows down for this one, but Marguerite Chapman figures briefly, and there's some fast action topped by a motorbike and car chase. The fist fight on top of the station wagon is repeated straight after the credits on 10, even though its effectiveness is undermined by an obvious process screen. Good to have the chase resumed however, and the clay factory makes a wonderfully arresting locale. In fact this ep seems to have been filmed entirely on location, apart from a couple of brief interiors -- and of course the process screen inserts. Good stunts make this ep a further stand-out. And this time the car chases the bike, reversing the formula from number 9. Oddly the cliffhanger is similar to Chapter 1, but it is more simply and realistically resolved in Chapter 11, an ep where finally Marguerite Chapman comes into her own. This one too is nonetheless crowded with action, even though, aside from the climax, mostly interior settings are used. The cliffhanger is one of the most unusual and bizarre in the entire history of the movie serial in that it's not resolved. There are no cheats, no last-second surprises. It actually happens just the way you see it.

The final act sees no let-up in chase and fight action. In fact Lydecker does some of his most thrilling work.

All told, a very cleverly made and most attractive serial which belies its rapid shooting time and modest negative cost. Full marks to solo debut director William Witney.

OTHER VIEWS: One of the best of the war-time Republic serials, with some marvelous action scenes, stuntwork and Lydecker explosions, set against striking natural backgrounds. The direction has both style and flair with some fine camera set-ups and visually exciting high angle shots. The plot, too, whilst following a well-worn path, rings some surprising changes on its well-worn theme (people are actually killed and the villains actually succeed in blowing up the munitions plant) and the ingenious device of twin brothers is effectively exploited in impressively realistic special effects. The cast too is a cut above the usual average, with a fine performance by Kane Richmond in his dual role.

Production values are first-class. Most of the film was made on location, with many changes of scene and an unusual number of interior sets.

**The Director:** William Witney is one of the kings of both the serial and "B" western. He regards his best film as *Stranger at My Door* (1956). Of his 88 other features and serials, the most famous are *Bells of San Angelo* (1947) starring Roy Rogers, *Adventures of Captain Marvel* (1941) starring Tom Tyler, *Jungle Girl* (1941) starring Frances Gifford, and *Perils of Nyoka* (1942) starring Kay Aldridge.

# Stagecoach to Monterey

**Allan Lane** (Chick Weaver/Bruce Redmond), **Peggy Stewart** (Jessie Wade), **Wally Vernon** (Throckmorton Snodgrass), **Twinkle Watts** (Inky Wade), **Tom London** (Charles Wade), **Roy Barcroft** (J. Rodney Stevens), **LeRoy Mason** (Blackjack Barstow), **Kenne Duncan** (Joe), **Bud Geary** (Gans), **Carl Sepulveda, Fred Graham** (henchmen), **Jack O'Shea** (Jim Boyd), **Jack Kirk** (bartender), **Henry Wills** (Buck), **Cactus Mack**.

Director: **LESLEY SELANDER**. Original screenplay: **Norman S. Hall**. Photography: **William Bradford**. Film editor: **Harry Keller**. Art directors: **Gano Chittenden, Russ**

**Kimball.** Music score: **Joseph Dubin.** Assistant director: **Bart Carre.** Sound recording: **Vic Appel.** RCA Sound System. Associate producer: **Stephen Auer.** Executive producer: **Herbert J. Yates.**

Copyright 3 August 1944 by Republic Pictures Corp. U.S. release: 15 September 1944. No New York opening. No U.K. or Australian release. 6 reels. 55 minutes.

SYNOPSIS: Government agent defeats mining swindle.

COMMENT: To judge by the last half-hour, this is a very tame, talky western, produced on a miniscule budget. The action climax is most ineptly staged and directed with stunt players clutching their breasts and crumpling to the ground and a wagon chase contrived through dull panning shots intercut with obvious studio action against a process screen. Lane's Frank Redmond is a whistle-clean hero, Wally Vernon a dull comic sidekick (Throckmorton Snodgrass), Miss Stewart a reasonably attractive heroine, Miss Twinkle Watts a juvenile thrown in for the "pleasure" of the sub-teen age group for whom the movie was obviously intended (though we cannot see even 1944 kiddies sitting still for all the talk, talk, talk), Tom London the heroine's too-eager-to-put-his-wrongs-right dad. In all, a waste of time except for the most rabid fans. Anyone who thinks Selander a notch above the usual run of "B" western hacks should see *Stagecoach to Monterey*.

# Stage to Thunder Rock

**Barry Sullivan** (Sheriff Horne), **Marilyn Maxwell** (Leah Parker), **Keenan Wynn** (Ross Sawyer), **Scott Brady** (Sam Swope), **Lon Chaney, Jr** (Henry Parker), **John Agar** (Dan Carrouthers), **Wanda Hendrix** (Mrs Swope), **Anne Seymour** (Myra Parker), **Allan Jones** (Mayor Ted Dollar), **Ralph Taeger** (Reese Sawyer), **Laurel Goodwin** (Julie Parker), **Robert Strauss** (Judge Bates), **Robert Lowery** (Seth Harrington), **Argentina Brunetti** (Sarita), **Rex Bell, Jr** ("Shotgun"), **Suzanne Cupito** (Sandy Swope), **Wayne Peters** (Toby Sawyer), **Paul E. Burns** (Joe Withers), **Roy Jenson** (Harkins).

Director: **WILLIAM F. CLAXTON.** Screenplay: **Charles A. Wallace.** Photographed in Techniscope and Technicolor by **W. Wallace Kelley.** Film editor: **Jodie Copelan.** Music: **Paul Dunlap.** Art directors: **Hal Pereira, Robert Smith.** Set decorators: **Sam Comer, James Edgar Roach.** Make-up: **Wally Westmore.** Hair styles: **Nellie Manley.** Dialogue coach: **Frank London.** Production manager: **William C. Davidson.** Process photography: **Farciot Edouart.** Assistant director: **Russ Haverick.** Sound recording: **Harold Lewis, John Wilkinson.** Producer: **A.C. Lyles.**

Copyright 31 December 1963 by A.C. Lyles Productions. Released through Paramount Pictures. New York opening: 10 November 1964. Not reviewed in the New York Times. U.S. release: 17 June 1964. U.K. release: 8 June 1964, in a version cut down to 62 minutes. Original and U.S. running time: 82 minutes.

Alternative U.S. title: *STAGECOACH TO HELL*.

SYNOPSIS: A sheriff captures a bank robber, but is stalked not only by his prisoner's father but by a hired gunman.

COMMENT: A slow-moving western with too many speeches, particularly from the sadly aged Marilyn Maxwell who has the lead part, and Anne Seymour who overdoes the money-pinching harridan. The British version doubtless cuts the talk to a minimum, whilst retaining the action spots and the guest appearances by such old-time favorites as Wanda Hendrix and Allan Jones (both look surprisingly fit). Claxton's monotonous, TV-style direction doesn't help, nor does a rather dirge-like music score. Still, Barry Sullivan handles Horne capably, Ralph Taeger (who seems to have made only a handful of movies) makes a strong antagonist, and it's always a pleasure to see Lon Chaney and Keenan Wynn. "B" hero Robert Lowery has a small role which he puts across with ease, whilst even such potential hams as Robert Strauss and Paul E. Burns make themselves welcome.

As mentioned earlier, director Claxton does little with the wide screen, except in his exteriors where he is helped out by Wallace Kelley's autumn-hued cinematography.

# the Star Packer

**John Wayne** (U.S. Marshal John Travers), **Verna Hillie** (Anita Matlock), **George ["Gabby"] Hayes** (Matt Matlock), **Yakima Canutt** (Yak, John's Indian partner), **Earl Dwire** (Mason), **Ed Parker** (Parker), **George Cleveland** (Old Jake, the Matlock cook), **William Franey** (Pete, town bum), **Tom Lingham** (Sheriff Davis), **Art Ortega** (deputy), **Tex Palmer** (stagecoach driver), **Davie Aldrich** (boy), **Glenn Strange**.

Director: **ROBERT N. BRADBURY**. Original screenplay: **Robert N. Bradbury**. Photography: **Archie Stout**. Film editor: **Carl Pierson**. Technical director: **E.R. Hickson**. Music director: **Abe Meyer**. Sound recording: **J.A. Stransky Jr**. Producer: **Paul Malvern**.

Copyright 15 August 1934 by Monogram Pictures Corp. A Lone Star Western. No New York showcase. U.S. release: 30 July 1934. U.K. release through Pathé: 24 June 1935. Never released in Australia. 54 minutes.

VIEWERS' GUIDE: Okay for all.

COMMENT: One of the best of the Lone Stars — not only action-packed and fast-moving, but utilizing an interesting cast in a fairly involving script, all filmed on a fair-sized budget.

John Wayne of course is the man who packs the star. In point of fact he wears **two** stars in his efforts to unmask The Shadow. There's a bit of mystery as to The Shadow's identity, though this soon becomes obvious. The seasoned fan will have no trouble, and even the casual picturegoer should tumble to it sooner rather than later. Nonetheless the actor concerned puts up a good show.

It's pleasing to report that not only is Wayne in top form, but that his mate Yakima Canutt has a major role in this one as the Duke's constant sidekick — an Indian named Yak. In fact Canutt is one of the chief joys of the movie, performing an astonishing number of increasingly spectacular stunts, including several leaps from horse to horse, a wagon plunge, and five or six Flying W's including one which catapults two riders off the one horse.

Bradbury directs the triple action climax with all stops out. Lots of running inserts add to the excitement as a fair-sized posse rounds ups a fair-sized gang of outlaws. Locations are reasonably picturesque. And we love those whip pans!

The support cast, led by slim heroine Verna Hillie, comes over as top-notch.

# Stick To Your Guns

**William Boyd** (Hopalong Cassidy), **Brad King** (Johnny Nelson), **Andy Clyde** (California), **Jacqueline Holt** (June Winters), **Henry Hall** (Winters), **Joe Whitehead** (Buck), **Bob Card** (Frenchy), **Jimmy Wakely** (Pete), **Johnny Bond** (Skinny), **Dick Rinehart** (Bow Wow), **Jack Trent** (Red), **Homer Holcomb** (Lanky), **Tom London** (Waffles), **Mickey Eissa** (Ed), **Jack Smith** (Tex), **Weldon Heyburn, Kermit Maynard, Frank Ellis, Jack Rockwell, Herman Hack, Dick Curtis, Ian MacDonald, Charles Middleton**.

Directed by **LESLEY SELANDER**. Associate producer: **Lewis J. Rachmil**. Original screenplay by **J. Benton Cheney**. Based on characters created by **Clarence E. Mulford**. Art director: **Ralph Berger**. Sound mixer: **Charles Althouse**. Supervising editor: **Sherman A. Rose**. Film editor: **Carrol Lewis**. Photography: **Russell Harlan**. Wardrobe: **Earl Moser**. Assistant director: **Glenn Cook**. Music score: **John Leipold**. Music director: **Irvin Talbot**. Producer: **Harry Sherman**. A Harry Sherman Production.

Copyright 19 September 1941 by Paramount Pictures Inc. U.S. release: 27 September 1941. No New York showcase. Australian release: 12 November 1942. 5,655 feet. 63 minutes.

SYNOPSIS: All the Bar-20 cowhands gather at a word from one of its former crew who has become a ranch owner and is systematically being robbed of his stock by a rustling gang. Hopalong Cassidy and his leathery lieutenant, California, submit a plan of action: they will proceed to Snake Buttes, locate the hideout and try to work into the gang's roster. If they are successful, they agree, a smoke signal and sage signs will lead to the outlaw nest.

While Hoppy's sidekick, Johnny Nelson, waits for the rest of the Bar-20 worthies to assemble at the ranch, Hopalong and California head for the desert town of Ojos Verdes. While California cadges a free lunch and resists all blandishments and entreaties from the bartender for a single purchase, Hoppy finds out the location of the rustlers' headquarters from Long Ben, a treacherous gambler who reveals the location because he has been caught cheating and beaten up by the rustlers and has a long-standing fear of Hoppy. Long Ben hopes each will wipe out the other.

NOTES: Number 40 of the 66-picture series.
  Locations scenes photographed in the Lone Pine region, California.
  Songs: "Blue Moon on the Silver Sage" and "On the Strings of My Guitar", both sung by Brad King, with the guitar-strumming accompaniment of the Jimmy Wakely Trio (Wakely, Bond and Rinehart).
  Jacqueline "Jennifer" Holt is the daughter of Jack Holt.

VIEWERS' GUIDE: Okay for all.

COMMENT: Hopalong Cassidy and California pose as a couple of outlaws and join a gang of cattle rustlers. There's a moderate amount of action in the last reel, some good location photography by Russell Harlan, some less painful comic interludes than usual, but some wet romantic footage instead.

# Sunset Trail

**Ken Maynard** (Jim Brannon), **Ruth Hiatt** (Molly), **Frank Rice** (Weller), **Philo McCullough** (Tater Bug), **Buddy Hunter** (Buddy), **Dick Alexander** (One-Shot), **Frank Ellis, Slim Whitaker, Jack Rockwell, Lew Meehan, Bud Osborne, Bud McClure**, and "Tarzan", the horse.

Director: **B. REEVES EASON**. Story and screenplay: **Bennett Cohen**. Photography: **Arthur Reed**. Film editor: **S. Roy Luby**. Art director: **Ralph De Lacy**. Sound recording: **John Stransky**. Producer: **Phil Goldstone**.

Not copyrighted. An Amity Production, released through Tiffany: 7 January 1932. 62 minutes.

VIEWERS' GUIDE: Okay for all.

COMMENT: Early Ken Maynard western has more curiosity value than anything else. The diffused quality of the photography indicates that the camera was enclosed in a sound-proof booth — an indication that is borne out by the fact that camera movement is limited to slight panning. Music is limited to the front and end credits and sound effects are poor. No attempt has been made to mix sound effects and dialogue tracks, all the dialogue in fact being recorded on a single track with no overlapping. These limitations give the film a rather primitive air which the flat photography and drab sets re-inforce.

Burdened with his cumbersome camera, B. Reeves Eason can do little with the direction. Later to become a specialist in shooting action sequences for major-budget spectacles, Eason reveals none of that talent in this film. The action sequences here are poorly staged. He even resorts to the lazy device of speeding up the climactic fist fight to give it a bit of punch — with a lamentable lack of success.

Even by Z-grade standards, the support cast is second-rate. Ruth Hiatt is especially poor. Ken Maynard himself displays a pleasing personality.

Whatever they lack, the script and direction have sufficient pace to put the film across for Maynard's fans who are willing to overlook its disabilities.

# Susanna Pass

**Roy Rogers** (Roy Rogers), **Dale Evans Slye** (Kay "Doc" Parker), **Estelita Rodriguez** (Rita Mendoza), **Martin Garralaga** (Carlos Mendoza), **Douglas Fowley** (Roberts/Johnson), **Robert Emmett Keane** (Martin Masters), **Lucien Littlefield** (Russell Masters), **David Sharpe** (Vince), **Robert Bice** (Bob Oliver), **George Lloyd** (prisoner), **Foy Willing** (himself), and **The Riders of the Purple Sage** (themselves), and "Trigger" (the smartest horse in the movies).

Director: **WILLIAM WITNEY**. Story and screenplay: **Sloan Nibley, John K. Butler**. Photographed in **Trucolor** by **Reggie Lanning**. Film editor: **Tony Martinelli**. Art director: **Frank Hotaling**. Set decorators: **John McCarthy Jr, Charles Thompson**. Costume supervisor: **Adele Palmer**. Make-up supervisor: **Bob Mark**. Special effects: **Howard Lydecker, Theodore Lydecker**. Optical effects: Consolidated Film Industries. Music director: **Morton Scott**. Orchestrations: **Stanley Wilson**. Songs: "Susanna Pass" (the Slyes, supported by Willing and his Riders; reprised by the same) by **Jack Elliott** and **Sid Robin**; "Two-Gun Rita" (Rodriguez, Lloyd) by **Clem White**; "A Good, Good Morning" (the Slyes, Willing and his Riders) by **Foy Willing**; "Brush Those Tears from Your Eyes" (L. Slye, Willing and Riders) by **Oakley Haldeman, Al Trace, Jimmy Lee**. Sound recording: **T.A. Carman**. RCA Sound System. Associate producer: **Edward J. White**. Executive producer: **Herbert J. Yates**.

Copyright 9 May 1949 by Republic Pictures Corp. No recorded New York opening. U.S. release: 29 April 1949. U.K. release: 20 August 1951 (sic). Australian release through 20th Century-Fox: 27 April 1951. 6,195 feet. 68 minutes.

SYNOPSIS: Two brothers fall out over a fish hatchery. One knows there is a money-making oil deposit at the bottom of the lake, but the other refuses to sell.

NOTE: The murky, poorly-graded video print under review from The Republic Pictures Collection is far short of the quality we would expect of a print "mastered from the original negative" as is claimed on the wrapper. It looks like a poor-quality dupe from a 16mm TV print.

COMMENT: A nothing western. I take that back. If you like mildly pleasant songs, and Miss Rodriguez occasionally shooting off her mouth, and Mr Garralaga's mildly tedious attempts at comic relief, plus a bit of mild action against some mildly attractive background scenery, you'll enjoy *Susanna Pass*.

   True, there is a bit of occasional stuntwork, thanks to David Sharpe (who has an on-screen role as well), but Douglas Fowley overplays the heavy and the climax is noticeably short on action. Nonetheless, there is a fair brawl between Rogers and Sharpe at Keane's newspaper office. However the best stunt has Sharpe doubling for Rogers transferring himself from a less noble steed to Trigger in mid-gallop during the final chase.

   Miss Evans, here making a return to the series, has a lively enough role, though she is not too attractively photographed. In fact the photography with its obvious-day-for-night shortcomings as well, is hardly a major asset.

   Still, fair entertainment if your expectations are not too high — and you're a rabid Rogers fan.

OTHER VIEWS: In their efforts to provide something new for Rogers to do, screenwriters Nibley and Butler have saddled the star with an improbable yet predictable, an overloaded yet somewhat labored plot. The Lydeckers let loose with no less than three explosions, there are at least the same number of hard-riding chases, plus a realistically staged fist fight and a murder or two. Yet we still feel cheated on action. Too much talking and plotting, too much comic reliefing and singing — and too many fish.

# Taggart

**Tony Young** (Kent Taggart), **Dan Duryea** (Jason), **Dick Foran** (Stark), **Elsa Cardenas** (Consuela Stark), **Jean Hale** (Miriam Stark), **Emile Meyer** (Ben Blazer), **David Carradine** (Cal Dodge), **Peter Duryea** (Rusty Bob Blazer), **Tom Reese** (Vince August), **Ray Teal** (Ralph Taggart), **Claudia Barrett** (Lola), **Stuart Randall** (sheriff), **Harry Carey, Jr** (Lieutenant Hudson), **Bill Henry** (army sergeant), **Sarah Selby** (Maude Taggart), **George Murdock** (army scout), **Arthur Space** (colonel), **Bob Steele** (cook).

Director: **R.G. SPRINGSTEEN**. Screenplay: **Robert Creighton Williams**. Based on the 1959 novel by **Louis L'Amour**. Photographed in Technicolor by **William Margulies**. Film editor: **Tony Martinelli**. Art directors: **Alexander Golitzen, Raymond Beal**. Set decorators: **John McCarthy, James M. Walters, Sr.** Make-up: **Bud Westmore**. Hair styles: **Larry Germain**. Music composed by **Herman Stein**. Music supervisor: **Joseph Gershenson**. Unit production manager: **Frank Parmenter**. Assistant director: **Carl Beringer**. Sound recording: **Waldon O. Watson, David H. Moriarty**. Westrex Sound System. Producer: **Gordon Kay**. A Gordon Kay and Associates Production.

Copyright 13 March 1964 by Universal Pictures Company, Inc. New York opening on a double bill at the Palace and other theatres: 24 December 1964. U.S. release: 1 February 1965. U.K. release: 28 March 1965. 7,650 feet. 85 minutes.

SYNOPSIS: Lone survivor of a family massacre is pursued by three hired gunmen into Apache territory.

COMMENT: Making extensive use of action footage from some 3-D feature (*Fort Ti?*) for its Indians-attack-the-fort climax, *Taggart* is a reasonably actionful "B" western, with a strong if over-talkative villain (Dan Duryea), a commanding if too briefly observed heroine's dad (Dick Foran), and a quite pretty if late-entering female lead (Jean Hale). There are other interesting players as well, though I would exclude the somewhat surly Tony Young, who seems to have only the one expression and to deliver his lines in a similar monotone.

Springsteen's direction and other credits are competent enough. The editor has done a reasonable job splicing in the stock material of cattle rustling and fort storming which gives the movie the air of a fair-sized budget.

The story is developed somewhat along television lines with our hunted hero involved in three different encounters. The first is with a widow desperately trying to make a go at being a bar-girl -- an appealing portrait here by Claudia Barrett.

Fans will recognise Bob Steele in a fleeting part as the Taggart cook.

Aside from the stock footage, lots of dialogue, repetitious and/or fixed camera positions, *Taggart* has other "B"-picture stratagems including the novel idea of having the hero remonstrate (at length of course) with his dad for not hiring enough men! It's a pity that some of this ingenuity wasn't devoted to developing and motivating the character played by Elsa Cardenas. This lack of conviction undermines the impact of the climax considerably.

# Tall in the Saddle

**John Wayne** (Rocklin), **Ella Raines** (Arly Harolday), **Audrey Long** (Clara Cardell), **George "Gabby" Hayes** (Dave), **Elisabeth Risdon** (Miss Martin), **Ward Bond** ("Judge" Garvey), **Don Douglas** (Mr Harolday), **Russell Wade** (Clint Harolday), **Frank Puglia** (Juan Tala), **Paul Fix** (Bob Clews), **Harry Woods** (George Clews), **Emory Parnell** (Sheriff Jackson), **Cy Kendall** (Cap the bartender), **Bob McKenzie** (Doc Riding), **Raymond Hatton** (Zeke), **Russell Simpson** (Pat), **Wheaton Chambers** (Ab Jenkins), **Walter Baldwin** (Stan), **Frank Orth** (Ferdy Davis), **George Chandler** (saddler), **Erville Alderson** (depot manager), **Hank Bell** ("Yes, it goes"), **Eddy Waller** (end-of-the-line depot man), **Russell Hopton** (Miss Martin's messenger), **Clem Bevans** (white-whiskered card-player), **William Desmond, Frank Darien**.

Director: **EDWIN L. MARIN**. Screenplay: **Michael Hogan, Paul Fix**. Based on a magazine story (later expanded into a novel) by **Gordon Ray Young**. Photography: **Robert de Grasse**. Supervising film editor: **Theron Warth**. Film editor: **Philip Martin Jr**. Art directors: **Albert S. D'Agostino, Ralph Berger**. Set decorators: **Darrell Silvera, William Stevens**. Gowns: **Edward Stevenson**. Music composed by **Roy Webb**, directed by **Constantin Bakaleinikoff**. Assistant director: **Harry Scott**. Special photographic effects: **Vernon L. Walker**. Sound recording: **John E. Tribby**. Sound re-recording: **James G. Stewart**. RCA Sound System. Associate producer: **Theron Warth**. Producer: **Robert Fellows**.

Copyright 6 October 1944 by RKO Radio Pictures, Inc. New York opening at the Palace: 14 December 1944. U.S. release: 29 September 1944. U.K. release: 7 May 1945. Australian release: 12 April 1945. 8,000 feet. 89 minutes.

SYNOPSIS: Cowboy uncovers conspiracy plot in small western town.

NOTES: Wayne's fist association with producer Robert Fellows with whom he was later to form Wayne-Fellows Productions. Wayne liked the script of this one (co-written by actor Paul Fix) so much he tried to persuade John Ford to direct. Although Ford declined, some members of the Ford stock company, notably Ward Bond and Russell Simpson, were signed on for the cast.

COMMENT: One of Wayne's best westerns, with plenty of vigorously staged action, an intriguing plot, lots of interesting characters, loads of atmosphere, and an agreeably honed characterization for the Duke himself. It's tempting to say what a pity Ford knocked back this assignment, but Marin has actually done quite a super job. Of course he was helped no end by experts like Theron Warth (a graduate of RKO's film editing department, making his debut here as associate producer) and cinematographer Robert de Grasse.

It's good to see Wayne re-united with some of the players from his early 30s career, most notably ultra-smooth villain Ward Bond, rough-house heavy Harry Woods, cowardly off-sider Paul Fix, helpful barkeep Cy Kendall and most particularly George Hayes, a real audience-pleaser here in a made-to-order role as a cantankerous, woman-hating stagedriver. (Wayne is also introduced as something of a cynical misogynist. "I never feel sorry for anything that happens to a woman," he answers an early leading question from Hayes, to that driver's surprise and evident delight. But his attitude noticeably softens later on in the presence of both ultra-feminine heroine Audrey Long and more masculine Ella Raines).

Elisabeth Risdon's remarkably forceful performance as Miss Martin deserves special praise. We also liked Emory Parnell's blustering sheriff and Walter Baldwin's slovenly coach-stop man. In fact, all the characters are most skilfully played. Although Wayne rightly dominates the action, at more than one stage there are so many interesting characters jostling around in the background, they threaten to spill off the screen.

Production values are A-1. In short, a first-class western.

OTHER VIEWS: Exciting, fast-paced western, with a brilliant opening sequence, a delightfully aggressive heroine, fine photography, and a script that is as rich in characterization as in action and originality. Wayne has one of his best roles as the charmingly gutsy if somewhat cynical hero.

# Terrors on Horseback

**Buster Crabbe** (Billy Carson), **Al "Fuzzy" St John** (Fuzzy), **Patti McCarty** (Roxie), **I. Stanford Jolley** (Grant Barlow), **Kermit Maynard** (Wagner), **Henry Hall** (Doc Jones), **Karl Hackett** (Ed Sperling), **Marin Sais** (Mrs Bartlett), **Budd Buster** (Sheriff Jed Bartlett), **Steve Darrell** (Jim Austin), **Steve Clark** (Cliff Adams), **George Chesebro** (Luke Gordon), **Frank Ellis** (Connors), **Bud Osborne** (Ben Taggart), **Jack Kirk, Lane Bradford, Al Ferguson**.

Director: **SAM NEUFELD**. Original story and screenplay: **George Milton**. Photography: **Jack Greenhalgh**. Film editor: **Holbrook N. Todd**. Music director: **Lee Zahler**. Unknown function (sets? production manager?): **Bert Sternbach**. Assistant director: **Stanley Neufeld**. Sound recording: **Lyle Willey**. Producer: **Sigmund Neufeld**.

A Newfield [Neufeld] Brothers Production, copyright 14 August 1946 by Pathé Industries, Inc. Released through P.R.C. Pictures, Inc. No New York showcase. U.S. release: 1 May 1946. No Australian theatrical release. 6 reels. 55 minutes.

SYNOPSIS: Billy Carson and Fuzzy Q. Jones track down a gang of stagecoach bandits.

VIEWERS' GUIDE: Okay for all.

COMMENT: By the humble standards of PRC's Billy Carson series, this one has an unusually strong, well-paced story. Using a thriller format, it introduces a large number of characters.

One of the most amazing things about this film is that the official cast list gives not the slightest indication of the importance of the players' roles. Patti McCarty heads the support list, but after an elaborately staged introductory scene disappears from the film altogether except for one tiny glimpse. Stanford Jolley has three largish scenes but Karl Hackett has only the one scene in which he says not more than half-a-dozen lines. Henry Hall has less than half-a-dozen words and has only two scenes, the first of which is but a tiny glimpse of his back. Kermit Maynard has also only a small amount of footage and plays a subsidiary role to Frank Ellis (who receives no credit at all) who has the lion's share of the dialogue as well as his customary fist tussle with Buster after Kermit is killed! Marin Sais has one unimportant scene as the sheriff's wife and takes precedence in the billing over Budd Buster who plays the sheriff and has easily the largest amount of footage of the entire support cast! Steve Darrell hovers around in the background of quite a few scenes but Steve Clark has only one scene of two or three lines.

One of the characters Billy and Fuzzy are tracking down is Ben Taggart and he turns out to be played by Bud Osborne, quite a large and important role, with Bud playing the heavy and snarling delightfully, uncredited. Then they go after Luke Gordon and who should be playing him, also uncredited, but another old friend, villainous George Chesebro!

Direction and other production credits strike a rare level of competence and production values are adequate.

# Three Faces West

**John Wayne** (John Phillips), **Charles Coburn** (Dr Braun), **Sigrid Gurie** (Leni Braun), **Spencer Charters** (Dr "Nunk" Atterbury, veterinarian), **Roland Varno** (Dr Eric Von Scherer), **Trevor Bardette** (Clem Higgins), **Helen MacKellar** (Mrs Welles), **Sonny Bupp** (Billy Welles), **Wade Boteler** (Harris), **Russell Simpson** (minister), **Charles Waldron** (Dr Thorpe), **Wendell Niles** (radio announcer), **Dewey Robinson** (bartender), **Si Jenks** (train conductor).

Director: **BERNARD VORHAUS**. Screenplay: **F. Hugh Herbert, Joseph Moncure March, Samuel Ornitz**. Uncredited script contributor: **Doris Anderson**. Photography: **John Alton**. Supervising film editor: **Murray Seldeen**. Film editor: **William Morgan**. Art director: **John Victor MacKay**. Wardrobe: **Adele Palmer**. Special effects: **Howard Lydecker**. Music: **Victor Young**. Production manager: **Al Wilson**. RCA Sound recording. Associate producer: **Solomon C. Siegel**. Executive producer: **Herbert J. Yates**.

Copyright 12 July 1940 by Republic Pictures Corp. New York opening at the Criterion: 18 August 1940. U.S. release: 12 July 1940. U.K. release through British Lion: 11 November 1940. No Australian theatrical release. 9 reels. 79 minutes.

Shooting title: *The REFUGEE*.

SYNOPSIS: Dust Bowl farmers move themselves and their North Dakota township 1,500 miles to Oregon.

VIEWER'S GUIDE: Downbeat but inspiring. Suitable for all.

COMMENT: John Alton's atmospheric cinematography is the major asset of this odd Americana drama. Although he has close to a characteristic role (a stubborn leader, a man of action and strong principles, yet comradely and romantic), John Wayne is not exactly going to please his present-day fans, most of whom will find the setting bizarre. At the time of the film's release, Republic capitalized on Fox's *The Grapes of Wrath*, but few 1995 viewers will make this connection. Another problem is that in order not to be accused of a direct steal from Steinbeck, this film's writers have clouded the central story with a major sub-plot about a refugee doctor, his beautiful daughter and (virtually right at the finish) a former suitor who turns out to be a Nazi. One feels that the story would have come across with more impact had some of these plot strands been eliminated and the Wayne character filled in and backgrounded instead. In fact, the focus of the film is firmly on Coburn for the first half, with Wayne playing a subsidiary role.

The location scenes still impress. The dust-storm episodes are unforgettable — even when Alton's striking images are undermined by obvious studio cut-ins.

Coburn handles the central role with his usual cunning authority, Sigrid Gurie is charming enough, while Spencer Charters makes the most of one of his biggest roles as Wayne's sidekick and town fixture. Bardette plays a minor villain with grumpy finesse, Russell Simpson over-acts the minister. The rest of the players, including thankfully Sonny Bupp (who I must admit is quite adequate here) have no more than cameos.

OTHER VIEWS: Strikingly photographed by John Alton in a tone that is appropriately bleak and gray, *Three Faces West* is a bit of an entertainment no-no. The script's two stories are imperfectly welded, with audience focus and character motivation changing abruptly. Director Vorhaus is not much help. He's a great fan of close-ups, but does precious little to help the story's pace and drama. What paltry action there is, he seems anxious to get over with as quickly as possible so he can get back to more humdrum, foregone-conclusion and beating about the bush dialogue.

# Thunder Over the Prairie

**Charles Starrett** (Dr Steven Monroe), **Cliff "Ukelele Ike" Edwards** (Bones Malloy), **Eileen O'Hearn** (Nona Mandan), **Stanley Brown** (Roy Mandan), **Danny Mummert** (Timmy), **David Sharpe** (Clay Mandan), **Joe McGuinn** (Hartley), **Donald Curtis** (Taylor), **Ted Adams** (Dave Wheeler), **Jack Rockwell** (Clayton), **Budd Buster** (Judge Merryweather), **Horace B. Carpenter, Carl Shrum and His Rhythm Rangers**.

Director: **LAMBERT HILLYER**. Screenplay: **Betty Burbridge**. Based on the 1935 novel *The Medico Rides* by **James L. Rubel**. Photography: **Benjamin Kline**. Film editor: **Bert Kramer**. Songs by **Carl Shrum, Billy Hughes**. Producer: **William Berke**.

Copyright 30 July 1941 by Columbia Pictures Corp. No recorded New York opening. (In fact no Starrett movie was reviewed in *The New York Times* after *Start Cheering* on 17 March 1938). U.S. release: 30 July 1941. 6 reels. 60 minutes.

SYNOPSIS: Frontier doctor clears an Indian youth of a trumped-up murder charge.

VIEWER'S GUIDE: Okay for all.

NOTES: Second of Columbia's three-picture Medico series. The others: *The Medico of Painted Springs and Prairie Stranger*.

COMMENT: Opens most promisingly when it reaches the west after a short prologue (is this the first of the Medic series?) with a breathtakingly long take and tracking shot and buckboard ride through a dust storm. But when a disastrously inept young kid is introduced, interest begins to wane. Still, there is plenty of hard riding and fist throwing though the climax is most disappointingly resolved with the villains brought to justice through a montage of newspaper headlines!

Cliff Edwards delivers some songs in his inimitable manner, it's good to see stuntman David Sharpe on-screen, but sad to find Danny Mummert of Columbia's *Blondie* series so poorly directed.

All told, a fairly entertaining outing, though only slightly above average by Columbia's "B" western standard.

# Tom Sawyer

**Jackie Coogan** (Tom Sawyer), **Junior Durkin** (Huckleberry Finn), **Mitzi Green** (Becky Thatcher), **Lucien Littlefield** (teacher), **Tully Marshall** (Muff Potter), **Clara Blandick** (Aunt Polly), **Mary Jane Irving** (Mary) **Ethel Wales** (Mrs Harper), **Jackie Searl** (Sid), **Dick Winslow** (Joe Harper), **Jane Darwell** (Widow Douglass), **Charles Stevens** (Injun Joe), **Charles Sellon** (minister), **Lon Puff** (Judge Thatcher).

Director: **JOHN CROMWELL**. Screenplay: **Sam Mintz, Grover Jones, William Slavens McNutt**. Based on the 1876 novel *The Adventures of Tom Sawyer* by **Samuel Langhorne Clemens**. Photography: **Charles Lang, Jr**. Film editor: **Alyson Shaffer**. Art directors: **Hans Dreier, Bernard Herzbrun, Robert A. Odell**. Sound recording: **Harold C. Lewis**. Western Electric Sound System. Producer: **Louis D. Lighton**.

Copyright 17 November 1930 by Paramount Publix Corp. New York opening at the Paramount: 19 December 1930. U.S. release: 15 November 1930. 9 reels. 7,648 feet. 85 minutes.

SYNOPSIS: Huck Finn and Tom Sawyer see Injun Joe murder a man while "resurrecting" a body in the church graveyard.

NOTES: Second film version of the Mark Twain classic. The first was directed by none other than William Desmond Taylor in 1917 for the Oliver Morosco Photoplay Co. It starred Jack Pickford, Louise Huff and Robert Gordon. (So successful was this movie that Taylor followed it up immediately with a sequel, *Huck and Tom*). David O. Sleznick produced a third version in 1938, Arthur P. Jacobs a fourth in 1973. The character Tom Sawyer also figures in numerous *Huckleberry Finn* adaptations plus Paramount's 1939 "B"-budgeted *Tom Sawyer, Detective*.

COMMENT: A faithful rendering of Mark Twain's classic, well directed by John Cromwell. I particularly like the way whole passages of Twain's original dialogue have been integrated into the screenplay and the way Cromwell keeps his cameras moving during some of these exchanges. Cromwell, too, has a real flair for creating atmosphere and sustaining it at a consistent level throughout the film. Notice how he resists the temptation to turn the graveyard sequence into a James Whale feat of horror. One cannot imagine Walt Disney having such respect for his audience! Fine photography by Charles Lang, Jr.

*Tom Sawyer* dates only from its lack of background music although Cromwell tries to make up for this by using natural sound effects (Tom twanging the Jew's harp) and by keeping the story moving at a brisk pace. The screenplay is remarkably faithful to the original novel and retains all its major incidents and characters — as well as a large share of its dialogue. Paramount has also wisely lensed the film on locations astonishingly similar to those described in the novel so that in atmosphere as well as story the film is supreme in its fidelity to its source. The cast too is well-nigh perfect. Coogan fits easily and naturally into the shoes (or rather feet) of Tom Sawyer and while he seems a little old for the part Junior Durkin brings a fair amount of conviction to the part of Huck Finn (of course, we do not see so much of him as he comes into his own in the sequel — as does Jane Darwell who has only two or three brief scenes here as the Widow Douglas). Lucien Littlefield is inclined to over-act the part of the schoolmaster but Mitzi Green as the curled and beribboned Becky Thatcher, Jackie Searl as the obnoxious Sidney and Clara Blandick as harassed Aunt Polly are absolutely perfect. Oddly enough, Charles Stevens who would seem to have a role right up his alley as Indian Joe, is not wholly convincing, especially in his earlier scenes but Tully Marshall as Muff Potter gives a memorably realistic portrayal. Cromwell often keeps his camera moving with tracking shots through the town following the boys as they converse or picking up snatches of conversation in the store as it darts from one corner to the other. He has chosen to play many of the scenes with restraint, probably in deference to his youthful audience. Even the graveyard scene with its rapid tracking shot through the broken and lopsided crosses at midnight is not played for horror and even the lost-in-the-caves sequence with the flight from Indian Joe reaches a speedy conclusion and altogether this sequence is on screen for less than a quarter of the time it occupies in the 1938 version. Charles Lang's soft photography and musty, dusty sets created by art director Hans Dreier capture the atmosphere of the novel more realistically than the heavily romanticized 1938 film.

# Topeka

**Wild "Bill" Elliott** (Jim Levering), **Phyllis Coates** (Marian Harrison), **Rick Vallin** (Ray Hammond), **John James** (Marv Ronsom), **Denver Pyle** (Jonas Bailey), **Dick Crockett** (Will Peters), **Harry Lauter** (Mack Wilson), **Dale Van Sickel** (Jake Manning), **Ted Mapes** (Cully), **Fuzzy Knight** (Pop Harrison), **I. Stanford Jolley** (doctor), **Michael Colgan, Michael Vallon, Edward Clark, Henry Rowland.**

Director: **THOMAS CARR**. Original screenplay: **Milton M. Raison**. Photography: **Ernest Miller**. Film editor: **Sam Fields**. Music: **Raoul Kraushaar**. Dialogue director: **Stanley Price**. Sets: **Ted Offenbecker, Ernst Erlich**. Special effects: **Ray Mercer**. Assistant director: **Melville Shyer**. Sound recording: **Tom Lambert**. Producer: **Vincent M. Fennelly**. A Westwood Production, originally released in sepia.

Copyright 9 August 1953 by Monogram Pictures Corp. An Allied Artists Production, released by Monogram. No New York opening. U.S. release: 9 August 1953. U.K. release through Associated British-Pathé: April 1955. No Australian theatrical release. 6,256 feet. 69 minutes.

SYNOPSIS: See below.

VIEWERS' GUIDE: Okay for all.

COMMENT: Considering that the B-western was then in its last days, the series Wild Bill Elliott made for producer Vincent Fennelly at Monogram in the early fifties was unexpectedly exciting. The scripts had basic plot lines that were familiar and predictable, but they were reasonably fast-moving and allowed plenty of scope for action, and they were often peopled with some interesting, audience-involving characters. Production values were also high, with a great deal of location shooting and occasionally imaginative direction.

*Topeka* is one of the best films in this series. Thomas Carr's direction is often startlingly inventive, with crane shots, tilted pans, tracking shots and through-window angles that are surprisingly effective. The staging of the numerous fight scenes seems a little contrived, though it is noticeable that no doubles are used. Miss Coates has little to do, but the cast is otherwise adequate.

OTHER VIEWS: After his class A productions at Republic, William Elliott switched to Allied Artists in the early fifties for his final Western series. Unfortunately the double-bill cowboy film format was coming to a close. Despite the fact that this batch of Elliott films was several notches above the average genre budget films of the period, it could not prevent the ebb tide of the theatrical B Western film.

Cast as an outlaw who comes to a small town and is hired as its sheriff in order to rid the area of varmints, the lawbreaker sees a chance to make some easy money. To accomplish his scheme, Elliott's anti-hero gathers together his old gang who in turn get rid of the villains. Later, Elliott is redeemed by the love of a nice girl (Coates) and he turns on his comrades. From now on the straight and narrow path is his! As a reward for his seeing the light he wins a pardon, the hand of the heroine in matrimony, as well as the money he had earned from his past nefarious deeds. Thus in many ways this plotline has a different twist from the usual run of Western programmers.

— Parish and Pitts: *The Great Western Pictures.*

A gripping western tale in which outlaw Elliott is hired by helpless townspeople to help them defend themselves against a gang of bandits. Elliott rounds up his former gang to lend a hand, putting down the attack. He very nearly turns evil again and takes over the town for his own benefit, but is tamed by the love of Coates. Interestingly photographed, with a moody use of crane shots.

— *The Motion Picture Guide.*

An active and adventurous horse opera.

— *Monthly Film Bulletin.*

# the Trail Beyond

**John Wayne** (Rod Drew), **Verna Hillie** (Felice Newsome), **Noah Beery, Sr** (George Newsome), **Noah Beery, Jr** (Wabi), **Iris Lancaster** (Marie), **Robert Frazer** (Jules La Rocque), **Earl Dwire** (Benoit), **Eddie Parker** (Mounted Policeman Ryan), **James Marcus** (John Ball), **Artie Ortego** (Towanga), **Reed Howes** (fake constable).

Director: **ROBERT NORTH BRADBURY**. Screenplay: **Lindsley Parsons**. Based on the novel *The Wolf Hunters* by **James Oliver Curwood**. Photography: **Archie Stout**. Film editor: **Charles Hunt**. Art director: **E.R. Hickson**. Music composed by **Sam Perry**. Music supervisor: **Lee Zahler**. Stunts: **Yakima Canutt, Eddie Parker**. Sound recording:

**Ralph Shugart.** Producer: **Paul Malvern**. A Paul Malvern Production. Presented by Lone Star Productions.

Copyright 15 September 1934 by Monogram Pictures Corp. No New York opening. U.S. release: 22 October 1934. U.K. release through Pathé: 27 May 1935. 55 minutes.

SYNOPSIS: Cowboy journeys to Canada to track down a missing heiress. His quest is complicated when a young friend accidentally kills a card sharp and the two are forced to flee across country.

COMMENT: Hard to believe this is a "Lone Star Western". Even the music is different and the budget is pretty close to borderline "A". True, director Bradbury is up to his usual editing tricks, including disconcerting whip pans that don't quite work and odd wipes, but otherwise technical credits, including music scoring and sound recording, are of a much higher standard than usual. The Canadian locations are mighty impressive, especially as an action background. There are plenty of chases both on horse and canoe, with running inserts and some truly spectacular stunts, leading up to an action-packed double climax in which the thrills are crosscut between the Mounties cleaning up the renegades and our hero pursuing the chief villain. Although heavy on co-incidence, the fast-moving plot holds the attention. Wayne is doubtless doubled for the high diving shots, but he does an impressive amount of swimming. Miss Hillie makes an attractive heroine, and it's good to see both Noahs, father and son. (Is this their only film together?)

On the other hand, Frazer makes a somewhat lackluster villain. This must be one of the few westerns in which the heavies are well and truly outclassed in charisma by the good guys. Admittedly the baddies are hampered by some pretty ridiculous dialogue and dopey accents.

Despite these examples of amateurish acting, *The Trail Beyond* all told is a superior western. In fact one of the best of Wayne's early "B"-hero career.

# Trailing the Killer

**Francis McDonald** (Pierre), **Heinie Conklin** (Windy), **Jose de la Cruz** (Pedro), **Peter Rigas** (Manuel), "Caesar", the wonder dog ("Lobo"), **Tom London** (sheriff).

Director: **HERMAN C. RAYMAKER**. Story: **Jackson Richards**. Photography: **Pliny Goodfriend**. Music: **Oscar Potoker**. Music supervised by **Abe Meyer**, directed by **Sam Wineland**. Production manager: **Louis Rantz**. Sound recording: **W.C. Smith**. Associate producer: **Charles Hunt**. Producer: **Bennie F. Zeidman**.

Copyright 27 November 1932 by Bennie F. Zeidman Productions, Ltd. New York opening at the Gaiety: 1 December 1932. U.S. release through World Wide Pictures. 7 reels. 64 minutes.

TV title: *CALL OF THE WILDERNESS.*

COMMENT: Despite his prominence in the credits, Conklin's part in the print under review has been reduced to a ten-second appearance in the film's very last shot! Still, to judge from Mordaunt Hall's notice in *The New York Times,* the human actors always did take a very back seat to the animals. Fortunately, these scenes are quite well photographed, briskly directed, and scored with music of a quaint, primitive appeal. And the dog is by far the best I've seen! However, there's not much left of Jackson Richard's original story.

Mr Raymaker made a career out of directing "Rin-Tin-Tin" (see *The Night Cry* in *Film Index 5* with Heinie Conklin cast again in a small part). The only other sound film I have for him is *Adventure Girl* (1934). Previous to this movie, he directed a version of Zane Grey's *Under the Tonto Rim* for Paramount, released early in 1928.

OTHER VIEWS: Caesar, not an emperor, but a sheep dog, is the stellar performer in *Trailing the Killer*, the new film at the Gaiety. It is too long a picture, but is quite well done and a feature that is suitable for both adults and children. Caesar may do only what he is told, but he enlists one's sympathy during the pictorial proceedings. He unfortunately has to submit to some unpleasant experiences, including facing a mountain lion and being caught in a trap and strung up.

It is a simple little tale of a Canadian trapper who is eventually killed by a mountain lion. Lobo, the trapper's dog, acted by Caesar, is not only blamed for the killing of sheep, but also for the death of his master. He is shot at while swimming across a lake and eventually rescues his mate when she is trapped.

Besides several astutely pictured sequences depicting Pierre La Plante, the trapper, catching wild cats, there are some humorous scenes of puppies at play and others in which Lobo shows his persistence in dealing with crabs.

One of Lobo's little sons is caught on a tree trunk and is borne across the water. When he swims ashore he is pursued by the ferocious mountain lion. The puppy, however, succeeds in getting into a hole in a tree and is thus saved, because the lion cannot get at him.

It is quite pathetic when, after his master's death, Lobo goes off to join his mate, which is supposed to be a wolf. There is a price on Lobo's head, but, as is surmised, the Sheriff and his men finally learn that the lion and not Lobo is responsible for the death of Pierre and the sheep.

Caesar expresses satisfaction, affection, sorrow and he can boast of being one of the handsomest dogs that have taken up motion picture work. Herman C. Raymaker, the director of this film, has kept within reasonable bounds in detailing the incidents. Francis McDonald makes a believable trapper.
— Mordaunt Hall in *The New York Times*.

# Trail to Mexico

**Jimmy Wakely, Lee "Lasses" White** (themselves), **Julian Rivero** (Don Roberto Lopez), **Delores Castelli** (Chinita Lopez), **Dora Del Rio** (Dolores), **Terry Frost** (Bart Thompson), **Forrest Matthews** (Fred Jackson), **Brad Slaven** (The Texas Kid), **Alex Montoya** (Captain Martinez), **Jonathan McCall** (Paymaster McGrath), **Juan Duval** (Francisco Valdez), **Arthur Fiddlin' Smith** (himself), **Cactus Mack** (Montana), **Wheaton Chambers** (padre), **Dee Cooper** (Mack), **Billy Dix** (Joe), **Jesse Ashlock, Jack Rivers** (musicians), **Don Weston, The Saddle Pals, The Guadalajara Trio**.

Director: **OLIVER DRAKE**. Original screenplay: **Oliver Drake**. Photography: **James Brown**. Film editor: **Ralph Dixon**. Settings: **Vin Taylor**. Music director: **Frank Sanucci**. Songs: "Rawhide Ray" by **Dimitri Tiomkin** (music) and **Ned Washington** (lyrics); "Little Rose of the Rancho" by **Ralph Rainger** (music) and **Leo Robin** (music); "Mexican Hat Dance" by **Felipe A. Partichela**; "Trail to Mexico" by **Johnny Lange** and **Lew Porter**. Assistant director: **Eddie Davis**. Sound recording: **Tom Lambert**. Western Electric Sound System. Associate producer: **Glenn Cook**. Producer: **Oliver Drake**.

Copyright 11 July 1946 by Monogram Pictures Corp. No New York showcase. U.S. release: 29 June 1946. No general theatrical release in the U.K. If the movie was shown in U.K. cinemas — and even that is not certain — it would have been a floating release. Never theatrically released in Australia. 6 reels. 56 minutes.

VIEWERS' GUIDE: Okay for all.

COMMENT: Director/producer Oliver Drake makes use of an unusually fluid (for him) camera in this one, with running inserts and tracking shots enlivening an otherwise mundane and not particularly exciting story of gold-hijacking in old Mexico.

There's enough action to satisfy the fans. However, despite the running inserts and a nice sample of well-timed stunt-work in which clever film editing makes it appear that Jimmy himself makes the leap from galloping horse to running wagon, the action is not staged in a particularly exciting manner. There's music and song as well though none of the songs are particularly memorable and Mr Wakely's delivery of a song is only slightly more wooden than his delivery of dialogue. Still, despite his expressionless demeanor, he is a passable singer. His looks and figure, however, are not what we might expect from a western hero. He is aided as usual by Lee "Lasses" White, a sometimes obnoxious and no more than bearable "comedian" (he is just tolerable in this film).

The support cast is unusually uninteresting. The heroine is a nonentity and is about as appealing as a frog-pond at noon. Indeed the only familiar face in the entire support cast is Terry Frost, though the guy who essays the part of the Texas Kid renders it with a delightfully villainous glumness.

Production credits like production values are very ordinary. There's a bit of location shooting but the locations are like the rest of the film, not particularly exciting.

# Two-Fisted Rangers

**Charles Starrett** (Thad Lawson), **Iris Meredith** (Betty Webster), **Bob Nolan** (himself), **Kenneth MacDonald** (Jack Rand), **Dick Curtis** (Dirk Hogan), **Hal Taliaferro [Wally Wales]** (Sheriff Hanley), **James Craig** (Kid), **Pat Brady, Hugh Farr, Karl Farr, Lloyd Perryman, Tim Spencer** (themselves, The Sons of the Pioneers), **Bill Cody Jr** (Silver), **Ethan Laidlaw, Dick Botiller, Buel Bryant, Forrest Burns, Clem Horton, Bob Woodward, Francis Walker** (henchmen), **Ted Mapes** (stunt double).

Director: **JOSEPH H. LEWIS**. Original screenplay: **Fred Myton**. Photography: **George Meehan**. Film editor: **Charles Nelson**. Music director: **Morris Stoloff**. Songs by **Bob Nolan** and **Tim Spencer**. Stunts: **Bob Woodward, Francis Walker**. Assistant director: **Milton Carter**. Sound recording: **George Cooper**. Producer: **Leon Barsha**.

Copyright 14 December 1939 by Columbia Pictures Corp. No New York opening. U.S. release: 4 January 1940. U.K. release: 1942. Not theatrically released in Australia. 6 reels. 62 minutes.

U.K. release title: *FORESTALLED*.

SYNOPSIS: Cowboy brings to justice the land baron who killed his brother, the local sheriff.

NOTES: Starrett's 33rd of his 132 starring westerns.

Lewis' nickname, which stuck to him throughout his entire career as a director, was "Wagon Wheel Joe". When Lewis was directing westerns like this, one of the editors at Universal complained to the studio brass that Lewis' shots were hard to cut because "he keeps putting these damn wagon wheels in front of everything."

VIEWERS' GUIDE: Okay for all.

COMMENT: A delight for both action fans and connoisseurs of director Joseph H. Lewis (whose sixth or seventh film this is). About half the action takes place at night (fine photography by George Meehan), which is unusual enough. There are some fine directorial compositions and effects, including a pan across the faces of the vigilantes and some splendid film editing (Charles Nelson) straight out of Eisenstein's theories of montage.

For the ordinary fan, there's action a-plenty, a trio of delightful villains, and some very pleasant musical interludes by the Sons of the Pioneers.

# Unconquered

**Gary Cooper** (Captain Christopher Holden), **Paulette Goddard** (Abigail Martha "Abby" Hale), **Howard da Silva** (Martin Garth), **Boris Karloff** (Guyasuta, chief of the Senecas), **Cecil Kellaway** (Jeremy Love), **Ward Bond** (John Fraser), **Katherine DeMille** (Hannah), **Henry Wilcoxon** (Captain Steele), **C. Aubrey Smith** (lord chief justice), **Victor Varconi** (Captain Simson Ecuyer), **Virginia Grey** (Diana), **Porter Hall** (Leach), **Mike Mazurki** (Dave Bone), **Richard Gaines** (Colonel George Washington), **Virginia Campbell** (Mrs John Fraser), **Gavin Muir** (Lieutenant Fergus McKenzie), **Alan Napier** (Sir William Johnson), **Nan Sunderland** (Mrs Pruitt), **Marc Lawrence** (Sioto, medicine man), **Jane Nigh** (Evelyn), **Robert Warwick** (Pontiac, chief of the Ottawas), **Lloyd Bridges** (Lieutenant Hutchins), **Oliver Thorndike** (Lieutenant Baillie), **Rus Conklin** (Mamaultee), **John Mylong** (Colonel Henry Bouquet), **Raymond Hatton** (Venango scout), **Julia Faye** (Widow Swivens), **Paul E. Burns** (Dan McCoy), **Clarence Muse** (Jason), **Jeff York** (wide-shouldered youth), **Dick Alexander** (slave), **Syd Saylor** (spieler for Dr Diablo), **Si Jenks** (farmer), **Bob Kortman** (frontiersman), **Edgar Dearing, Hugh Prosser, Ray Teal** (soldiers—Gilded Beaver), **Chief Thundercloud** (Chief Killbuck), **Noble Johnson** (big Ottawa indian), **John Merton** (corporal), **Buddy Roosevelt** (guard), **John Miljan** (prosecutor), **Jay Silverheels** (indian), **Lex Barker** (royal american officer), **Jack Pennick** (Joe Lovat), **Byron Foulger** (townsman), **Denver Dixon** (citizen), **Fred Kohler, Jr** (sergeant), **Tiny Jones** (bondswoman), **Charles B. Middleton** (Mulligan), **Dorothy Adams** (Mrs Bront), **Davison Clark** (Carroll), **Griff**

**Barnett** (Brother Andrews), **George Kirby** (Charles Mason), **Leonard Carey** (Jeremiah Dixon), **Frank R. Wilcox** (Richard Henry Lee), **Iron Eyes Cody** (Red Corn), **Mary Field** (Maggie), **Diane Wadelow** (Lancashire girl), **Sanders Clark** (Ben), **Matthew Boulton** (Captain Brooks), **Willa Pearl Curtis** (mammy), **Frank Moran** (heavy), **Olaf Hytten** (officer on "Star of London"), **Alec Harford** (bandit), **Fred Zendar** (trapper), **William Meader**, **Wallace Earl** (slaves), **Barbara Morrison, Lloyd Whitlock, Boyd Irwin** (passengers), **George Magrill** (ship's agent), **Budd Fine** (man in boat), **Valmere Barman** (girl at whipping post), **John Harmon, Earl Hodgins** (spielers), **Jack Weatherwax** (medicine man's assistant), **Alan Bridge** (militiaman), **Richard Reeves** (Joshua), **Hope Landin** (Joshua's mother), **Crane Whitley** (plantation master), **Robert Barron** (surveyor), **Jerry James** (villager), **Eric Alden** (Zeke), **Frank Hagney** (Jaie), **Sally Rawlinson** (brunette), **Bill Hall** (corporal), **Geraldine Wall** (Mrs Bitt), **Charles Victor** (officer), **Forrest Taylor** (shopkeeper), **Jack G. Lee** (Major Trent), **Dwight Butcher** (guard), **Henry Mowbray, John Goldsworthy** (policemen), **Gordon Richards** (sheriff), **Montague Shaw** (judge's assistant), **Crauford Kent** (chaplain), **Arthur Gould Porter** (clerk of the court), **Colin Kenny, Leyland Hodgson** (jailers), **Arthur Blake** (aristocrat), **Leslie Denison** (bailiff), **Boyd Davis** (Dr Boyd), **Charles Flynn** (Ensign Price), **Chuck Hamilton, Kenneth Gibson, James Carlisle, George Bunny, Carl Saxe, Sam Ash, George Anderson, Trevor Bardette, James Flavin, Gil Sullivan, William Bailey, Al Murphy, Harlan Miller, Joe Whitehead, Walter Baldwin, Bill Wallace, Jasper Palmer, Jim Nolan, Jim Drum, Don Lynch, Bill Murphy, Ted Mapes, Ethel Wales, Llorna Jordan, Besse Wade, Betty Farrington, Jane Everett, Donya Dean** (villagers), **Eddie Dunn, Bill Sundholme, Ray Spiker, John Northpole, Jack Clifford, Guy "Slim" Wilkerson, Francis McDonald, Francis Ford** (frontiersmen), **June Harris** (frontierswoman), **William Haade, Jeff Corey, Erville Alderson, John Mallon, Mike Lally, Larry Lawson, Charles Sullivan** (trappers), **Len Hendry, Carl Matthews** (indian trappers), **Jack Overman, Harry Cording, Bill Hunter, Clancy Cooper** (sentries), **Allan Ray** (soldier), **James Horne, Gus Tante, Ted Allan, David Ralston, Gilbert Wilson** (royal american officer), **Lee Phelps** (royal american sergeant), **Fred Coby** (royal american soldier), **Bert Moorhouse, Mike Killian** (virginia militia officers), **Lane Chandler** (pennsylvania militia officer), **Larry Thompson, Russ Clark, John James, Dick Elmore** (officers), **Eugene R. Eberle, Calvin Ellison, Robert Baughman** (drummer-boys), **J.W. Cody** (Chief Lesser), **Rodric "Rodd" Redwing, Albert Cavigga, Eric Alden, Jay Silverheels, Vaughn Anthony, Bob Kortman, Edvard Persson** (indians), **Isabel Chabling Cooper, Charmienne Harker, Bell Mitchell, Fernanda Eliscu, Claire Du Brey, Mimi Aguglia, Nenette Vallon, Inez Palange, Maxime Chevalier, Rose Higgins** (squaws), and **Louise Saraydar, Constance Purdy, Al Ferguson, Donna Courter, Ottola Nesmith, Greta Granstedt, Gertrude Valerie, Karolyn Grimes, Beatrice Gray, Fred Datig Jr, Anna Lehr, Christopher Clark**.

Narrated by **Cecil B. De Mille**.

Director: **CECIL B. DE MILLE**. Screenplay: **Charles Bennett, Fredric M. Frank, Jesse Lasky Jr**. Based on the novel by **Neil Harmon Swanson**. Photographed in Technicolor by **Ray Rennahan**. Film editor: **Anne Bauchens**. Art directors: **Hans Dreier, Walter Tyler**. Set decorators: **Sam Comer, Stanley Jay Sawley**. Costumes: **Gwen Wakeling, Madame Barbara Karinska**. Make-up: **Wally Westmore**. 2nd unit director: **Arthur Rosson**. Dialogue director: **Robert Foulk**. Special effects: **Farciot Edouart, W. Wallace Kelley, Paul K. Lerpae, Devereaux Jennings**, supervised by **Gordon Jennings**. Technicolor color consultants: **Natalie Kalmus, Robert Brower**. Music: **Victor Young**. Song, "Whippoorwill's-A-Singing", by **Ray Evans** and **Jay Livingston**. Dance director: **Jack Crosby**. Historical research. **Donald Hayne, Henry S. Noerdlinger**. Technical consultants: **Captain Fred F. Ellis, Iron Eyes Cody**. Special sound effects: **George Dutton**. Unit manager: **Roy Burns**. Assistant director: **Edward Salven**. Rehearsal director: **Arthur Pierson**. Sound recording: **Hugo Grenzbach, John Cope**. Western Electric Sound System. Producer: **Cecil B. De Mille**. Associate producer: **Henry Wilcoxon**.

Copyright 3 October 1947 by Paramount Pictures Inc. New York opening at the Rivoli: 10 October 1947. U.S. release: 24 September 1947. U.K. release: 30 August 1948. Australian release: 12 February 1948. 13,375 feet. 148 minutes.

SYNOPSIS: Abby Hale, a pretty English convict girl, is ordered deported as a potential slave to the American colonies. Captain Holden saves her from being auctioned into slavery, and when she is captured by Indians and subjected to a slow tortuous death, Captain Holden appears in a flash of gunpowder smoke, convincing the Indians that he is a god, so that they relinquish Abby to him. Abby is also pursued by Martin Garth, a villain engaged in selling illegal firearms to Indians. Captain Holden risks court-martial in exposing Garth as prodding Indians into massacring the white colonists, and Holden is able to lead a small band of men to the defense of Fort Pitt, fooling the attacking savages just when the beleaguered occupants of the Fort are about to surrender. Abby and Holden find peace and happiness finally when all the villains who pursue them are killed off.

NOTES: Nominated for an Academy Award for Special Effects, but lost to the only other nominee *Green Dolphin Street*.
 Negative cost: around $5 million.
 Location exteriors filmed near Pittsburgh (the forest scenes) and by Arthur Rosson's unit on the Snake River, Idaho (the canoe sequence).

VIEWER'S GUIDE: Adults.

COMMENT: No survey of Hollywood's treatment of big-budget westerns would be complete without a Cecil B. De Mille epic. What is curious about this one though is that it wasn't particularly popular at the boxoffice and actually lost money. This seems strange as most of the ingredients for popular success are here. True, the movie is overlong, but most cash-paying patrons will hardly object to this extra value for their money. (I thought the film would be improved if three or four of the long and rather pointless dialogue scenes between Cooper and Goddard were cut. My impression is that these scenes merely pad out the film as a sop to the two principals). True, the script is somewhat naive and juvenile. It reduces historical figures to pasteboard cut-outs and then hands them verbose dialogue of appropriate banality. (It says much for the players that most are able to rise above their material). But the plot does allow for plenty of incident and spectacle, including shooting the rapids on the Snake which anticipates *The River Wild*. (It's a pity that the "peg" on which all this drama is hung, namely the conflict between hero Cooper and heavy Da Silva, is so disappointingly resolved with the villain receiving very cursory if just desserts from Cooper's faster pistol). It's true too that neither Cooper nor Miss Goddard seem entirely comfortable in their roles. The script forces Coop to do some remarkably stupid things, so it's probably no cause for wonder that he often appears to be acting half-heartedly at half-steam. Miss Goddard seems far too elegant for a maid-of-all-work. Her make-up is too heavy. Her performance on the other hands seems too lightweight. Many of the support players seem likewise somewhat ill-at-ease. Fortunately Da Silva makes his villain really mean and nasty.

Technically, the film's tension is a bit undermined by some obvious process screen effects. Director De Mille's hand is most in evidence in the crowd and action scenes. Rennahan's fine Technicolor photography is a major asset.

OTHER VIEWS: Like David O. Selznick's *Duel in the Sun*, this one is so un-De Mille it's surprising. But, like *Duel*, it will get business. As a spec it has sufficient size and scope to command plenty of b.o.... Despite the ten-twent-thirt meller-dramatics and the frequently inept script, the performances are convincing, a great tribute to the cast because that dialogue and those situations try the best of troupers.

— *The Daily Variety*.

Spectacularly, stirringly and with full panoply of gaudy color, Cecil B. De Mille again screen-vitalizes a chapter out of American history in his picture *Unconquered*. One may also say that he has supplied both a boisterous and sensational delineation of the frontiersman's era with the full complement of De Mille devices, even to the famous bath sequence, a dip into the serial thrillers when the hero and heroine shoot the rapids to the edge of a waterfall, and the staging of the battle of Fort Pitt that far out-does any conflict that was ever dreamt up for a world's fair carnival.

— Edwin Schallert in *The Los Angeles Times*.

P.S. When asked about Fredric (or is it Frederic?) M. Frank, his co-screenwriter Charles Bennett said in an interview with Pat McGilligan, "A lovely guy, but he couldn't write his own name." Well, that last comment was literally true anyway!

# Undercover

**Charles Starrett** (Bob Hunter), **Adrienne Dore** (Betty Winton), **Kenne Duncan** (Blake Hardy), **Wheeler Oakman** (Inspector McCrae), **Eric Clavering** (Madigan), **Phil Brandon** (Jameson), **Elliott Lorraine** (Winton), **Austin Moran** (Sergeant Woods), **Grace Webster** (Mrs Jameson), **Gilmore Young** (Hyde), **Wilbur Freeman** (Hammond), **Muriel Deane** (lady in hardware store), **Farnham Baxter, Winn Barren, Polly Moran, George Fiefield**.

Director: **SAM NEWFIELD**. Story: **Kenne Duncan**. Screenplay: **Murison Dunne**. Photography: **Sam Leavitt**. Film editor: **Alex Meyers**. Art director: **Robert Hall**. Production manager and assistant director: **Jack Chisholm**. Sound recording: **Harry Belock**. Producer: **J.R. Booth**. Associate producer: **Arthur Gottlieb**. A Booth Dominions picture, produced on location in Ontario, with interiors at the Ravena Rink, Toronto.

Not copyrighted or theatrically released in the U.S.A. Released in Canada by Dominion Motion Pictures Ltd in 1935 and in the U.K. by M-G-M in January, 1936. 60 minutes.

Alternative title: *UNDERCOVER MEN.*

SYNOPSIS: A bank clerk is disgraced for failing to foil a hold-up. He joins the Mounties and tracks down the bandits.

NOTES: The first of Starrett's 132 westerns.

Supported by M-G-M and designed for the British quota market, this was the second of a planned twelve Canadian "B" features to be co-produced by Arthur Gottlieb. Only this one and *The King's Plate* (1935), a racing melodrama starring Kenne Duncan and Toby Wing, also directed by Newfield, were actually made.

According to the *Monthly Film Bulletin*, both films suffered from naive, clumsy direction and dialogue. Though better than *The King's Plate*, acting here was "barely competent". However, the magazine's critic did more or less commend the "he-man action."

Hardly a brilliant start to what must be the most prolific career of any "B" western star. Gene Autry, for instance, made only 92 features and one serial. Only 93! Hopalong Cassidy made a mere 66 pictures, whilst Roy Rogers starred in a niggardly 84.

Unlike some of the other western stars, Charles Starrett was just as popular in Australia as in the States. In England, he was never a great favorite. Some of his later Columbia westerns were not released at all. Many had title changes — often purposely to disguise the fact that they were westerns!

Here is a filmography of Starrett's career:

## FILMOGRAPHY OF CHARLES STARRETT
Includes 166 films, 34 non-Western and 132 Western films, a career spanning 27 years.

The name of the distributor or production company and the director follows the title of the film and the initial year of release.

1. *The Quarterback* — 1926
Paramount, Fred Newmeyer — Silent.
Richard Dix, Esther Ralston, Harry Beresford, David Butler, Robert W. Craig, Mona Palmer, and the Dartmouth football team of which Charles Starrett was a member. [*The New York Times* called it "another football comedy."]

2. *Fast and Loose* — 1930
Paramount, Fred Newmeyer, sound Movietone.
Miriam Hopkins, Carol Lombard, Frank Morgan, Charles R. Starrett (Henry Morgan, automobile mechanic who wins Miriam), Henry Wadsworth, Winifred Harris, Herbert Yost, David Hutcheson, Ilka Chase, Herschel Mayall. [*The New York Times* critic Mordaunt Hall reported at the time: "One of the most amusing episodes of this film, a stretch that is pictured with consummate artistry, is where Marion, portrayed by Miriam Hopkins, one night encounters Henry Morgan, acted by Charles Starrett. Marion has stopped her car on the wet sand, and while she is gazing across the sound she hears splashing in the water and then sees Henry. He tells her that she will have difficulty in

getting her car to move, but Marion is in no mood to take any man's advice, for she has just decided that she does not wish to become Lady Rockingham (Lord Rockingham played by David Hutcheson). The stalwart Henry takes to the water again, and when he returns Marion is experiencing no end of trouble with her automobile. Henry looks on amused, despite the fact that Marion is spoiling her light clothes, and before he consents to help her he makes her ask him to do so and also to admit that she does not know anything about automobiles. This young Hercules pries up the car and soon it is wheeled off the treacherous sand. Henry admits that he comes to that spot every evening for a swim, and Marion bids him goodbye with perfunctory thanks. The next evening she turns up ready to go for a swim with Henry and they have their first kiss. It may seem rather abrupt, but one has to admit that Henry is a pleasant individual without a suspicion of affectation." (Editor's note: This is about the only good review the *Times* gave Starrett. He appeared in their listings up to 1938, including one Western, getting reviews like "he acquits himself favorably", "he is out of his element", etc.)]

3. *The Royal Family of Broadway* — 1930
Paramount, George Cukor and Cyril Gardner.
Ina Claire, Fredric March, Marian Brian, Henrietta Crosman, Charles Starrett, Arnold Korff, Frank Conroy, Royal C. Stout, Elsie Edmond, Murray Alper, Wesley Stark, Herschel Mayall.

4. *Silence* — 1931
Paramount, Louis Gasnier and Max Marcin.
Clive Brook, Marjorie Rambeau, Peggy Shannon, Charles Starrett (as Arthur Lawrence), Willard Robertson, John Wray, Frank Sheridan, Paul Nicholson, John Craig, J. N. Sullivan, Charles Trowbridge, Ben Taggart, Wade Boteler, Robert Homans.

5. *Touchdown!* — 1931
Paramount, Norman Z. McLeod.
Richard Arlen, Peggy Shannon, Jack Oakie, Regis Toomey, Charles Starrett (Paul Gehring), George Barbier, J. Farrell MacDonald, George Irving, Charles D. Brown.

6. *The Viking* — 1931
J.D. Williams and Associates, George Melford. Louise Huntington, Charles Starrett (Luke), Captain Bob Bartlett, Arthur Vinton. [The Viking was an old sealer ship].

7. *Damaged Love* — 1931
Superior Talking Pictures (Sono Art-World Wide), Irvin Willat.
June Collyer, Charles R. Starrett (Jim Powell), Eloise Taylor, Betty Garde, Charles Trowbridge. [*The New York Times* said "Charles Starrett a young Dartmouth student... has begun a career on the screen."]

8. *The Age For Love* — 1931
United Artists, Frank Lloyd.
Billie Dove, Charles Starrett (Dudley Crome), Lois Wilson, Edward Everett Horton, Mary Duncan, Adrian Morris, Betty Ross Clarke, Jed Prouty, Joan Standing, Alice Moe,

Charles Sellon, Count Pierre de Ramey, Vivian Oakland, Andre Beranger, Cecil Cunningham.

9. *Sky Bride* — 1932
Paramount, Stephen Roberts.
Richard Arlen, Jack Oakie, Virginia Bruce, Robert Coogan, Charles Starrett (Jim Carmichael), Louise Closser Hale, Tom Douglas, Harold Goodwin.

10. *Lady and Gent* — 1932
Paramount, Stephen Roberts.
George Bancroft, Wynne Gibson, Charles Starrett (Ted Streaver), James Gleason, John Wayne, Morgan Wallace, James Crane, William Halligan, Billy Butts, Joyce Compton.

11. *The Mask of Fu Manchu* — 1932
M-G-M, Charles Brabin.
Boris Karloff (Dr Fu Manchu), Charles Starrett (Terrence Granville), Lawrence Grant (Sir Lionel Barton), Lewis Stone (Sir Nayland Smith of Scotland Yard), Jean Hersholt (Professor Von Berg), Myrna Loy (Fah Lo See), Karen Morley (Sheila Barton), David Torrence (McLeod). [Starrett is manacled to an operating table to have a serum introduced into his blood. Just one of the many perils faced by actors in this film, still being shown in 1997].

12. *Our Betters* — 1933
RKO, George Cukor.
Constance Bennett, Gilbert Roland, Charles Starrett (Fleming Harvey), Anita Louise, Phoebe Foster, Grant Mitchell, Hugh Sinclair, Alan Mowbray, Minor Watson, Violett Kemble-Cooper, Tyrrell Davis, Virginia Howell, Walter Walker, Harold Entwhistle.

13. *Mister Skitch* — 1933
Fox, James Cruze.
Will Rogers, ZaSu Pitts, Rochelle Hudson, Florence Desmond, Harry Green, Charles Starrett (Harvey Denby), Eugene Palette.

14. *The Jungle Bride* — 1933
Monogram, Harry O. Hoyt and Albert Kelly.
Anita Page, Charles Starrett (Gordon Wayne), Kenneth Thomson, Eddie Borden, Gertrude Simpson, Jay Emmett, Clarence Geldert. [Charles croons "That's the Call of the Jungle" to Anita in this film.]

15. *The Return of Casey Jones* — 1933
Monogram, J. P. McCarthy.
Charles Starrett (as Casey Jones, the railroad engineer), Ruth Hall, Jackie Searle, George Walsh, Margaret Seddon, Robert Elliott, George Hayes, G.D. Wood, George Nash, Anne Howard.

16. *Murder on the Campus* — 1933

Chesterfield, Richard Thorpe.
Charles Starrett, Shirley Grey, J. Farrell MacDonald.

17. *The Sweetheart of Sigma Chi* — 1933
Monogram, Edwin L. Marin.
Mary Carlisle, Buster Crabbe, Charles Starrett (Marley), Florence Lake, Sally Starr, Eddie Tamblyn, Russell Pratt, Burr McIntosh, Franklin Parker, Tommy Dugan.

18. *Desirable* — 1934
Warner Brothers, Archie Mayo.
Jean Muir, George Brent, Veree Teasdale, Arthur Aylesworth, Joan Wheeler, Barbara Leonard, Charles Starrett (Russell Gray), John Halliday, Jim Miller, Virginia Hammond, Doris Atkinson, Pauline True, Russell Hopton.

19. *The Silver Streak* — 1934
RKO, Thomas Atkins.
Charles Starrett (Tom Caldwell), Sally Blane, Hardie Albright, Edgar Kennedy, Irving Pichel, William Farnum, Arthur Lake, Guinn Williams, Doris Dawson, Theodore von Eltz, Murray Kinnell, Harry Allen, James Bradbury.

20. *This Man Is Mine* — 1934
RKO, John Cromwell.
Irene Dunne, Ralph Bellamy, Constance Cummings, Kay Johnson, Charles Starrett (Judd McCrea), Vivian Tobin, Sidney Blackmer, Louis Mason.

21. *One In a Million* — 1934
Invincible, Frank Strayer.
Charles Starrett, Dorothy Wilson, Holmes Herbert, Robert Frazer, Gwen Lee, Guinn Williams, Fred Santley.

22. *Gentlemen Are Born* — 1934
First National, Alfred E. Green.
Franchot Tone, Jean Muir, Margaret Lindsay, Ann Dvorak, Ross Alexander, Nick (later Dick) Foran, Charles Starrett (Stephen Hornblow), Russell Hicks, Robert Light, Arthur Aylesworth, Henry O'Neill, Addison Richards, Marjorie Gateson, Bradley Page.

23. *Three on a Honeymoon* — 1934
Fox, James Tinling.
Sally Eilers, Charles Starrett, Zasu Pitts, John Mack Brown, Henrietta Crosman, Irene Hervey, Howard Lally, Russell Simpson, Cornelius Keefe, Wini Shaw, Elsie Larson.

24. *Call It Luck* — 1934
Fox, James Tinling.
Pat Paterson, Herbert Mundin, Charles Starrett (Stan Russell), Gordon Westcott, Georgia Caine, Theodore von Eltz, Reginald Mason, Ernest Wood, Ray Mayer, Susan Fleming.

25. *Stolen Sweets* — 1934
Chesterfield, Richard Thorpe.
Sally Blane, Charles Starrett. [Sally Blane was a sister of Loretta Young].

26. *Green Eyes* — 1934
Chesterfield, Richard Thorpe.
Shirley Grey, Charles Starrett.

27. *Sons of Steel* — 1935
Chesterfield, Charles Lamont.
Charles Starrett (Phillip Mason), Polly Ann Young [another sister of Loretta Young], William Bakewell, Aileen Pringle, Walter Walker, Holmes Herbert, Richard Carlyle, Florence Roberts, Adolph Millar, Jack Shutta, Lloyd Ingraham, Edward LeSaint, Tom Ricketts, Edgar Norton, Barbara Bedford, Harry Semels, Al Thompson.

28. *A Shot in the Dark* — 1935
Chestefield, Charles Lamont.
Charles Starrett (Ken Harris), Robert Warwick, Edward Van Sloan, Marion Shilling, Doris Lloyd, Helene Jerome, Eddie Tamblyn, Robert McKenzie, George Morrell, Herbert Bunston, Broderick O'Farrell, John Davidson, Jane Keckley. [Based on the novel by Clifford Orr: *The Dartmouth Murders*.]

29. *What Price Crime?* — 1935
Beacon, Albert Herman.
Charles Starrett, Noel N. Madison, Virginia Cherrill, Charles Delaney, Jack Mulhall, Nina Guilberg, Henry Roquemore, Gordon Griffith, John Elliott, Arthur Loft, Earl Tree, Jack Cowell, Arthur Roland, Edwin Argus, Al Baffert, Monte Carter, Lafe McKee.

30. *One New York Night* — 1935
M-G-M, Jack Conway.
Franchot Tone, Una Merkel, Conrad Nagel, Harvey Stephens, Steffi Duna, Charles Starrett, Louise Henry, Tommy Dugan, Harold Huber, Henry Kolker.

31. *Make a Million* — 1935
Monogram, Lewis D. Collins.
Charles Starrett (Jones), Pauline Brooks, George E. Stone, James Burke, Guy Usher, Norman Houston, Monte Carter, Jimmy Aubrey, George Cleveland.

32. *So Red the Rose* — 1935
Paramount, King Vidor.
Margaret Sullavan, Walter Connolly, Randolph Scott, Elizabeth Patterson, Janet Beecher.

33. *Undercover* — 1935

All films from here on are Columbia Pictures unless specially noted.

34. *The Gallant Defender* — 1935
*1 (see P.S.)
David Selman.
[Charles' first American Western, but he would continue to make a few non-Westerns.]
Charles Starrett (Johnny Flagg), Joan Perry (Barbara McGrail), Harry Woods (Barr Munro), Edward LeSaint (Harvey Campbell), Jack Clifford (the sheriff), Al Bridge (Salty Smith), George Billings (Jimmy McGrail), George Chesebro (Swale), Edmund Cobb, Frank Ellis, Jack Rockwell, Tom London, Stanley Blystone, Lew Meehan, Merrill McCormick, Glenn Strange, Al Ferguson, Slim Whitaker, Bud Osborne, Sons of the Pioneers (Bob Nolan, Tim Spencer, Hugh Farr, Karl Farr, Len Slye). [Starrett was billed as "the new fighting favorite." Many of his early Westerns were based, roughly, on stories by popular author Peter B. Kyne.]

35. *Along Came Love* — 1936
Paramount, Bert Lytell.
Irene Hervey, Charles Starrett, Doris Kenyon, H.B. Warner, Irene Franklin, Bernadene Hayes, Ferdinand Gottschalk, Charles Judels, Frank Reicher, Mathilde Comont.

36. *The Mysterious Avenger* — 1936
*2 (see P.S)
David Selman.
Charles Starrett (Ranny Maitland and Ranny Morgan), Joan Perry (Alice Lockhart), Wheeler Oakman (Brophy), Edward LeSaint (Lockhart), Lafe McKee (Maitland), Hal Price (the sheriff), Charles Locher (later Jon Hall) (Lafe Lockhart), George Chesebro (Foley), Edmund Cobb, Dick Botiller, Jack Rockwell, and Sons of the Pioneers.

37. *Stampede* — 1936
*5 (see P.S.)
Ford Beebe.
Charles Starrett (Larry Carson), Finis Barton (Dale Milford), J.P. McGowan (Stevens), LeStrange Millman (Milford, rancher), Reginald Hincks (the sheriff), James McGrath (Brooks), Arthur Kerr (Gans), Jack Atkinson (Hodge), Michael Heppel (Kyle), Ted Mapes.

38. *Secret Patrol* — 1936
*3 (see P.S.)
David Selman.
Charles Starrett (Alan Barclay, RCMP), Finis Barton (Ann), J.P. McGowan (Barstow), Henry Mollinson (Gene), LeStrange Millman (McCord), James McGrath (Arnold), Arthur Kerr (Jordan), Reginald Hincks (superintendent), Ted Mapes.

39. *Code of the Range* — 1936
*4 (see P.S.)
C. C. Coleman Jr.

Charles Starrett (Lee Jamison), Mary Blake (Janet Parker), Ed Coxon (Angus McLeod), Allan Caven (Calamity Parker), Ed Peil Sr (the sheriff), Edmund Cobb (Ed Randall), Edward LeSaint (Adams), Ralph McCullough (Quigley), Albert J.S. Smith (Barney Ross), Art Mix, George Chesebro.

40. *The Cowboy Star* — 1936
*6 (see P.S.)
David Selman.
Charles Starrett (Spencer Yorke), Iris Meredith (Mary Baker), Si Jenks (Buckshot), Marc Lawrence (Johnny Sampson), Ed Peil Sr (Clem Barker), Wally Albright (Jimmy Baker), Ralph McCullough (Pretty Boy Hogan), Dick Terry (midget), Landers Stevens (Producer Jack Kingswell), Nick Copeland, Winifred Hari.

41. *Dodge City Trail* — 1936
*15 (see P.S)
C. C. Coleman Jr.
Charles Starrett (Steve Braddock), Donald Grayson (singer) (Slim Grayson), Marion Weldon (Marion Phillips), Russell Hicks (Kenyon Phillips), Si Jenks (Rawhide), Al Bridge (Dawson), Art Mix (Blackie), Ernie Adams (Dillon), Lew Meehan (Joe), Hank Bell (Red), Jack Rockwell, George Chesebro, Blackie Whiteford.

42. *Two-Gun Law* — 1937
*9 (see P.S.)
Leon Barsha.
Charles Starrett (Bob Larson), Peggy Stratford (Mary Hammond), Hank Bell (Cookie), Edward LeSaint (Colonel Ben Hammond), Dick Curtis (Len Edwards), Lee Prather (Sheriff Bill Collier), Charles Middleton (Wolf Larson), Alan Bridge (Kipp Faulkner), Victor Potel (Cassius), Art Mix, George Chesebro, George Morrell, Tex Cooper.

43. *Two-Fisted Sheriff* — 1937
*10 (see P.S.)
Leon Barsha.
Charles Starrett (Sheriff Dick Houston), Barbara Weeks (Molly Herrick), Bruce Lane (Bob Pierson), Ed Peil (Judge Webster), Alan Sears (Laughing Bill Slagg), Walter Downing (Doc Pierce), Ernie Adams (Sheriff Rankin), Claire McDowell (Miss Herrick), Frank Ellis (Gargan), Robert Walker (Lyons), George Chesebro (the prosecutor), Merrill McCormack (Hank Beasley), Richard Cramer (Taggart), Wally West (blacksmith), Edmund Cobb (deputy Jim), Art Mix, Al Bridge, Dick Botiller, George Morrell, Tex Cooper, Dick Alexander (Bull), Maston Williams (Dunn), Ethan Laidlaw (Burke), Steve Clark (Red).

44. *Westbound Mail* — 1937
*7 (see P.S.)
Folmer Blangsted.

Charles Starrett (Jim Bradley and Mule Skinner), Rosalind Kieth (Marion Saunders), Edward Keane (Gun Barlow), Arthur Stone (Andy), Ben Weldon (Steve Hickman), Al Bridge (Bull Feeney), George Chesebro (Slim), Art Mix (Shorty).

45. *Trapped* — 1937
*8 (see P.S.)
Leon Barsha.
Charles Starrett (Ted Haley), Peggy Stratford (Adele Roberts), Robert Middlemass (Sol Roberts), Allen Sears (Cal), Ted Oliver (Ike Britt), Lew Meehan (Moose Nelson), Ed Peil (Bill Ashley), Jack Rockwell (Tom Haggard), Edward LeSaint (the doctor), Francis Sayles (Chong), Art Mix.

46. *One Man Justice* — 1937
*11 (see P.S.)
Leon Barsha.
Charles Starrett (Larry Clarke), Barbara Weeks (Mary Crockett), Hal Taliaferro (Neal King), Jack Clifford (Sheriff Ben Adams), Al Bridge (Red Grindy), Walter Downing (Doc Willat), Mary Gordon (Bridget), Jack Lipson (Slim), Edmund Cobb (Tex Wiley), Dick Curtis (Hank Skinner), Maston Williams (Lefty Gates), Harry Fleischman (Joe Craig), Art Mix, Hank Bell, Steve Clark, Frank Ellis, Ethan Laidlaw, Eddie Laughton.

47. *Old Wyoming Trail* — 1937
*12 (see P.S.)
Folmer Blangsted.
Charles Starrett (Bob Patterson), Donald Grayson (Sandy), Barbara Weeks (Elsie Halliday), Dick Curtis (Ed Slade), Edward LeSaint (Jeff Halliday), Bob Nolan and Sons of the Pioneers, Guy Usher (Lafe Kinney), George Chesebro (Hank Barstow), Edward Peil (the sheriff), Edward Hearn (Hammond), Art Mix (Carson), Slim Whitaker, Alma Chester, Ernie Adams, Dick Botiller, Frank Ellis, Joe Yrigoyen, Charles Brinley, Fred Burns, Si Jenks, Curley Dresden, Ray Whitley, John P. (Blackie) Whiteford, Art Dillard, Ray Jones, Jerome Ward, Ed Javregi, Tex Cooper.

48. *Outlaws of the Prairie* — 1937
*13 (see P.S).
Sam Nelson.
Charles Starrett (Dart Colt, Texas ranger), Donald Grayson (Slim Grayson), Iris Meredith (Judy Garfield), Edward LeSaint (Lafe Garfield), Bob Nolan (Bob), Sons of the Pioneers, Dick Curtis (Dragg), Norman Willis (William Lupton), Edmund Cobb (Jed Stevens), Art Mix (Lawton), Steve Clark (Cobb), Hank Bell (Jim), Earle Hodgins (Neepah), Lee Shumway, Dick Alexander, Frank Shannon, Fred Burns, Jack Rockwell, Jack Kirk, George Chesebro, Charles LeMoyne, Frank Ellis, Frank McCarroll, Vernon Dent, Curley Dresden, Jim Corey, Blackie Whiteford, George Morrell, Buel Bryant, Ray Jones.

49. *Start Cheering* — 1938
Albert S. Rogell.

Jimmy Durante, Joan Perry, Walter Connolly, Charles Starrett, Broderick Crawford, E. Earle, Gertrude Niesen, Raymond Walburn, The Three Stooges, Hal LeRoy, Ernest Truex, Virginia Dale, Chaz Chase, Jimmy Wallington, Romo Vincent, Gene Morgan, Louise Stanley, Arthur Hoyt, Howard Hickman, Minerva Urecal, Arthur Loft, Nick Lukats, Louis Prima and Band, Johnny Greene and Orchestra.

50. *Cattle Raiders* — 1938
*16
Sam Nelson.
Charles Starrett (Tom Reynolds), Donald Grayson (Slim Grayson), Iris Meredith (Nancy Grayson), Bob Nolan (Bob), Sons of the Pioneers, Dick Curtis (Ed Munro), Allen Brook (Steve Reynolds), Edward LeSaint (John Reynolds), Edmund Cobb (Burke), George Chesebro (Brand), Ed Coxon (Doc Connors), Steve Clark (Hank), Art Mix (Keno), Clem Horton (Slash), Allan Sears (Hayes), Edward Peil (the sheriff), Jack Clifford (the judge), Jim Thorpe, Curley Dresden, Merrill McCormack, Hank Bell, Frank Ellis, George Morrell, Blackie Whiteford, Robert Burns, Wally West, Forrest Taylor, Horace B. Carpenter, James Mason.

51. *Law of the Plains* — 1938
*18
Sam Nelson.
Charles Starrett, Iris Meredith, Dick Curtis, Bob Nolan, Sons of the Pioneers, Robert Warwick, Edward LeSaint, Edmund Cobb, Art Mix, Jack Rockwell, George Chesebro.

52. *West of Cheyenne* — 1938
*19
Sam Nelson.
Charles Starrett, Iris Meredith, Dick Curtis, Bob Nolan, Sons of the Pioneers, Pat Brady, Edward LeSaint, Edmund Cobb, Art Mix, Ernie Adams, Jack Rockwell, John Tyrell.

53. *Colorado Trail* — 1938
*21
Sam Nelson.
Charles Starrett, Iris Meredith, Dick Curtis, Edward LeSaint, Edward Peil, Al Bridge, Robert Fiske, Bob Nolan, Sons of the Pioneers, Hank Bell, Edmund Cobb, Jack Clifford.

54. *Call of the Rockies* — 1938
*17
Allan James.
Charles Starrett, Iris Meredith, Donald Grayson, Dick Curtis, Edward LeSaint, Edmund Cobb, Art Mix, John Tyrell, George Chesebro, Glenn Strange.

55. *South of Arizona* — 1938
*20
Sam Nelson.

Charles Starrett, Iris Meredith, Dick Curtis, Bob Nolan, Sons of the Pioneers, Robert Fiske, Edmund Cobb, Art Mix.

56. *Rio Grande* — 1938
*22
Sam Nelson.
Charles Starrett, Ann Doran, Dick Curtis, Bob Nolan and the Sons of the Pioneers.

57. *West of the Santa Fe* — 1938
*24
Sam Nelson.
Charles Starrett, Iris Meredith, Dick Curtis, Robert Fiske, LeRoy Mason, Bob Nolan, Sons of the Pioneers, Hank Bell, Edmund Cobb, Clem Horton, Richard Botiller, Edward Hearn, Edward Le Saint, Buck Connor, John P. (Blackie) Whiteford).

58. *Spoilers of the Range* — 1939
*27
C.C. Coleman Jr.
Charles Starrett, Iris Meredith, Dick Curtis (Lobo Savage), Art Mix (Santos), Hank Bell (the sheriff), Kenneth MacDonald (Cash Fenton), Ethan Laidlaw (the bartender), Forrest H. Dillon, Carl Sepulveda, Buel Bryant, Clem Horton, George Russell, Horace B. Carpenter, Charles Brinley, Joe Weaver, Edward LeSaint, Forbes Murray, Edward Peil, Bob Nolan, Sons of the Pioneers.

59. *Western Caravans* — 1939
*28
Sam Nelson.
Charles Starrett (Sheriff Jim Carson), Iris Meredith (Joyce Thompson), Bob Nolan (Bob), Sons of the Pioneers, Dick Curtis (Mart Kohler), Russell Simpson (Winchester Thompson), Hal Taliaferro (Joel Winters), Hank Bell (Hank), Sammy McKim (Matt Winters), Ethan Laidlaw (Tip Scranton), Edmund Cobb (Tex Mays), Charles Brinley.

60. *The Man From Sundown* — 1939
*29
Sam Nelson
Charles Starrett (Larry Whalen, Texas ranger), Iris Meredith (Barbara Kellogg), Bob Nolan (Bob), Sons of the Pioneers, Richard Fiske (Tom Kellogg), Jack Rockwell (Hank Austin), Alan Bridge (Slick Larson), Richard Botiller (Rio Mason), Ernie Adams (Shorty Bates), Robert Fiske (Captain Prescott), Edward Peil (Sheriff Wiley), Clem Horton (Bat), Forrest H. Dillon (Kir), Edmund Cobb (Roper), Oscar Gahan.

61. *Riders of Black River* — 1939
*30
Norman Deming.
Charles Starrett, Iris Meredith, Bob Nolan, Sons of the Pioneers, Dick Curtis, Francis Sayles, Olin Francis, Stanley Brown, Edmund Cobb, Forrest Taylor.

62. *Texas Stampede* — 1939
*25
Sam Nelson.
Charles Starrett, Iris Meredith, Lee Prather, Fred Kohler Jr, Charles Brinley, Hank Bell, Bob Nolan, Sons of the Pioneers.

63. *Outpost of the Mounties* — 1939
*31
C. C. Coleman.
Charles Starrett, Iris Meredith, Dick Curtis, Stanley Brown, Kenneth MacDonald, Edmund Cobb, Bob Nolan, Sons of the Pioneers, Lane Chandler, Albert Morin, Hal Taliaferro, Pat O'Hara.

64. *The Stranger From Texas* — 1939
*32
Sam Nelson.
Charles Starrett (U.S. marshal), Lorna Grey, Richard Fiske, Dick Curtis, Jack Rockwell (the sheriff), Edmund Cobb, George Chesebro, Buel Bryant, Bob Nolan, Sons of the Pioneers.

65. *The Thundering West* — 1939
*23
Sam Nelson.
Charles Starrett, Iris Meredith, Dick Curtis, Art Mix, Ed Cobb, Hal Taliaferro.

66. *North of the Yukon* — 1939
*26
Sam Nelson.
Charles Starrett, Linda Winters, Lane Chandler, Kenne Duncan, Bob Nolan, Ed Cobb, Hal Taliaferro.

67. *Bullets For Rustlers* — 1940
*34
Sam Nelson.
Charles Starrett, Lorna Gray, Dick Curtis, Lee Prather, Francis Walker, Eddie Laughton (Shorty, the bartender), Bob Nolan, Sons of the Pioneers, Kenneth MacDonald, Jack Rockwell, Hal Taliaferro.

68. *Blazing Six Shooters* — 1940
*35
Joseph H. Lewis.
Charles Starrett, Iris Meredith, Bob Nolan, Sons of the Pioneers, Dick Curtis, George Cleveland, Al Bridge, Henry Hall, Stanley Brown, John Tyrell, Eddie Laughton, Francis Walker, Edmund Cobb, Bruce Bennett.

69. *Two-Fisted Rangers* — 1940
*33
Joseph H. Lewis.
Charles Starrett, Iris Meredith, Dick Curtis, Kenneth MacDonald, Bill Cody Jr, Bob Nolan, Pat Brady, Sons of the Pioneers, Hal Taliaferro.

70. *Texas Stagecoach* — 1940
*36
Joseph H. Lewis.
Charles Starrett, Iris Meredith, Dick Curtis, Francis Walker, Bob Nolan, Sons of the Pioneers, Kenneth MacDonald, Edward LeSaint, Harry Cording.

71. *West of Abilene* — 1940
*37
Ralph Cedar.
Charles Starrett, Marjorie Cooley, Bruce Bennett, William Pawley, William A. Kellogg, Don Beddoe, George Cleveland, Forrest Taylor, Bob Nolan, Sons of the Pioneers, Francis Walker, Eddie Laughton, Vestor Pegg, Bud Osborne.

72. *The Durango Kid* — 1940
*38
Lambert Hillyer.
Charles Starrett (The Durango Kid), Luana Walters, Bob Nolan, Pat Brady, Sons of the Pioneers, Kenneth MacDonald, Francis Walker, Forrest Taylor, Melvin Long, Frank LaRue.

73. *Thundering Frontier* — 1940
*39
D. Ross Lederman.
Charles Starrett, Iris Meredith, Fred Burns, Carl Stockdale, Raphael (Ray) Bennett, Alex Callam, Bob Nolan, Sons of the Pioneers, John Tyrell, Francis Walker, John Dilson.

74. *Outlaws of the Panhandle* — 1941
*41
Sam Nelson.
Charles Starrett, Frances Robinson, Richard Fiske, Ray Teal, Lee Prather, Norman Willis (Faro Jack Vaughn), Eddie Laughton, Jack Low, Stanley Brown, Bob Nolan, Sons of the Pioneers, Steve Clark, Bud Osborne.

75. *The Pinto Kid* — 1941
*40
Lambert Hillyer.
Charles Starrett, Louise Currie, Paul Sutton, Hank Bell, Ernie Adams, Bob Nolan, Sons of the Pioneers, Francis Walker, Richard Botiller, Jack Rockwell, Roger Grey.

76. *The Medico of Painted Springs* — 1941

*42

Lambert Hillyer.

Charles Starrett (as the Medico), Terry Walker, Ben Taggart, Richard Fiske, Edmund Cobb, Edythe Elliott, Bud Osborne, Steve Clark, Charles Hamilton, George Chesebro. [Starrett liked this role better than the Durango Kid.]

77. *Prairie Stranger* — 1941
*44
Lambert Hillyer.

Charles Starrett, Cliff Edwards, Patti McCarty, Forbes Murray, Frank LaRue, Archie Twitchell, Francis Walker, Edmund Cobb, James Corey, Russ Powell, Lew Preston.

78. *Thunder Over the Prairie* — 1941
*43
Lambert Hillyer.

Charles Starrett (as the Medico), Eileen O'Hearn, Cliff Edwards, Carl Shrum and his Rhythm Rangers, Horace B. Carpenter, Stanley Brown, Danny Mummert, David Sharpe, Joe McGuinn, Donald Curtis, Ted Adams, Jack Rockwell, Budd Buster.

79. *The Royal Mounted Patrol* — 1941
*45
Lambert Hillyer.

Charles Starrett (Tom Jefferies), Russell Hayden (Lucky Lawrence), Wanda McKay (Betty Duvalle), Donald Curtis (French Duvalle), Lloyd Bridges (Hap Andrews), Kermit Maynard (Sergeant Coburn), Evan Thomas (commander), Ted Adams (Pete), Harrison Greene (the manager), George Morrell (a trapper).

80. *Riders of the Badlands* — 1941
*46
Howard Bretherton.

Charles Starrett (Steve Langdon and Mac Collins), Russell Hayden (Lucky Barton), Cliff Edwards (Bones Mallory), Ilene Brewer (Flo), Kay Hughes (Celia), Roy Barcroft (Captain Martin), Rick Anderson (Sheriff Taylor), Edith Leach (Ellen Taylor), Ethan Laidlaw (Bill), Harry Cording (Higgins), Hal Price (Warden James), John L. Cason, Ted Mapes, Francis Walker, Edmund Cobb, George J. Lewis.

81. *West of Tombstone* — 1942
*47
Howard Bretherton.

Charles Starrett (Steve Langdon), Russell Hayden (Lucky Barnett), Cliff Edwards (Harmony Haines), Marcella Martin (Carol Barnett), Gordon DeMain (Wilfred Barnett), Clancy Cooper (Dave Shurlock), Jack Kirk (the sheriff), Budd Buster (Wheeler), Tom London (Morris), Francis Walker, Ray Jones, Eddie Laughton.

82. *Lawless Plainsmen* — 1942
*48

William Berke.

Charles Starrett (Steve Rideen), Russell Hayden (Lucky Bannon), Cliff Edwards (Harmony Stuggs), Luana Walters (Baltimore Bonnie), Ray Bennett (Seth McBride), Gwen Kenyon (Madge Mason), Frank LaRue (Bill Mason), Stanley Brown (Tascoa), Nick Thompson (Ochella), Eddie Laughton (Slim), Carl Mathews.

83. *Down Rio Grande Way* — 1942

*49

William Berke.

Charles Starrett (Steve Martin), Russell Hayden (Lucky Haines), Britt Wood (Britt Haines), Rose Anne Stevens (Mary Ann), Norman Willis (Vandall), Davison Clark (Colonel Baldridge), Edmund Cobb (Stoner), Budd Buster (Kearney), Joseph Eggerton (Judge Henderson), Paul Newlan (Sam Houston), Betty Roadman (Ma Haines), Tom Smith, Jim Corey, William Desmond.

84. *Riders of the Northland* — 1942

*50

William Berke.

Charles Starrett (Steve Bowie), Russell Hayden (Lucky Laidlaw), Cliff Edwards (Harmony Bumpas), Shirley Patterson (Sheila Taylor), Lloyd Bridges (Alex), Bobby Larson (Buddy Taylor), Kenneth MacDonald (Matt Taylor), Paul Sutton (Chris Larsen), Robert O. Davis (nazi agent), Joe McGuinn (Stacy), Francis Walker (Dobie), George Piltz (Luke), Blackjack Ward.

85. *Bad Men of the Hills* — 1942

*51

William Berke.

Charles Starrett (Steve Carlton), Russell Hayden (Lucky Shelton), Cliff Edwards (Harmony Haines), Luana Walters (Laurie Bishop), Alan Bridge (Sheriff Arnold), Guy Usher (Doctor Mitchell), Joel Friedkin (Judge Malotte), Norma Jean Wooters (Buckshot), John Shay (Marshal Upjohn), Dick Botiller (Brant), Art Mix, Jack Ingram, Ben Corbett.

86. *Overland To Deadwood* — 1942

*52

William Berke.

Charles Starrett (Steve Prescott), Russell Hayden (Lucky Chandler), Leslie Brooks (Linda Banning), Cliff Edwards (Harmony Hobbs), Norman Willis (Cash Quinlan), Matt Willis (Red Larsen), Francis Walker (Vince), Lynton Brent (Clipper), June Pickrell (Mrs Banning), Gordon DeMain (George Bullock), Art Mix, Bud Osborne, Herman Hack.

87. *Riding Thru Nevada* — 1942

*54

William Berke.

Charles Starrett, Shirley Patterson, Arthur Hunnicutt, Clancy Cooper, Davison Clark, Minerva Urecal, Edmund Cobb, Ethan Laidlaw, Art Mix, Kermit Maynard, Jimmie Davis and his Rainbow Ramblers.

88. *Pardon My Gun* — 1942
*55
William Berke.
Charles Starrett, Alma Carroll, Arthur Hunnicutt (Arkansas), Texas Jim Lewis and his Lone Star Cowboys, Dick Curtis, Noah Beery Sr, Lloyd Bridges, Ted Mapes, Dave Harper, Roger Grey.

89. *The Fighting Buckaroo* — 1943
*53
William Berke.
Charles Starrett, Kay Harris, Arthur Hunnicutt (Arkansas), Ernest Tubbs with Johnny Luther's Ranch Boys, Stanley Brown, Wheeler Oakman, Forrest Taylor, Robert Stevens, Norma Jean Wooters, Roy Butler.

90. *Cowboy in the Clouds* — 1943
*60
Benjamin Kline.
Charles Starrett, Dub Taylor, Julie Duncan, Dick Curtis, The Jesters, Jimmy Wakely and his Saddle Pals, Davison Clark, Hal Taliaferro, Edward Cassidy, Paul Zaremba, Charles King Jr, John Tyrell.

91. *Robin Hood of the Range* — 1943
*58
William Berke.
Charles Starrett, Arthur Hunnicutt (Arkansas), Kay Harris, Jimmy Wakely Trio, Kenneth MacDonald, Douglas Drake, Hal Price, Edward Peil, Frank LaRue, Bud Osborne, Stanley Brown.

92. *Frontier Fury* — 1943
*57
William Berke.
Charles Starrett, Roma Aldrich, Arthur (Arkansas) Hunnicutt, Jimmy Davis and his Singing Buckaroos, Clancy Cooper, I. Stanford Jolley, Edmund Cobb, Ted Mapes, Bruce Bennett, Bill Wilkerson, Stanley Brown, Joel Friedkin.

93. *Hail to the Rangers* — 1943
*59
William Berke.
Charles Starrett, Arthur (Arkansas) Hunnicutt, Robert Owen Atcher, Leota Atcher, Norman Willis, Lloyd Bridges, Ted Adams, Ernie Adams, Tom London, Jack Kirk, Davison Clark.

94. *Law of the Northwest* — 1943
*56
William Berke.

Charles Starrett, Shirley Patterson, Arthur (Arkansas) Hunnicutt, Stanley Brown, Douglas Leavitt, Donald Curtis, Donald Drake, Davison Clark, Reginald Barlow.

95. *Riding West* — 1944
*63
William Berke.
Charles Starrett, Shirley Patterson, Arthur Hunnicutt, Ernest Tubbs and his Singing Cowboys, Steve Clark, Wheeler Oakman, J.P. Whiteford, Clancy Cooper, Bill Wilkerson.

96. *Cowboy Canteen* — 1944
*61
Lew Landers.
Vera Vague, Guinn Williams, Jane Frazee, Charles Starrett, Tex Ritter, Tailor Maids, Walter (Dub) Taylor, Roy Acuff and his Smoky Mountains Boys and Girls, Bill Hughes, Edythe Elliott, Johnny Tyrell, Emmett Lynn, Max Terhune, Buck, Chickie and Buck. [Billed as a musical comedy.]

97. *Sundown Valley* — 1944
*62
Benjamin Kline.
Charles Starrett, Dub Taylor, Jeanne Bates, The Tennessee Ramblers, Jimmy Wakely and his Saddle Pals, Jessie Arnold, Clancy Cooper, Jack Ingram, Wheeler Oakman, Joel Friedkin, Grace Leonard, Eddie Laughton, Forrest Taylor.

98. *Cowboy From Lonesome River* — 1944
*64
Benjamine Kline.
Charles Starrett, Vi Athens, Dub Taylor, Ozie Waters, Jimmy Wakely and his Saddle Pals, Arthur A. Wenzel, Shelby D. Atchison, Foy Willingham, Al Sloey, Ian Keith, John Tyrell, Craig Woods, Bud Geary, Steve Clark, Kenneth MacDonald.

99. *Cyclone Prairie Rangers* — 1944
*65
Benjamine Kline.
Charles Starrett, Dub Taylor, Constance Worth, Jimmie Davis, Jimmy Wakely and his Saddle Pals, Robert Fiske, Clancy Cooper, Ray Bennett, I. Stanford Jolley, Edward M. Phillips, Edmund Cobb, Forrest Taylor, Paul Zaremba.

100. *Saddle Leather Law* — 1944
*66
Benjamine Kline.
Charles Starrett, Dub Taylor, Vi Athens, Lloyd Bridges, Jimmy Wakely and his Saddle Pals, Salty Holmes, Reed Howes, Robert Kortman, Frank LaRue, Ted French, Ed Cassidy, Steve Clark, Frank O'Connor, Budd Buster, Franklyn Farnum.

101. *Rough Ridin' Justice* — 1945
*68

Derwin Abrahams.

Charles Starrett, Dub Taylor, Betty Jane Graham, Jimmy Wakely, Wheeler Oakman, Jack Ingram, Forrest Taylor, Jack Rockwell, Edmund Cobb, Dan White, Robert Kortman, George Chesebro, Robert Ross.

102. *Return of the Durango* Kid — 1945
*69
Derwin Abrahams.

Charles Starrett (The Durango Kid), Tex Harding, Jean Stevens, John Calvert, Betty Rearden, Hal Price, Britt Wood, Ray Bennett, Paul Conrad.

103. *Both Barrels Blazing* — 1945
*70
Derwin Abrahams.

Charles Starrett, Tex Harding, Dub Taylor, Pat Parrish, The Jesters, Emmett Lynn, Alan Bridge, Charles King Jr, Edward M. Howard, Jack Rockwell, Robert Baron.

104. *Blazing the Western Trail* — 1945
*72
Vernon Keays.

Charles Starrett, Carole Mathews, Tex Harding, Dub Taylor, Bob Wills and his Texas Playboys, Alan Bridge, Nolan Leary, Virginia Sales, Steve Clark, Mauritz Hugo, Ethan Laidlaw, Edmund Cobb, Frank LaRue.

105. *Rustlers of the Badlands* — 1945
*73
Derwin Abrahams.

Charles Starrett, Tex Harding, Sally Bliss, Dub Taylor, Carl Sepulveda, George Eldredge, Edward M. Howard, Ray Bennett, Ted Mapes, Karl Hackett, James T. (Bud) Nelson, Frank McCarroll, Al Trace and his Silly Symphonists.

106. *Lawless Empire* — 1945
*74
Vernon Keays.

Charles Starrett (Durango Kid), Tex Harding, Dub Taylor, Mildred Law, Bob Wills and his Texas Playboys, Johnny Walsh, John Calvert, Ethan Laidlaw, Forrest Taylor, Jack Rockwell, George Chesebro, Boyd Stockman, Lloyd Ingraham, Jessie Arnold, Tom Chatterton.

107. *Outlaws of the Rockies* — 1945
*71
Ray Nazarro.

Charles Starrett, Tex Harding, Carole Mathews, Dub Taylor, Philip Van Zandt, I. Stanford Jolley, George Chesebro, Steve Clark, Jack Rockwell, Carolina Cotton, Spade Cooley.

108. *Sagebrush Heroes* — 1945
*67
Benjamine Kline.
Charles Starrett, Dub Taylor, Constance Worth, Jimmy Wakely and his Saddle Pals, Ozie Waters, Elvin Field, Bobby Larson, Forrest Taylor, Joel Friedkin, Lane Chandler, Paul Zaremba, Eddie Laughton, Johnny Tyrell.

109. *Texas Panhandle* — 1946
*75
Ray Nazarro.
Charles Starrett, Tex Harding, Nanette Parks, Walter (Dub) Taylor, Forrest Taylor, George Chesebro, Jody Gilbert, William Gould, Jack Kirk, Budd Buster, Hugh Hooker, Carolina Cotton, Spade Cooley.

110. *Frontier Gun Law* — 1946
*76
Derwin Abrahams.
Charles Starrett, Tex Harding, Dub Taylor, Jean Stevens, Weldon Heyburn, Jack Rockwell, Frank LaRue, John Elliott, Robert Kortman, Stanley Price, Al Trace and his Silly Symphonists.

111. *Gunning For Vengeance* — 1946
*78
Ray Nazarro.
Charles Starrett, Smiley Burnette, Marjean Neville, The Trailsmen, Robert Kortman, George Chesebro, Frank LaRue, Lane Chandler, Phyllis Adair, Robert Williams, Jack Kirk, John Tyrell.

112. *Roaring Rangers* — 1946
*77
Ray Nazarro.
Charles Starrett, Smiley Burnette, Adelle Roberts, Jack Rockwell, Edward Cassidy, Mickey Kuhn, Ed Cobb, Ted Mapes, Gerald Mackey, Bob Wilke, Merle Travis and his Broncho Busters.

113. *Galloping Thunder* — 1946
*79
Ray Nazarro.
Charles Starrett, Smiley Burnette, Adelle Roberts, Richard Bailey, Kermit Maynard, Ed Cobb, Ray Bennett, Curt Barrett, John Merton, Nolan Leary, Merle Travis and his Broncho Busters.

114. *Two-Fisted Stranger* — 1946
*80
Ray Nazarro.

Charles Starrett, Smiley Burnette, Doris Houck, Charles Murray, Lane Chandler, Ted Mapes, George Chesebro, Jack Rockwell, Herman Hack, Davison Clark, Maudie Prickett, Zeke Clements.

115. *The Desert Horseman* — 1946
*81
Ray Nazarro.
Charles Starrett, Smiley Burnette, Adelle Roberts, Walt Shrum and his Colorado Hillbillies, John Merton, Richard Bailey, George Morgan, Tommy Coates, Jack Kirk, Bud Osborne, Riley Hill.

116. *Heading West* — 1946
*82
Ray Nazarro.
Charles Starrett (Steve Randle and The Durango Kid), Smiley Burnette (as himself), Doris Houck, Hal Taliaferro (Jimmy Mallory), Jack Ingram, Hank Penny and the Plantation Boys, Nolan Leary, Norman Willis, Bud Geary, Tommy Coates, Frank McCarroll, Fenton Reynolds, Matty Roubert, Stanley Price, Harold Hensley, Noel Boggs, Sanford Williams, John Merton, Charles Soldani.

117. *Landrush* — 1946
*83
Vernon Keays.
Charles Starrett, Smiley Burnette, Doris Houck, Ozie Waters, Emmett Lynn, Bud Geary, Bud Osborne, Stephen Barclay, Robert Kortman, George Chesebro.

118. *Terror Trail* — 1947
*84
Ray Nazarro.
Charles Starrett, Smiley Burnette, Barbara Pepper, Ozie Waters and his Colorado Rangers, Lane Chandler, Zon Murray, Elvin Eric Field, Tommy Coates, George Chesebro, Robert Barron, Budd Buster, Bill Clark.

119. *The Fighting Frontiersman* — 1946
*85
Derwin Abrahams.
Charles Starrett, Smiley Burnette, Helen Mowery, Hank Newman and the Georgia Crackers, Emmett Lynn, Jacques J. O'Mahoney (later Jock Mahoney), Robert W. Filmer, George Chesebro, Zon Murray, Jim Diehl, Maude Prickett, Russell Meeker, Frank Ellis, Ernie Adams, Frank LaRue.

120. *South of the Chisholm Trail* — 1947
*86
Derwin Abrahams.

Charles Starrett, Smiley Burnette, Nancy Saunders, Hank Newman and the Georgia Crackers, Jacques J. O'Mahoney, Frank Sully, Jim Diehl, Jack Ingram, George Chesebro, Edwin Parker.

121. *West of Dodge City* — 1947
\*88
Ray Nazarro.
Charles Starrett, Smiley Burnette, Nancy Saunders, Mustard and Gravy, Fred Sears, Glenn Stuart, Stan Jolley, George Chesebro, Bob Wilke, Nolan Leary, Steve Clark, Zon Murray, Marshall Reed.

122. *The Lone Hand Texan* — 1947
\*87
Ray Nazarro.
Charles Starrett, Smiley Burnette, Mary Newton, Fred Sears, Maude Prickett, George Chesebro, Robert Stevens, Bob Cason, Jim Diehl, George Russell, Jasper Weldon, Mustard and Gravy (guitarists).

123. *Law of the Canyon* — 1947
\*89
Ray Nazarro.
Charles Starrett, Smiley Burnette, Nancy Saunders, Buzz Henry, Fred Sears, George Chesebro, Edmund Cobb, Zon Murray, Jack Kirk, Bob Wilke, Frank Marlo, Texas Jim Lewis and his Lone Star Cowboys.

124. *Prairie Raiders* — 1947
\*90
Derwin Abrahams.
Charles Starrett, Smiley Burnette, Nancy Saunders, Robert Scott, Ozie Waters and his Colorado Rangers, Hugh Prosser, Lane Bradford, Ray Bennett, Doug Coppin, Steve Clark, Tom Coates, Frank LaRue, Bob Cason.

125. *The Stranger From Ponca City* — 1947
\*91
Derwin Abrahams.
Charles Starrett, Smiley Burnette, Virginia Hunter, Paul Campbell, Forrest Taylor, Jim Diehl, Ted Mapes, Jock Mahoney, Tom McDonough, John Carpenter, Texas Jim Lewis and his Lone Star Cowboys.

126. *Buckaroo From Powder River* — 1947
\*93
Ray Nazarro.
Charles Starrett, Smiley Burnette, Eve Miller, Forrest Taylor, Paul Campbell, The Cass County Boys, Doug Coppin, Philip Morris, Casey MacGregor, Ted Adams, Ethan Laidlaw, Frank McCarroll.

127. *Last Days of Boot Hill* — 1947
*94
Ray Nazarro.
Charles Starrett, Smiley Burnette, Virginia Hunter, Paul Campbell, Mary Newton, Bill Free, J. Courtland Lytton, Bob Wilke, Al Bridge, The Cass County Boys.

128. *Riders of the Lone Star* — 1947
*92
Derwin Abrahams.
Charles Starrett, Smiley Burnette, Virginia Hunter, Steve Darrell, Edmund Cobb, Mark Dennis, Lane Bradford, Ted Mapes, George Chesebro, Peter Perkins, Edwin Parker, Curley Williams and his Georgia Peach Pickers.

129. *Phantom Valley* — 1948
*96
Ray Nazarro.
Charles Starrett, Smiley Burnette, Virginia Hunter, Joel Friedkin, Robert W. Filmer, Mikel Conrad, Zon Murray, Sam Flint, Teddy Infuhr, Fred Sears, Jerry Jerome, Ozie Waters and his Colorado Rangers.

130. *West of Sonora* — 1948
*97
Ray Nazarro.
Charles Starrett, Smiley Burnette, Anita Castle, The Sunshine Boys, Steve Darrell, George Chesebro, Hal Taliaferro, Bob Wilke, Emmett Lynn, Lynn Farr.

131. *Whirlwind Raiders* — 1948
*98
Vernon Keays.
Charles Starrett, Smiley Burnette, Nancy Saunders, Fred Sears, Little Brown Jug, Jack Ingram, Philip Morris, Patric Hurst, Edwin Parker, Lynn Farr, Doyle O'Dell, The Radio Rangers.

132. *Six-Gun Law* — 1948
*95
Ray Nazarro.
Charles Starrett, Smiley Burnette, Nancy Saunders, Paul Campbell, Hugh Prosser, Curly Clements and his Rodeo Rangers, George Chesebro, Billy Dix, Bob Wilke, Bob Cason, Ethan Laidlaw, Pierce Lyden, Bud Osborne, Budd Buster.

133. *Blazing Across the Pecos* — 1948
*99
Ray Nazarro.
Charles Starrett (Steve Blake and D.K.), Smiley Burnette, Jock Mahoney, Patricia White (Lola Carter), Paul Campbell (Jim Traynor), Red Arnall and the Western Aces, Charles Wilson (Ace Brockway), Thomas Jackson (Matt Carter), Jack Ingram (Buckshot

Thomas), Chief Thundercloud, Pat O'Malley, Frank McCarroll, Pierce Lyden, Paul Conrad.

134. *Trail To Laredo* — 1948
*100
Ray Nazarro.
Charles Starrett, Smiley Burnette, Jim Bannon, Virginia Maxey, Tommy Ivo, Hugh Prosser, George Chesebro, John Merton, Bob Cason, Bob Wilke.

135. *El Dorado Pass* — 1948
*101
Ray Nazarro.
Charles Starrett, Smiley Burnette, Elena Verdugo, Steve Darrell, Rory Mallinson, Ted Mapes, Stanley Blystone, Shorty Thompson and his Saddle Rockin' Rhythm.

136. *Challenge of the Range* — 1949
*103
Ray Nazarro.
Charles Starrett, Smiley Burnette, Paul Raymond, William Halop, Steve Darrell, Henry Hall, Robert Filmer, George Chesebro, John McKee, Frank McCarroll, John Cason, The Sunshine Boys.

137. *Quick on the Trigger* — 1949
*102
Ray Nazarro.
Charles Starrett, Smiley Burnette, Lyle Talbot, Helen Parrish, The Sunshine Boys, George Eldredge, Ted Adams, Alan Bridge, Russell Arms.

138. *The Blazing Trail* — 1949
*106
Ray Nazarro.
Charles Starrett, Smiley Burnette, Jock Mahoney, Marjorie Stapp, Steve Pendleton, Steve Darrell, John Merton, Fred Sears, Trevor Bardette, Robert Malcolm, John Cason, Hank Penny, Slim Duncan.

139. *Desert Vigilante* — 1949
*104
Fred F. Sears.
Charles Starrett, Smiley Burnette, Peggy Stewart, Tristram Coffin, The Georgia Crackers, Mary Newton, Paul Campbell, Tex Harding, Jack Ingram.

140. *South of Death Valley* — 1949
*107
Ray Nazarro.
Charles Starrett, Smiley Burnette, Gail Davis, Fred Sears, Lee Roberts, Tommy Duncan and his Western All Stars, Richard Emory, Clayton Moore, Jason Robards.

141. *Horsemen of the Sierras* — 1949
*108
Fred F. Sears.
Charles Starrett, Smiley Burnette, Lois Hall, Tommy Ivo, John Dehner, Jason Robards, Daniel M. Sheridan, Jock Mahoney, T. Tex Tyler.

142. *Laramie* — 1949
*105
Ray Nazarro.
Charles Starrett, Smiley Burnette, Fred Sears, Tommy Ivo, Elton Britt, Bob Wilke, George Lloyd, Myron Healey, Shooting Star, Jay Silverheels.

143. *Bandits of El Dorado* — 1949
*109
Ray Nazarro.
Charles Starrett, Smiley Burnette, George J. Lewis, Mustard and Gravy, Fred Sears, John Dehner, Clayton Moore, Jock Mahoney, John Doucette, Max Wagner, Henry Kulky.

144. *Renegades of the Sage* — 1949
*110
Ray Nazarro.
Charles Starrett, Smiley Burnette, Leslie Banning, Jock Mahoney, Trevor Bardette, Douglas Fowley, Fred Sears, Jerry Hunter, George Chesebro, Frank McCarroll, Selmer Jackson.

145. *Outcast of Black Mesa* — 1950
*112 (see NOTES)
Ray Nazarro.
Charles Starrett, Smiley Burnette, Martha Hyer, Richard Bailey, Stanley Andrews, William Haade, Lane Chandler, William Gould, Bob Wilke, Charles Roberson, Ozie Waters.

146. *Texas Dynamo* — 1950
*113 (see NOTES)
Ray Nazarro.
Charles Starrett (Steve Drake and D.K.), Smiley Burnette, Lois Hall, Jock Mahoney, John Dehner, Gregg Barton, George Chesebro, Marshall Bradford, Emil Sitka, Fred Sears.

147. *Trail of the Rustlers* — 1950
*111 (see NOTES)
Ray Nazarro.
Charles Starrett, Gail Davis, Smiley Burnette, Myron Healey, Tommy Ivo.

148. *Streets of Ghost Town* — 1950
*114 (see NOTES)
Ray Nazarro.

Charles Starrett, Smiley Burnette, Stanley Andrews, George Chesebro, Mary Ellen Kay, Frank Fenton, Don Reynolds, John Cason, Jack Ingram, Ozie Waters and his Colorado Rangers.

149. *Across the Badlands* — 1950
*115 (see NOTES)
Fred Sears.
Charles Starrett, Smiley Burnette, Dick Elliott, Stanley Andrews, Charles Evans, Helen Mowery, Bob Wilke, Hugh Prosser, Robert S. Cavendish, Paul Campbell.

150. *Lightning Guns* — 1950
*117 (see NOTES)
Fred F. Sears.
Charles Starrett, Smiley Burnette, Gloria Henry, William Norton Bailey, Jock Mahoney, Edgar Dearing, Raymond Bond, Chuck Roberson, Frank Griffin, Joel Friedkin, George Chesebro, Ken Houchins.

151. *Raiders of Tomahawk Creek* — 1950
*116 (see NOTES)
Fred F. Sears.
Charles Starrett, Smiley Burnette, Kay Buckley, Edgar Dearing, Billy Kimbley, Paul Marion, Paul McGuire, Bill Hale, Lee Morgan.

152. *Frontier Outpost* — 1950
*118 (see NOTES)
Ray Nazarro.
Charles Starrett, Lois Hall, Smiley Burnette, Robert Wilke, Jock Mahoney.

153. *Prairie Roundup* — 1951
*119
Fred F. Sears.
Charles Starrett (Steve Carson), Smiley Burnette (himself), Mary Castle (Toni Eaton), Frank Fenton (Buck Prescott), The Sunshine Boys, Frank Sully (the sheriff), Paul Campbell (Poker Joe), Forrest Taylor (Dan Kelley), Don Harvey (Hawk Edwards), George Baxter (Jim Eaton), Lane Chandler (Red Dawson), John Cason (Drag Barton), Al Wyatt (masked man), Glenn Thompson (Pete), Ace Richman (Curtis).

154. *Riding the Outlaw Trail* — 1951
*120
Fred F. Sears
Charles Starrett, Smiley Burnette, Sunny Vickers, Edgar Dearing, Peter Thompson, Jim Bannon, Lee Morgan, Chuck Roberson, Pee Wee King.

155. *Fort Savage Raiders* — 1951
*121
Ray Nazarro.
Charles Starrett, Smiley Burnette, Fred Sears, John Dehner, Trevor Bardette, Peter Thompson, John Cason, Frank Griffin, Sam Flint.

156. *Snake River Desperadoes* — 1951
*122

Fred F. Sears.

Charles Starrett, Smiley Burnette, Don Reynolds, Tommy Ivo, Monte Blue, Boyd (Red) Morgan, George Chesebro, John Pickart, Charles Horvath, Sam Flint, Duke York.

157. *Bonanza Town* — 1951
*123
Fred F. Sears

Charles Starrett, Smiley Burnette, Fred Sears, Luther Crockett, Myron Healey, Charles Horvath, Ted Jordan, Al Wyatt, Paul McGuire, Vernon Dent.

158. *Cyclone Fury* — 1951
*124
Ray Nazarro.

Charles Starrett, Smiley Burnette, Fred Sears, Clayton Moore, Bob Wilke, Louis Lettieri, George Chesebro, Frank O'Connor, Merle Travis.

159. *The Kid From Amarillo* — 1951
*125
Ray Nazarro.

Charles Starrett, Smiley Burnette, Harry Lauter, Fred F. Sears, Don Megowan, Scott Lee, Guy Teague, Charles Evans, George Lewis, Henry Kulky, Jerry Scroggins, Cass County Boys.

160. *Pecos River* — 1951
*126
Fred F. Sears.

Charles Starrett (Steve Baldwin), Smiley Burnette (as himself), Jack Mahoney (as Jack Mahoney), Delores Sidener (Betty Coulter), Steve Darrell (Whip Rockland), Edgar Dearing (Ol' Henry), Frank Jenks (Sheriff Dennig), Paul Campbell (Sniffy), Zon Murray (Mose), Maudie Prickett (Mrs Peck), Edward Featherstone (Mr Grey), and Harmonica Bill. [The pressbook brags that it is Starrett's 200th Western!]

161. *Smoky Canyon* — 1952
*128
Fred F. Sears.

Charles Starrett, Smiley Burnette, Jack Mahoney, Dani Sue Nolan, Tristram Coffin, Larry Hudson, Chris (also Cris) Alcaide, Sandy Sanders, Forrest Taylor, Charles Stevens, Boyd (Red) Morgan, Leroy Johnson.

162. *The Rough Tough West* — 1952
*130
George Archainbaud.

Charles Starrett, Smiley Burnette, Jock Mahoney, Carolina Cotton, Marshall Reed, Fred Sears, Bert Arnold, Tommy Ivo, Valeria Fisher, Pee Wee King, Boyd (Red) Morgan.

163. *Junction City* — 1952
*131
Ray Nazarro.

Charles Starrett, Smiley Burnette, Kathleen Case, Robert Bice, Jock Mahoney, John Dehner, Steve Darrell, George Chesebro, Anita Castle, Mary Newton, Hal Price, Hal Taliaferro, Chris Alcaide, Bob Woodward.

164. *Laramie Mountains* — 1952
*129
Ray Nazarro.
Charles Starrett (Steve Holden), Smiley Burnette (as himself), Jack Mahoney (Swift Eagle), Fred Sears (Major Markham), Marshall Reed (Lieutenant Pierce), Rory Mallinson (Paul Drake), Zon Murray (Carson), John War Eagle (Chief Lone Tree), Bob Wilke (Mandel).

165. *The Hawk of Wild River* — 1952
*127
Fred F. Sears.
Charles Starrett, Smiley Burnette, Jack Mahoney, Clayton Moore, Edwin (also Eddie) Parker, Jim Diehl, Lane Chandler, Syd (also Sid) Saylor, John Cason, LeRoy Johnson, Jack Carry, Sam Flint, Donna Hall.

166. *The Kid From Broken Gun* — 1952
*132
Fred F. Sears.
Charles Starrett, Smiley Burnette, Jack Mahoney, Tristram Coffin, Angela Stevens, Chris Alcaide, Myron Healey, Mauritz Hugo, Edgar Dearing. [Released 19 August 1952. This was Starrett's 132nd Western and his last film. It was his 166th movie.]

## BRITISH TITLE CHANGES

The following is a listing of the United Kingdom title changes for the Charles Starrett Westerns as reported by author Allen Eyles in *The Western*, (c) 1975 by publisher A. S. Barnes & Co., South Brunswick and New York.

1936: Secret Patrol (On Secret Patrol), Stampede (Shooting Showdown).

1939: Western Caravans (Silver Sands), The Man From Sundown (A Woman's Vengeance), Outpost of the Mounties (On Guard), The Stranger From Texas (The Stranger), Two-Fisted Rangers (Forestalled).

1940: Bullets For Rustlers (On Special Duty), Blazing Six-Shooters (Stolen Wealth), Texas Stagecoach (Two Roads), West of Abilene (The Showdown), The Durango Kid (The Masked Stranger), The Pinto Kid (All Square).

1941: Outlaws of the Panhandle (Faro Jack), The Medico of Painted Springs (The Doctor's Alibi), Prairie Stranger (The Marked Bullet), The Royal Mounted Patrol (Giants A'Fire).

1942: Lawless Plainsmen (Roll On), Down Rio Grande Way (The Double Punch), Riders of the Northland (Next In Line), Bad Men of the Hills (Wrongly Accused), Overland to Deadwood (Falling Stones).

1943: Hail to the Rangers (Illegal Rights).

1944: Riding West (Fugitive from Time), Cowboy Canteen (Close Harmony), Cowboy From Lonesome River (Signed Judgment), Saddle Leather Law (The Poisoner),

1945: Rough Ridin' Justice (Decoy), Return of the Durango Kid (Stolen Time), Both Barrels Blazing (The Yellow Steak), Blazing the Westward Trail (Who Killed Waring?), Rustlers of the Badlands (By Whose Hand), Lawless Empire (Power of Possession), Outlaws of the Rockies (A Roving Rogue).

1946: Frontier Gun Law (Menacing Shadows), Gunning For Vengeance (Jail Break), Roaring Rangers (False Hero), Galloping Thunder (On Boot Hill), Two-Fisted Stranger (High Stakes), The Desert Horseman (Checkmate), Headin' West (The Cheat's Last Throw), Landrush (The Claw Strikes), Terror Trail (Hands of Menace), The Fighting Frontiersman (The Golden Lady).

1947: South of the Chisholm Trail (Strange Disappearance), West of Dodge City (The Sea Wall), Lone Hand Texan (The Chest), Law of the Canyon (The Price of Crime), Prairie Raiders (The Forger).

1948: Whirlwind Raiders (State Police), Blazing Across the Pecos (Under Arrest), Trail to Laredo (Sign of the Dagger), El Dorado Pass (Desperate Men), Quick on the Trigger (Condemned in Error).

1949: Challenge of the Range (Moonlight Raid), The Blazing Trail (The Forged Will), South of Death Valley (River of Poison), Horsemen of the Sierras (Remember Me), Bandits of El Dorado (Tricked), Renegades of the Sage (The Fort).

1950: Outcast of Black Mesa (The Clue), Texas Dynamo (Suspected), Trail of the Rustlers (Lost River), Across the Badlands (The Challenge), Lightning Guns (Taking Sides), Raiders of Tomahawk Creek (Circle of Fear).

1951: Bonanza Town (Whip Hand, later changed to Two-Fisted Agent), The Kid From Amarillo (Silver Chains), Pecos River (Without Risk).

1952: Laramie Mountains (Mountain Desperadoes).

## PLAYER NAME CHANGES

From Bill McDowell: A number of the supporting players in the Starrett Westerns later changed their names. Stanley Brown became Brad Taylor at Republic. Charles Locher became Jon Hall. Linda Winters became Dorothy Comingore. Roy Harris later was Riley Hill. Doris Houch was known as Doris Colleen. Boyd Morgan, of course, became Red Morgan. Patricia White became Pat Barry. Bruce Lane was formerly Yancey Lane.

## STARRETT REMAKES

Starrett remakes: *Texas Stampede* was a remake of Buck Jones' *The Dawn Trail*. *Two-Fisted Sheriff* was from Tim McCoy's *Trapped*. *The Mysterious Avenger* was remade by Starrett as *The Stranger From Texas*. *Riders of Black River* was from McCoy's *The Revenge Rider*. McCoy's *Texas Cyclone* became *One Man Justice* with Starrett.

NOTES: Charles Starrett is such a popular star that at least three of his fans have published filmographies of his complete or western work. Jim Ward compiled the pioneering complete list in his magazine, *Wild West Stars*. This is substantially the list reprinted above, with a bit of additional information here and there, plus a few corrections (mainly typos). Like the beautifully illustrated monograph written and compiled by Mario DeMarco, Jim's list is complete. There is an earlier list by that brilliant researcher John Stoginski, published in *Western Film Collector*, but this details only Starrett's western movies. (Only! 132 films). Unlike the Ward and DeMarco listings in which films are arranged within their respective years in an ad hoc fashion, Stoginski's work places all the movies in their order of release. An admirable idea, which only falls down when Columbia provided an incorrect date for *Frontier Outpost*. This movie was actually released on 29 December 1949. This makes its correct numbering 111, not 118.

Intermediate films also require re-numbering. Stoginski's number appears after the asterisk (*). Using this numbering, the western films can be placed in their correct release order.

Mario DeMarco interviewed Starrett at length and obtained some interesting information. The negative cost of Starrett's first Columbia western, *The Gallant Defender* was a quite respectable $150,000. The shooting schedule was no less than three weeks. Over the years, budgets became tighter and schedules were trimmed. The 1952 films were each shot in ten or twelve days, though budgets were still comparatively "quite high". Locations were mainly photographed "on a rocky terraced landscape near Chatsworth, about 26 miles north of Hollywood." The films were produced so quickly, they often didn't have a name, just a production number or a shooting title. The completed movies were shown to the office staff who competed for a $15 prize to think up something suitably catchy for a title.

Asked to name whom he considered his best director, Starrett immediately nominated Ray Nazarro. "He knew the camera well and could kind of cut the picture as he shot and went along [though] he wasn't an actor's director." The star also cited Buddy Coleman and Sam Nelson as good men with a camera. When asked about Lambert Hillyer, however, Starrett became really enthusiastic. "Now there was a fine director. He directed Tom Mix. He had the camera background, and also he understood acting. Lambert was a fine director and was sympathetic with actors."

P.S. There is also an error in Stoginski's numbering of the first fifteen Starrett westerns. Stoginski omits *Undercover* but adds a non-existent movie he calls *Quick Trigger Law* which was probably a shooting title for *Two Gun Law* and he misplaces *Dodge City Trail*. The correct numbering is as follows:

1. UNDERCOVER.
2. GALLANT DEFENDER.
3. MYSTERIOUS AVENGER.
4. SECRET PATROL.
5. CODE OF THE RANGE.
6. STAMPEDE.
7. COWBOY STAR.
8. DODGE CITY TRAIL.
9. WESTBOUND MAIL.
10. TRAPPED.
11. TWO GUN LAW.
12. TWO FISTED SHERIFF.
13. ONE MAN JUSTICE.
14. OLD WYOMING TRAIL.
15. OUTLAWS OF THE PRAIRIE.

# Valley of the Giants

**Wayne Morris** (Bill Cardigan), **Claire Trevor** (Lee Roberts), **Frank McHugh** ("Fingers" McCarthy), **Alan Hale** ("Ox" Smith), **Donald Crisp** (Andy Stone), **Charles Bickford** (Howard Fallon), **Jack LaRue** (Ed Morrell), **John Litel** (Hendricks), **Dick Purcell** (Creel), **El Brendel** (Fats), **Russell Simpson** (McKenzie), **Cy Kendall** (Sheriff Graber), **Harry Cording** (Greer), **Wade Boteler** (Joe Lorimer), **Helen MacKellar** (Mrs Lorimer), **Addison Richards** (Hewitt), **Jerry Colonna** (saloon singer).

Director: **WILLIAM KEIGHLEY**. Screenplay: **Seton I. Miller, Michael Fessier**. Based on the 1918 novel by **Peter Bernard Kyne**. Photographed in Technicolor by **Sol Polito**. Technicolor cameraman: **Allen M. Davey**. Technicolor consultants: **Natalie Kalmus, Morgan Padelford**. Film editor: **Jack Killifer**. Art director: **Ted Smith**. Costumes: **Milo Anderson**. Make-up: **Perc Westmore**. Dialogue director: **Jo Graham**. Music composed by **Adloph Deutsch**, orchestrated by **Hugo F. Friedhofer**, directed by **Leo F. Forbstein**. Song, "Only a Bird in a Gilded Cage" (Colonna). Sound recording: **Oliver S. Garretson**. Associate producer: **Lou Edelman**.

Copyright 27 July 1938 by Warner Bros. Pictures, Inc. New York opening at the Strand: 9 September 1938. U.S. release: 17 September 1938. Australian release: November 1938. 8 reels. 79 minutes.

SYNOPSIS: Unscrupulous logger has his heart set on wasting California's giant redwood trees.

NOTES: Fourth of five film versions of Kyne's novel. The others: a Paramount silent directed by James Cruze in 1919, starring Wallace Reid; a First National silent directed by Charles Brabin in 1927, starring Milton Sills; *God's Country and the Woman* (1936), which although allegedly based on a novel by James Oliver Curwood, uses an identical storyline to the 1927 picture; *The Big Trees* (1952) which though allegedly based on a story by Kenneth Earl is an obvious remake of the present *Valley of the Giants*.

COMMENT: After being dismissed from *The Adventures of Robin Hood* for working too slowly, Keighley was anxious to prove to the studio that he could turn out an outdoorsy "A" spectacle in minimum time.

True, Keighley had handled a similar theme in *God's Country and the Woman*, but that picture was lensed in his usual meticulous style and cost the studio a packet. True, it made money, but that was not the point. His working methods had been questioned. He wanted to show the studio bosses they were wrong. His being fired was unjustified. It wasn't his fault *Robin Hood* was over-budget. The blame lay with over-priced, unreliable actors like Errol Flynn, and cameraman Tony Gaudio who took forever and a day to set up his lights. It was no mere whim that the first thing Mike Curtiz had done on taking over *Robin Hood* was to insist on the slow-working Gaudio being replaced by Sol Polito. So now Keighley also wanted Polito and a cast of professional but cut-price players. No star temperaments, just actors who always knew their lines and could rattle them off on the first take.

So what we have here is a "B"-picture cast in an "A"-picture action spectacle. No fancy camerawork or particularly stylish direction. Just good solid action — and plenty of it. Lots of crowd scenes, fights, a saloon smashed up, a real two-storey building burnt down, a real lumber train wrecked, a real dam dynamited, and lots of colossal redwood trees crashing to the ground. Big indoor sets, expansive outdoors locations, and lots of colorful extras milling about in almost every scene.

If the direction is little more than functional and the acting merely competent (though Alan Hale has a grand time as a rampaging lumberjack), the plot is fast-moving and the dialogue reasonably sharp.

And the theme of course has an environmental edge which will appeal to today's greenies as well.

All told, an "A"-grade western, produced on a lavish and exciting scale.

Miss Trevor's fans will probably not toss their hats in the air, though she has a showy enough role. Morris makes a reasonably personable hero, Bickford a fairly menacing heavy, whilst McHugh provides some mild comic relief.

One of the highlights of the entertainment is Jerry Colonna's highly individualistic impression of "She's Only a Bird in a Gilded Cage".

And incidentally, despite the official cast list, that is not Cy Kendall playing the sheriff. Is Hewitt the land agent? If so, he's definitely not Addison Richards. If not, why isn't such a major role credited?

OTHER VIEWS: Early 3-strip Technicolor films are always interesting. This one is no exception. Unfortunately something seems to have gone wrong with the first seven or eight minutes of the 2006 TV print. Bickford's hair is far too red, yet Trevor's red gown looks rather dull. Some of the greens are blurred. Fortunately, as Trevor steps along the street towards the second "Prairie Pullman", the colors suddenly come right and stay that way for the rest of the film. Great location scenery. And the vividly revealing color makes Trevor look properly in character too.

# the Vanishing Riders

**Bill Cody** (Bill Jones), **Bill Cody, junior** (Tim Lang), **Ethel Jackson** (Joan Stanley), **Wally Wales** (Wolf Larson), **Donald Reed** (Frank Stanley), **Budd Buster** (Hiram McDuff), **Roger Williams** (Joe Lang), **Ace Cain** (Kentuck), **Colin Chase** (Luke), **Buck Morgan** (Red), **Bert Young** (Jed), **Barney Beasley** (Peevers), **Milburn Morante** (Hank), **Bud Pope** (sheriff), **Oscar Gahan, Francis Walker** (henchmen).

Director: **BOB HILL**. Original story and screenplay: **Oliver Drake**. Photography: **Bill Hyers**. Film editor: **Holbrook N. Todd**. Stunts: **Francis Walker**. Producer: **Ray Kirkwood**.

Not copyrighted by Spectrum Pictures Corp. U.S. release on 3 July 1935 through States Rights Independent Exchanges. 58 minutes.

SYNOPSIS: Sheriff "adopts" orphaned lad and then comes to the aid of a pretty girl whose ranch is in danger from a well-organized gang of rustlers, led by the notorious outlaw, Wolf Larson (sic).

COMMENT: Not one of Bill Cody's better efforts. The script veers an uneasy course between suspense and cornball comedy, finally electing for plain slapstick. Mind you, Budd Buster never has the slightest doubt where the script is headed. He plays all his scenes in a disconcertingly broad, hammy style. On another level, the young lad is also consistently awful. However, it's sad to see a fine actor like Wally Wales attempting to make something of the ridiculous script. The super-lovely Ethel Jackson also deserves better. Bob Hill's direction never amounts to anything more than mercilessly routine. Even by the humble standards of a kids' matinee offering, production values are miniscule. In short, our *Vanishing Riders* are a bore.

# the Vigilantes Return

**Jon Hall** (Johnny Taggart), **Margaret Lindsay** (Kitty), **Andy Devine** (Andy), **Robert Wilcox** (Clay Curtwright), **Jonathan Hale** (Judge Holden), **Arthur Hohl** (sheriff), **Wallace Scott** (bartender), **Joan Fulton [Shawlee]** (Ben's girl), **Lane Chandler** (messenger), **Jack Lambert** (Ben), **John Hart, Monte Montague, Robert J. Wilke** (henchmen), **Tex Cooper** (townsman).

Director: **RAY TAYLOR**. Original screenplay: **Roy Chanslor**. Photographed in CineColor by **Virgil Miller**. Film editor: **Paul Landres**. Art directors: **Jack Otterson, Frank A. Richards**. Set decorators: **Russell A. Gausman, Don Webb**. Costumes: **Rosemary Odell**. Make-up: **Jack P. Pierce**. Dialogue director: **William Holland**. Music: **Paul Sawtell**. Song, "One Man Woman" (Lindsay) by **Jack Brooks** and **Milton Schwarzwald**. CineColor color consultant: **Arthur E. Phelps**. Assistant director: **William Tummel**. Sound supervisor: **Bernard B. Brown**. Sound engineer: **William Hedgcock**. Western Electric Sound System. Producer: **Howard Welsch**.

Copyright 12 August 1947 by Universal Pictures Co., Inc. New York opening at the Rialto: 30 June 1947. U.S. release: July 1947. Never theatrically released in the U.K. Australian release: 27 November 1947. 5,999 feet. 67 minutes.

SYNOPSIS: Undercover agent bests stagecoach bandits.

COMMENT: The main appeal of this film is CineColor. Despite its limited color range, its pastel tones are so attractive here, every frame of the movie is a pleasure to look at. Margaret Lindsay of course adds to that pleasure, even if her new upswept hair style makes her less recognisable. Paula Drew is also a winning lass, the villains — particularly Arthur Hohl's crooked sheriff and Jack Lambert's surly Ben — are heavy enough to please most fans (Bob Wilke has no dialogue but he can be spotted now and again helping to balance out the background compositions), and Andy Devine is along for a bit of mild yet agreeable comedy relief.

Hero Jon Hall handles his chores in his usual competent if colorless manner, whilst the action spots are helped out by a couple of great stunts. The plot is entertaining enough and it all comes to a satisfactory final free-for-all.

Veteran serial director Ray Taylor had moved to Universal after being fired from Republic's *The Painted Stallion*. When Universal discontinued its serial line-up in 1946, Mr Taylor was obviously at a loose end. This is the last film I have for him, though he may have directed some more in the "B" class before his death in 1952.

All told, by "B" standards, this is a creditable effort, nicely paced, attractively photographed and at times vigorously staged. The sharply-edited, many-angled stagecoach rescue is as thrilling as a top serial highlight, whilst the spectacular climactic fall through the balcony is one of the best stunts we've ever seen in the double-bill western.

OTHER VIEWS: Perennial good girl Margaret Lindsay is a slightly shady saloon lady in this fascinatingly CineColored western. She even has a jaunty song, though her singing voice is doubtless dubbed. Otherwise she fills her role agreeably enough, though most viewers will have their eyes on Andy Devine who does his usual sterling job of turning thin material into more humorously substantial cloth.

# Wagon Master

**Ben Johnson** (Travis Blue), **Harry Carey, Jr** (Sandy Owens), **Joanne Dru** (Denver), **Ward Bond** (Elder Wiggs), **Charles Kemper** (Uncle Shiloh Clegg), **Jane Darwell** (Sister Ledeyard), **Alan Mowbray** (Dr A Locksley Hall), **Ruth Clifford** (Fleuretty Phyffe), **Russell Simpson** (Adam Perkins), **Kathleen O'Malley** (Prudence Perkins), **James Arness** (Floyd Clegg), **Fred Libby** (Reese Clegg), **Hank Worden** (Luke Clegg), **Mickey Simpson** (Jesse Clegg), **Francis Ford** (Mr Peachtree), **Cliff Lyons** (sheriff of Crystal City), **Don Summers** (Sam Jenkins), **Movita Castenada** (Navajo woman), **Jim Thorpe** (Navajo), **Chuck Hayward** (Jackson).

Director: **JOHN FORD**. Screenplay: **Frank S. Nugent, Patrick Ford**. Original screen story: **John Ford**. Photography: **Bert Glennon**. 2nd unit director: **Cliff Lyons**. 2nd unit photography: **Archie Stout**. Film editor: **Jack Murray**. Assistant film editor: **Barbara Ford**. Art director: **James Basevi**. Set decorator: **Joe Kish**. Men's wardrobe: **Wes Jeffries**. Women's wardrobe: **Adele Parmenter**. Make-up: **Don Cash**. Hairdresser: **Anna Malin**. Special effects: **Jack Caffee**. Miniatures: **Ray Kellogg**. Properties: **Jack Golconda**. Costume research: **D.R.O. Hatswell**. Songs: "Shadows in the Dust", "Song of the Wagon Master", "Wagons West", "Chuckawalla Swing" by **Stan Jones**, recorded by the **Sons of the Pioneers**. Music director: **Richard Hageman**. Assistant director: **Wingate Smith**. Sound recording: **Frank Webster, Clem Portman**. RCA Sound System. Associate producer: **Lowell Farrell**. Producers: **John Ford, Merian C. Cooper**. An Argosy Pictures production.

Copyright 19 April 1950 by Argosy Pictures Corp. Released by RKO Radio Pictures. New York opening at the Globe: 17 June 1950. U.S. release: 17 April 1950. U.K. release: 18 September 1950. Australian release: 8 December 1950. 7,921 feet. 88 minutes.

SYNOPSIS: Mormons hire a couple of young horse traders to guide their wagon train to the promised land.

NOTES: Filmed in Monument Valley and in Professor Valley, Utah.
  Negative cost: around $700,000. Initial net worldwide rentals $635,000.

COMMENT: It's hard to believe but there are actually some people who don't like *Wagon Master*. Not enough action is one of the claims. It's true that the final shoot-out with the Cleggs is a little abruptly terminated. It's over almost as soon as it starts. But any feeling of slight disappointment is quickly dissipated by the marvelous pictorial reprise with which the film proper concludes.
  Another objection is where are the stars? People want John Wayne and Maureen O'Hara.
  But frankly I am glad there are no superstars in this movie. They would spoil it. Here we have believable characterizations all the way down the line. Not just the usual captivating turns from the Ford Stock Company of character players, but from the leads as well.
  "What's the point of the movie?" ask others. The answer's simple. *Wagon Master* is a poem. A narrative poem, a lyric poem, a comic poem, a moral poem, an historical poem. It is all of these, and more. So if you don't like poetry, give *Wagon Master* a miss. Not that the characters go around mouthing blank verse at each other, but they are the natural, real, believable, sympathetic and hateful people of the best poetry. Ordinary men and women. Most are called upon to be heroic, but they accept their heroism lightly. A few are cast as irredeemably cruel, and they embrace their meanness with fervor.
  But in addition to the people, the beloved Fordian types in their moments of trial and triumph, there's the impressive desert scenery against which also they are forced to force themselves to struggle.
  The music by Richard Hageman and the recurring songs by Stan Jones (rendered by the Sons of the Pioneers) blend atmospherically and dramatically into the narrative. The cinematography is likewise superb.

OTHER VIEWS: Along with *The Fugitive* and *The Sun Shines Bright*, I think *Wagon Master* came closest to being what I had wanted to achieve.

— John Ford, quoted by Peter Bogdanovich in *John Ford* (Studio Vista, London, 1967).

# Wagon Wheels

**Randolph Scott** (Clint Belmet), **Gail Patrick** (Nancy Wellington), **Billy Lee** (Sonny Wellington), **Leila Bennett** (Hetty Masters), **Jan Duggan** (Abby Masters), **Monte Blue** (Murdock), **Raymond Hatton** (Jim Burch), **Olin Howland** (Bill O'Meary), **J.P. McGowan** (Couch), **James A. Marcus** (Jed), **Helen Hunt** (Mrs Jed), **James B. "Pop" Kenton** (Masters), **Alfred Delcambre** (Ebe), **John Marston** (orator), **Sam McDaniel** (black coachman), **Howard Wilson** (permit officer), **Michael S. Visaroff** (Russian), **Julian Madison** (Lester), **Eldred Tidbury** (Chauncey), **E. Alyn Warren** (the factor), **Fern Emmett** (settler), **Clara Lou [Ann] Sheridan** (extra), **Lew Meehan** (listener), **Harold Goodwin** (Nancy's brother), **Colin Tapley** (mountaineer), **Lorraine Bridges, Earl Covert, "The Singing Guardsmen", Pauline Moore** (members of the wagon train).

Director: **CHARLES T. BARTON**. 2nd unit director: **Otto Brower**. Screenplay: **Jack Cunningham**. Adapted by **Charles Logue** and **Carl A. Buss** from the 1929 novel *Fighting Caravans* by **Zane Grey**. Photography: **William C. Mellor**. 2nd unit photography: **Henry Gerrard**. Film editor: **Jack Dennis**. Art director: **Earl Hedrick**. Songs: "Wagon Wheels" (Earl Covert and "The Singing Guardsmen"; reprised by the whole cast including Scott, Patrick and most enthusiastically by Lee) by **Billy Hill**; "Estrellita" (Bridges) by **Manuel Ponce**; "Under the Daisies, The Snowy White Daisies" (Duggan). Music director: **Irvin Talbot**. Western Electric Sound System. Producer: **Harold Hurley**. Executive producer: **Adolph Zukor**.

Copyright 21 September 1934 by Paramount Productions, Inc. New York opening at the Mayfair: 3 October 1934. U.S. release: 15 September 1934. U.K. release: 23 March 1935. 6 reels. 56 minutes.

Alternative U.S. TV title: *CARAVANS WEST*.

SYNOPSIS: Fur trappers stir up Indians to attack a wagon train headed for Oregon in 1844.

NOTES: A re-make of *Fighting Caravans* (1931) which starred Gary Cooper as Clint Belmet, Fred Kohler as Murdock and Lily Damita as the heroine.

Charles Barton's first film as full director.

COMMENT: You would naturally expect William A. Wellman's close friend and longtime minor associate to model his first film after the master. But Hollywood is usually so unpredictable and illogical, it's actually a surprise to find this surmise actually happening.

Barton never became a really class "A" director and his later films with the likes of Abbott & Costello and Donald O'Connor are just about as far away from Wellman territory as it's possible to get. But here he makes a reasonable attempt to follow Wellman's foot-steps with a slice of historical saga. Although the plot is different, notice how close in mood and structure and atmosphere this movie is not only to Wellman's *Westward the Women* (1951), but even more to Ford's *Wagon Master* (1950).

It's said that this movie uses out-takes from *Fighting Caravans*, which is probably correct though the footage is so skillfully integrated and matched that most people will assume that a lot of money was spent on *Wagon Wheels*. It certainly looks mighty impressive. Not only ruggedly picturesque, but vividly, colorfully realistic.

The action spots are vigorously staged, and though there is room for romance and sentiment, these elements are for the most part subordinated.

With three exceptions, the approach is unvarnished and unglamorously realistic. The exceptions are a bit of amusing comic by-play between Jan Duggan's over-romantic spinster and Raymond Hatton's rough-hewn frontiersman, three or four rousing musical interludes (a device which certainly brings *Wagon Master* to mind), and some unfortunate but fortunately limited encounters between our hero and a typically Hollywood precocious ankle-biter, over-enthusiastically played by Billy Lee.

The rest of the cast is much more agreeable, with Randolph Scott contributing his usual stalwartly ingratiating performance, Gail Patrick making a surprisingly spirited heroine, and solid character studies from the likes of Jan Duggan, Leila Bennett, Raymond Hatton, villainous Monte Blue, and Olin Howland doing more than justice to a major role.

All told, Barton's direction has the necessary sweep and pace, whilst production values are by "B" standards outstandingly lavish.

OTHER VIEWS: It seems a contradiction in terms to talk about a "B" epic, but that's exactly what this remarkable film is. In fact were it not for its short running time, *Wagon Wheels* could make every claim to being a class "A" feature — and no audience would argue the point.

The scriptwriters have packed an astonishing amount of incident into 56 minutes, and yet seem to have found plenty of time and opportunity not only for lavish pictorial effects of the multi-wagoned train stretching clear to the horizon but for rich characterizations and three or four appropriately realistic musical interludes as well... In fact the emphasis throughout is firmly on realism. The film conveys not only a vivid record of the rigors of the trek, but an unvarnished look at the pioneers themselves: heroes certainly, but with feelings and dreams, lusts and emotions strangely recognizable as akin to our own.

# West of Abilene

**Charles Starrett** (Tom Garfield), **Marjorie Cooley** (Judith Burnside), **Bruce Bennett** (Frank Garfield), **William Pawley** (Chris Matson), **Don Beddoe** (Forsyth), **George Cleveland** (Bill Burnside), **Forrest Taylor** (sheriff), **William A. Kellogg** (deputy), **Bob Nolan** (Bob), **Francis Walker** (Bat), **Eddie Laughton** (Poke), **Vestor Pegg** (Kennedy), **Bud Osborne** (Wilson), **Frank Ellis** (settler), **Ted Mapes** (stunt double for Charles Starrett), and the Sons of the Pioneers: **Bob Nolan, Pat Brady, Hugh Farr, Carl Farr, Lloyd Perryman**.

Director: **RALPH CEDER**. Screenplay: **Paul Franklin**. Photography: **George Meehan**. Film editor: **Charles Nelson**. Music director: **Morris W. Stoloff**. Songs by **Bob Nolan** and **Tim Spencer**. Stunts: **Francis Walker**. Assistant director: **Wilbur McGaugh**. Associate producer: **Leon Barsha**.

Copyright 29 June 1940 by Columbia Pictures Corp. No New York opening. U.S. release: 21 October 1940. 57 minutes.

U.K. release title: The *SHOWDOWN*.

SYNOPSIS: Settlers battle with land-grabbers.

NOTES: Starrett's 37th western.

COMMENT: Quite passable "B" western. The direction is efficient — at times even a trifle imaginative (the first encounter with Chris Matson — so skilfully played by William Pawley — with his back to Starrett; the climax with the ticking clock) and there is enough action to get by, though the script is inclined to be talky and there is too much footage inside some very cheesy studio interiors. The songs are mediocre.

# West of Wyoming

**Johnny Mack Brown** (Johnny), **Gail Davis** (Jennifer), **Myron Healey** (Brody), **Dennis Moore** (Dorsey), **Stanley Andrews** (Simon Miller), **Milburn Morante** (Panhandle), **Mary Gordon** (Nora), **Carl Mathews** (Ray), **Paul Cramer** (Terry), **John Merton** (sheriff), **Mike Ragan** (Chuck), **Steve Clark** (Dalton), **Cliff Taylor** (old-timer), **Frank McCarroll**, **Bud Osborne**.

Director: **WALLACE W. FOX**. Screenplay: **Adele Buffington**. Photography: **Harry Neumann**. Film editor: **John C. Fuller**. Music director: **Edward J. Kay**. Settings: **Vin Taylor**. Set continuity: **Helen McCaffrey**. Assistant director: **Harry O. Jones**. Sound recording: **John Kean**. Western Electric Sound System. Supervisor: **Eddie Davis**.

Copyright 19 February 1950 by Monogram Pictures Corp. No New York opening. U.S. release: 19 February 1950. U.K. release through Associated British-Pathe: 7 July 1952 (sic). No Australian theatrical release. 57 minutes.

SYNOPSIS: A scheming rancher, employer of a gang of thugs, rebels against the opening of the Wyoming territory to homesteaders.

VIEWERS' GUIDE: Okay for all.

COMMENT: Johnny Mack Brown may be getting on in years but he can still ride bareback at a gallop. Clever film editing also makes him seem to stop a team of runaway horses and lasso one of the villains from the back of his horse. The fights are realistically staged too and although the climax is somewhat abruptly terminated and tame there is probably enough action to satisfy the fans — though many are going to find the script more than a trifle garrulous especially with such word-chewing characters as Milburn Morante and Mary Gordon on hand.

Congratulations to all involved for finding yet another method to eke out a scene long beyond its normal running time. One of the players has to read a letter and has lost her specs, so she has to pause and squint before every word as she says it aloud. This scene was extended so long that the film editor has had the mercy to interpolate a cross-cut scene in the middle of it.

The heroine Gail Davis has a negligible part, limited to six or seven words, while ham players like Morante, Gordon and Stanley Andrews are allowed to chew up the scenery for miles around. The villains are led by those old stand-bys Myron Healey and Dennis Moore; and while Dennis and Johnny have a fair dust-up, the climax with Healey is very tame indeed. John Merton is on the right side of the law for once as the honest local sheriff, a role to which he brings no distinction whatever.

Speaking of lack of distinction — the same phrase might be used about the direction and all other production credits — they are competent but completely lacking in vitality and inventiveness — but with a script like that what could you expect? Production values are no more than fair.

OTHER VIEWS: There's gold where the settlers want to settle. Badmen discover it, which brings on a lot of ambushing, sniping from behind rocks and general bad temper. Until Johnny Mack Brown arrives.

There's nothing oppressively original about the piece, but after all, with plenty of hard ridin' and hard shootin' who'd want — or expect — originality?

— D.U.H.

# Westward Bound

**Ken Maynard** (Ken), **Hoot Gibson** (Hoot), **Bob Steele** (Bob), **Betty Miles** (Enid Barrett), **John Bridges** (Ira Phillips), **Harry Woods** (Roger Caldwell), **Karl Hackett** (Henry Wagner), **Weldon Heyburn** (Albert Lane), **Hal Price** (Jasper Tuttle), **Roy Brent** (Will), **Frank Ellis** (Judd), **Curley Dresden** (Monte), **Al Ferguson, Dan White**.

Director: **ROBERT EMMETT TANSEY**. Screenplay: **Elizabeth Beecher, Frances Kavanaugh**. Story: **Robert Emmett Tansey, Frances Kavanaugh**. Photography: **Marcel Le Picard**. Film editor: **John C. Fuller**. Music director: **Frank Sanucci**. Producer: **Robert Emmett Tansey**.

Copyright 3 December 1943 by Monogram Pictures Corp. U.S. release: 17 January 1944. No New York opening. No Australian theatrical release. 6 reels. 54 minutes.

SYNOPSIS: Shoddy, formula-type "Trail Blazers" entry in which Maynard, Gibson, and Steele play the heroes in a valley where Woods and Hackett are trying to scare the existing ranchers off their land. Production standards were so low that the makers stooped to borrowing footage for the dynamiting climax. An astute viewer (though this is by no means a prerequisite) may catch proof of the slack production techniques in a scene where a stick of dynamite that is supposed to cause an explosion is kept in full view of the camera while the explosion takes place. The stick of dynamite remains intact throughout this shot.

— *Motion Picture Guide*.

VIEWERS' GUIDE: Okay for all.

COMMENT: As a general rule, action scenes are not producer/director Robert Tansey's particular forte. As a matter of fact, it's difficult to say just exactly what is Mr Tansey's specialty. It certainly doesn't lie in inspiring his players either. For in this one, the usually reliable Ken Maynard gives a very unconvincing performance. True, Maynard and his cohorts are not helped by the atrociously amateurish dialogue handed them by screenwriters Elizabeth Beecher and Frances Kavanaugh.

Still, music director Frank Sanucci does his best to whip up some excitement, photographer Marcel Le Picard contributes adequate work and the heroine is passably attractive.

OTHER VIEWS: A nasty cartel is trying to take the land away from honest ranchers. Into this cliched situation, Maynard and company do not enter for at least fifteen minutes. However, once on, they do provide a bit of action. The climax isn't bad, by the humble standards of the Trail Blazers, with Hoot Gibson throwing dynamite all over the place and even blowing himself up for the fade-out! And as for the dialogue, it's a must for all connoisseurs of the deathless cliche. Some choice samples:

"Looks like those raiders will never stop, Mr Tuttle."

"Did you recognise any of them?"

"Not a one."

"Well, looks like this will just about finish Tuttle."

"Hello, Lane, you mixed up in this? I always thought you were a crook. Now I know it!"

"They never surrender peaceful. Any sign of the others yet?"

"No, and we're plenty out-numbered!"

"Well, here we go again!"

— G.A.

# Westward Ho

**John Wayne** (John Wyatt), **Sheila Mannors** (Mary Gordon), **Frank McGlynn Jr** (Jim Wyatt), **Jack Curtis** (Ballard), **Yakima Canutt** (Red), **Bradley Metcalfe** (young John Wyatt), **Dickie Jones** (Young Jim Wyatt), **Hank Bell** (Mark Wyatt), **Mary MacLaren** (Mrs Hannah Wyatt), **James Farley** (Lafe Gordon), **Glenn Strange** (Carter), **The Singing Riders** (themselves), **Lloyd Ingraham, Fred Parker, Hal Price, Henry Hall, Edward Coxen** (state officials), **Frank Ellis** (Russell), **Earl Dwire, Silver Tip Baker, Edward Hearn, James Sheridan** (townsmen), **Tex Palmer, Al Taylor, Eddie Parker, Herman Hack, Cactus Mack** (henchmen), **Jack Kirk** (singing rider), **Fred Burns, Bob Burns, Charles Brinley, Ray Henderson, Jack Ingram, Clyde McClary** (vigilantes), **Arthur Thalasso** (barttender).

Director: **ROBERT N. BRADBURY**. Screenplay: **Lindsley Parsons, Robert Emmett Tansey**. Story continuity: **Harry Friedman**. Original screen story: **Lindsley Parsons**. Photography: **Archie Stout**. Film editor: **Carl Pierson**. Technical director: **E.R. Hickson**. Music: **Heinz Roemheld, Clifford Vaughan**. Songs: "Westward Ho" (The Singing Riders; reprised twice), "Ridin' Down That Rocky Road To Town" (Singing

Riders), "The Girl That I Found In My Dreams" (Wayne dubbed by Jack Kirk). Sound recording: **Dave Stoner**. Producer: **Paul Malvern**. Executive producer: **Trem Carr**.

Copyright 7 August 1935 by Republic Pictures Corp. No New York opening. U.S. release: 19 August 1935. U.K. release through British Lion: May 1936. 7 reels. 61 minutes.

SYNOPSIS: Loner organizes a vigilante group to hunt for his younger brother who was kidnapped by outlaws twelve years previously.

NOTES: Dedicated to the Vigilantes... builders of the New Empire of the West... stern frontiersmen of the days of '49. Men who gave their lives to purge the new frontier of lawlessness.

Republic's first film. Negative cost: a mere $37,000. However, that is largesse indeed compared to the sixteen Lone Star westerns, which were brought in at no more than $11,000 a-piece. More than three times the Lone Star budget here, and all that extra money is right up there on the screen.

COMMENT: Despite some oddities (Wayne serenading the heroine with a dubbed basso profundo) and technical shortcomings (jerky continuity, tacky indoor sets, primitive sound recording), this is not only one of the best of Wayne's pre-superstar westerns, but a worthwhile addition to any permanent collection in its own right. The locations are truly breathtaking. Bradbury is a director (and Stout a photographer) who knows how to get both the dramatic and pictorial best out of them. The movie is full of sweeping images (the outlaw band, lined up across the frame, silhouetted vividly against sky and sand; the black-shirted singing riders, all mounted on white horses, encircling the renegades on a boulder-strewn mountainside) and no expense has been spared in staging the many action highlights, with lots of thrilling stuntwork, falls and running inserts. This is not a movie that saves all its action for the final reel either. In fact, if one has any complaint against the film, it's so full of action, there's little chance for the heroine. Never mind, Wayne acquits himself nobly, and there's an excellent performance from Frank McGlynn Jr as the outlaw brother. The villains, led by Curtis and Canutt are appropriately nasty.

One critic has complained recently that the action scenes are undermined by the lack of background music. I didn't find this a problem. There is music in the film — under montages — plus no less than three songs (including the title number which is rendered no less than three times).

By the humble standards of the "B" western, production values are outstanding.

# Where Trails End

**Tom Keene** (himself), **Frank Yaconelli** (Pierre), **Joan Curtis** (Joan Allen), **Charles King** (Jim Regan), **Donald Stewart** (Don Bedford), **Steve Clark** (Steve Allen), **Fred Hoose** (Wade), and **William Vaughn, Horace B. Carpenter, Nick Moro, Gene Alsace, Sherry Tansey, Steve Clensos, Tex Palmer, Tom Seidel, Chick Hannon**, and "Prince" (Keene's famous horse).

Director: **ROBERT EMMETT TANSEY**. Screenplay: **Robert Emmett Tansey, Frances Kavanaugh**. Photography: **Robert Cline**. Film editor: **Fred Bain**. Music director: **Frank Sanucci**. Production manager: **Fred Hoose**. Assistant director: **Don Verk**. Sound recording: **Corson Jowett**. Producer: **Robert Emmett Tansey**.

Copyright 1 May 1942 by Monogram Pictures Corp. No New York opening. U.S. release: 1 May 1942. Not theatrically released in Australia. 6 reels. 55 minutes.

COMMENT: This Monogram western gets my vote as the worst of that genre ever made. In fact it's so bad, it's almost entertaining. The villain, would you believe, is a Nazi-type German in the Old West? As if this were not ambivalent enough, we are also provided with some atrociously unfunny comic relief by Frank Yaconelli pretending to be a Frenchman! All the characters of course are sorely afflicted with the "B"-grade shuffle. And needless to say, producer/co-writer/director Robert Tansey does not miss a single opportunity to pad out the film's running time! His only interesting trick is to foreshadow the introduction of CinemaScope by arranging his characters in a triptych and panning from one to the other. The acting is unbelievably bad and there is a young boy in the film whose performance must surely be a classic of ineptitude. And as for the climax... hero and villain advance on each other, guns blazing like wet blankets. The villain stands ten feet away from Keene and fires at least ten times! And does he hit the hero once? or even crease his shirt? You guessed it! he does not. And as if this wasn't breathtakingly inept enough, they then repeat the whole performance with the subsidiary villain!

# Wild Horse Canyon

**Jack Randall** (Jack "Wild Horse" Gray), **Dorothy Short** (Jean Hall), **Frank Yaconelli** (Lopez Valdesto), **Dennis Moore** (Pete Hall), **Ed Cassidy** (Tom "Dad" Hall), **Warner Richmond** (Travers), **Walter Long** (Rosco), **Charles King** (Red, henchman), **Tom London** (Arnold), **Earl Douglas** (Lopez's brother), **Hal Price** (sheriff), **Post Park** (wrangler), **Sherry Tansey** (barfly), **Buzz Barton** (pool player), **Milburn Morante** (bartender), **Tex Palmer** (henchman), **Chick Hannon** (barfly/henchman), **Fred Parker** (ranch owner), **Foxy Callahan** (cowhand), **Tom Steele** (stunt double for Jack Randall), and "Rusty" (the wonder horse).

Director: **ROBERT HILL**. Original story and screenplay: **Robert Emmett Tansey**. Photography: **Bert Longenecker**. Film editor: **Howard Dillinger**. Art director: **E.R. Hickson**. Music director: **Abe Meyer**. Assistant director: **Eddie M. Saeta**. Production manager: **Charles J. Bigelow**. Producer: **Robert Emmett Tansey**. Executive producer: **Scott R. Dunlap**.

Copyright 4 January 1939 by Monogram Pictures Corp. No New York opening. U.S. release: 21 December 1938. 56 minutes.

COMMENT: Rustlers run into trouble in this well above average Jack Randall western (the tenth of twenty-two entries for Monogram). This one has some exciting action including a saloon brawl with thrilling stuntwork (muffled slightly by poor sound effects), some of it performed by Randall himself; a fast horse chase commencing with spinning 360° pans through the foliage then going into running inserts head on and ending with a stunt spill; a double shoot-out climax with Jack stalking the two villains in some effective tracking shots. The cast is interesting too. Walter Long is one of our favorite villains -- he makes a late entrance but once on screen he relishes his work. The fort is held down until Long's arrival by Warner Richmond a delightfully crooked foreman (Charles King has a small role as one of his henchmen) and Dennis Moore doing another of his corrupt son impersonations. Tom London has a brief uncredited part as the crooked horse trader who has a fight with Jack. Frank Yaconelli plays the hero's sidekick but it is virtually a straight part and he is nothing like his usual obnoxiously "comic" self. Dorothy Short is a passable heroine. Production values are remarkably high by Monogram B-feature standards. The photography sparkles in both interior and exterior and the sets are reasonably appealing The music direction too is superior with effective use of silences. Oddly enough, there is one song but it is not rendered by Mr Randall but by Frank Yaconelli! One odd point about the direction is that a reverse angle is not used when Randall is explaining how the brand was faked; surely this could have been shot and inserted later! Otherwise the direction is capable during the dialogue scenes and more than capable in the action spots. It is good to see some real horses used in the film though the herd scenes doubtless are stock footage.

# Wild Horse Range

**Jack Randall** (Jack Wallace), **Dorothy Short** (Jean Hall), **Phyllis Ruth** (Ann Morgan), **Frank Yaconelli** (Manny), **Charles King** (Stoner), **Tom London** (Arnold), **Marin Sais** (Harriet Morgan), **Ralph Hoopes** (Buddy Mitchell), **Forrest Taylor** (Mitchell), **George Chesebro** (Ed Baker), **Carl Mathews** (Frank), **Steve Clark** (sheriff), **Ed Cassidy** (Hall), **Warner Richmond** (Travers), **Tex Palmer** (henchman), **Foxy Callahan** (townsman and stunt double for Tom London), **Herman Hack, Victor Adamson** (townsmen), and "Rusty" (the wonder horse).

Director: **RAYMOND K. JOHNSON** (pseudonym of **Bernard B. Ray**). Screenplay: **Carl Krusada, Bennett Cohen**. Story: **Tom Gibson**. Photography: **Edward A. Kull, William Hyer**. Film editor: **Robert Golden**. Music directors: **Johnny Lange, Lew Porter**. Songs: "Home on the Range" by **Daniel E. Kelly** (music) and **Brewster M. Higley** (lyrics); "When I Come Home" by **Johnny Lange** and **Lew Porter**. Production manager: **Harry Gordon**. Assistant director: **William Nolte**. Sound recording: **Glen Glenn**. Producer: **Harry S. Webb**.

Copyright 24 June 1940 by Monogram Pictures Corp. No New York opening. U.S. release: 25 June 1940. 58 minutes.

SYNOPSIS: Rustlers run into trouble again.

NOTES: The above credits (which are transcribed from the film itself and the copyright entry in the Library of Congress) must be qualified by the remarks below.

VIEWER'S GUIDE: Particularly suitable for younger childre who are either congenitally inattentive or simply not over-bright.

COMMENT: Although the writing credits give absolutely no indication of the fact, this is a remake of *Wild Horse Canyon* released only 18 months previously! And what an extraordinary re-make it is too! Key incidents, such as Randall's fight with Arnold and his escape with the connivance of the sheriff are omitted although they are referred later on in the plot.

This film starts with a totally irrelevant chase after a runaway buckboard driven by the 12-year-old son of the horse buyer Mitchell. Despite this elaborate introduction and his prominence in the cast list, said son disappears after his introductory scene — and so does his father disappear after **his** introductory scene. Then Jack Randall once again playing the part of Jack Wallace gets involved with the Halls by rescuing the daughter who is being chased by villain Charles King (some nice running inserts and fast riding here — could be they are speeded up — ending with a not bad stunt as the double plucks the girl from her saddle as her horse stumbles). But the Halls are not the proprietors of the Arrowhead Ranch in this one so before we know where we are we have abruptly left the Halls and Warner Richmond and Ed Cassidy and Dorothy Short — all repeating their previous roles without credit here which leads us to believe that all these scenes — the chase, the rescue, the bronc-busting are **actually out-takes from** *Wild Horse Canyon*. This explains then why we do not see some of the key scenes from the previous film such as King's dismissal. So we find ourselves abruptly at the Arrowhead Ranch which is run in this film by Marin Sais as a wheel-chair case. Charles King is the ranch foreman, though how he came to obtain this position which he was apparently holding concurrently with his other position as one of Hall's ranch-hands is a dilemma that the ingenuity of the new scriptwriters have been unable to solve. No explanation for King's peculiar conduct is offered, just as Jack offers no reason for leaving the Halls. While Tom London repeats his part of Arnold and Steve Clark once again plays the sheriff, Frank Yaconelli's Mexican saddle-pal is called Manny here and his part is more comic than it was in *Wild Horse Canyon*. Phyllis Ruth gets the heroine billing though her footage is limited and is in fact confined to the one indoor set — a confinement which she shares with Marin Sais. New members of the cast also include George Chesebro as a particularly nasty henchman of King's.

Like the previous film, Jack does not sing a note in this either — in fact there are no songs at all despite the musical credit in the Library of Congress which I believe to be incorrect. There is no credit for music on the film itself and the opening consists of a rendition of "Home on the Range" which sounds like an old gramophone record, as fact that is confirmed by a distinct sound on the track as if the record were being played over again — which it is. The multiple photography credit indicates that Kull almost undoubtedly did the exteriors while Hyer did the interiors (the out-takes from *Wild Horse Canyon* were photographed by Bert Longnecker). The direction by Raymond K. Johnson (whoever he might be — a pseudonym?) is akin to that of Robert Hill — capable but above the level of mere capability only in some action spots — Jack has a tussle or two with Charles King and a real herd of horses led by a white stallion figures in the action.

Aside from the writing and odd continuity editing, production credits are competent and production values are above average — good exteriors for a "B"-feature!

# Wild Horse Stampede

**Ken Maynard** (Ken), **Hoot Gibson** (Hoot), **Betty Miles** (Betty Wallace), **Ian Keith** (Carson), **Don Stewart** (Donny), **Si Jenks** (Rawhide), **Bob Baker** (Cliff Tyler), **John Bridges** (Colonel Black), **Glenn Strange** (Tip), **Reed Howes** (Tex), **Kenneth Harlan** (Borman), **Tom London, Tex Palmer** (outlaws), **Augie Gomez, Chick Hannon, Tex Palmer, George Sowards** (henchmen), **Forrest Taylor** (Marshal Tyler), **I. Stanford Jolley** (Commissioner Brent), **Kenne Duncan** (Hanley), **Robert McKenzie** (Puckett), **Ben Corbett** (stunt double for Ken Maynard), **Cliff Lyons** (stunt double for Hoot Gibson), and **Jim Keene.**

Director: **ALAN JAMES**. Screenplay: **Elizabeth Beecher**. Original screen story: **Frances Kavanaugh**. Photography: **Marcel Le Picard**. Film editor: **Fred Bain**. Music director: **Frank Sanucci**. Production manager: **Fred Hoose**. Assistant director: **Robert Emmett Tansey**. Sound recording: **Glen Glenn**. Producer: **Robert Tansey**.

Copyright 16 April 1943 by Monogram Pictures Corp. U.S. release: 16 April 1943. 6 reels. 59 minutes.

SYNOPSIS: Indians on the warpath against railroad workers again. This time rustlers are stirring the pot.

COMMENT: Although Glenn Strange must be the only member of the cast who bothers to aim his pistol before pressing the trigger, there is otherwise plenty of fairly effective action and stuntwork in this Trail Blazers western. Director James tries his best to infuse a bit of energy into the tired plot with occasional flurries of camera movement, despite lighting photography that is mostly as flat and uninteresting as the dreary studio sets. True, Frank Sanucci's music score is even more flat-footed and pedestrian. All the same this entry is slightly above average by Monogram's humble standards.

# Wyoming Outlaw

**John Wayne** (Stony Brooke), **Ray Corrigan** (Tucson Smith), **Raymond Hatton** (Rusty Joslin), **Donald "Red" Barry** (Will Parker), **Adele Pearce [Pamela Blake]** (Irene Parker), **LeRoy Mason** (Balsinger), **Charles Middleton** (Luke Parker), **Katherine Kenworthy** (Mrs Parker), **Elmo Lincoln** (U.S. marshall), **Jack Ingram** (sheriff), **David Sharpe** (Newt), **Jack Kenny** (radio operator), **Yakima Canutt** (Ed Sims), **Dave O'Brien** (park warden), **Curley Dresden** (himself), **Tommy Coats** (Shorty), **Ralph Peters** (newspaper reader), **Jack Kirk, Al Taylor** (posse men), **Bud McTaggert** (park ranger), **Budd Buster** (bank teller), **Ed Payson** (townsman), **Jack Rockwell** (rancher), **Frankie Marvin** (cowhand), **George DeNormand, John Beach** (henchmen), **Allan Cavan** (Senator Roberts), **Bob Burns** (man at hearing).

Director: **GEORGE SHERMAN**. Screenplay: **Betty Burbridge, Jack Natteford**. Story: **Jack Natteford**. Based on characters created by **William Colt MacDonald**. Photography: **Reggie Lanning**. Film editor: **Tony Martinelli**. Music score: **William Lava**. Stunts: **George Montgomery, Kermit Maynard, Tommy Coats, George DeNormand**. Production manager: **Al Wilson**. Assistant director: **Harry Knight**. RCA

Sound System. Associate producer: **William Berke**. Executive producer: **Herbert J. Yates**.

Copyright 27 June 1939 by Republic Pictures Corp. No recorded New York opening. U.S. release: 27 June 1939. U.K. release in 1940 through British Lion. Never released theatrically in Australia. 6 reels. 62 minutes.

SYNOPSIS: The mesquiteers meet up with a dust-bowl family impoverished by a local politician.

NOTES: Number 24 of the 52-picture series.

VIEWER'S GUIDE: Too depressing and downbeat in mood for young children.

COMMENT: An interesting precursor to several later films. The dust-bowl setting reminds us of Wayne's *Three Faces West*, whilst the climax with the outlaw trapped on the hilltop by the posse, as reporters cover the story, is very reminiscent of *High Sierra*.

The story in fact is not only very unusual by "B" western standards, but it provides some uncommonly bright opportunities for solid acting. Donald "Red" Barry is particularly memorable as the hard-luck outlaw. Also giving the best performance of his entire career is Charles Middleton, forsaking his normally stiff and heavy-handed mannerisms, to pen a searing sketch of an honest man, hard done by yet scrupulously resigned to his fate. Adele Pearce, a startlingly realistic heroine, makes the most of her opportunities; whilst Wayne has not one but two all-in fist fights, the first with his old nemesis Yakima Canutt (in which, aside from a single shot, both men do all their own tussling), the second with chief villain LeRoy Mason. David Sharpe is oddly miscast in the role of a bartender, but it's good to see Elmo Lincoln (the screen's first Tarzan) as the marshal.

The story synopsis in the studio press book is the same as the script as filmed — with one notable exception. Wayne was originally to pursue and best the villain. Doubtless for economy reasons a different ending was used, the villain disposed of in a most uncommon manner, leading into a somewhat abrupt riding-off farewell.

Although the production credits have been removed from the TV print under review, there is certainly nothing for anyone to be ashamed of in this creditable entry, which was actually filmed after Wayne's huge success in *Stagecoach*. It's odd to find Wayne still being cast in a "B", though he has the lion's share of the action. Both Corrigan and Hatton (replacing ventriloquist Max Terhune who retired from the series after the previous "Three Mesquiteers", namely *Three Texas Steers*) are obligated to provide no more than perfunctory support. Wayne does all the fighting as well as the thinking.

# Wyoming Roundup

**Whip Wilson** (himself), **Phyllis Coates** (Terry Howard), **Tommy Farrell** (Bob Burke), **Henry Rowland** (Bill Howard), **House Peters Jr** (Randolph), **I. Stanford Jolley** (Earl Craven), **Richard Emory** (Jack Craven), **Stanley Price** (Clark), **Frank Jaquet** (doctor), **Lyle Talbot** (saloon owner), **Robert J. Wilke** (Wyatt), **Roy Bucko, Herman Hack** (cowhands), **Artie Ortego** (barfly).

Director: **THOMAS CARR**. Original screenplay: **Dan Ullman**. Photography: **Ernest Miller, Charles Van Enger**. Film editor: **Sam Fields**. Music composed and conducted by **Raoul Kraushaar**. Art director: **David Milton**. Set decorator: **Ted Offenbecker**. Dialogue supervisor: **Stanley Price**. Set continuity: **Emilie Erlich**. Special photographic effects: **Ray Mercer**. Assistant director: **Melville Shyer**. Sound recording: **John Kean**. Associate producer: **Harry Mandell**. Producer: **Vincent M. Fennelly**. A Silvermine Production.

Copyright 31 October 1952 by Monogram Pictures Corp. No New York opening. U.S. release: 9 November 1952. No U.K. or Australian theatrical release. 53 minutes.

SYNOPSIS: A plot to ruin a rancher by rustling his cattle is foiled by a couple of deputy marshals.

COMMENT: This Whip Wilson western is a bit better than his usual effort. The reason is mainly in the cast. Bob Wilke is one of our favorite villains and he gets a large share of the action in this one (which followed soon after his success in *High Noon*). And Phyllis Coates, although she doesn't have all that much footage here, is one of the most fetching of the "B"-picture heroines. And then there are such faithful stand-bys as Lyle Talbot and I. Stanford Jolley.

Another reason this film is better than most is that Mr Wilson himself is less wooden and is not so unattractively photographed (though his fans will be disappointed that he neither uses nor even wears his whip in this one).

Yet another reason is that there's a bit more action and that the land-grabbing plot has a couple of original twists. Alas, there are no chases with running inserts and the exteriors were photographed in the familiar Hollywood backblocks (the only cattle we see are in a snip of stock footage), but there's a saloon brawl at the beginning, a couple of ambushes and a big shoot-out at the end.

Carr's direction has pace and a small trace of style and the film is short too (though one must admit it seems just as long as usual). Photography is above average (doubtless explained by the presence of Charles Van Enger though the photographic style of the film is pretty consistent. If the two cameramen didn't work in tandem, maybe Van Enger shot the exteriors. Then again the scene in the jail is better lit than the one in the saloon). Other credits and production values are up to standard.

# Zorro's Fighting Legion

**Reed Hadley** (Don Diega Vega/Zorro), **Sheila Darcy** (Volita), **William Corson** (Ramon), **Leander de Cordova** (Governor Felipe), **Edmund Cobb** (Gonzales), **John Merton** (General Manuel), **C. Montague Shaw** (Pablo), **Billy Bletcher** (voice of Don del Oro), **Budd Buster** (Juan), **Carleton Young** (Benito Juarez), **Guy D'Ennery** (Don Francisco), **Paul Marion** (Kala), **Joe Molina** (Tarmac), **Jim Pierce** (Moreno), **Helen Mitchel** (Donna Maria), **Curley Dresden** (Tomas), **Charles King** (Valdez), **Al Taylor** (Rico), **Charles B. Murphy** (Pepito), **Joe Delacruz** (bridge heavy), **Jason Robards** (cantina owner), **Theodore Lorch** (Carlos), **Jack O'Shea, Jerome Ward, Millard McGowan** (cave heavies), **Augie Gomez** (cave Indian), **Cactus Mack** (Cisco), **Bud**

**Geary** (dungeon heavy), **Jack Moore** (Fernando), **George Plues** (Garcia), **Jack Carrington** (Antonio Gomez), **Victor Cox** (gun heavy), **Bob Wilbur** (Hernandez), **John Wallace** (jailer), **Burt Dillard** (Jaime), **Jimmy Fawcett** (Jose), **Martin Faust** (Mabesa), **Ken Terrell** (Martin), **Wylie Grant** (Martinez), **Carl Sepulveda** (Orlando), **Eddie Cherkose** (Pedro), **Charles Murphy** (Pepito), **Max Marx** (presidio guard), **Buel Bryant** (Renaldo), **Norman Lane** (Ricardo), **Ralph Faulkner** (Rodriguez), **Alan Gregg** (Salvador), **Ernest Sarracino** (Sebastian), **Yakima Canutt, Reed Howes, Barry Hays, Joe McGuinn** (soldiers), **Bill Yrigoyen** (stage-driver), **Jerry Frank** (throne guard), **Gordon Clark** (Miguel Torres), and **Frank Ellis, Ted Mapes, Henry Wills, Joe Yrigoyen**.

Directors: **WILLIAM WITNEY, JOHN ENGLISH**. Screenplay: **Ronald Davidson, Franklyn Adreon, Morgan Cox, Solomon Shor, Barney A. Sarecky**. Based on the 1919 novel *The Curse of Capistrano* by **Johnston McCulley**. Photography: **Reggie Lanning**. Film editors: **Edward Todd, William Thompson, Bernard Loftus**. Music score: **William Lava**. Song, "We Ride" (male chorus), by **William Lava** (music), **Eddie Cherkose** (lyrics). Production manager: **Al Wilson**. Unit manager: **Mack D'Agostino**. RCA Sound System. Associate producer: **Hiram S. Brown Jr**. Executive producer: **Herbert J. Yates**.

Copyright 16 December 1939 by Republic Pictures Corp. Chapter titles: *The Golden God, The Flaming "Z", Descending Doom, The Bridge of Peril, The Decoy, Zorro to the Rescue, The Fugitive, Flowing Death, The Golden Arrow, Mystery Wagon, Face to Face, Unmasked*. 12 Chapters in all. Each chapter has 2 reels, excepting number one which has three. U.S. release: December 1939.

SYNOPSIS: Mexico, 1824. Juarez needs gold from the San Mendolito mines, but a ursurper, disguising himself as a Yaqui god, Don del Oro, diverts the gold in a bid to make himself Emperor of Mexico.

NOTES: 16th of Republic's 66 serials. Negative cost: $144,419 (slightly over the budget estimate of $137,826).

Republic's 2nd serial using the Zorro character (or a direct derivation). The others: *Zorro Rides Again* (1937), *Zorro's Black Whip* (1944), *Son of Zorro* (1947), *Ghost of Zorro* (1949).

For a discussion of feature films derived from Johnston McCulley, see *The Mark of Zorro*.

VIEWER'S GUIDE: Suitable for all.

COMMENT: The first chapter is a must. It's a bit wordy, true, but it starts off with a lively montage of stock Mexican battle footage and once it warms to its theme with a couple of great sword duels involving Hollywood tutor Ralph Faulkner, we get a rousing sequence as the Legion gathers and the song is belted out right through all four verses for the only time in the serial. (We only hear snatches and the odd verse or two in other eps). Director Witney who handled all the action and location footage has a field day on the camera truck here. We also enjoyed our introduction to Don del Oro, though his stentorian "voice" is likely to be an irritation as the serial progresses. The cliff-hanger with an exploding landslide is okay, despite obvious cheating. Episode 2 though is a bit of a let-down. Dull old John English who directed most of the dialogue scenes just lets his players sit around and talk. It's not until the Legion gathers at the wonderfully designed San Nicholas Mission that interest really perks up. But would you believe, here's a cliff-hanger using exactly the same device as the introductory episode -- and resolved of course in exactly the same cheating way, though we must admit the plunge through the stained-glass window is quite spectacular. Yes, this episode 3 turns out to be the most exciting and action-packed so far. The sequence in which Budd Buster is lined up for number checking by Ed Cobb is pretty suspenseful and we love the cliff-hanger in which Hadley fends off Pierce and King only to be trapped in a lift-shaft. Of course, this too is disappointingly resolved, but Witney redeems himself with some more well-staged action at the chase climax with our hero trapped on a rope bridge that a wounded Yaqui severs with his knife.

Incidentally, Witney was helped out on some of the action by expert stuntman Yakima Canutt who either staged or himself doubled a number of great gags. It's untrue, however, as reported elsewhere that the diminutive Canutt doubled the tall Hadley as Zorro. Most if not all the many sword duels were doubled by Ralph Faulkner.

Reggie Lanning's fine camerawork and the expertly paced film editing of Todd, Thompson and Loftus (this was the last of only 3 serials in which Republic employed no less than three editors) are again in thrilling evidence in chapter five. This episode is really packed with action, fortunately leaving little time for corny dialogue, although there are still one or two choice examples. Number six also has plenty of action, this time made even more interesting by the return of the heroine whom, if my memory is correct, we haven't seen since Chapter two. The cliffhanger here is a favorite serial device that never fails to thrill: Zorro is cornered in a dungeon with a sliding wall that moves inexorably towards him as the credits flash with details of next week's episode.

Many critics regard chapter seven as the best of the serial. Personally, I prefer eight, though I must admit seven runs it close for thrills with Merton's brilliantly edited stagecoach escape and chase. Seven ends right in the middle of Canutt's famous under-the-coach stunt. Eight has the stunt complete, plus a marvellous sequence with Ramon trapped in a blazing jail by a wonderfully vicious peg-legged turnkey.

Nine is the economy episode, most of it consisting of footage from chapters one and two featuring Merton, plus a bit of Cobb from chapter three. The tie-in council conference is all directed by English in his usual lacklustre style, including would you believe the cliffhanger itself which is the weakest of the entire eleven.

Ten is certainly an improvement, as we get back to a bit of Witney action and Lydecker miniature work. Eleven is one of the best. The ceremonial cave atmosphere is creepy enough, while the cliffhanger is a real humdinger.

Twelve has the longest introductory reprise of any of the episodes. The final unmasking of Don Del Oro is reasonably exciting. Zorro also unmasks, would you believe? And for the heroine yet! For someone who receives billing right after Hadley, Miss Darcy has certainly had an easy time. She figures briefly in but four or five of the twelve episodes. Very briefly. She seems a very nice girl too. Never mind. The serial is wound up to all our satisfactions by the re-appearance of Carleton Young's Juarez and a few rousing bars of "We Ride".

One or two odd lapses in continuity (the mission that is blown up at the end of an early ep is magically restored much later on) plus a few of the usual cliffhanging "cheat" shots would not have worried the serial's original Saturday matinee fans. Nor would the generally no more than passable acting; nor some unintentionally risible examples of corny, cliched, amateurish, explaining-the-obvious dialogue.

Full of energy and gusto, *Zorro's Fighting Legion* deserves its number one choice among many critics as the best serial ever made. It's not my favorite (that's *Jungle Girl*), but it certainly rates in my Top Ten.

**The Directors:** See *Spy Smasher* for William Witney. The question I'm always asked is did English direct any other serials other than those on which he collaborated with Witney. The answer to this question is, yes. Two: *Daredevils of the West* (1943) starring Allan Lane and Kay Aldridge, for which he received a sole director credit. And *Captain America* (1943) on which he collaborated with Elmer Clifton.

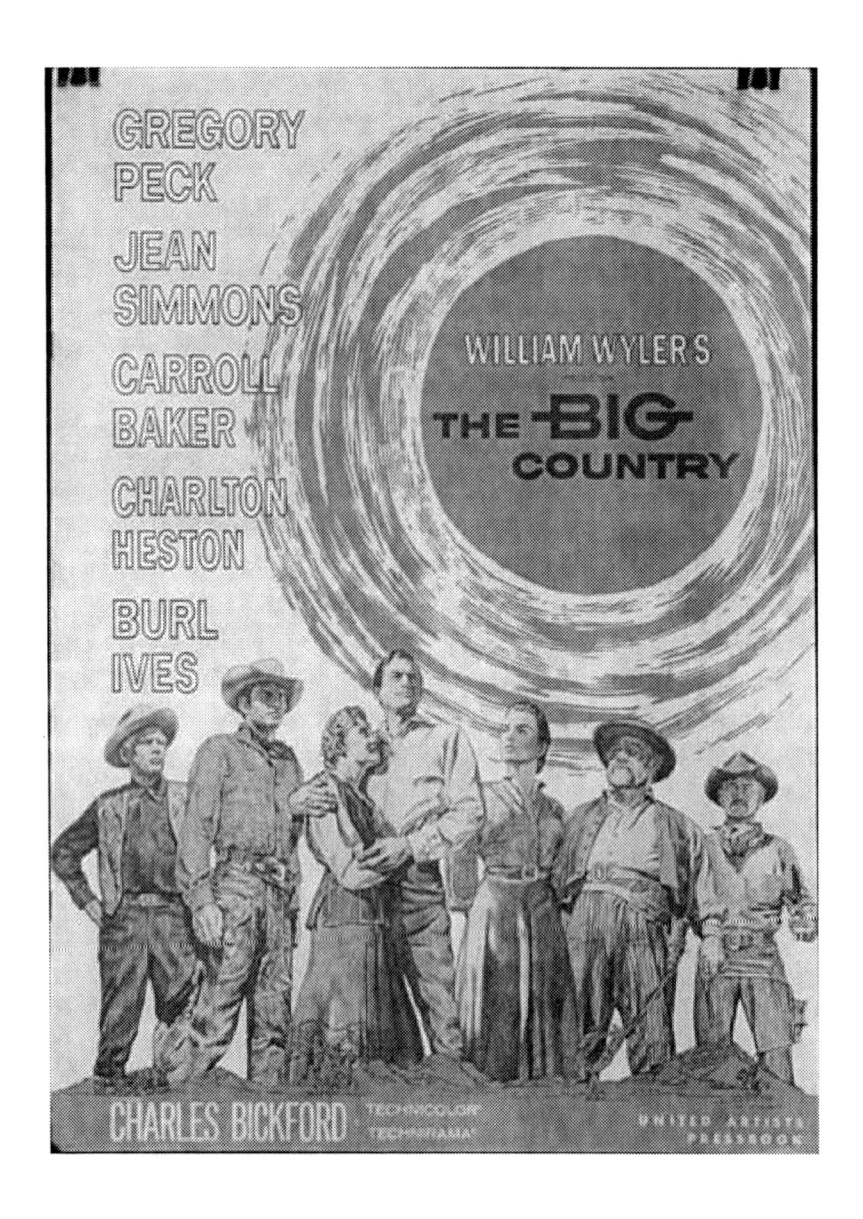

# The Most Popular Western Stars of 1931—1932

*surveyed by Don Miller*

1. Buck Jones
2. Ken Maynard
3. George O'Brien
4. Harry Carey
5. Bob Steele
6. Tom Mix
7. Tim McCoy
8. Tom Keene
9. Tom Tyler
10. John Wayne

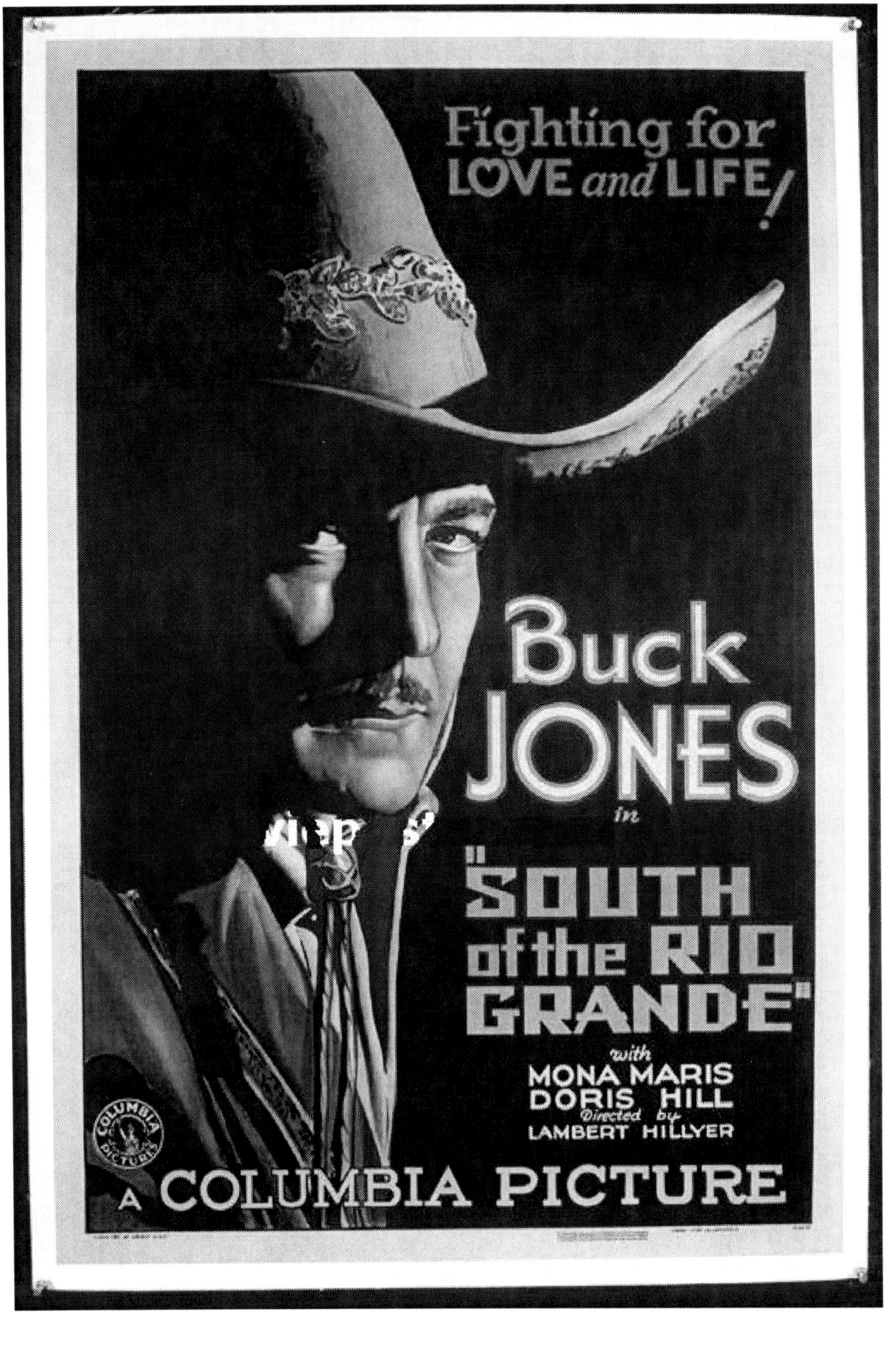
Fighting for
LOVE and LIFE!
Buck
JONES
in
"SOUTH
of the RIO
GRANDE"
with
MONA MARIS
DORIS HILL
Directed by
LAMBERT HILLYER
COLUMBIA PICTURES
A COLUMBIA PICTURE

# The "Western" Money-Makers

*as voted by American exhibitors
in 19 annual polls conducted by
the Motion Picture Herald*

1936—1954

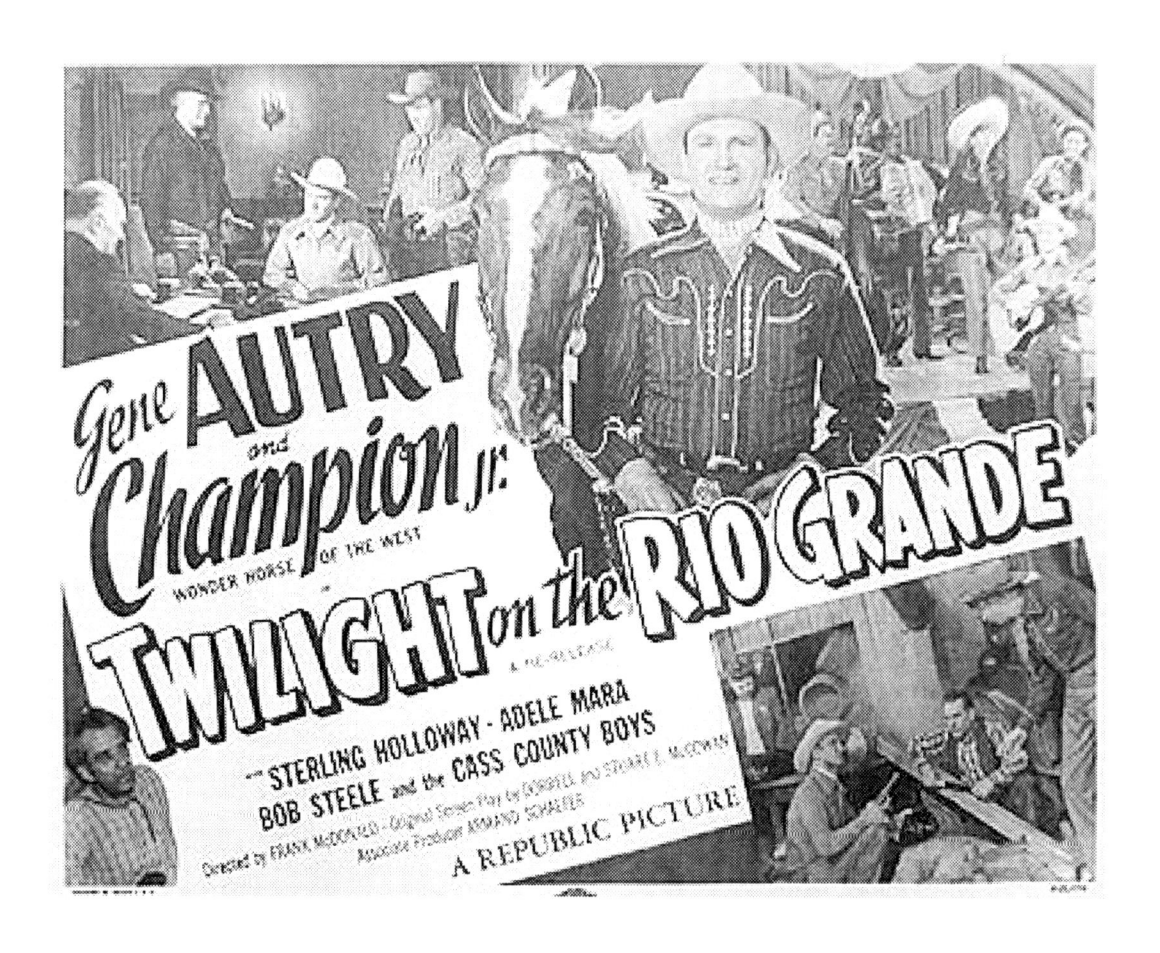

# 1936

1. Buck Jones
2. George O'Brien
3. Gene Autry
4. William Boyd
5. Ken Maynard
6. Dick Foran
7. John Wayne
8. Tim McCoy
9. Hoot Gibson
10. Buster Crabbe

[The first poll — and Gene Autry's first year on it. He was to continue right through, in never less than third position, aside from his three years of service in World War 2]

# 1937

1. Gene Autry
2. William Boyd
3. Buck Jones
4. Dick Foran
5. George O'Brien
6. Tex Ritter
7. Bob Steele
8. Three Mesquiteers (Robert Livingston, Ray Corrigan, Max Terhune)
9. Charles Starrett
10. Ken Maynard

[Last appearance on the lists of Ken Maynard, a top money-maker in the late silent period]

# 1938

1. Gene Autry
2. William Boyd
3. Buck Jones
4. George O'Brien
5. Three Mesquiteers (Robert Livingston/John Wayne, Ray Corrigan, Max Terhune)
6. Charles Starrett
7. Bob Steele
8. Smith Ballew
9. Tex Ritter
10. Dick Foran

[Only appearance on the list of Smith Ballew]

# 1939

1. Gene Autry
2. William Boyd
3. Roy Rogers
4. George O'Brien
5. Charles Starrett
6. Three Mesquiteers (John Wayne/Robert Livingston, Ray Corrigan/ Duncan Renaldo, Max Terhune/Raymond Hatton)
7. Tex Ritter
8. Buck Jones
9. John Wayne
10. Bob Baker

GEORGE
O'BRIEN
STAGE
TO CHINO
VIRGINIA VALE and "PALS of the GOLDEN WEST"
Produced by BERT GILROY • Directed by EDWARD KILLY

# 1940

1. Gene Autry
2. William Boyd
3. Roy Rogers
4. George O'Brien
5. Charles Starrett
6. Johnny Mack Brown
7. Tex Ritter
8. Three Mesquiteers (Robert Livingston, Duncan Renaldo/Bob Steele, Raymond Hatton/Rufe Davis)
9. Smiley Burnette
10. William Elliott

[First appearance on the lists of Wild Bill Elliott, who was set to continue right through until the polls were discontinued after 1954]

# 1 9 4 1

1. Gene Autry
2. William Boyd
3. Roy Rogers
4. Charles Starrett
5. Smiley Burnette
6. Tim Holt
7. Johnny Mack Brown
8. Three Mesquiteers (Bob Livingston/Tom Tyler, Bob Steele, Rufe Davis)
9. William Elliott
10. Tex Ritter

[First appearance on the lists for Tim Holt. His career was interrupted by World War 2 in which he displayed such daring and courage he won numerous medals and citations. On resuming in movies, he looked set to challenge both Autry and Rogers in 1951, but RKO discontinued his series in 1952]

# 1942

1. Gene Autry
2. Roy Rogers
3. William Boyd
4. Smiley Burnette
5. Charles Starrett
6. Johnny Mack Brown
7. William Elliott
8. Tim Holt
9. Don "Red" Barry
10. Three Mesquiteers (Tom Tyler, Bob Steele, Rufe Davis/Jimmie Dodd)

[First appearance on the lists of Donald Barry]

[Also first appearance of Jimmy/Jimmie Dodd, an actor who was never quite sure how to spell his name]

# 1943

1. Roy Rogers
2. William Boyd
3. Smiley Burnette
4. George "Gabby" Hayes
5. Johnny Mack Brown
6. Tim Holt
7. Three Mesquiteers (Tom Tyler, Bob Steele, Jimmie Dodd)
8. Don "Red" Barry
9. William Elliott
10. Russell Hayden

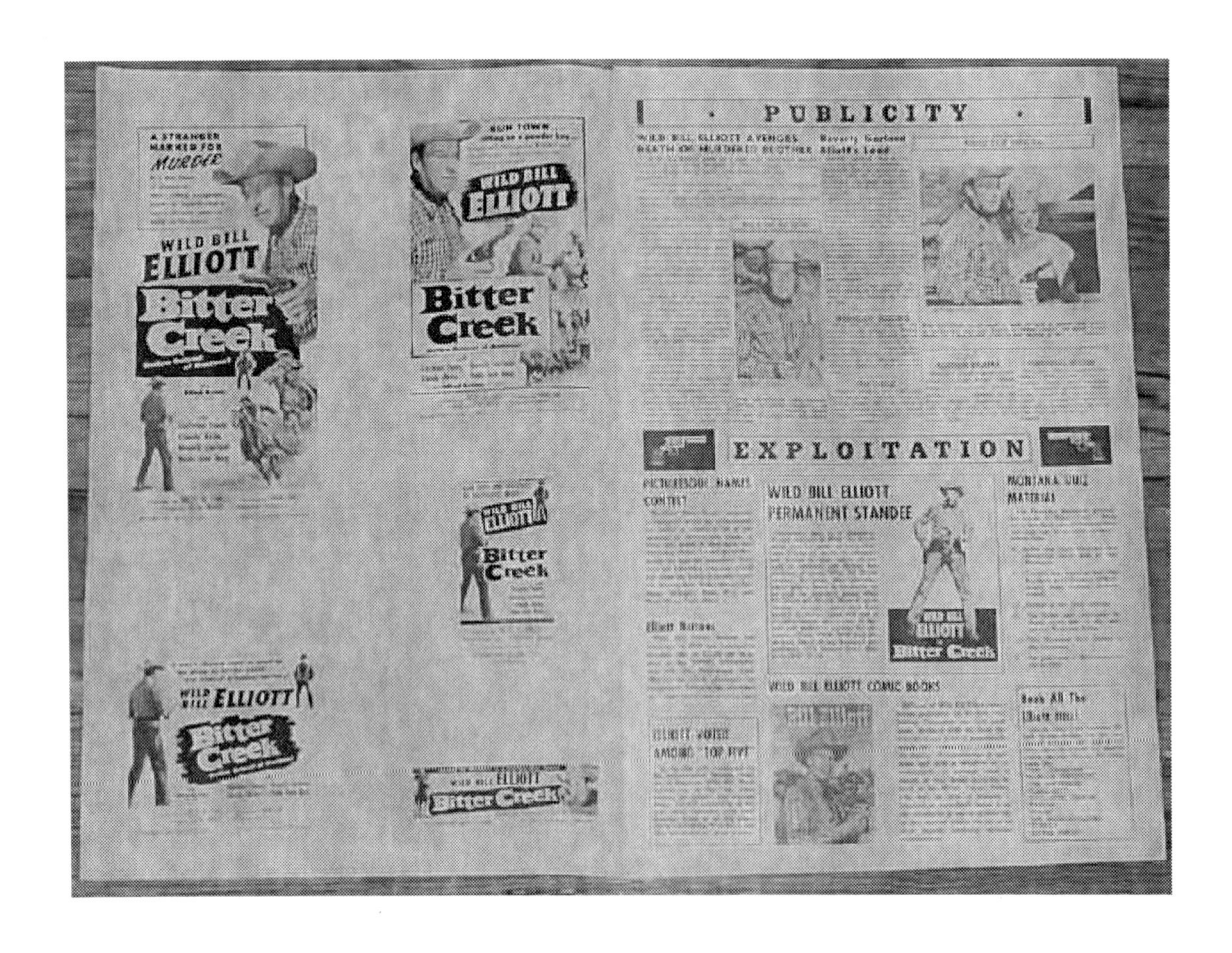

[Last year for the Three Mesquiteers. The 52-picture series wound up in 1943]

TIM
HOLT
BORDER TREASURE
RICHARD MARTIN
JANE NIGH
Produced by HERMAN SCHLOM
Directed by GEORGE ARCHAINBAUD
Written by NORMAN HOUSTON
RKO RADIO

# 1944

1. Roy Rogers
2. William Boyd
3. Smiley Burnette
4. George "Gabby" Hayes
5. William Elliott
6. Johnny Mack Brown
7. "Red" Barry
8. Charles Starrett
9. Russell Hayden
10. Tex Ritter

TEX
RITTER
WITH HIS HORSE "WHITE FLASH" IN
"THE PIONEERS"
INSPIRED BY JAMES FENIMORE COOPER'S NOVEL
FEATURING
RED FOLEY and his SADDLE PALS
"ARKANSAS" SLIM ANDREWS
DOYE O'DELL
A MONOGRAM PICTURE
An Edward Finney Production
Directed by AL HERMAN
Screenplay by CHARLES ANDERSEN

TEX RITTER
See THE WILD STAMPEDE OF 6,000 ELK!
"DOWN THE WYOMING TRAIL"
WITH HIS HORSE WHITE FLASH
AN EDWARD FINNEY PRODUCTION

[Sidekick Smiley Burnette's popularity peaked in 1943 and 1944. Thereafter he yielded in every year except 1951 to George "Gabby" Hayes]

# 1945

1. Roy Rogers
2. George "Gabby" Hayes
3. William Boyd
4. William Elliott
5. Smiley Burnette
6. Johnny Mack Brown
7. Charles Starrett
8. "Red" Barry
9. Tex Ritter
10. Rod Cameron

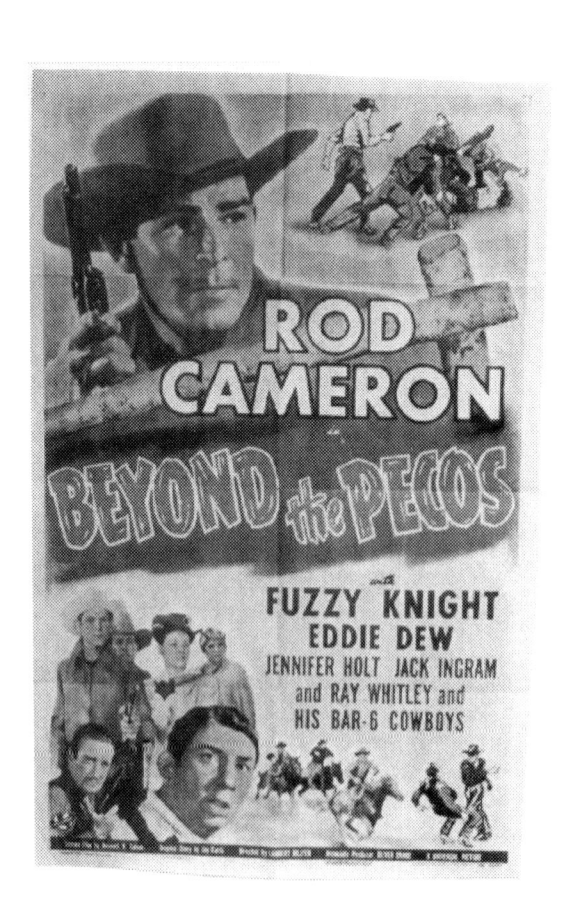

[Rod Cameron just made the list for 1945, his only representation]

# 1946

1. Roy Rogers
2. William Elliott
3. Gene Autry
4. George "Gabby" Hayes
5. Smiley Burnette
6. Charles Starrett
7. Johnny Mack Brown
8. Sunset Carson
9. Fuzzy Knight
10. Eddie Dean

[Only appearances in the lists for both Sunset Carson and Fuzzy Knight]

# 1947

1. Roy Rogers
2. Gene Autry
3. William Boyd
4. William Elliott
5. George "Gabby" Hayes
6. Charles Starrett
7. Smiley Burnette
8. Johnny Mack Brown
9. Dale Evans
10. Eddie Dean

[Dale Evans was the only female star ever to make the lists of western money-makers]

# 1948

1. Roy Rogers
2. Gene Autry
3. William Elliott
4. George "Gabby" Hayes
5. William Boyd
6. Charles Starrett
7. Tim Holt
8. Johnny Mack Brown
9. Smiley Burnette
10. Andy Devine

## THRILL ROUND UP

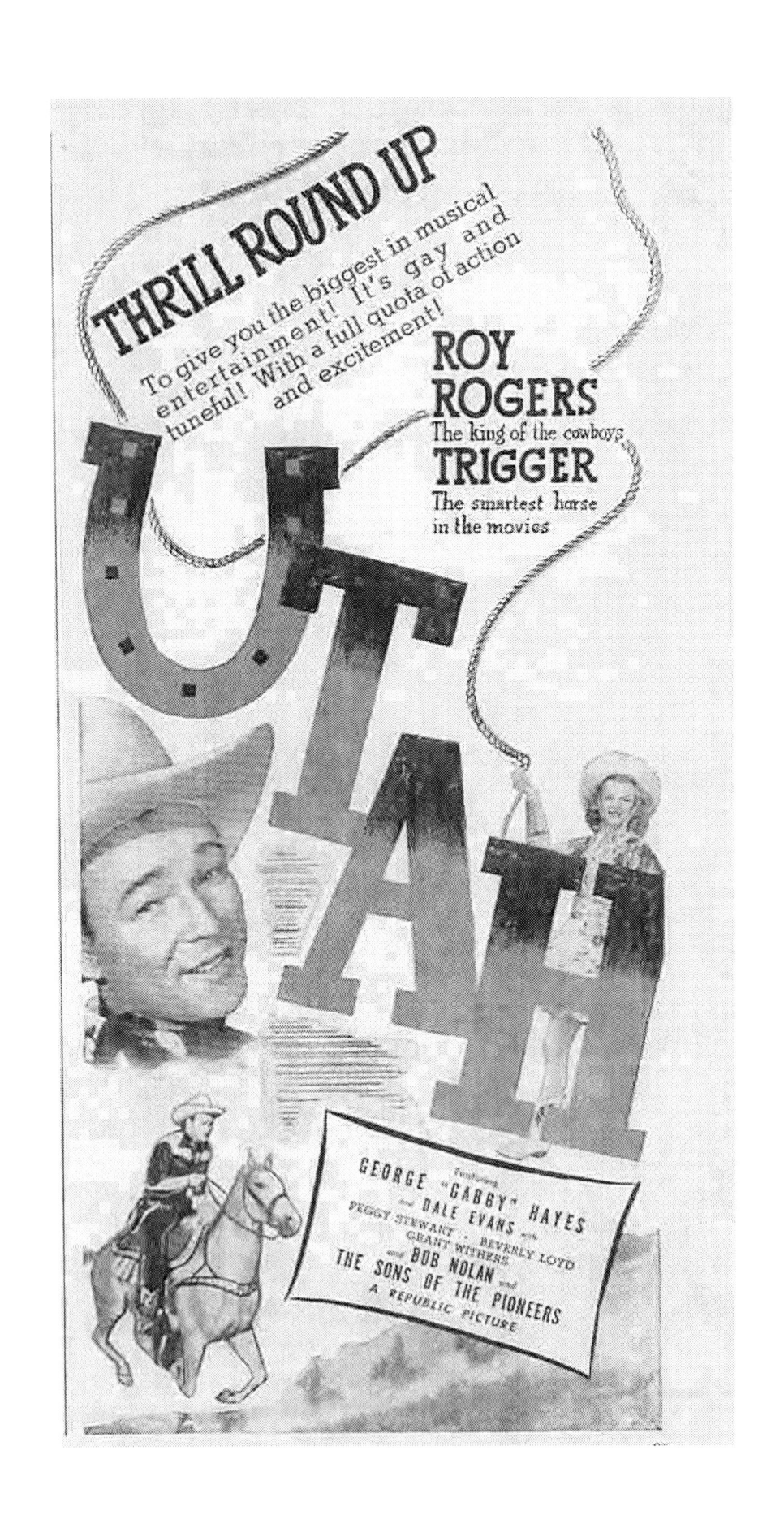

To give you the biggest in musical entertainment! It's gay and tuneful! With a full quota of action and excitement!

**ROY ROGERS**
The king of the cowboys

**TRIGGER**
The smartest horse in the movies

# UTAH

featuring
GEORGE "GABBY" HAYES
and DALE EVANS with
PEGGY STEWART • BEVERLY LOYD
GRANT WITHERS
and BOB NOLAN and
THE SONS OF THE PIONEERS
A REPUBLIC PICTURE

ROY
ROGERS
TRIGGER
TWILIGHT
IN THE
SIERRAS
in TRUCOLOR
DALE EVANS
ESTELITA RODRIGUEZ
PAT BRADY
A REPUBLIC PRODUCTION

# 1949

1. Roy Rogers
2. Gene Autry
3. George "Gabby" Hayes
4. Tim Holt
5. William Elliott
6. Charles Starrett
7. William Boyd
8. Johnny Mack Brown
9. Smiley Burnette
10. Andy Devine

# 1950

1. Roy Rogers
2. Gene Autry
3. George "Gabby" Hayes
4. William Elliott
5. William Boyd
6. Tim Holt
7. Charles Starrett
8. Johnny Mack Brown
9. Smiley Burnette
10. Dale Evans

# 1951

1. Roy Rogers
2. Gene Autry
3. Tim Holt
4. Charles Starrett
5. Rex Allen
6. William Elliott
7. Smiley Burnette
8. Allan Lane
9. Dale Evans
10. George "Gabby" Hayes

[Initial appearances on the lists for both Rex Allen and Allan "Rocky" Lane]

# 1952

1. Roy Rogers
2. Gene Autry
3. Rex Allen
4. William Elliott
5. Tim Holt
6. George "Gabby" Hayes
7. Smiley Burnette
8. Dale Evans
9. Charles Starrett
10. William Boyd

[Last appearance on the lists for Charles Starrett who had made every year from 1937, except 1943]

ROY ROGERS
KING OF THE COWBOYS
TRIGGER
THE SMARTEST HORSE IN THE MOVIES
SONS OF THE PIONEERS
GEORGE "Gabby" HAYES · MARIS WRIXON
THE SONS OF THE PIONEERS
M. COATES WEBSTER · MAURI GRASHIN ROBERT T. SHANNON JOSEPH KANE
MAURI GRASHIN ROBERT T. SHANNON
A REPUBLIC PICTURE
R55-416

# 1953

1. Roy Rogers
2. Gene Autry
3. Rex Allen
4. William Elliott
5. Allan Lane

[As the days of the "B" western drew to a close, only five places were voted for in 1953]

# 1954

1. Roy Rogers
2. Gene Autry
3. Rex Allen
4. William Elliott
5. George "Gabby" Hayes

[The poll was discontinued after 1954]

# Favorite Western Stars in the U.K.

a 1950 editorial survey by

The Western Film Annual

1. Gene Autry
2. Randolph Scott
3. John Wayne
4. Roy Rogers
5. Joel McCrea
6. William Boyd
7. Tim Holt
8. Alan Ladd
9. Johnny Mack Brown
10. Smiley Burnette

# Favorite Western Stars in Australia

a 1960s survey of "Ranch Nights"

<u>by Hoyts Theatres Ltd</u>

1. Audie Murphy
2. James Stewart
3. Randolph Scott
4. Joel McCrea
5. Rory Calhoun
6. Alan Ladd
7. John Wayne
8. Gary Cooper
9. Jock Mahoney
10. George Mongomery

# Index

Across the Badlands (1950)
Adventures of Chico (1937)
Ambush (1949)
Ambush Trail (1946)
Ambush Valley (1936)
Americana (1939)
American Empire (1942)
Angel and the Badman (1946)
Appaloosa (1966)
Arizona (1940)
Arizona Bad Man (1935)
Arizona Legion (1939)

Bad Men of Arizona (1942)
Belle Starr's Daughter (1948)
Bells of San Angelo (1947)
Big Country (1958)

Big Jack (1949)
Big Stampede (1932)
Billy the Kid Returns (1938)
Bitter Creek (1954)
Black Aces (1937)
Black Bart (1948)
Blazing Across the Pecos (1948)
Blue Montana Skies (1939)
Borderland (1937)
Border Patrol (1942)
Border Romance (1930)
Boy from Oklahoma (1954)
Brimstone (1949)

Cabin in the Cotton (1932)
Call of the Wilderness (see Trailing the Killer)
Canyon Passage (1946)
the Capture (1950)
Caravans West (see Wagon Wheels)
Carolina (1934)
the Challenge (see Across the Badlands)
Challenge of the Range (1949)
Code of the West (1947)
Colorado Sunset (1939)
Colorado Trail (1938)

Dead Man's Trail (1952)
Deputy Marshal (1949)
Desert Pursuit (1953)
the Desperado (1954)
Destry Rides Again (1939)
Down on the Farm (see On Our Selection)
Duel at Silver Creek (1952)
Dumb Bell of the Yukon (1946)

Five Came Back (1939)
Forestalled (see Two-Fisted Rangers)
Frontier Horizon (see New Frontier)
Frontier Marshal (1939)
Frontiersman (1938)

Frontiersmen (see Frontiersman)
Fury at Furnace Creek (1948)

Give and Take (see Singin' in the Corn)
Grand Canyon (1949)
Great Barrier (1937)
Guns of the Timberland (1960)

Haunted Gold (1933)
Heaven Only Knows (1947)

Indian Paint (1965)
In Old California (1942)
In Old Monterey (1939)

Jack McCall Desperado (1953)
Jedda (1955)
Jivaro (1954)
Juarez (1939)

Kettles in the Ozarks (1955)
King of Dodge City (1941)

Last of the Mohicans (1920)
Lawless Nineties (1936)
Lawless Range (1935)
Lawless Street (1955)
Law of the Badlands (1950)
Law of the 45's (1935)
L'il Abner (1940)
Lonely Trail (1936)
Lost Trail (1945)
Lost Treasure of the Amazon (see Jivaro)
Lucky Texan (1934)

Ma and Pa Kettle (1949)
Man from Laramie (1955)
Mark of Zorro (1940)
Men in Exile (1937)
Men of Destiny (see American Empire)

Mexicali Rose (1939)
Montana (1950)
Montana Mike (see Heaven Only Knows)
Moonlight Raid (see Challenge of the Range)
Mountain Justice (1936)
My Son Alone (see American Empire)
Mysterious Mr Sheffield (see Law of the 45's)

'Neath Arizona Skies (1934)
New Frontier (1939)
Night Riders (1939)

On Our Selection (1932)
Owd Bob (1938)

Painted Stallion (1937)
Paradise Canyon (1935)
Paradise Ranch (see Paradise Canyon)
Prairie Moon (1938)
Public Cowboy Number One (1937)
Pursued (1947)

Rawhide (1938)
Red River (1948)
the Refugee (see Three Faces West)
Ride 'Em Cowboy (1941)
Riders of Black River (1939)
Riders of Destiny (1933)
Riding Shotgun (1954)
Rio Rita (1942)
Robbery Under Arms (1957)
Robin Hood of Texas (1947)
Robin Hood of the Range (1943)
Rolling Home (1946)
Romance of a Horse Thief (1971)
Rough Riders' Round-Up (1939)
Round-Up Time in Texas (1937)
Rovin' Tumbleweeds (1939)
Sagebrush Trail (1933)
San Antonio (1946)

the Searchers (1956)
Seminole Uprising (1955)
Seventh Cavalry (1956)
Shootout at Medicine Bend (1957)
Showdown (see West of Abilene)
Silent Barriers (see Great Barrier)
Silly Billies (1936)
Silver Dollar (1933)
Singin' in the Corn (1946)
Six-Gun Law (1947)
Sons of the Pioneers (1942)
Southwest to Sonora (see Appaloosa)
the Spoilers (1942)
Spy Smasher (1942)
Stagecoach to Hell (see Stage to Thunder Rock)
Stagecoach to Monterey (1944)
Stage to Thunder Rock (1964)
Star Packer (1934)
Stick To Your Guns (1941)
Sunset Trail (1931)
Susanna Pass (1949)

Taggart (1964)
Tall in the Saddle (1944)
Terrors on Horseback (1946)
Three Faces West (1940)
Thunder over the Prairie (1941)
Tombstone, the Town Too Tough To Die (see Bad Men of Arizona)
Tom Sawyer (1930)
To the Victor (see Owd Bob)
Trail Beyond (1934)
Trailing the Killer (1932)
Trouble Chaser (see L'il Abner)
Two-Fisted Rangers (1939)

Unconquered (1947)
Undercover {Men} (1935)
Under Arrest (see Blazing Across the Pecos)

Valley of the Giants (1938)

Vanishing Riders (1935)
Vigilantes Return (1947)

Wagon Master (1950)
Wagon Wheels (1934)
West of Abilene (1940)
West of Wyoming (1950)
Westward Bound (1943)
Westward Ho (1935)
Where Trails End (1942)
Wild Horse Canyon (1938)
Wild Horse Range (1940)
Wild Horse Stampede (1943)
Wyoming Outlaw (1939)
Wyoming Round-Up (1952)

Zorro's Fighting Legion (1939)

he had to find her... he had to find her...
WARNER BROS.
JOHN WAYNE
"THE SEARCHERS"
VISTAVISION
JEFFREY HUNTER · VERA MILES
WARD BOND · NATALIE WOOD
JOHN FORD

MONOGRAM PICTURES
present
John
WAYNE
IN
"PARADISE CANYON"
Directed By CARL PIERSON Story By LINDSLEY PARSONS
Screen Play By ROBERT EMMETT
A PAUL MALVERN PRODUCTION

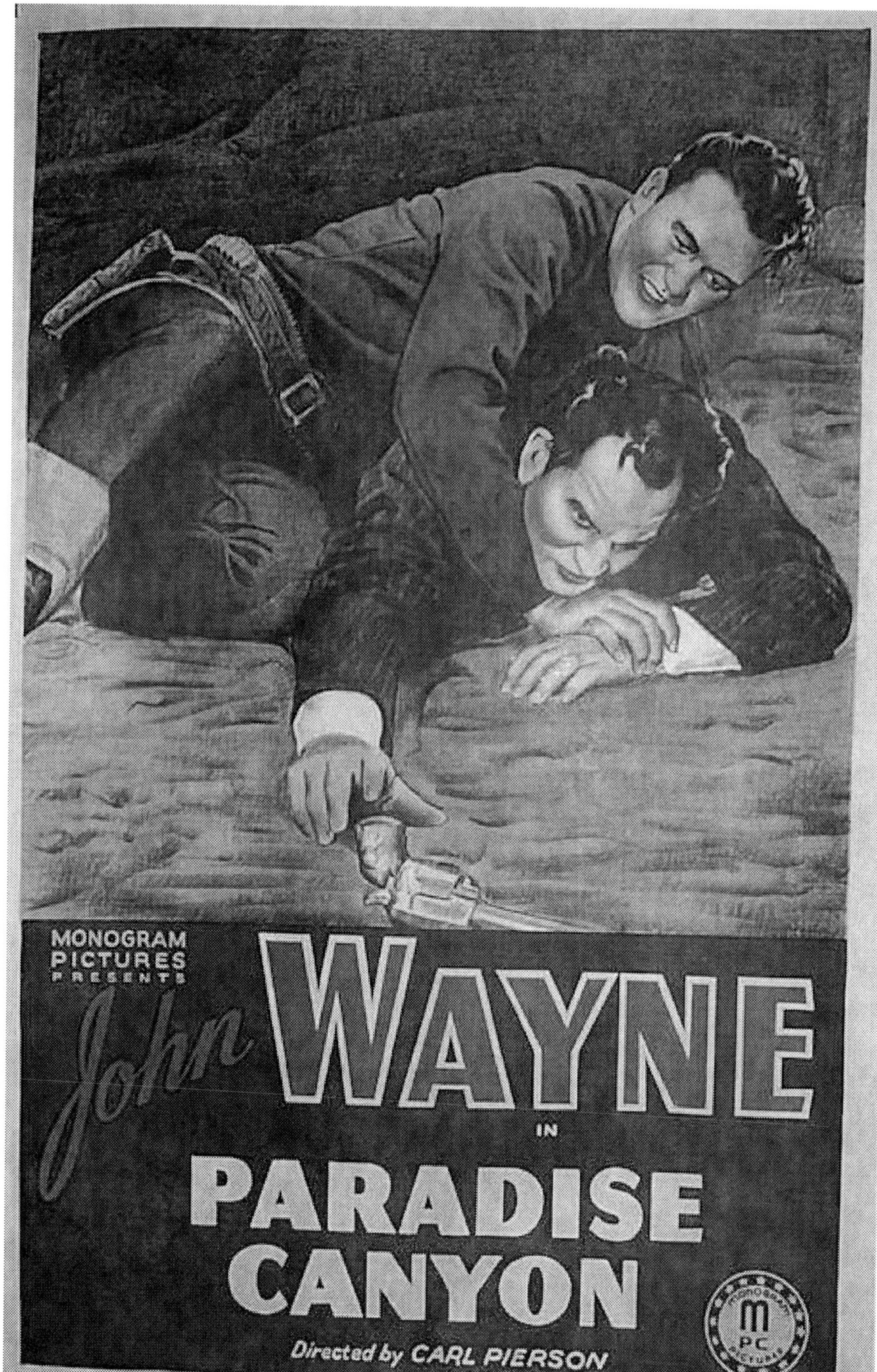
MONOGRAM
PICTURES
PRESENTS
John
WAYNE
IN
PARADISE
CANYON
Directed by CARL PIERSON
MPC

GUILTY
OF DARING TO LOVE
AND LIVE
THREE FACES WEST
with
JOHN WAYNE · SIGRID GURIE
CHARLES COBURN
BERNARD VORHAUS
Director
A Republic PICTURE

MONTGOMERY
CLIFT
JOHN
WAYNE
JOANNE DRU
IL FIUME
ROSSO
Un film prodotto e diretto da HOWARD HAWKS

JOHN WAYNE
LA PRISONNIÈRE
DU DÉSERT
JEFFREY HUNTER · VERA MILES
WARD BOND · NATALIE WOOD
VISTAVISION

THEIR BULLETS RIVETED A NEW STAR TO THE FLAG!
MONTANA
NEW TRIUMPH FROM WARNER BROS. IN
TECHNICOLOR
ERROL FLYNN
ALEXIS SMITH
DIRECTED BY RAY ENRIGHT
James R. Webb
Borden Chase
Charles O'Neal

UNIVERSAL presents
The VIGILANTES RETURN
in CINECOLOR
with
JON HALL MARGARET LINDSAY
ANDY DEVINE
PAULA DREW ROBERT WILCOX
JONATHAN HALE JACK LAMBERT
Original Screenplay by ROY CHANSLOR · Directed by RAY TAYLOR · Produced by HOWARD WELSCH · A UNIVERSAL PICTURE

Charles STARRETT · Smiley BURNETTE
ACROSS the BADLANDS
HELEN MOWERY · DICK ELLIOT
HARMONICA BILL
Written by BARRY SHIPMAN
Produced by COLBERT CLARK
Directed by FRED F. SEARS
A COLUMBIA PICTURE

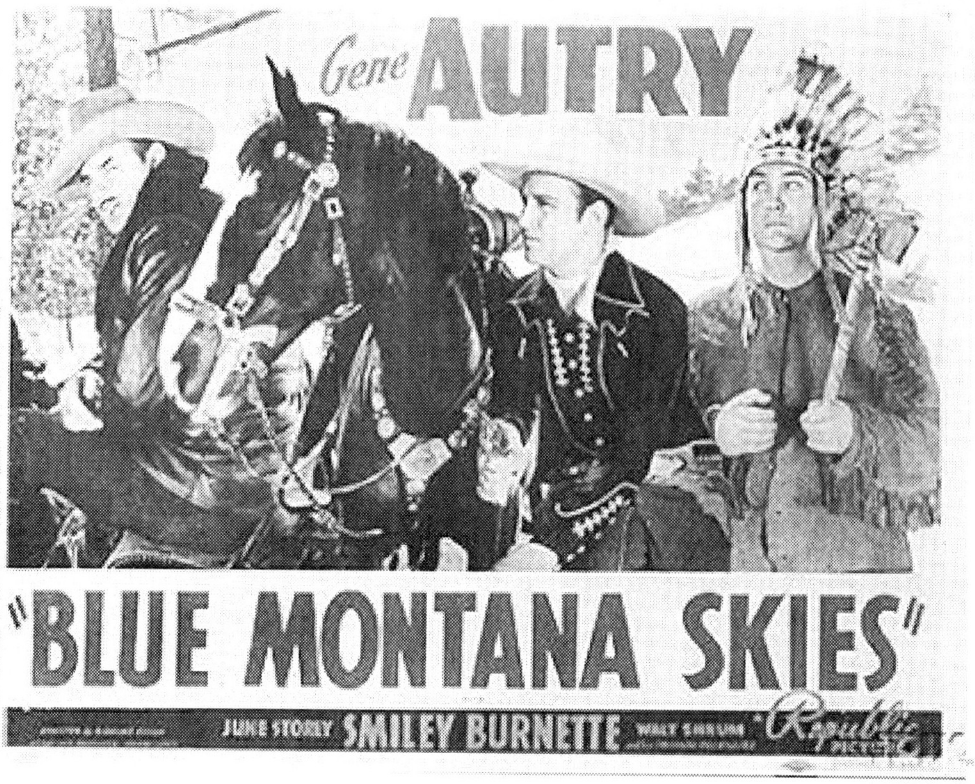
Gene AUTRY
"BLUE MONTANA SKIES"
JUNE STOREY SMILEY BURNETTE